FOUNDATIONS OF LABOR AND EMPLOYMENT LAW

By

SAMUEL ESTREICHER

Professor of Law
New York University

STEWART J. SCHWAB

Professor of Law
Cornell Law School

New York, New York
FOUNDATION PRESS
2000

Foundation Press, a division of West Group, has created this publication to provide you with accurate and authoritative information concerning the subject matter covered. However, this publication was not necessarily prepared by persons licensed to practice law in a particular jurisdiction. Foundation Press is not engaged in rendering legal or other professional advice, and this publication is not a substitute for the advice of an attorney. If you require legal or other expert advice, you should seek the services of a competent attorney or other professional.

TEXT IS PRINTED ON 10% POST CONSUMER RECYCLED PAPER

INTRODUCTION

The workplace is not what it used to be. Labor unions have declined dramatically, with members constituting 10 percent of the private-sector workforce today, compared with 35 percent in the 1950s. Women and minorities are working in record numbers. The explosion of information technology has fueled the shift from manufacturing to service jobs. The rise of the global economy has put increasing pressure on firms to increase productivity, cut costs, and reduce waste. Temporary workers, leased workers, and quality circles are growing in importance.

Legal regulation has responded to the changing workplace with varying degrees of success. Federal laws regulating unions and collective bargaining have not changed significantly since 1959. These laws are now commonly criticized as being ineffectual or out-of-date. In well-publicized remarks a few years ago, Lane Kirkland, then head of the AFL-CIO, proclaimed (undoubtedly with tongue in cheek) that the union movement might be better off with the "law of the jungle" than with current labor laws. In contrast, employment law at the state and federal level has exploded in recent years. Congress passed major statutes beginning in 1964 regulating employment discrimination, and then in the mid-1970s regulating occupational safety and health, as well as pensions and other fringe benefits. More recent federal regulations cover polygraphs, plant closings, civil rights, and family and medical leave. At the state level, significant common law and legislative developments now regulate wrongful termination, drug testing, and privacy in the workplace—and arguably are eroding conventional assumptions of "at will" employment.

Legal scholars have struggled to assimilate these turbulent changes in the workplace and its legal regulation. A mundane but revealing sign of assimilation comes from the increasingly accepted distinction in terminology between *employment law*, meaning laws that protect individual workers, and *labor law*, meaning laws that regulate labor unions and collective bargaining. Among practitioners, the field is increasingly called *labor and employment law*, to capture the growing importance of regulations of employment decisions that apply to all employees whether or not they have chosen collective representation.

Scholars are vigorously questioning basic assumptions in both labor and employment law. Why are unions and collective bargaining declining in importance, and what can or should law do about the decline? How has the expansion in employment law affected the nonunionized workplace? Answers to these questions require an understanding of the law as it has evolved thus far, but they also require familiarity with the tools of policy analysis.

As the workplace itself has changed so dramatically, many of the insights about the proper role of law are increasingly found outside traditional legal scholarship. That is where this book comes in. Interdisciplinary labor and employment law scholarship is more important than ever before. There exists a rich literature in industrial relations, labor economics, industrial sociology, labor history, and related fields that can illuminate the study of labor and employment law. Legal scholars indeed have much to learn from this scholarship. But they also have much to offer. The devil is in the institutional arrangements. Details of the law matter; and practical issues of procedure and access to remedies are necessary to a full account of the law "on the ground." In short, there needs to be a two-way exchange between scholars in industrial relations, labor economics, and labor history, on the one hand, and legal scholars, on the other. This book attempts to provide an accessible text that might promote such an exchange.

This edited collection of articles displays the leading interdisciplinary thinking in regard to both the unionized and the nonunionized workplace—in both labor and employment law. Part I examines structural changes in the workplace. These include changes in career employment and the rise of contingent work, along with the decline of unions. Ironically, as unions have declined, scholars have increasingly appreciated the productive potential of unions, particularly their ability to solve collective goods problems in the workplace. So Part I, particularly Chapter 3, includes discussions of this second "voice" face of unions, as it is sometimes called (monopoly unionism being the first face).

Part II examines the legal regulation of unions. We examine existing legal arrangements in terms of their contribution to efficiency, redistribution, and democratic participation—with a particular emphasis on the growing "labor law and economics" literature.

Part III turns to legal regulation of the nonunion workplace. Essays presented there critically examine the rise in employment law regulating nonunion and union workplaces alike, particularly laws regulating termination of workers, minimum wages, and pensions.

Part IV attempts to glimpse the future. We include comparative assessments of the industrial relations and employment law systems of our leading competitors—including Canada, Japan, and Germany—and developments pursued under the "Social Charter" of the European Union. Our final two chapters evaluate reform proposals that seek to shape the future role of unions and the future legal regulation of the nonunion workplace.

This book is intended for use in basic labor law and employment law courses as well as in advanced seminars. We believe it could also be profitably used in undergraduate and graduate offerings in schools of business, management, and industrial relations. Indeed, lawyers, union leaders, and human-resource specialists should find it helpful. Our hope is that the book sparks greater interaction among all these groups.

SAMUEL ESTREICHER
STEWART J. SCHWAB

FOUNDATIONS OF LAW SERIES

ROBERTA ROMANO, GENERAL EDITOR

Foundations of Administrative Law
Edited by Peter H. Schuck, Yale Law School

Foundations of Contract Law
*Edited by Richard Craswell, Stanford Law School and
Alan Schwartz, Yale Law School*

Foundations of Corporate Law
Edited by Roberta Romano, Yale Law School

Foundations of Criminal Law
*Edited by Leo Katz, Michael S. Moore and Stephen J. Morse,
all of the University of Pennsylvania Law School*

Foundations of The Economic Approach to Law
Edited by Avery Wiener Katz, Columbia Law School

Foundations of Employment Discrimination Law
Edited by John Donohue, III, Stanford Law School

Foundations of Environmental Law and Policy
Edited by Richard L. Revesz, New York University Law School

Foundations of Labor Law
*Edited by Samuel Estreicher, New York University Law School
and Stewart J. Schwab, Cornell Law School*

Foundations of Tort Law
Edited by Saul Levmore, University of Chicago Law School

CONTENTS

*

FOUNDATIONS OF LABOR AND EMPLOYMENT LAW

*

Part I

Frameworks for Analyzing Labor Markets

This Part presents models and data about the variety of labor markets in the economy. Chapter 1 examines spot markets and long-term internal labor markets and presents data on contingent worker and income distribution. Chapter 2 examines theory and evidence about the role of labor unions in labor markets. Chapter 3 explores the relative decline of labor unions.

1

Models of the Labor Market

The U.S. labor market is huge. In 1996, it included nearly 127 million employees and 6 million employers. The average employer, therefore, has about twenty employees. Since some employers are huge, however, the median employer has far fewer than twenty employers. In addition, more than 10 million workers are self-employed, and another 7 million persons are looking for work but cannot find it—the unemployed. Total compensation to employees in 1994 was nearly $3.7 trillion, compared with $2 trillion for all other forms of income, such as investments, self-employment, pensions, and welfare programs. See U.S. Bureau of the Census, *Statistical Abstract of the United States: 1997* (Washington, D.C.: U.S. GPO, 1997), Tables 621, 636.

1

As well as being huge, the American labor market is complex and diverse. In contrast to the relatively homogeneous labor markets of Germany, Japan, and most other industrialized nations, a high proportion of American workers are members of racial or ethnic minorities. African Americans comprise 11 percent of all workers; Hispanic Americans, 9 percent; and Asian Americans and others, 4 percent. Women account for 46 percent of the workforce. See Howard N. Fullerton, Jr., "The 2005 Labor Force: Growing, but Slowly," 118 *Monthly Labor Review* 30, Table 1 (Nov. 1995).

This chapter provides a framework for understanding how this complex market works—an understanding necessary to a sophisticated evaluation of its legal regulation. Section A begins with what economists call a "price-theory" model of the labor market. In this section emphasis is placed on ways in which the labor market is similar to and different from other markets, as well as ways in which this market "works" or "fails." Section B then discusses internal labor markets, which are made up of employees who are attached to a single employer for long stretches of their working lives. In Section C we look at the contingent workforce, which consists of workers with a less permanent attachment to a single employer, such as independent, temporary, leased, part-time, and home workers. Section D provides data on the distribution of income from the labor market.

A. Price–Theory Model of the Labor Market

The neoclassical, or *price-theory*, model of labor markets consists of a supply, demand, and equilibrium story. For a fuller discussion, see Ronald G. Ehrenberg and Robert S. Smith, *Modern Labor Economics*, 6th ed. (Reading, Mass.: Addison–Wesley, 1997).

Supply of Labor. A labor supply curve shows how much people want to work as the offered wage increases. The amount of work is usually measured in total hours, weeks, or years of all workers combined. A full study of labor supply involves complicated issues such as whether people work less as they become wealthier, how family members share time working at home and in the labor force, and how retirement decisions change in relation to government Social Security policy. For our purposes, however, we can adopt a simple story of labor supply for a particular industry—say, the market for bank tellers. As the wage rises, more people will want to work in that market. This leads to the upward-sloping market supply curve shown in Figure 1–1.

Supply and Demand in a Competitive Market

Two points are worth noting about this simple supply curve. First, in mapping how wage changes alter the supply of labor, the curve holds constant all other factors that could influence labor supply. For example,

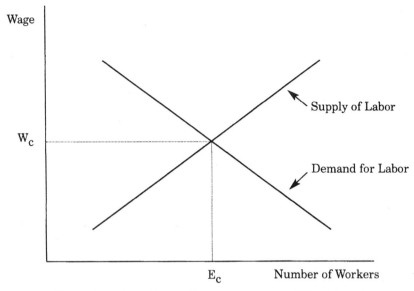

Figure 1–1. Supply and Demand in a Competitive Market

if this is the supply curve for bank tellers, it assumes that the wages remain constant for occupations requiring comparable skills, such as secretaries. If the secretary wage rises, fewer people prefer to be bank tellers, and more people prefer to be secretaries. This rise in the secretary wage would cause the entire supply curve for bank tellers to shift to the left, showing that fewer people would want to work as bank tellers for any given wage.

Second, this market-level supply curve differs from the supply curve faced by an individual firm in the market. The market supply curve for bank tellers shows, for each wage, the number of persons willing to work as bank tellers rather than work in some other occupation or not work at all. Having decided to become a bank teller, the worker must decide which bank to work for. The price-theory model of competitive markets assumes that many banks offer virtually identical jobs, that many workers bid for the work, and that everyone knows the available choices. Under these conditions, all banks offer the same wage, which is the "market" wage. If a particular bank offers a below-market wage, it will attract no workers. On the other hand, because each particular bank is small relative to the market, any one bank attracts all the workers it wants at the market wage. Thus, at the market wage rate, the supply curve for a particular firm is a horizontal line. The individual-firm supply curve is the same as the market supply curve when only one firm hires workers—that is, when the firm is a monopsonist. The market imperfections from monopsony are discussed below.

Demand for Labor. The individual-firm demand curve shows the maximum number of workers the firm wants to hire at each wage. A firm is willing to hire additional workers so long as the additional revenue from an extra worker (formally called the marginal revenue product of labor) exceeds the additional wages and other costs (e.g., payroll taxes, training) associated with hiring that worker. An equivalent way to conceptualize the demand curve is that it is the line that shows, for each level of employment, the extra revenue the firm obtains by hiring another worker. A fundamental conclusion of price theory is that the demand for labor (or any other commodity) is downward sloping. As the wage falls, the price of labor relative to other inputs, such as capital, falls. In that circumstance, banks are more willing to hire additional tellers rather than purchase more automatic teller machines.

Two points about the labor demand curve are worth noting. First, both the individual-firm demand curve and the industry demand curve are downward sloping. The maximum number of workers the individual firm will hire increases as the wage falls. The total number of workers that all firms in the industry are willing to hire is the sum of the number of workers that each firm is willing to hire. This total also increases as the wage falls.

Second, the reason for the downward slope of the demand curve is not that the additional workers hired are less skilled than workers hired earlier. The price-theory model assumes that workers are interchangeable, and the "marginal" worker should not be viewed as the one hired last in time. Rather, the declining additional output occurs because the firm's capital (which is assumed to remain constant) must be shared among more workers. Further, after a while, extra workers become less useful (in technical terms, they yield diminishing returns), even if they are given additional capital to work with. For example, the first bookkeeper hired might add a lot to the firm's revenues by keeping better track of inventory. A second bookkeeper might be even more valuable than the first, since together they might be able to run a more sophisticated inventory system. The eighth bookkeeper, however, probably adds less to the firm than bookkeepers hired earlier did, both because she has to wait for time on the computer and because, even if she is given a computer, the undone tasks are less critical. The diminishing returns occur even though the eighth bookkeeper is as skilled as the others. Because the wage of a particular worker does not depend solely on his or her individual skill but depends also on the amount of capital and the number of other workers in the firm, some philosophers have argued that skilled workers have no moral claim to their high wages. The prospect of high wages helps allocate skilled workers to jobs where they are most productive, and thus makes the economy more efficient, but that is a society-wide goal rather than an individual moral claim. See, for example, Amartya Sen, "The Moral Standing of the Market," in Ellen F.

Paul, Jeffrey Paul, and Fred D. Miller, Jr., eds., *Ethics and Economics* (New York: Basil Blackwell, 1985), 1, 14–17.

Market Equilibrium. The wage rate at which the demand for labor equals the supply of labor is the market-clearing wage (W_c in Figure 1–1). At this wage, neither a shortage nor a surplus of workers exists. If the wage rate exceeds W_c, the number of persons seeking work exceeds the number of workers that firms are willing to hire. Unemployment results, leading to downward pressure on wages. If the wage rate falls below W_c, a labor shortage exists. Firms will increase wages to attract more workers until the market-clearing equilibrium wage is reached, and E_c workers are employed in this market.

. . .

While the price-theory model of labor markets is stylized, it can provide insights into a variety of labor policies. One important issue is whether employers or employees "pay" a payroll tax. Many social insurance programs are financed by payroll taxes. Social Security retirement, disability, and medical insurance programs, for example, are funded by a tax nominally paid equally by employers and employees. Other programs, such as unemployment insurance and workers' compensation, are financed by payroll taxes paid only by employers. What is the real impact of these programs on labor costs and the demand for labor? Consider the following discussion by Ronald G. Ehrenberg and Robert S. Smith.

"Who Bears the Burden of a Payroll Tax?"*
RONALD G. EHRENBERG and ROBERT S. SMITH

In the United States several social insurance programs are financed by payroll taxes. Employers, and in some cases employees, make mandatory contributions of a fraction of the employees' salaries, up to a maximum level (or taxable wage base), to the social insurance trust funds.... [I]t is not clear just why payroll taxes on *employers* are so heavily used in the social insurance area. There seems to be a prevailing notion that such taxes result in employers' "footing the bill" for the relevant programs, but this is not necessarily the case.

With our simple labor market model, we can show that the party making the social insurance payment is not necessarily the one that bears the burden of the tax. Suppose for expository convenience that only the employer is required to make payments and that the tax is a fixed amount (X) per labor hour rather than a percentage of payroll. Now consider the market demand curve D_0 in Figure [1–2], which is drawn in such a way that desired employment is plotted against the wage *employees receive*. Prior to the imposition of the tax, the wage

* Reprinted by permission from Ehrenberg and Smith, *Modern Labor Economics*, 6th ed., (Reading, Mass.: Addison–Wesley, 1997), 84–87, © by Addison–Wesley.

employees receive is the same as the wage employers pay. Thus if D_0 were the demand curve before the tax was imposed, it would have the conventional interpretation of indicating how much labor firms would be willing to hire at any given wage. However, *after* imposition of the tax, employer wage costs would be X above what employees received.

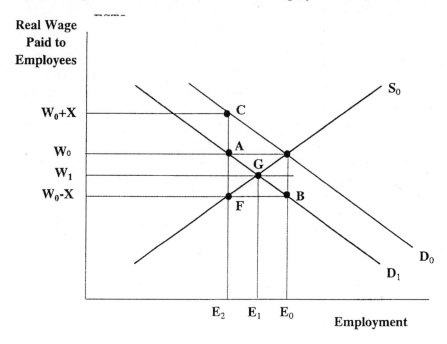

**Figure 1–2. The Market Demand Curve and Effects
of an Employer–Financed Payroll Tax**

Thus, if employees received W_0, employers would face costs of $W_0 + X$. They would no longer demand E_0 workers; rather, because their costs were $W_0 + X$, they would demand E_2 workers. Point A (where W_0 and E_2 intersect) would become a point on a new market demand curve formed when demand shifted down because of the tax (remember, the wage on the vertical axis of Figure [1–2] is the wage *employees receive*, not the wage employers pay). Only if employee wages fell to W_0-X would firms want to continue hiring E_0 workers, for then *employer* costs would be the same as before the tax. Thus, point B would also be on the new, shifted demand curve. Note that with a tax of X, the new demand curve (D_1) is parallel to the old one and the vertical distance between the two is X.

Now, the tax-related shift in the market demand curve to D_1 implies that there would be an excess supply of labor at the previous equilibrium wage of W_0. This surplus of labor would create downward pressure on the *employee* wage, and this downward pressure would continue to be exerted until the employee wage fell to W_1, the point at which the quantity of labor supplied just equaled the quantity demanded. At this point, employment would also have fallen to E_1. Thus, *employees* bear part of the burden of an employer payroll tax in the form of *lower wage rates and lower employment levels*. The lesson is clear: The party legally liable for the contribution (the employer) is not necessarily the one that bears the full burden of the actual cost.

Figure [1–2] does suggest, however, that employers may bear at least *some* of the tax, because the wages received by employees do not fall by the full amount of the tax (W_0—W_1 is smaller than X, which is the vertical distance between the two demand curves). The reason for this is that with an upward-sloping labor market supply curve, employees withdraw labor as their wages fall, and it becomes more difficult for firms to find workers. If wages fell to W_0—X, the withdrawal of workers would create a labor shortage that would serve to drive wages to some point (W_1 in our example) between W_0 and W_0—X. Only if the labor market supply curve were *vertical*—meaning that lower wages have no effect on labor supply—would the *entire amount of the tax* be shifted to workers in the form of a decrease in their wages by the amount of X. . . .

In general, the extent to which the labor market *supply* curve is sensitive to wages determines the proportion of the employer payroll tax that gets shifted to employees' wages. The less responsive labor supply is to changes in wages, the fewer the employees who withdraw from the market and the higher the proportion of the tax that gets shifted to workers in the form of a wage decrease. . . . It must also be pointed out, however, that to the degree employee wages do *not* fall, employment levels *will*; when employee wages do not fall much in the face of an employer payroll-tax increase, employer labor costs are increased—and this increase reduces the quantity of labor employers demand.

A number of empirical studies have sought to ascertain what fraction of employers' payroll-tax costs are actually passed on to employees in the form of lower wages (or lower wage increases). Although the evidence is somewhat ambiguous, a comprehensive review of these studies led to at least the tentative conclusion that most of a payroll tax is eventually shifted to wages, with little long-run effect on employment. Government policies, however, are frequently judged by their near-term results, and there is also research indicating that imposing a payroll tax could cause employer wage costs to rise, and employment therefore to fall, for a period of five to ten years before the tax is fully shifted to employee wages. It is not surprising, therefore, that payroll taxes have been suspected as a possible cause of the rise in European, relative to North American, unemployment during the 1980s.

Notes and Questions

1. *Key Assumptions.* The price-theory model is based on several critical assumptions outlined here. We further examine various market imperfec-

tions in Chapter 6, in exploring the justifications for laws mandating minimum terms.

   a. *Absence of Monopsony.* The model assumes that each employer is such a small part of the market that it can hire as many workers as it wants without affecting the wage rate. Suppose, however, that a firm is the only employer in its region (i.e., a monopsonist). Such a firm faces the market supply curve for labor and cannot expand its workforce without raising the wage rate. (See Figure 1–3.) Presumably, if the monopsonist pays higher wages to attract new workers, it must raise the wages for current workers as well. Thus, the marginal cost of hiring another worker exceeds the market wage. The monopsonist will hire workers until the marginal revenue product of another worker equals the marginal cost of hiring that worker (which for a monopsonist is above the market wage). In Figure 1–3, the monopsonist will hire E_m workers and pay them W_m. A monopsonist, thus, will hire fewer workers and pay a lower wage than firms in a competitive market would hire and pay.

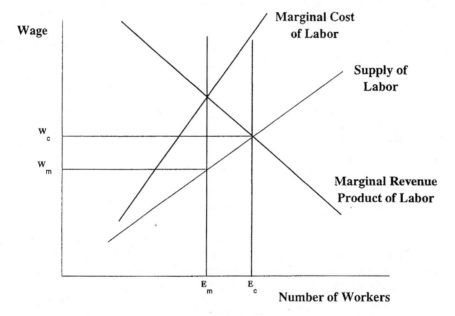

Figure 1–3. Labor Market Outcome for a Monopsonist

   In explaining the general economic theory of monopsony, Roger D. Blair and Jeffrey L. Harrison give as an example a textile mill in an isolated North Carolina town. *Monopsony: Antitrust Law and Economics* (Princeton, N.J.: Princeton University Press, 1993), 36–39. The textile mill dominates the local labor market. Domination, in the economic theory of monopsony, means that some workers will work at the mill for low wages, because they have limited alternatives. But the mill must raise wages if it wants to hire more workers. In other words, the mill affects the local wage by deciding how many workers to employ. To keep the wage low, a monopsonist will hire fewer workers than optimal, even though additional workers could produce revenues for the firm that would more than cover their additional wages. By assumption, the monopsonist would have to raise wages for current workers as well, thus making the additional workers too costly.

Traditionally, economists have thought that monopsony rarely occurs in the modern American economy. More recently, however, they have argued that firms in competitive labor markets may sometimes confront upward-sloping supply curves. This could occur when long-term workers have limited mobility between firms or when high wages induce greater effort from workers (the so-called efficiency wage model, discussed later in this chapter). See William M. Boal and Michael R. Ransom, "Monopsony in the Labor Market," 35 *Journal of Economic Literature* 86, 110 (1997): "Monopsonistic exploitation arising from supply frictions ... is probably widespread but small on average."

b. *Absence of Monopoly.* The price-theory model also assumes that individual workers take the wage rate as given in making their supply decisions. This assumption is violated if workers can act as monopolistic suppliers of labor. Unions are commonly thought to function as monopolists, effectively controlling the labor supply rather than allowing individual workers to decide whether and at what price to work. As we shall see in Chapter 2, a major prediction of the union-as-monopolist model is that fewer workers will be hired and the wage will be higher than in the competitive, nonunion equilibrium.

Under the price-theory model, monopolists or monopsonists create an efficiency loss. By reducing employment below competitive levels, workers who would be most productive in the monopolized or monopsonized industry are prevented from working there. Instead, they must settle for a second-best alternative, be it unemployment, taking a less productive job, or quitting the labor force entirely.

c. *Maximization of Profits.* The price-theory model also assumes that employers base personnel decisions solely on the maximization of profits. Most employers are corporations or other legal entities operating through agents. Supervisors who hire and fire are agents of the employer and often have agendas other than maximizing the profits for distant shareholders. For example, a supervisor may fire a surly but productive employee to "show who is boss" rather than because the firing would maximize firm profits. Whether this divergence of interests between principal/stockholders and agent/supervisors can justify governmental scrutiny of terminations is part of the current debate over wrongful-termination law, which is explored in Chapter 7. Similarly, the profit-maximizing assumption is problematic for governments, which now employ over 16 percent of the American workforce. Finally, the older industrial relations literature often questioned whether firms attempted to maximize profits, arguing instead that firms merely tried to reach a satisfactory level of profits, and concentrated on growth or market share or other goals. The classic article here is Richard Lester, "Shortcomings of Marginal Analysis for Wage/Employment Problems," 36 *American Economic Review* 63 (1946). Lester argued that because firms did not slavishly seek to maximize profits, they would not necessarily curtail employment when wages rose. For a sympathetic critique of the views of "institutionalist" labor economists who questioned the suitability of price theory for labor markets, see Bruce E. Kaufman, "The Postwar View of Labor Markets and Wage Determination," and Richard B. Freeman, "Does the New Generation of Labor Economists Know More Than the Old Generation?," both in Bruce E. Kaufman, ed., *How Labor Markets Work: Reflections on Theory and Practice* (Lexington, Mass.: Lexington Books, 1988).

2. *Unemployment and Price Theory.* Unemployment is the major bugaboo of the price-theory model of labor markets. The essence of that supply-and-demand model is that wages will rise or fall until an equilibrium level of employment is reached. Equilibrium is a situation where no surplus or shortage of labor exists. Every qualified person willing to work at the market wage can find an employer willing to hire the person, and every job will be filled. Involuntary unemployment should not exist.

Several modifications of price theory have arisen to explain unemployment. "Cyclical" unemployment occurs when consumer demand and production fall during a recession, causing firms to terminate workers. Some cyclical unemployment is "wait" unemployment, workers on temporary layoff, who often receive unemployment benefits while waiting to return to their jobs. Unemployment occurs, however, even in a "full employment" economy. Many theorists emphasize that unemployment is often voluntary. Some workers are between jobs and therefore unemployed. Information about job vacancies is limited, and job seekers take time to find a good match rather than accept the first available job. This type of unemployment is sometimes labeled "frictional" unemployment. By contrast, "structural" unemployment arises from a geographic or skill mismatch between workers and available jobs. The jobs may exist, but the workers cannot get them because they lack the necessary skills. When a major employer in a community goes out of business, for example, many workers, particularly older workers, are unwilling or unable to learn new skills or to relocate to new jobs.

3. *The Controversial Word "Market."* Many commentators over the years have protested a model of the labor market that treats human beings as commodities. This sentiment was emphatically registered by Congress in 1914, when it declared in Section 6 of the Clayton Act that "the labor of a human being is not a commodity or article of commerce." 15 U.S.C. § 17. Congress enacted this section to ensure that the Sherman Act's prohibitions against monopolies were not applied to labor unions. For a good analysis of the troubled intersection between the labor laws and the antitrust laws, see Douglas Leslie, "Principles of Labor Antitrust," 66 *Virginia Law Review* 1183 (1980).

Certainly the labor market differs in many ways from, say, the market for wheat. Foremost, the labor market is a rental market only. Workers are not bought and sold. Of course, other markets are only rental markets as well. Second, nonpecuniary factors are uniquely important in the labor market. The person selling labor services must physically accompany the services, so the lighting, safety, pleasantness, and friendships at work are sometimes as important as the wage. While labor economists are apt to say that unpleasant working conditions can be compensated by higher wages, others protest that these divergent qualities are incommensurable with wages. Other unique features of labor markets include the relative immobility of workers (it is harder to move workers than wheat when a shortage occurs on the other side of the country) and the inability of workers to diversify their investments.

In the following reading, Professor Fischel compares labor markets and capital markets. While acknowledging that labor markets have unique features, Fischel ultimately concludes that the similarities outweigh the differences.

"Labor Markets and Labor Law Compared with Capital Markets and Corporate Law"*

DANIEL R. FISCHEL

... Two assumptions seem to me—a nonspecialist in the field—to underlie much of contemporary labor law: (1) employers, left to their own devices, will oppress workers; and (2) this problem of worker exploitation is best handled by a federal labor policy administered by an administrative agency. Corporate law, by contrast, makes the opposite assumptions. Firms are for the most part free to adopt whatever institutional arrangement they choose; and state, not federal, law controls. What accounts for these fundamental differences?

While some differences between labor and capital markets do exist, I argue that they do not justify the differences between labor and corporate law. In particular, the tendency of firms to reach efficient contractual arrangements, and to economize on transaction costs by choosing to be governed by a particular set of standard-form contractual terms embodied in state law, is relevant to both labor and capital markets....

Imagine an entrepreneur who wants to undertake a new venture and who thus needs to raise capital. Because potential investors always have the opportunity to invest elsewhere, the entrepreneur will have to provide them with credible information about the venture in order to demonstrate its superiority over alternative investments. Potential investors will also be concerned about use of the proceeds by the entrepreneur once the funds are invested. At the extreme, potential investors are concerned that the entrepreneur will simply pocket all the proceeds and leave investors with nothing. Less extreme agency problems range from self-dealing of various sorts to a simple lack of hard work by the entrepreneur. The greater the investors' concerns over these agency

* Reprinted from 51 *University of Chicago Law Review* 1061 (1984).

problems, the less they are willing to pay for a given percentage of the income generated by the firm's assets. In order to convince investors to pay more, the entrepreneur has to enter into institutional arrangements that limit his discretion to further his own interests at the expense of investors.

Though oversimplified and abstract, this discussion fairly describes the actual operation of capital markets. Firms that wish to raise capital from lenders enter into detailed contractual arrangements describing the nature of the project and limiting the ability of the borrower to behave in ways that are detrimental to the lender. Similarly, firms employ a variety of monitors and informational intermediaries such as independent accountants, investment bankers, and independent directors in order to convince suppliers of capital (lenders and shareholders) that the project is worthwhile and that agency problems will be kept to a minimum.

It is worth emphasizing that these voluntary concessions by those who want to raise capital are motivated purely by self-interest. All firms (entrepreneurs) want to minimize their cost of capital, just as they want to minimize the cost of all other factors of production. Because it is the firm (the entrepreneur) that bears the cost of institutional arrangements that operate to the detriment of investors, the firm is able to lower its cost of capital by adopting institutional arrangements that minimize the resources wasted by investors in determining the suitability of investments and in monitoring the behavior of the firm's agents. Society as a whole also suffers when inefficient governance structures are adopted because fewer goods and services are produced. But investors do not suffer: they are indifferent between investing at a lower price in a firm with an inefficient institutional arrangement and investing at a higher price in a firm where they are better protected.

This important insight—that it is in the interest of the firm (entrepreneur) to adopt efficient contractual arrangements because the firm pays for inefficiencies through a higher cost of capital—is implicitly recognized by corporate law. Under modern enabling statutes, firms are for the most part free to adopt whatever structures they choose. State corporate statutes provide a set of standard-form terms, but firms are generally free to alter these terms in their charters or bylaws. The judicial function is largely confined to enforcing the agreement (sometimes implicit) between the parties. The federal securities laws impose upon firms mandatory obligations that cannot be varied by agreement, but their focus is on disclosure; in the main, they do not restrict firms' ability to adopt whatever institutional arrangements they wish, so long as the arrangements are disclosed....

Labor law is strikingly different. The assumption dominant in corporate law—that firms have incentives to adopt contractual provisions that maximize investors' wealth—is completely alien to labor law.

Rather, labor law generally assumes that unless firms are subjected to direct regulation, they will adopt governance mechanisms that oppress labor. Firms, for example, are forbidden to create company unions, to require workers to forgo union affiliation as a condition of employment, to have an announced policy of firing all employees who engage in concerted activity, or to disseminate certain types of truthful information during unionization campaigns. The freedom of firms, under corporate law, to enter into whatever contractual arrangements they choose is generally absent in labor law. . . .

What accounts for the fundamental distinction between the regulation of labor and capital markets? Labor and capital are two different inputs to the production processes of particular firms. If a self-interested firm has incentives to adopt the contractual arrangements that shareholders prefer, why doesn't the identical firm have the same incentives with respect to workers? Initially, it would seem that similar tendencies would be at work. If workers (for simplicity I am ignoring differences among workers) prefer compensation to take the form of fringe benefits or safer working conditions rather than higher wages, the firm has a strong incentive to accommodate their preferences. If workers as a class prefer unions or some other type of collective representative to individual bargaining, firms will contract with unions voluntarily; indeed, firms would compete for labor by advertising their willingness to deal with unions in the same manner that firms compete for capital by advertising their willingness to be subject to scrutiny by independent, third-party auditors. Firms would voluntarily enter into both types of arrangements in order to minimize the cost of a factor of production. Nothing turns on whether the firm is seeking to minimize its cost of capital or its cost of labor.

Despite the obvious similarities between the operation of capital and labor markets, some possible differences between the two might be thought to justify the greater bias toward regulation in labor markets. The three most important differences are that capital markets are closer to the ideal of perfect competition than labor markets; that possibilities of firm-specific investments exist in labor markets that do not exist in capital markets; and that participants in labor markets have less ability to diversify risk. The implications of these differences, however, are ambiguous.

Investors in capital markets are protected by the virtually infinite number of investment substitutes. Firms compete for investment dollars, and investors who are dissatisfied with a particular investment can sell it without difficulty. Nor is it necessary for each investor to be aware of the characteristics of particular firms. So long as market prices of securities reflect the relevant characteristics of particular firms—and the evidence indicates that they do—it is very hard for an investor to make what is ex ante a bad deal. By accepting the market price, investors are protected.

Labor markets exhibit far different characteristics. Apart from competition for labor among firms, fewer substitutes exist for labor opportunities. Being self-employed, in other words, is for workers a less efficient substitute than placing money in the bank is for investors. Moreover, because of the difficulties associated with relocating, the exit option is much more costly for workers than for investors. Finally, labor is a more heterogeneous good than capital; as a result, accepting the market wage of a particular firm without search might be a less rational strategy for workers than accepting the market price of a security is for investors.

One possible effect of these differences between labor and capital markets is that firms might be able to offer a different and inferior package, particularly lower wages, than would prevail under perfect competition. But the magnitude of this effect might also be very small. It is not necessary that there be an infinite number of competitors for a market to behave competitively; indeed, industries with a few large firms can and often do exhibit the characteristics of a competitive industry. Nor is it necessary that all participants in a particular market be well-informed for the market to behave competitively. So long as there is a sufficient number of informed shoppers, firms will not be able to offer inferior products (conditions of employment) or charge supracompetitive prices (pay below-market wages). And if employment terms are competitively set, the uninformed will tend (at least if price discrimination is rare) to be protected....

The possibility of firm-specific investments of human capital in labor markets raises a somewhat different problem. It suggests that although labor markets may be competitive at the time of the original negotiation, they may not remain competitive after one of the parties becomes dependent on the other (or at the very least faces the cost of relocation). At the extreme, a firm could hire a worker and then reduce his wage to a level just above the worker's opportunity wage minus the worker's cost of relocation. Workers in competitive labor markets realize this possibility, however, and demand compensation ex ante. In order to allay workers' rational concerns and thereby reduce the amount of compensation that must be paid, firms have incentives to adopt governance mechanisms that reduce the probability of opportunistic behavior by the firm ex post. One possibility is for firms to strengthen the "voice" alternative for workers: grievance-resolution mechanisms of various kinds decrease the ability of firms to engage in opportunistic behavior at workers' expense.

The third major difference between capital and labor markets is the relative inability of participants in labor markets to diversify risk. Human capital, unlike capital investments in particular firms, is notoriously difficult to diversify. But again, the implications of this point for the regulation of labor markets are obscure. In competitive labor markets, inefficient risk-bearing is of little consequence for workers with no firm-specific investment of human capital. Apart from the costs of relocating, this class of workers has the ability to shift its labor to other firms if one particular firm suffers an economic downturn. Relative inability to bear risk is relevant, however, for risk-averse workers whose firm-specific investments of human capital constitute a large percentage of their wealth. These workers will demand compensation for having to bear risk; conversely, firms will attempt to design contractual arrangements—providing such risk-shifting devices as long-term contracts or severance-pay provisions—in order to minimize the risk borne by workers. In short, we should observe different governance mechanisms in labor markets than in capital markets, but there is no reason to believe that workers will be systematically worse off than investors.

It is worth emphasizing that I am not claiming that workers will never enter into bargains that do not work out well ex post; I am not even claiming that all workers will make prudent bargains as judged ex ante. Investors do not always make perfect bargains either. My point is that it is extremely unlikely that either workers or investors will be systematically exploited in any meaningful sense. The interest of the firm in minimizing the cost of all inputs in the production process will cause it to adopt the contractual mechanisms that best allay workers' and investors' rational concerns.

Note

1. *Federal versus State Regulation.* In an omitted section of the paper, Professor Fischel notes that most labor legislation is at the federal level, while most corporate law is at the state level. Many corporate-law commentators have suggested that state regulation leads to a "race to the bottom," whereby states seeking to have firms incorporate in their state enact more and more lax laws that favor management over shareholders. Fischel insists, however, that state competition will produce optimal laws: managers want to attract investors, and one way of doing so is incorporating in a state whose laws favor investors. The corporate race-to-the-bottom debate is reviewed in Roberta Romano, *Foundations of Corporate Law* (New York: Oxford University Press, 1993), 85–99. She finds that the issue boils down to the empirical question of the efficiency of product markets and takeover markets; her review of the empirical evidence favors state regulation over national regulation.

An analogous debate on whether state environmental regulation would result in a destructive race to the bottom is explored in Richard L. Revesz, *Foundations of Environmental Law* (New York: Oxford University Press, 1997), Chapter 7. Revesz distinguishes race-to-the-bottom fears, whereby states underregulate in an effort to attract industry, from interstate-externality concerns, whereby states underregulate because much of the benefit of, say, clean-air legislation would accrue to downwind states.

Fischel argues that competition among state employment laws for firm relocations should make workers better off, just as competition among state incorporation laws for firm incorporation revenues makes investors better off. Fischel concedes, however, that the greater immobility of workers compared with investors weakens his argument. In the United States, labor law is handled at the federal level and preempts state law; but employment discrimination and employment laws enacted by Congress generally may be supplemented by equally or more protective state legislation. Whether regulation should be set at the state or the national level is an underdeveloped topic in labor and employment law.

B. Internal Labor Markets and Relational Employment Contracts

The price-theory model of labor markets envisions many workers and many employers bidding for work. A day laborer may be the archetypal worker in that model. But many workers have a long-term relationship with a single employer for much of their working life. These workers do not determine daily whether the current wage matches their labor supply schedule, and the employers do not check daily whether current marginal productivity exceeds their workers' wage. In short, the "spot" market envisioned by the price-theory model does not seem to fit these workers well.

Since the 1970s, a rich literature has developed that examines the "internal labor markets" of firms that employ workers for much of their careers. Career employment provides benefits for employees who value job security and for firms that believe seniority will help them attract and motivate a skilled workforce. A major difficulty of career employment is that outside conditions, such as technology, consumer preferences, and foreign competition, can change dramatically in even a decade, much less the span of a career. Workers and employers locked in long-term relationships are vulnerable to exploitation or dashed expectations. Much employment regulation—particularly the regulation of pensions and terminations—attempts to protect workers in these career jobs.

With these risks, why would workers and an employer enter into a long-term relationship? The basic reason is that a long-term relationship can be more productive, allowing both the employer and its employees to earn more than they would in a series of short-term relationships. The greater productivity comes from firm-specific investments (e.g., the worker learns the company approach) and from the greater work effort of properly monitored long-term employees.

The simplest model of career employment arises from firm-specific investments (i.e., investments in worker skills that add to the value of the firm but not to the value of a worker who is forced to leave the firm). Without firm-specific investments, a worker has only general skills and always receives a wage that equals his productivity. Some workers, however, take the time and effort to learn skills that are especially valuable to one employer. The worker and firm share in on-the-job training costs early in the worker's career. The worker invests in training by accepting lower pay than he could get from another job in the early years. The employer invests in training by paying the worker more than he currently produces for the firm. When training is complete, the worker's productivity is enhanced and both parties share the benefits. The worker is paid more than he would receive in a noncareer job, but less than he currently produces. (A graphical analysis of this model appears in Stewart J. Schwab, "Life–Cycle Justice: Accommodating Just Cause and Employment at Will," 92 *Michigan Law Review* 8, 14 (1993), reproduced in Chapter 7 of this volume, Figure 7–1.)

The key point to this simple investment model is that the agreement is self-enforcing. Neither the employer nor the employee wants to end the relationship because once it begins, both sides recoup benefits after they make investments. Because the contract is self-enforcing, the law has no special role to play in monitoring the relationship. The contract would not be self-enforcing if, for example, the parties agreed that the worker would be paid more than his current productivity late in the relationship. In that case, the employer would benefit by ending the relationship at the point where wages exceed productivity. Symmetrically, the contract would not be self-enforcing if the parties agreed that the employee would receive above the noncareer wage early and below the noncareer wage later. In that case, the employee would want to quit and take a higher-paying job in the external market after being trained.

In addition to encouraging firm-specific investments, many career employment relationships arise from attempts to control and reward worker effort. Typically, output depends on the worker's effort as well as on factors outside the worker's control. Greater effort leads to greater output and profits, allowing for higher wages. An ideal contract would specify the optimal level of worker effort and the wage. Workers are willing to work harder so long as the extra discomfort is less than the extra pay. At the optimal level of effort, the extra effort just equals the extra productivity and wage. Note that optimal effort is less than maximum effort, because at some point the worker prefers an easier job to extra pay. If a risk-neutral employer could easily observe effort, and workers were risk averse, the optimal contract would have the worker give the optimal effort and be paid a constant wage that does not depend on output. This contract is self-enforcing, in that neither side has an incentive to break it.

Problems of asymmetric information may induce the parties to make agreements about effort that are not fully self-enforcing. For example, in many jobs the employer cannot easily observe how hard the employee is working. One solution is to pay the worker based on output rather than effort, but this places on the worker the risk of adverse outside conditions beyond the worker's control (e.g., weather). Another solution is to have the employee post a bond that he forfeits if the employer eventually discovers he is shirking on the optimal effort. As long as the probability of detection times the bond exceeds the value of shirking, the employee will continue to work hard. In addition to the fear that employers might expropriate the bond, another problem is that workers often cannot afford to post actual bonds.

A third solution is to have the worker agree to work hard in the early years of his or her career in return for moderate pay. Eventually the employer will discover the worker's level of effort. If the worker's effort is optimal, the worker is rewarded with a promotion, bonus, pension, and the like. If the worker's effort is suboptimal, the worker is fired. Such an agreement can induce optimal effort by the worker. The danger is that the agreement is not self-enforcing. Employers have an incentive to receive the worker's hard effort in the early years of the career, and then renege on the later bonus. The employer's concern for a good reputation is one check on such opportunism. Legal constraints on termination may be another. (For a graphical analysis of this "efficiency-wage" model, see Stewart J. Schwab, "Life–Cycle Justice: Accommodating Just Cause and Employment at Will," 92 *Michigan Law Review* 8, 18 (1993), reproduced in Chapter 7 of this volume, Figure 7–2.)

The following article by Michael Wachter and Randall Wright amplifies on these basic features of internal labor markets.

"The Economics of Internal Labor Markets"*
MICHAEL L. WACHTER and RANDALL D. WRIGHT

... In the textbook model of the labor market, firms and workers make few investments in the job or in the relationship. Hence, firms can discharge workers, and workers can quit, at little cost. In the extreme case, sunk investments are zero, so the parties lose nothing by terminating their relationship.

The distinguishing characteristic of the internal labor market [ILM], on the other hand, is that firms and workers incur substantial sunk cost investments. Since these investments are not portable across firms, job immobility results. If workers were to switch jobs or firms were to discharge workers, the sunk investments would be lost. Minimizing these sunk cost losses encourages the parties to maintain their ongoing relationship.

The external labor market [ELM] is the benchmark for any analysis of the ILM. It provides the opportunity costs of alternative employment for workers, and of alternative workers for firms. Workers in the ILM always have opportunities to find jobs with other firms, and these external opportunities provide limits below which their rewards cannot fall. Similarly, firms can hire new workers from the ELM and discharge workers who fail to meet work standards. Although the wages and other terms and conditions of employment are set administratively by the firm,

* 29 *Industrial Relations* 240–62 (1990).

they must ultimately rest on the opportunities for hiring new workers into port-of-entry ILM jobs from the external market. Hence, ELM economic pressures on the ILM are not repealed; they are simply rechanneled through these port-of-entry jobs.

[F]our central economic factors ... affect an ongoing employment relationship: (1) firm or match-specific training, (2) risk aversion, (3) asymmetric information, and (4) transaction costs. Our thesis is that all four of these factors need to be considered simultaneously in order to provide a view of the ILM that is consistent with the broad "stylized facts" of ongoing employment relations....

Match-specific capital. The central rationale for long-term attachments rests on firm-specific investments. Narrowly defined, these refer to investments in training that make workers more productive with their current firm than with alternative firms. In the polar case, such training only increases the marginal product of workers on their current job and has a zero impact on their productivity with other firms. The result is an incentive to continue the employment relationship.

Match-specific investments is a somewhat broader category. It refers to firm-specific investments in human capital via on-the-job training, learning-by-doing, etc.; to worker-specific investments; and generally to the case in which a firm and a worker may simply have formed a "good match." This match implies a greater expected "surplus" than would result if a new random worker was inserted into the slot, or if the worker was assigned a new random job.

The surplus consists of the firm's profit derived from its current employees over and above what could be earned by recourse only to an external labor market, and the utility of the workers from the employment compensation package over and above what they could derive on the external market. The goal of the worker-firm coalition is to maximize this surplus subject to constraints imposed by technology, information, and other features of the environment.

Workers enter a firm with general (i.e., portable across firms) training. However, productivity often benefits from match-specific investments, so the size of the surplus becomes a function of the return on those investments. The first investments in the match are the expenditures on hiring and screening that allocate workers to jobs in which their productivity is likely to be highest. Specific training can then be undertaken at a level which maximizes the value of the match.

A difficulty with match-specific investments is that although the ILM is disciplined *ex ante* by the usual market forces, *ex post* there is a lock-in effect due to the investments that have been sunk into the relationship. This makes the *ex post* ILM a bilateral bargaining situation. In this context, inefficient rent seeking is possible. A particular problem involves quits or discharges designed to prevent a party from recouping past investments. To encourage joint surplus maximization, rather than self-interested or counterproductive rent seeking, the ILM must design enforceable contractual arrangements to deal with such turnover....

The ILM's answer to turnover is to deal with it *indirectly* through wage or compensation policy. In his seminal study on human capital, Becker suggests that rent-seeking behavior (quits or discharges to gain a larger proportion of the surplus) could be reduced if both parties shared in the investment costs, with the goal of making their contract self-enforcing. For example, workers would invest in their own specific training to the extent that their current wage (w) is lower than their opportunity wage (ow) in the external market. The firm's investment is similarly measured by the difference between the worker's marginal product (mp) and w. The worker would be deterred from quitting, and the firm would be deterred from laying off the worker, because such behavior would result in the loss of future returns on these investments.

Thus, a central result of the specific-training literature is a wedge between the marginal product and the wage (the firm's investment) and between the wage and the opportunity wage (the workers' investments). The wedge reflects the fact that the returns on investments occur later than the investment costs. A continuing pattern of such investments produces the familiar upward-sloping age-earnings profile. Internal promotions can similarly be explained by this investment pattern....

Risk aversion.... Whether due to better access to financial capital markets or simply to different attitudes toward fluctuations in income, ... employers are assumed in these models to be typically less risk averse than workers.

Efficient risk sharing thus requires that compensation be smoothed. Smoothing means that mp will vary by more than w, and at any point in time mp need not equal w. Hence, the risk-sharing model, like the match-specific investment model, predicts divergence between mp and w. This divergence has different implications in the two models in terms of the sequencing of pay. Only match-specific investments explain why wages increase with age. However, the profile could also exhibit a high variance. Indeed, absent risk aversion on the part of workers, wages may vary as much as profits.

There are trade-offs, as well as complementarities, between match-specific investments and risk aversion. The deferred compensation that is used to make contracts self-enforcing conflicts with the goal of smoothing workers' income (unless deferred compensation can be perfectly insured against future exogenous events).

Asymmetric information.... If both parties cannot observe work effort or product market conditions at equal cost, cost minimization suggests allocating the collection of such information to the low-cost party. Although it seems efficient to simply have that party report the results, incentive problems arise because the party with the informational advantage can use that information to achieve opportunistic aims. For a contract to be efficient, it must resolve this dilemma: It must not only assign the information gathering to the low-cost party, but also provide a mechanism which prevents the information from being used strategically. We call a contract that resolves this dilemma a self-enforcing contract or an incentive-compatible contract.

Contracts that control workers' strategic behavior. It is generally assumed that workers know their own work effort, while the firm can only learn about the quality of the workers' input through costly monitoring. Since workers prefer leisure to work, they have an incentive to overstate their effort if left to monitor it themselves. Modeled as a principal-agent problem, consider a worker (agent) who produces output (y) according to the function $y = f(e,x)$, where e is effort and x is a random variable. Neither x nor e is observed by the firm (principal), although we will assume that it can observe y. If e (or x) is public information, then assuming the worker is risk averse and the firm is risk neutral, the optimal contract would have the worker expend a certain efficient level of effort in return for *constant* wage w. The effect is to make w independent of y.

When information is distributed asymmetrically, however, an opportunity arises for strategic behavior by the worker. The worker is able to put forth a very low level of e (assuming leisure is preferable to hard work) and claim that the resulting low level of y is due to a bad realization of x, so she/he is entitled to the same level of w. Hence, there is no incentive to supply the correct effort.

The optimal contract in this case (under certain fairly mild regularity conditions) sets w as an increasing function of output, $w = w(y)$, $w' > 0$. This provides incentives for more appropriate effort, although it also exposes the worker to uncertain income, which is a problem if she/he is risk averse. This illustrates an important tradeoff between allocating income risk and providing the correct incentives in contracts. It is the extension of this simple model that leads to the broad problem of motivating work effort through incentive pay....

Contracts that control firms' strategic behavior. There are also models in which firms have the informational advantage, usually with respect to the state of product demand or technology....

Appropriate work incentives would encourage workers to work harder when product market conditions are favorable and mp is higher. But if w were constant due to income smoothing, the firm would have an incentive to misreport the product market as being favorable, hence forcing greater work effort. As above, the misreporting problem is alleviated by making compensation (as in bonuses or profit sharing) vary with work effort. Such contracts have important self-enforcing properties because the firm does not gain by misreporting product market conditions. Here again, however, income smoothing is traded off against appropriate work incentives....

A second problem relates to the sequencing of w and mp .... In this case, workers (but not firms) are in the recoupment phase on their sunk investments in later years (with $w > mp$). By misreporting its product market conditions as unfavorable, a firm could seek to discharge workers who are recouping on their deferred compensation. One solution is to restrict the way in which a firm can adjust to changes in product market conditions. Seniority schedules are partly a response to this problem. When the firm is investing in workers, forcing it to lay off workers according to a seniority schedule means that it must accept a loss on investment in junior workers before senior workers (with $w > mp$) can be laid off. ....

Transaction costs.... If the parties inside the firm attempt to maximize the coalition's surplus, they must obviously attempt to reduce transaction costs as much as possible (or, more accurately, as much as it is efficient to do so). Since negotiating, writing, and enforcing contracts often incur high transaction costs, complex state-contingent contracts might not be joint profit maximizing.

In place of this state-contingent contract, the parties could reach an understanding on general principles, but not on specifics. This agreement could be either implicit or explicit, although in most nonunion firms it is entirely implicit. In this contracting framework, the parties deal with new events by rolling over their general understanding to these new factors.

Incomplete contracts might seem to worsen problems of asymmetric information. Absent detailed, state-contingent contracts, what factors prevent opportunistic behavior by either of the parties? Perhaps the most important disincentive for strategic behavior is the repeated nature of the ILM relationship. Repeated transactions are less subject to opportunism than are short-run relationships. An opportunity for gain that results in a breakdown of the relationship is not likely to be pursued if there is much surplus to be lost or significant fixed costs to be incurred in terminating or restarting the relationship. Long-term relationships sometimes can reduce opportunities to misrepresent the outcomes of stochastic events due to the application of the law of large numbers; it is simply not acceptable to report that a certain advantageous outcome has occurred too often.

Reputational considerations are also frequently cited as critical in restraining strategic behavior. Obviously firms are more likely than workers to acquire reputations in the external labor market. To the extent that firms engage in strategic behavior at the cost of workers, their reputation in the external market will suffer. These firms will have to pay higher wages to attract new workers or will find it more costly to continue the contract provision that requires the workers to post a bond in the form of deferred compensation.

A second control over strategic behavior is the potential for retaliation by the other party. Firms can obviously discharge workers. The more difficult issue concerns redress for workers. By deciding to shirk in response to perceived unfairness, workers can prevent a firm from realizing profits generated by strategic behavior. In the extreme, workers can engage in sabotage. Using such methods, however, clearly reduces the joint profits of the parties.

Perhaps the most powerful redress available to workers is to insist that their contracts be made more explicit and more enforceable by third parties. This effectively means that the workers will become unionized. Third-party enforcement generates transaction costs that reduce the joint profits generated by an employment relationship. Moreover, when the underlying issue is one of misreporting asymmetric information, third-party enforcement would necessitate that any asymmetric information be provided to the third party.

The efficiency argument for labor unions is that there are potential gains in having workers choose an exclusive agent-auditor to represent them in bargaining with the employer. In this context, unions lower the transaction costs by replacing worker-by-worker bargaining with a single agent. The agent also acts as an auditor who monitors the firm's use of its (asymmetric) information and reduces the potential for inefficient rent seeking. This view of unions has been stressed by Freeman and Medoff [as we shall see in Chapter 2—eds.].

Notes and Questions

1. *Dual Labor Markets.* The detailed theory of internal labor markets grew out of the broader theory of "dual labor markets." Dual-labor-market theory divides the labor market into two noncompeting sectors. Internal labor markets govern primary-sector jobs. These jobs have high wages, stable employment, and good working conditions. Secondary-sector jobs, by contrast, are low-paying, unstable, and dead-end. Jobs in the secondary sector do not require much education or experience, and workers are not rewarded for having either of them. The sectors do not compete directly with each other; secondary workers tend to be locked in secondary jobs, with little chance of moving to the higher-paying primary sector. Without competition from secondary workers, primary jobs can remain high paying. See Michael J. Piore and Peter Doeringer, *Internal Labor Markets and Manpower Analysis* (Lexington, Mass.: D.C. Heath, 1971); Michael J. Piore, "Jobs and Training," in Samuel H. Beer and Richard E. Barringer, eds., *The State and the Poor* (Cambridge, Mass.: Winthrop, 1970).

Some empirical evidence supports the existence of two separate sectors of the economy, one in which education and experience result in higher wages and one in which they do not, with wage differentials that persist over time. See William Dickens and Kevin Lang, "A Test of Dual Labor Market Theory," 75 *American Economic Review* 792 (1985), and "The Reemergence of Segmented Labor Market Theory," 78 *American Economic Review (Papers*

& *Proceedings)* 129 (May 1988). Still, many economists are troubled by the failure of dual-labor-market theory to adequately explain why secondary workers with appropriate education cannot enter the primary sector, given that they presumably are willing to work at wages below the primary-sector wage.

2. *"Efficiency Wage" Theory.* Will workers work harder if they receive higher wages? The basic price-theory model of labor markets assumes the causality runs the other way. Competitive firms pay their workers their marginal productivity, but the pay does not influence productivity. This is the standard assumption for other markets as well. Consumers pay more for higher-quality bread, but paying a higher price does not increase the quality of a particular loaf.

Two separate ideas suggest why a firm that pays higher wages might have more productive workers. First, better workers will apply for jobs as the wage rises. This is similar to other markets; consumers get better-quality bread as they pay more. The difference is that, in general, consumers can determine the quality of bread by inspecting it, and do not have to rely indirectly on the high price. For many jobs, however, firms have difficulty directly determining the quality of job applicants, and a higher wage helps attract a better applicant pool. The basic point of this first idea, however, is that the higher wages attract better workers but do not make particular workers more productive.

The second idea suggests that, for a given worker or workforce, raising the wage can induce greater productivity. There are several reasons for this. First, workers are less likely to quit because of the high wage. This allows firms to spend more money on training workers, knowing they will have time to recoup their investment. Second, workers are more motivated when they are treated fairly, and will view the firm as fair if it pays them well. Third, workers will work harder at the high-paying job to avoid being fired because the penalty of losing the high pay is larger.

The idea that wages influence productivity is the key concept in the "efficiency-wage" model. In this model, firms increase wages so long as the extra gain in productivity exceeds the extra wage. This efficiency wage, as it is called, is higher than the market-clearing wage of the price-theory model because it equals the marginal productivity of labor, recognizing that the wage itself increases this productivity.

The efficiency-wage model was first applied to developing economies. The argument there was that increasing wages above the market-clearing level would improve the health and nutrition of workers, making them more productive. The model was later applied to advanced economies as well. Among the important implications of the efficiency-wage model is that it helps explain involuntary unemployment. Firms will not lower wages to market-clearing levels (wages are "sticky" downward), because doing so would reduce the productivity of its workforce. For an excellent introduction to efficiency-wage models, see George A. Akerlof and Janet L. Yellen, eds., *Efficiency Wage Models of the Labor Market* (New York: Cambridge University Press, 1986).

3. *Complexity of Internal Labor Markets*. Economists have had difficulty empirically distinguishing firm-specific-capital explanations from efficiency-wage explanations for long-term employment. For example, efficiency-wage theory suggests that the employer will institute back-loaded compensation schemes to encourage effort, but many other possible explanations for these schemes also exist. Wachter and Wright's main point is that ILMs arise for a variety of reasons; thus, we should not expect any one reason to explain how they operate. In particular, they emphasize "(1) firm or match-specific training, (2) risk aversion, (3) asymmetric information, and (4) transaction costs" as economic factors that may affect the creation of an ILM.

C. Changing Employment Markets

Internal labor markets focus on career or primary workers. The paradigmatic case, whereby a worker spent the bulk of his working life with a single employer, never described most workers. The average worker in the 1970s, for example, held ten jobs during his or her lifetime. Slightly over a quarter (28 percent) of the workforce were currently in jobs that would last twenty years or more, and nearly a quarter (23 percent) were in jobs that would last less than two years. See Robert E. Hall, "The Importance of Lifetime Jobs in the U.S. Economy," 72 *American Economic Review* 716 (1982). Today, many scholars detect a trend toward less job attachment. Richard S. Belous, for example, reports a dramatic increase between 1980 and 1988 in temporary, part-time, and subcontracted workers—what he terms "contingent" workers as opposed to "core" workers. See Belous, *The Contingent Economy: The Growth of the Temporary, Part–Time and Subcontracted Workforce* (Washington D.C.: National Planning Association, 1989). As Belous explains, core workers have relatively stable employment with a single employer. Firms expand their workforce around these core workers in boom times by hiring contingent workers, and then let the contingent workers go in slack times. These contingent workers, then, provide firms with flexibility. The rise in the contingent workforce in recent years comes from the greater importance of the global economy, which puts a premium on management flexibility in responding to shifts in market conditions. Compared with core workers, contingent workers typically have lower pay and fewer health-care, pension, and other benefits. Some scholars, however, have questioned the basic assertion that lifetime jobs are disappearing in the United States. See Henry S. Farber, "Are Lifetime Jobs Disappearing? Job Duration in the United States: 1973–1993," in John Haltiwanger, Marilyn Manser, and Robert Topel, eds., *Labor Statistics Measurement Issues* (University of Chicago Press, 1998) 157–203.

In 1993, President Clinton appointed a blue-ribbon commission, chaired by Harvard economist and former Secretary of Labor John Dunlop, to examine labor markets and make policy recommendations. One of their major areas of concern was with the contingent workforce, as the following reading shows.

"Contingent Workers"*

U.S. DEPARTMENTS OF LABOR AND COMMERCE

1. General Observations

As employers seek new ways to make the employment relationship more flexible, they increasingly rely on a variety of arrangements popularly known as "contingent work." The use of independent contractors and part-time, temporary, seasonal, and leased workers has expanded tremendously in recent years. The Commission views this change as both a healthy development and a cause for concern.

On the positive side, contingent employment relationships are in many respects a sensible response to today's competitive global marketplace. The benefits are clear that various forms of contingent work can offer to both some management and some workers. Contingent arrangements allow some firms to maximize workforce flexibility in the face of seasonal and cyclical forces and the demands of modern methods such as just-in-time production. This same flexibility helps some workers, more of whom must balance the demands of family and work as the numbers of dual-earner and single-parent households rise. Workers benefit when a diversity of employment relationships is available. For example, temporary work provides a mechanism for transitions between jobs, affording employers and workers an opportunity to size each other up before deciding to enter into a more stable employment relationship. Manpower Incorporated CEO Mitchell S. Fromstein told the Commission that his firm transitioned approximately 150,000 "temps" into permanent jobs with client companies in 1993 alone.

On the negative side, ... contingent arrangements may be introduced simply to reduce the amount of compensation paid by the firm for the same amount and value of work, which raises some serious social questions. This is particularly true because contingent workers are drawn disproportionately from the most vulnerable sectors of the workforce. They often receive less pay and benefits than traditional full-time or "permanent" workers, and they are less likely to benefit from the protections of labor and employment laws. A large percentage of workers who hold part-time or temporary positions do so involuntarily. The expansion of contingent work has contributed to the increasing gap between high and low wage workers and to the increasing sense of insecurity among workers....

Unfortunately, current tax, labor, and employment law gives employers and employees incentives to create contingent relationships not for the sake of flexibility or efficiency but in order to evade their legal obligations. For example, an employer and a worker may see advantages

---

* *Report and Recommendations of the Commission on the Future of Worker–Management Relations* (The Dunlop Commission, Dec. 1994), 35–41.

wholly unrelated to efficiency or flexibility in treating the worker as an independent contractor rather than an employee. The employer will not have to make contributions to Social Security, unemployment insurance, workers' compensation, and health insurance, will save the administrative expense of withholding, and will be relieved of responsibility to the worker under labor and employment laws. The worker will lose the protection of those laws and benefits and the employer's contribution to Social Security, but may accept the arrangement nonetheless because it gives him or her an opportunity for immediate and even illegitimate financial gains through underpayment of taxes. Many low-wage workers have no practical choice in the matter. The federal government loses billions of dollars to underpayment of taxes by workers misclassified as independent contractors.

Notes

1. *Uniform Statutory Definition of Employee.* The Dunlop Commission recommends a single definition of employee for all employment laws and the Internal Revenue Code. The Commission advocates an "economic realities" test, under which workers who are economically dependent on a single entity should generally be treated as employees. "Factors such as low wages, low skill levels, and having one or few employers," the Commission opines, "should all militate against treatment as an independent contractor." A single economic-realities test will reduce the incentives to evade legal obligations by labeling the worker an independent contractor rather than an employee.

2. *The Diversity of Contingent Workers.* One problem with a single definition of employee for all statutes is that it lumps together all contingent workers and all statutes without confronting the variety of concerns to which the "contingent worker" label is attached. One concern might be that many part-time workers do not qualify for their company's health insurance. The policy response might be to amend the federal laws regulating employee benefits. A quite different concern is that child-care workers and other domestic workers, often now labeled independent contractors, are paid less than the minimum wage. A third concern is that home workers, many of whom spend long hours at computer keyboards, face oppressive conditions. A unifying theme is that additional regulation of contingent workers will raise costs and eliminate jobs. A central point of the Dunlop Commission report is that tightening the definition of independent contractor would be good policy because these workers are exploited. But government regulation to eliminate or discourage such jobs will hurt the many workers who want part-time or part-year work to meet family or educational demands or who do not want (or want to pay for) health insurance and other benefits because they are covered under a spouse's policy. The Dunlop Commission's recommendations do not confront the subtlety of the issues here. For an amplification of the dangers of lumping all contingent workers together, see Stewart J. Schwab, "The Diversity of Contingent Workers and the Need for Nuanced Policy," 52 *Washington & Lee Law Review* 915 (1995).

3. *Estimating the Contingent Workforce*. Dr. Richard S. Belous estimates that the contingent workforce is 25–30 percent of the American workforce, and growing. Belous, "The Rise of the Contingent Workforce: The Key Challenges and Opportunities," 52 *Washington & Lee Law Review* 863 (1995). Belous obtained his estimates by taking Bureau of Labor Statistics (BLS) data and adding up the percentages of workers who were part-time (18.8), temporary (1.3), self-employed (8.2), and in business services (4.5). Belous reached his lower bound by not counting some workers in order to reduce any double-counting. Double-counting problems grow as the number of categories included in the contingent workforce increases.

4. *Defining and Surveying the Contingent Workforce*. Recognizing that existing data were poor, the Bureau of Labor Statistics added a supplement about the contingent workforce and alternate-arrangement workforce in its 1995 and 1997 Current Population Surveys (CPS), surveys of about 50,000 households conducted by the U.S. Census Bureau for BLS. The BLS defined contingent workers as those "who do not have an explicit or implicit contract for long-term employment." The first two questions in the supplement to the CPS were:

1. Some people are in temporary jobs that last only for a limited time or until the completion of the project. Is your job temporary?

2. Provided the economy does not change and your job performance is adequate, can you continue to work for your current employer as long as you wish?

Follow-up questions distinguished between workers holding temporary jobs and workers who left ongoing jobs for personal reasons, such as returning to school.

In its broadest estimate of the contingent workforce, the BLS found that 4.4 percent of the workforce (5.6 million workers) view their jobs as temporary. In a narrower estimate, the BLS found that 1.9 percent of the workforce were wage and salary workers on the job for one year or less who expected their job to end within a year. Some demographic evidence suggests that contingent workers are more "exploited" than noncontingent workers. As Table 1–1 shows, compared with noncontingent workers, contingent workers are young, female, of Hispanic origin, poorly paid, and without employer-provided health insurance plans. On the other hand, Table 1–1 also reveals that contingent workers are more likely than noncontingent workers to be in school or college educated, and are no more likely to be black. Other survey results indicate that nearly two-thirds of all contingent workers have health insurance, often obtained through family policies or private purchase. Table 1–2 shows that most contingent workers (56 percent) say they would prefer permanent employment, although a substantial number (36 percent) prefer their arrangement to permanent employment.

Table 1-1. Selected Characteristics of the Contingent and Alternative-Arrangement Workforces

Characteristic		Contingent	Non-Contingent	Alternative Arrangements				
				Independent Contractor	On-Call Worker	Temporary Help Agency	Contract Firm	Traditional Arrangement
Percent of U.S. Workforce		4	96	6.7	1.6	1.0	0.6	90
					%			
Age	16 to 24	30	13	3	22	23	10	15
	25 to 34	25	25	18	23	30	34	25
	35+	45	62	78	56	47	56	60
Gender	Male	49	54	67	49	45	70	53
	Female	51	46	33	51	55	30	47
Race[a]	White	82	85	91	89	75	82	85
	Black	11	11	5	8	21	13	11
	Hispanic Origin	12	9	7	13	12	6	10
Education Status (ages 16 to 24)	In School	64	40	31	50	16	26	43
	Not In School	36	60	69	50	84	74	57
Education (ages 25 +)	College Degree +	36	30	34	26	22	33	30
	<College Degree	64	71	66	74	78	67	71
Health Insurance Coverage	Employer-Provided	21	54	N/A	20	7	50	58
	Covered by Any	66	82	73	67	46	82	83
Pension	Included in Plan	15	44	2	19	4	36	47
	Eligible for Plan	23	49	4	27	10	48	52
Hours	Full-time	58	82	34	47	80	83	82
	Part-time	42	18	66	53	20	17	18
Median Weekly Salary		$417	$510	$523	$432	$329	$619	$510

[a] As the BLS explains, percentages for Race may not sum to 100 percent because data for the "other races" group are not presented and Hispanics are included in both the white and black population groups. Other details may not add to totals because of rounding.
Source: Bureau of Labor Statistics, news release, "Contingent and Alternative Arrangements" (Dec. 2, 1997), available at <ftp://ftp.bls.gov/pub/news.release/History/conemp.020398.news>.

Table 1–2. Job Satisfaction of the Contingent and Alternative–Arrangement Workforce

| | | Alternative Arrangements | | |
Preference	Contingent Workers	Independent Contractor	On–Call Worker	Temporary Help Agency
		------------------------------------- % -------------------------------------		
Own Employment	56	84	40	34
Noncontingent/Traditional Employment	36	9	50	59
It Depends/Not Available	8	7	10	7

Source: Bureau of Labor Statistics, news release, Contingent and Alternative Arrangements (Dec. 2, 1997), available at <ftp://ftp.bls.gov/pub/news.release/History/co-
nemp.020398.news>.

5. *Alternative–Arrangement Workers.* The BLS definition of contingent
workers emphasizes the short-term nature of the relationship. The BLS also
surveyed workers who might have long-term jobs, but whose jobs differ from
"typical" jobs. These "alternative employment arrangements" include independent contractors, on-call workers, temporary help agency workers, and
workers employed by contract firms. The largest group by far is independent
contractors, comprising 6.7 percent of the overall workforce. These include
independent consultants and free-lance workers. Most are self-employed
(and about half of all self-employed workers are independent contractors, the
others being business operators such as shop or restaurant owners), but 12
percent are wage and salary workers. On-call workers are people called in to
work only when needed, although they can be scheduled for several weeks in
a row. Examples include substitute teachers or construction workers supplied by a union hiring hall. Temporary help agency workers are persons
paid by a temporary help agency. The BLS survey distinguishes them from
contract workers, defined as persons working for a company that provides
employees or services to others under contract, and who usually work for
only one customer at the customer's work site.

These categories of alternative arrangements should not be lumped
together. Independent contractors and contract workers tend to have good
jobs. As Table 1–1 shows, they are more likely than workers in traditional
arrangements to be male, white, older, college educated, and well paid. The
vast majority (84 percent) of independent contractors prefer their arrangement to traditional work (Table 1–2). By contrast, temporary help agency
workers and on-call workers tend to be young, female, Hispanic or black,
without a college degree, and poorly paid. More would prefer a traditional
work arrangement than prefer their alternative arrangement.

The only common characteristics among alternative arrangements are
that, compared with traditional arrangements, workers are less likely to
work full-time or be covered by health insurance or a pension plan. Even so,
most work full-time (except for on-call workers) and most are covered by
health insurance (except for temporary help agency workers).

6. *Contingent Workers and Underemployment.* In a new reconceptualiza-
tion, Professor Lester insists that the root problem underlying contingent
work is not the degree of attachment to any single employer, or the unusual
nature of the legal arrangements, but whether the worker is underemployed.
Lester defines an underemployed worker as having "(1) inferior quality of

employment relative to other workers with the same level of education, skills or experience (human capital) and endowments; and (2) a preference for a job better matched to the worker's particular human capital and abilities, yet an inability to obtain a more suitable job." Gillian Lester, "Careers and Contingency," 51 *Stanford Law Review* 73, 87 (1998). Thus, a self-employed computer analyst who moves from place to place is not underemployed, nor is a high school graduate who take a temporary job with a personnel firm to acquire word processing skills. But the downsized worker forced to take a job without benefits outside her area of training is underemployed.

> At core is the fear that a class of workers is forced outside of the system of traditional jobs, in which workers have job security, benefits, and access to promotion ladders by which they may advance along a career path. The claim also seems to be that these "externalized" workers have worse jobs than they deserve and desire—otherwise, law reformers would not seek improvements through regulation....

> Studies like Belous's, which aggregate workers within certain labor market categories (e.g., part-time) in which there is a high prevalence of insecure or dead-end jobs, may understate the heterogeneity of workers in each class and thus overstate the problem. The BLS definition of contingency, which focuses on job security, identifies a narrower group, but may be both too narrow and too broad. Many workers who expect their jobs to last for more than one year may be trapped in a bad labor market path that will lead to labor market harms. Moreover, some who work on temporary and other short-term assignments experience no real economic insecurity, expecting to be at least as "employable" as traditional workers. A third approach focuses on the root harms sought to be avoided, rather than the facial characteristics of a particular worker's employment contract. I suggest that this root harm is "underemployment," i.e., when a worker is not matched to a job that exploits her human capital and motivations as fully as for comparably skilled and motivated workers. This creates a labor market problem that policymakers should try to solve if feasible.

Gillian Lester, "Careers and Contingency," 51 *Stanford Law Review* 86, 90 (1998).

D. The Level and Distribution of Earnings

How much money do Americans make? How much have earnings risen over time? What is the degree of inequality? These are important questions, and the answers require careful attention to definitions. In this section, we provide an introduction to these issues. These are labor market issues, because nearly three-quarters of all income comes from labor; the remaining quarter comes from dividends, rent, or profit from capital. As measured in the National Income and Product Accounts, labor's share of total national income increased from 68.9 percent in 1963 to 73.1 percent in 1972. Its share remained at 73.1 percent in 1995. Robert J. Gordon, "The American Real Wage Since 1963: Is It Unchanged or Has It More Than Doubled?" 2 (mimeo; December 17, 1995). The scholarly literature of the widening income disparity is vast. Among the well-known works is Bennett Harrison and Barry Bluestone, *The Great U–Turn: Corporate Restructuring and the Polarizing of America* (New York: Basic Books, 1988), claiming that earnings inequality fell through much of the 1970s but then had a "great U-turn" and began to rise sharply after 1978. For an overview of the literature, see Frank Levy and Richard J. Murnane, "U.S. Earnings Levels and Earnings Inequality: A Review of Recent Trends and Proposed Explanations," 30 *Journal of Economic Literature* 1333 (1992).

Definitions. In assessing income statistics, several key definitions arise. First, one must define earnings and income. For example, consider a worker who earns a $40,000 salary, has employer-paid health insurance worth $4,000, works in her own side business earning $5,000, and receives stock dividends and bank interest of $1,000. She also receives child support of $10,000 from her ex-husband. She lost her job for part of the year and received $2,000 in unemployment benefits and $1,000 in food stamps. The Current Population Survey of the Census Bureau, which provides the most commonly cited income figures, defines money earnings as wages and salary and net income from self-employment, before taxes. It does not include fringe benefits. Income includes earnings plus income from all other sources, including unemployment compensation, Social Security, interest and dividends, and alimony and child support. Not included are noncash benefits such as food stamps and subsidized lunches. If one is particularly interested in fringe benefits, other data sources, such as the BLS Employment Cost Index, would be more appropriate.

Second, an analyst of income statistics must distinguish between means and medians. Mean income is calculated by dividing total income by the number of units in the group. Median income is the income that divides the group in half, so that 50 percent of the units have greater than the median and 50 percent have less. If an above-median person earns more money, the mean will rise but the median will not. Typically, mean income is larger than median income, because some people have extremely high incomes that raise the mean, while no one earns less than $0 and thus no one drags the mean down too far. For example, in 1998 the mean income of year-round, full-time workers was $47,459 for men and $32,714 for women. The corresponding median numbers were lower, $36,252 for men and $26,855 for women. See Table 1–3.

Third, one must notice the time unit of earnings. Sometimes statements are made about average hourly earnings. For example, according to the Bureau of Labor Statistics, in 1996 the average hourly earnings in the United States were $11.82. At other times, statements are made about weekly, monthly, or annual earnings. The smaller the unit of time, the higher earnings appear to be. For example, as a rough cut, weekly earnings can be converted to annual earnings by multiplying by 52, but generally this will be an overestimate, because it ignores weeks of unemployment or other weeks without payment.

Fourth, in judging trends over time, one must recognize whether the statistics are reported in "current" or "real" terms. In 1970, actual per capita income was only $3,177. By 1998, income had risen to $20,120. But much of this increase did not improve the lot of workers, because the price of goods rose by 163.0/41.3 or approximately 395 percent over that time. (See Table 1–3, column 10.) The real, or inflation-adjusted, increase in wages was much less. To track the economic progress of workers over time, the standard method is to convert actual wages to a base-year's wages through use of the BLS Consumer Price Index. For example, to convert the 1970 income to 1998 dollars, we can multiply by 163.0/41.3. In 1998 dollars, then, the 1970 per capita income was $12,539. The accuracy of the Consumer Price Index (CPI) is critical in judging income trends over time. We discuss the controversy surrounding the CPI methodology below.

Table 1–3. Income Trends over Time

	Per Capita		Full-Time, Full-Year Workers				Median Household Income	Median Family Income	
			Male		Female				
Year	Current $	1998 $	Median	Mean	Median	Mean	Income	Income	CPI-U-XI
(1)	(2)	(3)	(4)	(5)	(6)	(7)	(8)	(9)	(10)
1998	20,120	20,120	36,252	47,459	26,855	32,714	38,885	46,737	163.0
1997	19,241	19,541	35,797	46,838	26,434	31,850	37,581	45,262	160.5
1996	18,136	18,841	34,842	45,889	25,904	31,277	36,872	43,945	156.9
1995	17,227	18,425	34,439	45,269	25,431	30,104	36,446	43,436	152.4
1994	16,555	18,208	34,769	45,203	25,588	30,594	35,486	42,655	148.2
1993	15,777	17,797	35,056	44,965	25,346	30,139	35,241	41,691	144.5
1992	14,847	17,249	35,820	43,216	25,668	29,325	35,593	42,490	140.3
1991	14,617	17,493	36,299	43,153	25,425	29,090	36,054	43,011	136.2
1990	14,387	17,942	36,141	43,744	25,680	29,173	37,343	44,090	130.7
1989	14,056	18,477	37,357	45,674	25,814	29,352	37,997	44,974	124.0
1988	13,123	18,082	37,673	44,969	25,552	29,034	37,512	44,354	118.3
1987	12,391	17,779	38,283	45,133	25,202	28,733	37,394	44,438	113.6
1986	11,670	17,356	38,510	44,807	25,049	28,135	37,027	43,811	109.6
1985	11,013	16,683	37,870	43,548	24,620	27,401	35,778	42,015	107.6
1984	10,328	16,203	37,658	42,731	24,194	26,777	35,165	41,469	103.9
1983	9,494	15,537	36,835	42,144	23,696	26,175	34,179	40,226	99.6
1982	8,980	15,311	36,922	42,300	23,296	25,817	34,392	39,954	95.6
1981	8,476	15,334	37,434	42,006	22,536	25,092	34,507	40,502	90.1
1980	7,787	15,423	37,973	42,455	22,957	25,214	35,076	41,637	82.3
1979	7,168	15,789	38,501	43,911	23,197	25,217	36,259	43,144	74.0
1978	6,455	15,588	38,787	44,203	23,281	25,121	36,377	42,597	67.5
1977	5,785	14,920	38,867	43,662	22,732	24,592	35,004	41,289	63.2
1976	5,271	14,464	38,031	43,085	22,809	24,576	34,812	41,046	59.4
1975	4,818	13,974	37,513	42,676	22,388	23,963	34,224	39,790	56.2
1974	4,445	13,960	38,197	43,206	22,531	24,133	35,166	40,521	51.9
1973	4,141	14,300	39,603	43,578	22,406	23,870	36,302	41,617	47.2
1972	3,769	13,837	38,687	43,309	22,222	23,958	35,599	40,809	44.4
1971	3,417	12,923	36,424	40,973	21,561	23,104	34,143	38,897	43.1
1970	3,177	12,539	36,247	40,699	21,470	23,112	34,471	38,942	41.3

Note: All income figures, except for column 2, are in 1998 dollars as adjusted by the CPI-U-X1 index.
a This index is identical to CPI-U, commonly called the inflation rate, from 1983 on. Before 1983, the X1 series used revised weights on housing expenditures to provide an historically consistent inflation rate.
Source: U.S. Census Bureau, Current Population Surveys (March), Tables P–1, P–36, P–37, H–5, F–5, available at http://www.census.gov/hhes/income/histinc/

Finally, one must notice how the statistics group people together. The three most common groupings are by person, family, and household. Table 1–3 lists these income figures for each group over time. For example, in 1998 the median personal income for year-round, full-time workers was $36,252 for men and $26,855 for women. The well-being represented by these figures depends greatly on whether the income supports a family or single person, or is combined with other incomes to support a family. Family income (defined as the total income of two or more persons related by blood, marriage, or adoption who live together) ignores the income of single people. Household income (defined as the total income of all people living in the same housing unit) considers both single people and families. In general, because family income excludes single people, it will exceed household income.

Basic Facts About Income.

1.   *Great Inequality of Income.* Table 1–4 gives a snapshot of the current household and family income distribution in the United States. An individual with a $75,000 income makes more than 80 percent of American households. A married couple with a combined income of $145,199 makes more than 95 percent of American families.

Table 1–4. Distribution of Household and Family Income, 1998

Income Percentile	Household	Family
95th	$132,199	$145,199
80th	$75,000	$83,693
60th	$48,337	$56,020
50th (Median)	$38,885	$46,737
40th	$30,408	$37,692
20th	$16,116	$21,600

Source: U.S. Bureau of the Census, Current Population Survey (March 1998), Tables H–1, H–5, F–1, F–5, available at http://www.census.gov/hhse/income/histinc.

The American level of income inequality is the greatest in the industrialized world. A common measure of income inequality is the Gini ratio, a statistical measure of the fraction of a country's income that would have to be redistributed to achieve equal household or family income. A Gini score of 0 indicates that all households have the same income, and 1 indicates that a single household receives all the income.

For the United States in 1997, the Gini ratio for household income was 0.459, up from 0.397 in 1973. U.S. Census Bureau, *Historical Income Tables—Households,* Table H–4, available at <http://www.census.gov/hhes/income/histinc/h04.html>.

2. *Education and Earnings.* A key predictor of income and earnings is education. By 1998, about 30 percent of all workers over age twenty-five had a college degree or more. For full-time, year-round workers with a bachelor's degree or more, median earnings were $52,313 for men and $37,417 for women. By contrast, full-time, year-round workers with only a high school diploma had earnings of only $30,865 for men and $21,963 for women. U.S. Census Bureau, *Historical Income Tables—People,* Tables P–20, P–24, available at <http://www.census.gov/hhes/income/histinc>.

3. *Income Gap is Widening.* Since the 1970s, top households and families are doing increasingly better than average or poor families. In 1980, the bottom 80 percent of households received over 56 percent of the nation's income; by 1998, they received less than 51 percent. In other words, the top quintile now receives almost half of the nation's income. The top 5 percent of households alone receives 21 percent of the income. U.S. Census Bureau, *Historical Income Tables—Households,* Table H–2, available at <http://www.census.gov/income/h02.txt>.

Figure 1–4 shows the change in income distribution for households since 1967. The income for the bottom two quintiles has declined in real terms since the early 1970s, and the income of the next two quintiles has barely increased. By contrast, the income of the top quintile, and particularly of the top 5 percent of households, exploded in the 1990s.

4. *Incomes of Average and Poor Workers Are Stagnating or Falling.* In the more than quarter-century since the first oil price shock of 1973, wages and income of the average American worker have stagnated, according to a variety of official government statistics. For example, the median real income for male full-time, full-year workers rose from $36,247 in 1970 (in 1998 dollars) to $36,252 in 1998. (See Table 1–3, column 4.) Median household and family incomes managed to creep up slightly over that period, largely because people are working longer hours and the fraction of two-income households has increased dramatically. (See Table 1–3, columns 8 and 9.)

More disturbing is what has happened to the bottom 40 percent of households. As Figure 1–4 shows, these households have no more income, in real terms, than they did in the early 1970s. For example, the mean household income of the bottom quintile was $9,002 in 1974 (in 1997 dollars) and $8,872 in 1997. For the second quintile, the 1974 mean was $21,564 and the 1997 mean was $22,098.

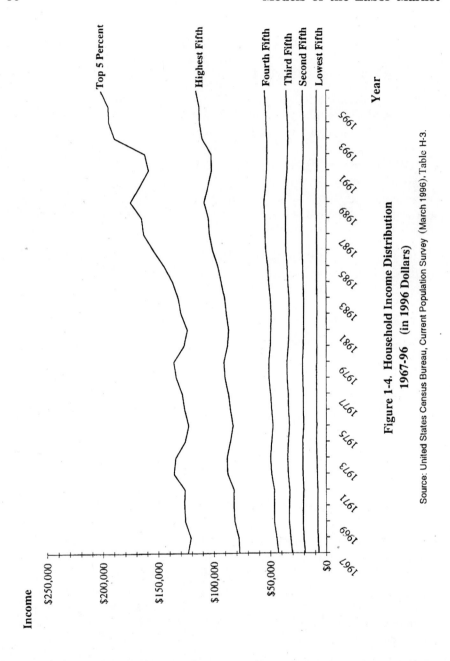

**Figure 1-4. Household Income Distribution
1967-96 (in 1996 Dollars)**

Source: United States Census Bureau, Current Population Survey (March 1996), Table H-3.

    Also troubling are the persistent income differences between races, as shown in Figure 1–5. Median household income for blacks is consistently below that for other races, although Hispanic and black incomes have converged in recent years. Median household income is 55 percent higher for whites than for blacks and 80 percent higher for Asian and Pacific Islanders than for blacks.

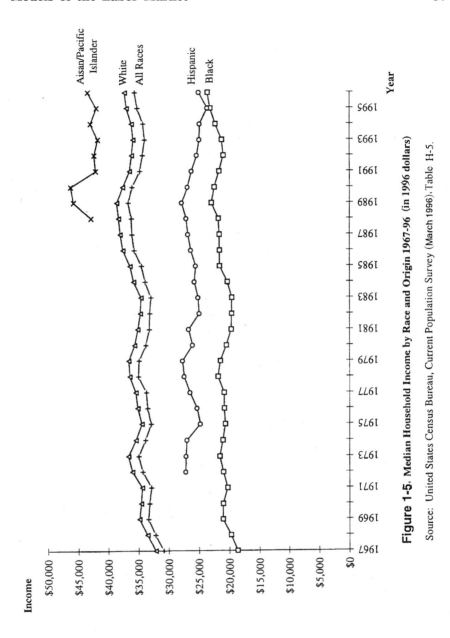

Figure 1-5. Median Household Income by Race and Origin 1967-96 (in 1996 dollars)

Source: United States Census Bureau, Current Population Survey (March 1996), Table H-5.

5. *Controversy over the Consumer Price Index.* The actual income of almost all households, poor and rich, rises over time. But the price of goods likewise rises. When comparing changes in income distribution between rich and poor, one can use actual incomes without accounting for price changes. But to compare the value of particular incomes over

time (say, of the bottom fifth or the median), analysts typically use the Consumer Price Index to convert all incomes to constant dollars.

The Consumer Price Index (CPI) is designed to answer the question, "How much more income will consumers need to be just as well off with the new set of prices as the old?" Michael J. Boskin et al., "Consumer Prices, the Consumer Price Index, and the Cost of Living," 12 *Journal of Economic Perspectives* 3, 10 (1998). The official CPI is constructed by the Bureau of Labor Statistics on the basis of a monthly survey of the prices of 71,000 goods and services at 22,000 retail outlets, plus rents from 35,000 rental units.

In recent years, the CPI has been criticized for overstating inflation. In 1996, a five-member commission appointed by the Senate Finance Committee concluded that the CPI overstates inflation by about 1.1 percentage points each year. Michael J. Boskin, Ellen R. Dulberger, Robert J. Gordon, Zvi Griliches, and Dale W. Jorgenson, *Toward a More Accurate Measure of the Cost of Living*, Final Report to the Senate Finance Committee, December 4, 1996. The Boskin Commission identified three separate sources of bias. A 0.4 point "product substitution bias" occurs because the CPI monitors a fixed basket of goods, the contents of which are changed only about once a decade. It thus ignores the fact that consumers avoid price increases by switching, for example, from beef to chicken when beef prices rise. A 0.1 point "retail outlet substitution bias" occurs because the CPI compares prices in the same stores over time and collects price data during the week. It thus ignores major shifts in retailing as consumers save by shopping in superstores and discount chains and during weekend sales. Finally, and numerically most important, a 0.6 point "quality and new goods bias" occurs because the CPI does not fully account for the gains to consumers from new products and quality changes in existing products. For example, the CPI did not survey VCRs, microwave ovens, and personal computers until a decade after they penetrated the market, and thus failed to notice the 80 percent price fall. At a more mundane level, one respected economist has determined that the CPI overestimated inflation in breakfast cereals by 25 percent through ignoring the gains to consumers from the introduction of apple-cinnamon Cheerios and other new brands. See Jerry A. Hausman, "Valuation of New Goods Under Perfect and Imperfect Competition," in Timothy F. Bresnahan and Robert J. Gordon, eds., *The Economics of New Goods* (Chicago: University of Chicago Press, 1997), 209–37.

The political implications of a downward CPI adjustment are enormous. For example, a reduced CPI would reduce retirement income for Social Security recipients, since their benefits are tied to the CPI. More broadly, growing income inequality is a minor topic when the poor are better off over time in absolute terms. If the rich are getting richer while the poor are getting poorer, however, social tensions are likely to rise. The current official CPI suggests that the "poor are getting poorer" view is correct. A revised CPI along the lines recommended by the Boskin Commission would suggest a rosier scenario: while income disparity has increased since the mid–1970s, median household income and mean household income of the bottom fifth have increased as well. See Michael J. Boskin and Dale W. Jorgenson, "Implications of Overstating Inflation for Indexing Government Programs and Understanding Economic Progress," 87 *American Economic Review (Papers & Proceedings)* 89 (May 1997) (which states that revising CPI downward by 1.1 points shows that real median income has increased 35.7 percent from 1973 to 1995, rather than by 4.3 percent, using the official CPI).

For a review of the technical and political issues involved in the Consumer Price Index, see Symposium, "Measuring the CPI," 12 *Journal of Economic Perspectives* 3–78 (1998); Jeff Madrick, "The Cost of Living: A New Myth," *New York Review of Books* 19, 23 (March 6, 1997), which points out that the Boskin Commission methodology would imply that average incomes in the 1950s were below the poverty line; "The Cost of Living: An Exchange," *New York Review of Books* 64–67 (June 26, 1997), an exchange between Madrick and two Boskin Commission members.

2

Models of Unions

This chapter examines the role of unions in the American economy. Views on this issue are polarized, as emphasized by Harvard economists Richard Freeman and James Medoff in "The Two Faces of Unionism," 57 *Public Interest* 69 (1979). The "monopoly face" characterizes unions as entities that increase wages of their members above competitive market levels by gaining monopoly control of the labor supply. Under this view, unions create inflation, retard the introduction of new technology, and inefficiently distort the allocation of labor away from its most productive uses. The "collective-voice face" argues that unions can foster an efficient workplace by providing a mechanism other than quitting whereby workers can communicate their preferences to management. This view emphasizes that many workplace issues, such as the level of safety or the grievance system, involve collective goods—goods that, once provided for one worker, are necessarily provided for many other workers. Unions can promote efficiency by helping firms set the efficient level of collective goods.

A. The Monopoly Face

1. The Theory of Monopoly Unions

Economists—particularly those who emphasize the benefits of competitive markets—have long argued that unions are monopolies trying to increase wages (and thereby inevitably decreasing employment) for their members. In the standard price-theory model, two basic effects arise from a monopolist's increased price. First, income is transferred from consumers to the monopolist. Second, resources are wasted. In a fully efficient economy without monopolies, prices reflect the (marginal) cost of all products and resources flow to their highest valued use. When monopoly power raises certain prices above cost, consumers inefficiently turn to less-valued items.

Under the monopoly theory, monopolist labor unions, like other monopolists, have two effects: first, they redistribute income to unionized workers from nonunion workers, corporate profits, or consumers; second, by raising wages in certain industries above the next highest wage, unions lower overall wealth because labor and capital do not go to their most productive uses.

One way to visualize the transfers and losses of monopoly unions is through a simple graph of supply and demand. (See Figure 2–1.) Without unions, the competitive equilibrium occurs where supply meets demand, at wage W_c and employment level E_c. Suppose a monopoly union forces wages up to W_u, so that employers reduce employment to E_u. This redistributes money to workers who remain employed, shown by the rectangle $W_u W_c DA$. It also creates an overall loss in output, shown by the triangle ABC. This triangle represents jobs that workers would be willing to work at wages employers would be willing to pay, but are not offered because of the monopoly setting of the wage. The steeper the demand curve (more "inelastic" is the technical term), the more union-ized workers will gain and the smaller the efficiency loss for a given increase in the wage. Some of the implications of monopoly theory for unions are explored in the following article by Nobel prize winning economist Milton Friedman.

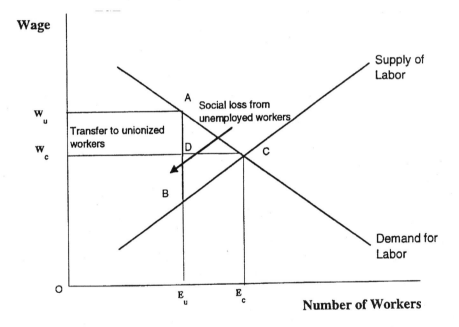

**Figure 2–1. Monopoly Union Effects
on Labor Supply and Demand**

"Some Comments on the Significance of Labor Unions for Economic Policy"*

MILTON FRIEDMAN

... The power of unions, as of any other monopoly, is ultimately limited by the elasticity of the demand curve for the monopolized services. Unions have significant potential power only if this demand curve is fairly inelastic at what would otherwise be the competitive price. Even then, of course, they must also be able to control either the supply of workers or the wage rate employers will offer workers.

Demand for Labor

The theory of joint demand developed by Marshall is in some ways the most useful tool of orthodox economic theory for understanding the circumstances under which the demand curve will be inelastic. It will be recalled that Marshall emphasized that the demand for one of a number of jointly demanded items is the more inelastic, (1) the more essential the given item is in the production of the final product, (2) the more inelastic the demand for the final product, (3) the smaller the fraction of total cost accounted for by the item in question, and (4) the more inelastic the supply of cooperating factors. Alfred Marshall, *Principles of Economics*, 8th ed. (London: Macmillan, 1920), 385–86. The most significant of these items for the analysis of unions are the essentiality of the factor and the percentage of total costs accounted for by the factor. Now, a factor is likely to be far more essential in the short run than in the long run. Let a union be organized and let it suddenly raise the wage rate. Employment of the type of labor in question is likely to shrink far less at first than it will over the longer run, when it is possible to make fuller adjustment to the change in wage rate. This adjustment will take the form of substitution of other factors for this one, both directly in the production of each product, and indirectly in consumption as the increased price of the products of unionized labor leads consumers to resort to alternative means of satisfying their wants. This simple point is, at one and the same time, important in understanding how unions can have substantial power and how their power is sharply limited in the course of time.

The importance of the percentage of total cost accounted for by the factor leads one to predict that a union may be expected to be strongest and most potent when it is composed of a class of workers whose wages

* In David McCord Wright, ed., *The Impact of the Union* (New York: Harcourt, Brace, 1951), 204, 207–23.

make up only a small part of the total cost of the product they produce—a condition satisfied, along with essentiality, by highly skilled workers. This is the reason why economic theorists have always been inclined to predict that craft unions would tend to be the most potent. This implication of the joint-demand analysis seems to have been confirmed by experience. While industrial unions have by no means been impotent, craft unions have in general been in a stronger economic position and have maintained it for longer periods. . . .

Supply of Labor and Control Over Wage Rates

Another line along which orthodox economic analysis has some interesting implications is the role of so-called restrictive practices. It is clear that if a union can reduce the supply of persons available for jobs, it will thereby tend to raise the wage rate. Indeed, this will be the only way of raising the wage rate if the union cannot exercise any direct control over the wage rate itself. . . .

This line of reasoning has led to the view that, in general, unions may be regarded as exercising control over the wage rate primarily by controlling the supply of workers and that, in consequence, the so-called restrictive practices—high union initiation fees, discriminatory provisions for entrance into unions, seniority rules, etc.—have the economic function of reducing the supply of entrants so as to raise wage rates. This is an erroneous conception of the function of these restrictive practices. They clearly cannot serve this function without a closed or preferential shop, which already implies control over employers derived from sources other than control over entrance into unions. To see the function of these practices and the associated closed shop, let us suppose that the wage rate can be fixed above its competitive level by direct means, for example, by legal enactment of a minimum wage rate. This will necessarily mean that fewer jobs will be available than otherwise and fewer jobs than persons seeking jobs. This excess supply of labor must be disposed of somehow—the jobs must be rationed among the seekers for jobs. And this is the important economic function the so-called restrictive practices play. They are a means of rationing the limited number of jobs among eager applicants. Since the opportunity to work at a wage rate above the competitive level has considerable economic value, it is understandable that the restrictive practices are important and the source of much dispute.

The question remains how the wage rate can be controlled directly by means other than legal enactment of a minimum wage rate. To do this, unions must be able to exercise control over employers—they must be able to prevent existing employers from undercutting the union wage rate, as well as the entry of new employers who would do so. They must somehow be able to force all employers to offer the union wage rate and no less. The devices whereby this is done are numerous and can hardly be fully enumerated here. However, one feature of the various devices whereby wage rates are directly enforced or entry into an occupation limited is essential for our purposes, namely, the extent to which they depend on political assistance. Perhaps the extreme example is again medicine, in which practice of the profession is restricted to those licensed by the state and licensure in turn is in general placed in the hands of the profession itself. State licensure applies in similar fashion to dentists, lawyers, plumbers, beauticians, barbers, morticians, and a host of other occupations too numerous to list. . . . Only slightly removed from this kind of licensure provision and in many ways far more effective is local political support through building codes, health regulations, health ordinances, and the like, all of which serve numerous craft unions as a means of preventing nonunion workers from engaging in their fields through substitution or elimination of materials or techniques, and of preventing potential employers from undercutting the union wage rate. It is no accident that strong unions are found in railways, along with federal regulation. Again, union actions involving actual or potential physical violence or coercion, such as mass picketing and the like, could hardly take place were it not for the unspoken acquiescence of the authorities. Thus, whether directly in the form of specific laws giving power to union groups or indirectly in the form of the atmosphere and attitude of law enforcement, direct control over union wage rates is closely connected to the degree of political assistance unions can command.

Here again, there is a very close parallel between labor unions on the one hand and industrial monopolies on the other. In both cases, widespread monopolies are likely to be temporary and susceptible of dissolution unless they can call to their aid the political power of the state.

Notes and Questions

1. *What are Union Goals?* As Friedman recounts, the monopoly model has two variations on the source of union power. Often it is said that the union restricts the labor supply, so that competing firms will bid up the price of unionized labor. Alternatively, the union sets a wage rate. In response, firms hire fewer workers. In either variation, the resulting wage-employment combination is a point on the employer's labor demand curve (point A in Figure 2–1).

How high a wage will the monopolistic union seek? This depends on the union's goal, which is often unclear. Most of the strategies discussed in this note were first examined in John T. Dunlop, *Wage Determination Under Trade Unions*, 2nd ed. (New York: Augustus M. Kelley, 1950), 32–50.

a. *Maximize Wages.* The union goal might be "Higher wages, above all else!" This goal has costs, however: a union can increase the wage only by losing jobs. As labor becomes more expensive, employers will respond by reducing output or substituting machinery or cheaper nonunion labor. Because a wage maximization goal does not care about job loss, it seems an unlikely goal for unions with some unemployed members. It is often suggested, however, that the United Mine Workers (UMW) pushed for wage maximization. Certainly UMW leader John L. Lewis recognized the employment trade-offs of demanding high wages:

> The policy of the United Mine Workers of America [of "maintaining wage standards"] will inevitably bring about the utmost employment of machinery of which coal mining is physically capable.... Fair wages and American standards of living are inextricably bound up with the progressive substitution of mechanical for human power. It is no accident that fair wages and machinery will walk hand-in-hand.

Lewis, *The Miners' Fight for American Standards* (Indianapolis: Bell, 1925), 108.

Professor Farber, in a careful empirical study of UMW contracts, has questioned whether this union actually followed a high-wage policy, having found that UMW agreements show a high degree of risk aversion and emphasize employment. Henry S. Farber, "Individual Preferences and Union Wage Determination: The Case of the United Mine Workers," 86 *Journal of Political Economy* 923 (1978).

b. *Maximize the Wage Bill.* Another possibility is that unions try to maximize the total earnings of their members. In terms of Figure 2–1, the goal here is to maximize the rectangle $W_u AE_u 0$. If the demand curve is elastic at the competitive wage, however, this goal would imply setting a wage below the competitive wage. No union has such a goal, nor would it last long if it did. See Albert Rees, *The Economics of Work and Pay*, 2nd ed. (New York: Harper & Row, 1979), 118.

c. *Maximize Rents.* Alternatively, unions may try to maximize the gains (sometimes called rents) from unionization. If the union ignores unemployment, this would be the amount their employed members receive above what they would receive in a nonunion firm. In Figure 2–1, this is the rectangle $W_u ADW_c$. The difference between maximizing rents and maximizing the wage bill arises if unions recognize that their actions indirectly affect wages and employment in the nonunion sector.

d. *Maximize Union Dues.* The previous goals all concern the wages or employment of union members. This goal assumes that unions have as their principal objective some notion of improving the welfare of their members. Alternatively, the union may try to maximize its own income through dues or some other measure of the utility to the union or the union leaders. For an analysis in this spirit, see Donald L. Martin, *An Ownership Theory of the Trade Union* (Berkeley: University of California Press, 1980).

2. *Offsetting Benefits.* Economist Albert Rees agrees with Friedman that unions are an obstacle to optimum performance of the economy:

[The union] alters the wage structure in a way that impedes the growth of employment in sectors of the economy where productivity and income are naturally high and that leaves too much labor in low-income sectors of the economy like southern agriculture and the least skilled service trades. It benefits most those workers who would in any case be relatively well off, and while some of this gain may be at the expense of the owners of capital, most of it must be at the expense of consumers and the lower-paid workers. Unions interfere blatantly with the use of the most productive techniques in some industries, and this effect is probably not offset by the stimulus to higher productivity furnished by some other unions.

Albert Rees, *The Economics of Trade Unions*, rev. ed. (Chicago: University of Chicago Press, 1977), 186.

Nevertheless, Rees emphasizes that unions should not be judged solely on their efficiency effects:

If, as most of us believe, America should continue to have political democracy and a free enterprise economy, it is essential that the great mass of manual workers be committed to the preservation of this system and that they should not, as in many other democracies, constantly be attempting to replace it with something radically different. Yet such a commitment cannot exist if workers feel that their rights are not respected and they do not get their fair share of the rewards of the system. By giving workers protection against arbitrary treatment by employers, by acting as their representative in politics, and by reinforcing their hope of continuous future gain, unions have helped to assure that the basic values of our society are widely diffused and that our disagreements on political and economic issues take place within a broad framework of agreement. If the job rights won for workers by unions are not conceded by the rest of society simply because they are just, they should be conceded because they help to protect the minimum consensus that keeps our society stable. In my judgment, the economic losses imposed by unions are not too high a price to pay for their successful performance of this role.

Id. at 187.

3. *Can Unions Control Labor Supply?* In recent decades, at least, it seems implausible that any union controls the bulk of workers in a particular occupation or industry. The percentage of workers who are unionized rarely rises to monopoly levels.

In the following reading, Professor Kenneth Dau–Schmidt offers an alternative explanation for the ability of unions to increase wages. The union organizes firms or industries already enjoying supracompetitive, or monopoly, profits (whether due to natural or governmental monopoly, or perhaps simply by being the best in an industry), and forces employers to split these "rents" with the unionized workers.

"A Bargaining Analysis of American Labor Law and the Search for Bargaining Equity and Industrial Peace"*

KENNETH G. DAU–SCHMIDT

It seems very doubtful that cartelization of the labor market is the sole, or even the primary, source of union wage increases in the American economy. The establishment of a labor cartel in any market without licensure would seem very difficult. Workers are the consummate atomistic competitors. Moreover, if labor cartel power were the only source of union wage increases, an organizing campaign that proceeded to organize one competitive employer at a time would get nowhere because there would be only costs of unionization, but no benefits, to show employees until the requisite number of employers was organized. A labor cartel in a competitive product market without employer rents or productivity increases associated with unionism would have to be simultaneously organized across many employers in order to survive—like Athena springing full-grown from Zeus's head.

. . . . If the requisite barriers to entry to a product market exist, the employers would be more likely to exploit them than would a labor cartel. The employers are much more concentrated than individual employees; moreover, normal economic profits sustain employers while they organize their cartel or increase their grasp on market share through expansion or merger. Indeed, when significant economies of scale exist in an industry, the employers, as producers, will naturally gravitate toward oligopoly or monopoly. No such anticompetitive gravity compels the workers to combination. Finally, it seems much more plausible that unions could organize employers who enjoy monopoly rents, Ricardian rents, or quasi-rents, because such organization could be undertaken on a more manageable basis, one employer at a time. . . .

Empirical evidence also suggests that labor cartel power is less important than other sources of union wage increases. Based on available statistics, there seem to be few product markets in the United States that contain a percentage of organized workers that might even be imagined a labor cartel. Nationally, the proportion of private sector employees represented by a union is currently about 14 percent. Among industry groups and occupations for which such statistics are collected by the Bureau of Labor Statistics, the highest representation in any industry group on a national basis is 39 percent [communications and public utilities], while the highest representation in any particular occupation on a national basis is 42 percent [protective services]. Although the percent organized in particular industries, such as automobiles or steel, is undoubtedly higher, typically such industries suffered from

* 91 *Michigan Law Review* 419, 468–473 (1992).

product market concentration prior to organization. Similarly, the highest percentage organized in any state is 36 percent [New York and Michigan], although variations undoubtedly exist among local product markets.

Notes and Questions

1. *Countervailing Power*. Dau–Schmidt views monopoly unions grabbing profits from firms that themselves have monopoly power in product markets. This vision of monopoly unions squaring off against monopoly firms is reminiscent of the countervailing-power justification for unions popularized by John Kenneth Galbraith. Writing in 1952, Galbraith gave a classic description of unions as forces counterbalancing the power of capital:

> As a general though not invariable rule there are strong unions in the United States only where markets are served by strong corporations. And it is not an accident that the large automobile, steel, electrical, rubber, farm-machinery and non-ferrous metal-mining and smelting companies all bargain with powerful [former] CIO unions. Not only has the strength of the corporations in these industries made it necessary for workers to develop the protection of countervailing power, it has provided unions with the opportunity for getting something more as well. If successful they could share in the fruits of the corporation's market power. By contrast there is not a single union of any consequence in American agriculture, the country's closest approach to the competitive model. The reason lies not in the difficulties in organization; these are considerable, but greater difficulties in organization have been overcome. The reason is that the farmer has not possessed any power over his labor force, and at least until recent times has not had any rewards from market power which it was worth the while of a union to seek....

Galbraith, *American Capitalism: The Concept of Countervailing Power* (Boston: Houghton Mifflin, 1952), 122.

However, in the introduction to the 1993 edition of *American Capitalism*, Galbraith acknowledged that a vision of all-powerful corporations and the countervailing powerful unions seems anachronistic in an era of global markets:

> The core thesis that an established and effective answer to economic power is the building of countervailing power is, indeed, still valid. There is still the great supermarket chain as the answer to the market power of the big food companies.... The trade union remains an equalizing force in the labor markets.... But one cannot doubt that, over all, the role of exploitive market power, that of the monopoly or trust with which countervailing power contends, has, for other reasons, also diminished. International competition—in fashionable modern reference, the globalization of markets—has been a central factor....
>
> More subtle, but I think more important, has been the progressive bureaucratization, as perhaps it may be called, of the great industrial

enterprise. Once the great firm was respected and feared for its external power; now very often it is the victim of its own internal weakness. We now know that we may have less to fear from corporate power than from corporate incompetence.

Competition and bureaucratic weakness have, in their turn, had a notable effect on the trade union, the classic example of countervailing power. To put the matter bluntly, strong trade unions require strong employers. Nothing so weakens a union as an employer who cannot afford to pay and is closing plants or going entirely out of business. This is what, in these last decades, has driven the unions into the shadows. Countervailing power, the *raison d'être* of the trade union, requires that there be a power to countervail.

Galbraith, *American Capitalism: The Concept of Countervailing Power* (New Brunswick, N.J.: Transaction Publishers, 1993), ix–x.

2. *Unions and Rents.* Galbraith and Dau–Schmidt correctly observe that unions are strongest in highly concentrated industries, where firms earn rents from the power they have in the product market. Market-power rents are the extra profits, earned because the firm has no or only a few competitors, above the profits necessary to keep the firm in that industry. For example, if the return on capital in competitive industries were 10 percent, and the return on capital in a highly concentrated industry were 15 percent, firms in that industry would be earning rents of 5 percent. Even if unions were to grab some of that 5 percent for their members, the return to capital would still exceed that in other industries, and the firms would choose to stay in the concentrated industry.

A major source of monopoly rents comes from government regulation that sets prices or otherwise prevents firms from fully competing with each other. Beginning in the 1970s, extensive deregulation in industries such as airlines, trucking, and communications has increased competition. Unions in those industries came under severe pressure to become more flexible and modify their demands, and concession bargaining became common.

In addition to market-power rents, Dau–Schmidt discusses Ricardian rents and quasi-rents as possible sources of union gains. A Ricardian rent is the extra profit earned because an unusually productive resource is not generally available in the market. Examples include exceptionally fertile soil or a particularly rich vein of ore. Quasi-rents, unlike market-power or Ricardian rents, are not payments in excess of a competitive rate of return. Instead, they arise when the employer has already invested in resources that are highly specialized and hard to transport. Once locked in, the employer will stay in business even if the union forces wages up and thereby reduces the employer's level of profits. In the long run, such a union strategy will discourage employers from making highly specialized investments. See Armen A. Alchian, "Decision Sharing and Expropriable Specific Quasi–Rents: A Theory of First National Maintenance Corporation v. NLRB," 1 *Supreme Court Economic Review*, 235 (1982).

3. *Benign Union Wage Gains.* Under Dau–Schmidt's view, most union wage gains come only at the expense of supracompetitive profits. Unions are

appropriating part of the gains from a firm's market power or from its ownership of a uniquely valuable resource. If this view is accurate, union wage gains should require no trade-off with slower growth rates or higher prices for consumers. If the union wage gain comes from appropriating quasi-rents, the overall harm to the economy is greater. We address this issue further in the last section of this chapter when discussing evidence about union effects on profitability.

2.   *Efficient Collective Bargaining, or the "Off the Demand Curve" Model*

Even if the union is a monopolistic cartel, the resulting wage increase may not be inefficient, depending on whether the wage bargain is on or off the employer's demand curve. On-the-demand-curve bargaining occurs when the union sets a wage and allows the employer freely to choose employment, given the wage. Off-the-demand-curve bargaining occurs when the parties bargain simultaneously over wages and employment levels.

The standard monopoly model of unions assumes that the wage-employment agreement is a point on the firm's demand curve. The labor demand curve shows, for every wage, the amount of labor that maximizes the firm's profits. A particular model of bargaining is envisioned: Starting from the nonunion or competitive wage-employment outcome (which is the intersection of the labor supply and demand curves), the union demands a higher wage. After negotiations fix the wage, the employer unilaterally sets the level of employment. The employer will maximize profits, given the higher wage constraint, by reducing employment and substituting machinery or reducing output. Call this the "monopoly union" result.

What's wrong with this on-the-demand-curve monopoly-union outcome? It is inefficient, in the sense that other agreements exist that both labor and management would prefer. True, unionized workers prefer the monopoly-union result to the competitive result (otherwise they would not have demanded a higher-than-competitive wage in the first place). But other wage-employment combinations exist that workers prefer even more—combinations that employers, too, would prefer to the monopoly-union result.

The inefficiency of the monopoly-union result occurs because, by assumption, the parties bargain only over the wage, leaving the level of employment to the employer. The employer naturally picks the level which maximizes profits for that wage. At this wage and employment level, small reductions in the workforce are as harmful to the employer as small additions. Equally important, the firm would be willing to add workers for a very small reduction in the wage. But unless the union does not care about employment, it would prefer a somewhat lower wage in return for more jobs. Both parties can benefit, then, from a move off the demand curve.

A graphical analysis may make the argument clearer. Figure 2–2(A) shows a labor demand curve, line d_L, which we have seen before. In this figure, the labor demand curve is created by first drawing lines (called isoquants) that connect wage-employment combinations that give the firm the same level of profits. For example, consider an isoquant that shows all the ways an employer can earn profits of 100. It can earn 100 by paying a low wage to a very few workers (who cannot produce much because they are so few). Or it can earn 100 by paying a higher wage to more workers (who now produce more). Finally, it can earn 100 by hiring lots of workers (who now practically trip over themselves and so produce less) at a low wage. Lower isoquants (by which employers pay lower wages for the same amount of labor) give greater profits. The labor demand curve is created by asking, for every wage, what employment level the firm wants. The answer is that the firm picks the lowest obtainable isoquant for that wage, which occurs at the peak of an isoquant. The critical insight is that, at any point on the demand curve, the employer is indifferent between hiring or firing an additional worker at that wage.

Figure 2–2(B) illustrates the union's preferences for wages and employment by drawing lines (called indifference curves) connecting wage-employment combinations that the union values equally. The union wants to be on as high an indifference curve as possible. Under the monopoly-wage model of bargaining, the union picks its preferred wage, knowing the firm will then pick the employment level that maximizes profits for that wage. In the diagram, the union will pick the wage at A, which gives it the most preferred wage-employment package on the employer's demand curve. This point A is what we labeled the monopoly result. The critical insight is that, at this point, unions are willing to trade lower wages for more employment.

Figure 2–2(C) combines the prior two figures. It shows that point A is inefficient: both the union and the firm would prefer other agreements with more employment and lower wages. At point A, the union values employment relatively highly and the firm values lower wages relatively highly. Both sides are better off, then, if employment is traded for lower wages. For example, the union would find point C'' as good as point A (because it lies on the same indifference curve) and the firm makes higher profits at point C'' (because it lies on a more profitable isoquant). Similarly, the union prefers point C''' to point A while the firm makes equal profits. The points on the line between C and C''' form the contract curve. Each point on the contract curve is Pareto-optimal, in that only here is it impossible to improve one side's position without harming the other. On the contract curve, the firm's willingness to trade employment for wages just matches the union's willingness to make the same trade-off. Because both sides value employment and wages to the same degree, no more gains from trade can occur.

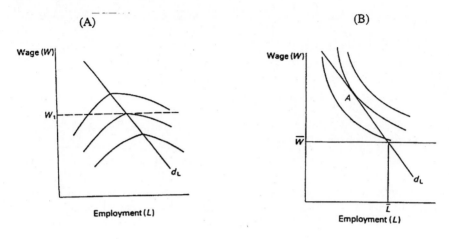

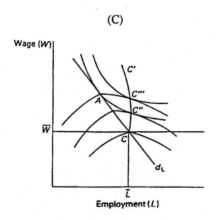

Figure 2–2

Wage and Employment Outcomes:
Off–the–Demand Curve Case*

In general, unless in the relevant range the union cares only about wages (which would make the indifference curve flat), there are always agreements off the demand curve that both parties prefer to an agreement on the demand curve. Conversely, any agreement on the contract curve is Pareto-efficient, in that one party's position can be improved only at the expense of the other's. The union wants to be as high on the contract curve as possible, while the firm wants to be as low as possible.

* Adapted from Barry T. Hirsch & John T. Addison, The Economic Analysis of Unions: New Approaches and Evidence 15 (Winchester, MA: Allen & Unwin, Inc., 1986).

The relative bargaining powers of the union and the firm determine where on the contract curve the agreement will be.

A critical issue is whether the competitive equilibrium (point C in Figure 2–2(C)) is on the contract curve. If it is, the competitive equilibrium is only one of many efficient points, and is not Pareto-superior to any other point on the contract curve. In general, it will be on the contract curve. Technically, the reason is that no union indifference curve dips below the competitive wage rate (in Figure 2–2(B), they are all asymptotic to the horizontal line at W), because the union would gain nothing by agreeing to below-market wages. By assumption, jobs are available to anyone willing to work at the competitive wage, and the wage is viewed broadly to include all aspects of the job of interest to the worker. See Ian M. McDonald and Robert M. Solow, "Wage Bargaining and Employment," 71 *American Economic Review*, 896 (1981); Andrew J. Oswald, "The Economic Theory of Trade Unions: An Introductory Survey," 87 *Scandinavian Journal of Economics*, 160 (1985). Therefore, a (horizontal) union indifference curve will be tangent to the (horizontal) firm-profit isoquant at the competitive equilibrium. If that is the case, the competitive equilibrium is a point on the contract curve.

Intuitively, the idea is that the union in an efficient collective-bargaining contract will not reduce the size of the pie, but merely grab a larger slice. If the nonunion firm would maximize profits with a certain labor/capital ratio, for example, the union will agree to the same ratio but bargain for a more preferable wage and employment package. In sum, when someone asserts that unions create inefficiencies, the conversation-stopping comeback is, "You must be assuming that all agreements are on the demand curve."

To bargain off the demand curve, the union must be able to bargain over the level of employment as well as wages. Firms generally are reluctant to negotiate ironclad job creation or job retention guarantees. One reason for retaining flexibility is that at any given wage, the firm can increase profits by cutting employment and returning to its demand curve. Unions attempt to stop this by insisting on contractual clauses defining minimum staffing arrangements and limiting technological changes. Such clauses can indirectly fix employment. But whether these agreements are sufficient to make contracts efficient is an unresolved empirical issue. The basic analysis is provided by Barry T. Hirsch and John J. Addison, *The Economic Analysis of Unions* (Boston: Allen & Unwin, 1987), 14–18; and Ronald G. Ehrenberg and Robert S. Smith, *Modern Labor Economics*, 6th ed. (Reading, Mass.: Addison–Wesley, 1997), 482–86.

Kenneth G. Dau–Schmidt, summarizing the recent empirical evidence, concludes that off-the-demand-curve bargaining is more likely:

> Although transaction costs may prevent optimal bargaining in some individual cases, studies examining whether organized employers operate on their

labor demand curve or at some higher negotiated level of employment consistently reject the labor demand curve response. The shape of the contract curve between the parties will vary from case to case, and studies have found examples of both rightward- and leftward-leaning contract curves. [A leftward-leaning contract curve shows a willingness of the union to trade employment for wages; a rightward-leaning curve shows a willingness to trade wages for employment.] Although further work needs to be done, perhaps the best characterization of the impact of unions in this regard, based on the available empirical evidence, is that unions negotiate optimal contracts that have little impact on the capital-labor mix or the level of output by organized employers. This characterization is based primarily on two studies, one by Kim Clark ["Unionization and Firm Performance: The Impact on Profits, Growth, and Productivity," 74 *American Economic Review* 893, 918 (1984)], the other by John Abowd ["The Effects of Wage Bargains on the Stock Market Value of the Firm," 79 *American Economic Review* 774 (1989)]. Clark examined a sample of over 900 union and nonunion businesses to gauge the impact of employee organization on various measures of firm performance, including return on capital, growth, and capital-labor mix. He found that, although organized firms tend to earn substantially lower returns on capital than non-union firms operating in comparable technological and competitive environments, employee organization had little effect on firm growth and the capital-labor mix. Abowd examined the effect of unexpected changes in collectively bargained labor costs on the value of common stock for a broadly representative sample of organized businesses. He found that, on average, unexpected increases in wealth to workers corresponded to decreases of similar size in the value of the common stock to shareholders. This equal and opposite relationship in worker and shareholder wealth is consistent with the bargaining analysis and the characterization of the contract curve between employers and unions [the line *CC'''* in Figure 2-2(C)] as typically vertical over the economy as a whole.

Dau–Schmidt, supra, 475–76.

3. *Median Voter Models of Unions*

The monopoly and efficient contract models discussed above assume that the union has clear preferences between wages and employment. If all workers are alike, a union can easily add up the preferences of individual workers to get a collective preference. But if workers vary in how they value wages and employment (or, more generally, in how they value the many items that unions bargain for, such as safety, pensions, grievance systems, etc.), the union has a difficult task in aggregating these preferences into coherent general goals. The median voter model offers an approach that recognizes the political character of unions. Under this model, workers can be clearly ranked from low to high on, say, their desired fraction of compensation paid as contributions to their pension plan. The union leaders seek that fraction desired by the median voter (50th percentile). Any other "platform" could be defeated by one closer to the median voter's preferences, and once the median platform is adopted, no other platform could gain a majority vote. The following reading by Bruce Kaufman and Jorge Martinez–Vazquez compares the median voter model with the monopoly and efficient contract models of unions. Although all three models have flaws, they argue that the median voter model best captures the goals of unions.

"Monopoly, Efficient Contract, And Median Voter Models of Union Wage Determination: A Critical Comparison"*

BRUCE E. KAUFMAN AND JORGE MARTINEZ–VAZQUEZ

. . .

II. *The Three Models: An Overview*

The monopoly, efficient contract, and median voter models are the three most frequently used theoretical models of union wage determination. . . .

The Monopoly Model. . . . The monopoly model assumes that the union has sufficient bargaining power to unilaterally and costlessly raise the wage from the market-determined wage to its preferred level . . . , but that the firm is then free to set the level of employment where profit is maximized. . . .

The Efficient Contract Model. Leontieff was the first to point out that the monopoly union outcome is not efficient or Pareto optimal. A labor contract is efficient if it is not possible to find another combination of W and L that makes at least one of the bargaining parties better off without making the other worse off. The importance of this observation is that if a contract is not efficient, then there are strong incentives for the parties to adopt a different W/L combination, because one or both of the parties can gain a higher level of utility.

. . . Compared to the monopoly model, the efficient contract model predicts a lower union wage rate but a higher level of employment. Also of importance, at [this point] the firm is no longer on its labor demand curve D but, rather, has agreed to hire more workers at the bargained wage than it would if given the freedom to set employment at the profit-maximizing level. Because the firm has an obvious incentive to cheat on the agreement by cutting employment back to the demand curve, for an efficient contract to be feasible the union must have some device (such as restrictive work rules) to prevent such an occurrence.

The Median Voter Model. A key difference between the monopoly and efficient contract models and the median voter model is in the nature of the union objective function. Given the assumption of homogeneous preferences among the membership, the monopoly and efficient

* 11 *Journal of Labor Research* 401 (1990).

contract models are able to derive an aggregate union utility function and a corresponding set of union indifference curves. In the median voter model, however, it is assumed that the membership has heterogeneous preferences with respect to wages and employment. The source of this heterogeneity in preferences is the assumption that the order of layoff is by inverse seniority. In this situation, the order of layoff gives rise to a corresponding distribution of most preferred wage demands on the part of the membership. In a one-period model, each union member would want the union to raise the wage until he or she was the next to be laid off. . . .

Given the distribution of most preferred wage demands among the membership, which wage rate will the union seek to obtain? [U]nder certain conditions it can be shown that the union's preferred wage will be that of the median voter in the union. These conditions are that the union's electoral process is perfectly democratic with elections determined by majority vote and that individual preferences are a function of only a single variable, well-ordered, and single-peaked. Given these assumptions, the political pressure on the union leadership to win re-election to office and ratification of new contracts will lead them to select . . . the preferred wage of the median voter, as the union's optimal wage. Assuming that the union has the bargaining power to obtain this wage, employment falls. . . .

III.   *Evaluation of the Models: Assumptions and Implications*

. . . We first focus on the assumptions and implications of the monopoly, efficient contract, and median voter models. Five theoretical problems seriously limit the descriptive and predictive power of the three models. In some cases, these problems affect one model but not another. These problems are:

Aggregation of Preferences. Every model of union wage determination, if it is to be more than *ad hoc*, must spell out how the preferences of individual rank-and-file members are aggregated to form the union's objective function. All three models do this, but each is subject to significant limitations.

Consider first the union objective function in the monopoly and efficient contract models. It is reasonably assumed that each union member is concerned with his or her wage rate and employment. How are these individual preferences aggregated to give rise to *the* union utility function? The key assumption is that individual preferences are homogeneous. This assumption is typically justified, in turn, by assuming that the order of layoff is by random draw or, alternatively, that reductions in labor demand are accommodated through work-sharing (reduced work hours). The essential problem with this approach is that the large majority of union contracts mandate layoff by inverse seniority. It is evident that a seniority rule gives rise to quite diverse wage/employment preferences among the rank and file.... It is not obvious how these diverse preferences can meaningfully be aggregated to form union indifference curves or why maximization of the wage bill or economic rents would be the preferred outcome for each union member.

One implication, then, is that the monopoly and efficient contract models presume some type of union objective function that, in most cases, is not likely to exist even as a first approximation. The issue of aggregation poses yet another problem for the efficient contract model in that there may exist no unique wage/employment outcome that can be said to be "efficient." An efficient contract outcome is a W/L combination in which none of the parties to the bargain can be made better off without making at least one party worse off. In a union where layoff is by seniority, every point on the labor demand curve is an "efficient" W/L combination, because it is impossible to find another W/L combination where (in the absence of side payments) at least one union member is not worse off.

A virtue of the median voter model is that, given certain conditions, it provides a consistent method to aggregate over the heterogeneous preferences of the rank and file. Unfortunately, however, the conditions for a unique voting equilibrium are fairly restrictive. In particular, the union's preferred wage will equal that of the median voter if (a) the electoral process in the union is perfectly democratic; (b) referenda are determined by majority vote among all possible pairs of outcomes; and (c) preferences are well-ordered (single-peaked) and a function of only a single variable. Violation of assumptions (a) and (b) may result in a union wage different from the median voter's to the degree that it insulates the union leadership from political competition or allows the leadership to set the voting agenda, while violation of assumption (c) may result in there being no unique equilibrium but, rather, a series of cyclic voting majorities.

Assumptions (a) through (c) are violated in nearly all real-world collective-bargaining negotiations. The important issue then becomes the degree to which these assumptions are violated and the sensitivity of the actual voting outcome to such violations. These questions would seem to be prime candidates for experimental laboratory testing, but as of yet none exists in the collective-bargaining area.

With regard to the aggregation of preferences, all three models face serious limitations. We believe, however, that of the three models, the objective function assumed in the median voter model is likely to approximate most closely the actual objectives of labor unions. Outside of a few hiring hall industries, such as longshoring, it is doubtful that the job allocation rules assumed in the monopoly and efficient contract models even closely resemble those employed in unionized firms. Given the prevalence of seniority arrangements, the median voter model, although restrictive, does capture the political nature of union decision making in an environment of heterogeneous and conflicting preferences.

The Principal–Agent Problem. A second limitation of the three models is that none of them ... make allowance for the principal-agent problem. As Ross first emphasized (Arthur Ross, *Trade Union Wage Policy*, Berkeley: University of California Press, 1948), union wage policy is shaped by two distinct groups: the union leadership and the union rank and file. The union leadership, according to Ross, is constrained by political pressure to negotiate a wage/employment level that broadly serves the interests of a majority of the rank and file. In most unions, however, limited information on the part of the membership, imperfections in the electoral process, and high policing costs give the leadership some discretion to negotiate a wage/employment level that satisfies its own goals (e.g., maximization of dues income) at the expense of the preferences of the rank and file. The greater the degree of this discretion, the greater will be the divergence between the predicted wage/employment outcomes ... and those actually negotiated in collective bargaining situations.

Empirical evidence, particularly of a recent vintage, is rather limited regarding the degree to which the principal-agent problem is a significant factor in union wage policy. It is clear, nevertheless, that a complete model of union wage determination should incorporate both separate objective functions for the union rank and file and the leadership and the political constraints that limit discretion on the part of the leadership.... It is unclear how either the monopoly or the efficient contract model could adequately incorporate the principal-agent problem, because neither makes explicit allowance for the electoral process in unions. The median voter model, on the other hand, is better suited for this task. Whether or not omitting the principal-agent problem significantly biases the predicted wage/employment outcomes of any of these three models, however, remains an empirical issue.

Strike Costs. A third limitation of the three models is that none incorporates the bargaining process and, more specifically, strike costs into the analysis. Each model assumes that the union can unilaterally set the wage rate at the desired level. This completely ignores, however, firm resistance and the constraint that strike costs place on the union's optimal wage. In reality, the union's optimal wage is likely to be affected by *two* separate constraints: the relationship between the union's wage demand and (1) the level of employment and (2) the size of strike costs that must be incurred to obtain that demand. The employment constraint is incorporated in the three models under consideration here, while the strike cost constraint is omitted....

As with the principal-agent problem, it can be debated on empirical grounds whether or not the omission of strike costs leads to a significant degree of error in the predictive ability of the simple versions of the monopoly, efficient contract, and median voter models. We believe that it probably does. We base this conclusion on evidence that the incidence of strikes varies considerably by industry and that higher strike rates, other things equal, lead to high union wage settlements.

If this conjecture is valid, the actual negotiated wage/employment outcomes in American industry may differ significantly from those predicted by the three models. A pressing research agenda item, therefore, is the integration of the employment and strike costs constraints in one formal model of wage determination.... In principle, this integration of employment and strike cost constraints could be accomplished in either the monopoly, efficient contract, or median voter model. We suspect, however, that the median voter model may provide greater insight on this issue, because it can better show under what conditions employment versus strike costs will be the binding constraint on union wage policy....

Dynamics. A fourth issue concerning the three models is their dynamic properties with respect to the behavior of union wages and employment over time. The monopoly and efficient outcomes ... are equilibrium points if the union's success in raising the wage from the market level does not thereby change the preferences of the membership regarding W and L and, thus, the shape of the indifference curves. One reason for suspecting that it might is that the higher union wage will cause more workers to join the union, expanding the total size of union membership. Will the larger union still have the same preference structure as before? Farber considered this issue and showed that with a random draw type of job allocation rule the preferred wage of each worker is independent of union size, but that with a work-sharing allocation rule the optimal wage is not. An equilibrium union wage with a work-sharing job allocation rule, therefore, requires that there be some restriction on entry into the union.

With respect to the median voter model, it has long been recognized that under certain conditions the wage/employment outcome ... is not an equilibrium point. By raising the wage, the size of employment is cut in half. In the next negotiation (assuming that laid-off union members lose their voting rights), the [least senior worker with a job] will lose his or her job as the union again raises the wage to the preferred wage of the new median voter. Over time, therefore, the union gradually shrinks until there are at most a handful of workers in the union.

Although this extreme form of dynamic instability is often cited as a serious defect of the median voter model, the issue is not so clear-cut. First, under certain plausible conditions, the model does yield a stable equilibrium wage. One condition is if the laid-off workers remain union members and retain their voting rights. Another is if the firm's minimum "breakeven" level of profit is at a point on the demand curve below [the preferred wage of the median worker in the original union]. Second, there are at least three reasons why the union's movement up the labor demand curve may be much slower than is suggested by the most simple version of the model. For example, ... when demand is uncertain and workers are risk-averse then the preferred wage of the median voter will be [reduced.] Second, the dynamic instability of the model is reduced if it is broadened to a multi-period framework so that the median voter's preferred wage is determined through an optimization process that takes into account his or her age and years to retirement. In this case, the median voter's preferred wage would rise gradually ... , so that he or she would be the next to be laid off at the time of retirement. Finally, a third approach is to incorporate strike costs into the model so that employer resistance prevents the union from moving up the labor demand curve as rapidly.

Although it is difficult to make a definitive statement concerning the dynamic properties of the three models, it seems fair to say that the monopoly and efficient contract models strongly suggest that the collective bargaining process should give rise to an equilibrium union/nonunion wage differential, while the median voter model suggests that it is likely (but not certain) that, *ceteris paribus*, union/nonunion wage differentials should increase over time. Available evidence, while not conclusive, does seem to support the prediction of the median voter model in this regard.

Incentive Compatibility. A final issue that affects the predictive ability of the models is the incentive compatibility of the contract outcomes. In the efficient contract model, the union agrees to a lower wage ... but obtains a higher level of employment.... The firm is to the right of its demand curve and would ... desire to reduce employment back to the demand curve. For the union to agree to trade off a lower wage for higher employment, there must clearly be some mechanism that prevents the firm from cheating *ex post* on the agreement. Without such protection, the outcome is not incentive compatible and the union would not agree to it. The obvious solution—to require in the contract that the firm employ [a specific number of] workers—is generally not feasible, because every firm needs the flexibility to reduce its work force in response to declining sales. An alternative approach ... is for the union to negotiate such work rules as manning requirements and minimum crew sizes. These contract rules are more easily policed and could, if properly structured, force the firm off its labor demand curve to [the higher employment level]. But there are practical reasons to doubt that restrictive work rules can overcome the incentive compatibility problem, further calling into question the predictive accuracy of the efficient contract model. On the other hand, both the monopoly and [median voter] outcomes are incentive compatible because each is on the firm's labor demand curve.

V. *Explanatory Power of the Models: The Cyclical Behavior of Union Wages*

A second criterion we propose to use to evaluate the three models is their ability to explain observed patterns of union wage/employment determination. While a number of specific features of union wage setting could be examined, we limit the analysis to two. The first one is the cyclical behavior of union wage rates.

Union money wage rates exhibit an asymmetric pattern over the business cycle, increasing during periods of business expansion but seldom decreasing in all but the most severe business contraction. Economists have used each of the monopoly, efficient contract, and median voter models to explain this pattern. We briefly evaluate the ability of each to do so....

Evaluation. Which of the three models offers the most convincing explanation of the cyclical pattern of union wages? The explanation offered by both the monopoly and the efficient contract models for the downward rigidity of union wages is essentially *ad hoc*. In the monopoly model, wage rigidity arises from the asymmetric shape of the union indifference curves, but there is no indication how the underlying preferences of the union membership give rise to such curves. Likewise, wage rigidity in the efficient contract model occurs only in the special case where the shifts of the equity locus and contract curve are of roughly equal magnitude. There is no obvious reason, however, why this restriction should hold true. In addition, neither model offers a logically satisfying explanation for why unions will agree to wage cuts in some situations and not in others.

The median voter model, on the other hand, largely overcomes these problems. It shows, for example, that rigid union wages are to be expected in cyclical downturns, for, in most cases, the layoffs that result do not threaten the job security of the majority of senior union members. When layoffs do threaten a majority of the membership, however, the model shows that the union will actively consider a wage cut. Although these types of explanations seem more convincing to us, there are shortcomings with the median voter model as well. The predicted path of union wages in a cyclical upswing, for example, is critically affected by the dynamic instability of the model noted earlier, as well as by the omission of strike costs.

VI. *The Incidence of Featherbedding Requirements*

The second feature of union wage/employment determination considered here is the conditions under which a union will seek to expand or protect employment opportunities by adopting featherbedding or "make-work" requirements. The essence of featherbedding is that through some type of restriction, such as a minimum crew size requirement or a fixed worker per machine ratio, the union forces the firm to hire more labor at the prevailing wage than it desires, in effect forcing the firm off its labor demand curve. Classic examples of featherbedding include the insistence of railroad unions that the companies continue to use firemen on diesel locomotives and the "bogus" rule of International Typographical Union that required a newspaper to reset any advertising copy obtained from another newspaper.

One test of the explanatory power of the three models under consideration here is their ability to explain what motivates unions to bargain for featherbedding requirements and whether this motivation will be greater for some unions than for others. The implications of each model in this regard are briefly discussed below.

The Monopoly Model. The monopoly model implies that featherbedding requirements should not be an important feature of wage determination in the union sector. Because the model assumes that the employer can unilaterally set the level of employment, the predicted wage/employment outcome is on the firm's labor demand curve. In this case, there is no featherbedding, because all workers have a marginal revenue product greater than or equal to the wage rate.

The Efficient Contract Model. The efficient contract model implies much the opposite. A central feature of an efficient contract is that the union trades off a lower wage for a promise by the firm to employ additional labor. Because the efficient contract outcome is to the right of the demand curve, it implies that, in general, a certain degree of featherbedding will exist in unionized firms.

There is a question of whether an efficient contract is feasible since the firm has an incentive to cheat on the agreement by reducing employment back to the labor demand curve. This may explain, in turn, Oswald's finding that few unions explicitly bargain over both wage rates and employment levels. [A]n efficient contract solution can still be approximated if the union imposes a more indirect type of restrictive work rule. One possibility is for the union to fix the ratio of labor to capital; a second is to fix the ratio of labor to output. Both types of restrictive work rules are far more easily policed by the union, substantially reducing the problem of feasibility. . . .

The Median Voter Model. . . . In a perfectly democratic union, the union's bargaining agenda is shaped by the preferences of the median voter. . . . If the union has unlimited bargaining power, then the median voter will always want the union to negotiate a featherbedding rule and, interestingly enough, the optimal rule will be [to] restrict the firm to the initial capital/labor ratio.

Evaluation. The monopoly model predicts that union contracts should not contain featherbedding requirements, and the efficient contract model predicts that all union contracts should contain some type of restrictive work rule. The median voter model gives the same prediction if the union has unlimited bargaining power. Which model best fits the facts? Unfortunately, the answer seems to be "none of them." The most authoritative study on union featherbedding is provided by Sumner Slichter, James Healy, and E. Robert Livernash, *The Impact of Collective Bargaining on Management*, Washington, D.C.: The Brookings Institution, 1960. Contrary to the prediction of the monopoly model, they conclude that featherbedding or make-work requirements are an important part of negotiated contracts in certain industries; but, contrary to the predictions of the efficient contract and median voter models, such rules are found only in a minority of unionized firms, principally those organized by craft unions or in declining industries or industries experiencing rapid technological change.

How can this seemingly aberrant result be explained? We believe that neither the monopoly nor the efficient contract model can shed much light on this issue. Slightly amending the median voter model, however, allows a solution to the paradox. The key requirement is to incorporate strike costs or, more generally, bargaining power into the model.

It is obvious that no union has unlimited bargaining power, a fact that Slichter et al. attested to when they observed that a union must generally give up a certain amount of wages in order to gain a make-work rule. If a union's bargaining power is sufficiently weak that it cannot obtain a wage higher than [the wage preferred by the median worker], it is clear that the median voter will have no interest in a make-work rule, because the cost to him or her would be a reduction in wages with no corresponding benefit in increased job security. Assume, however, that the union is sufficiently powerful that it could induce the employer to pay [a higher] wage rate. In this situation, the median voter would favor some type of featherbedding requirement. . . .

This revised model suggests two things. First, most unions do not pursue make-work requirements because they are not able to raise the wage high enough to threaten the job security of the senior majority of workers. . . . For this reason, the predictions of the efficient contract model can be called into serious question. Second, the median voter model explains why featherbedding requirements are largely found among craft unions and in declining industries or industries experiencing rapid technological change. Craft unions, for example, tend to have considerable bargaining power but memberships that are numerically smaller. In this case, it often makes sense for the union to bargain for featherbedding rules, since they allow the union to push up wages without threatening the job security of the senior majority of the membership. Likewise, if technological change allows a firm to move to a much higher capital/labor ratio in the long run, the senior majority of the union membership may again perceive it to be in their self-interest to use some of the union's bargaining power to restrict the firm's substitution possibilities in production, lest layoffs threaten those workers' job security.

Notes and Questions

1. *Median Voter and Efficiency.* The median voter model assumes that all workers are bound by a single contract, and that each worker votes for the leader who proposes a contract closest to his or her preferred contract. This single contract is a collective good. As discussed later in this chapter in the collective-voice view of unions, markets of individual workers generally fail to provide the optimal level of a collective good. Unfortunately, the outcome predicted by the median voter model, while different from the outcome in a market of individual workers, is not necessarily any closer to the efficient level of the collective good. The problem is that the collective agent operating under the median voter model does not care about how highly the nonmedian voters value the item, even though factoring in intensity of preferences is critical to determining the efficient level of the collective good. See Hirsch and Addison, *The Economic Analysis of Unions*, 26. A richer model of union representation whereby leaders do not simply count members' votes but recognize intensity avoids this problem, but the model quickly becomes indeterminate.

2. *Problems with Union Democracy.* The median voter model assumes that a well-functioning democratic union exists, whereby the officer preferred by a majority of workers will be elected. But individual union members have great difficulty monitoring and controlling the leaders who ostensibly act in their interest. Labor law regulates unions to ensure a certain level of democracy. The Labor–Management Reporting and Disclosure Act of 1959, 29 U.S.C. §§ 401–531, gives union members extensive voting and free speech rights, and mandates various political procedures, such as the length of time between elections. Still, the political analogy is imperfect. Unlike political voters, union members have no free press to keep them informed and no organized alternative party to criticize the incumbents. The ability of union leaders to control agendas, limit alternatives, and limit information keeps unions from meeting the democratic ideal assumed by the median voter model. Classic analyses of the possibilities of union democracy include William M. Leiserson, *American Trade Union Democracy* (New York: Columbia University Press, 1959); Seymour M. Lipset, Martin A. Trow, and James S. Coleman, *Union Democracy: The Internal Politics of the International Typographic Union* (Glencoe, Ill.: Free Press, 1956); Archibald Cox, "The Role of Law in Preserving Union Democracy," 72 *Harvard Law Review* 609 (1959); and Clyde W. Summers, "Democracy in a One–Party State: Perspectives from Landrum–Griffin," 43 *Maryland Law Review* 93 (1984). For a synthesis of legal doctrines affecting union democracy that draws extensively on disciplines other than law, see Roger C. Hartley, "The Framework of Democracy in Union Government," 32 *Catholic University Law Review* 13 (1982).

Shareholders in corporations have an analogous problem in controlling the corporate managers ostensibly working on their behalf. Corporate law gives shareholders various electoral rights. But in recent decades, scholars have emphasized the market for corporate control—whereby rival firms take over badly run corporations and oust incumbent management—as the prime mechanism that induces corporations to act on behalf of their shareholders. Could a market for union control exist? Unions occasionally do raid rival unions, and presumably are most successful when the workers are dissatisfied with the incumbent leadership. Several factors minimize the threat of interunion competition, however. First is the no-raid pact of articles III, § 4, and XX, § 2, of the AFL–CIO Constitution, whereby unions within the federation promise not to raid each other. See Lea B. Vaughn, "Article XX of the AFL–CIO Constitution: Managing and Resolving Inter–Union Disputes," 37 *Wayne Law Review* 1 (1990). Second, the nonprofit nature of unions and the nontransferability of union membership limit the financial gains from a raid. For an argument that a weak market for union control exists, see Stewart J. Schwab, "Union Raids, Union Democracy, and the Market for Union Control," 1992 *University of Illinois Law Review* 367.

B. Evidence on Union Wage Effects

Labor economists have devoted much effort to measuring the economic effects of unions. At the center of the inquiry has been the extent to which unions increase wages and other compensation, as predicted by the monopoly union model. The techniques used to carry out this inquiry have changed dramatically in the last generation. Much of this change comes from the availability of large data sets and the ability to analyze them through computers. Prior generations of labor economists emphasized personal experience and the case study as methods of testing hypotheses about labor markets. Today, labor economists study data sets based both on surveys of large samples of firms or workers designed to be representative of the labor force (cross-sectional studies), and on surveys that follow the same workers over time (longitudinal studies). Among the most widely used data sets are the Current Population Survey (a monthly cross-sectional survey of some 65,000 households conducted by the Bureau of the Census); the Expenditures for Employee Compensation Survey (a survey of firms conducted by the Bureau of Labor Statistics of the U.S. Department of Labor); the Panel Study on Income Dynamics (PSID) (a longitudinal survey, conducted by the University of Michigan, of 5,000 persons); and the National Longitudinal Survey (a survey broadly similar to the PSID, conducted by Ohio State University). Labor economists then analyze these data sets with computer programs, running regression equations that control for such variables as industry or region of the country.

Most estimates suggest that unionized workers have wages 10 to 30 percent higher than otherwise comparable nonunion workers. The wage differential varies greatly among groups of workers and over the business cycle. The wages of unionized workers are generally less sensitive to booms or busts than nonunion wages, and thus the wage differential tends to be highest during recessions. These studies have been surveyed and critiqued by H. Gregg Lewis, an acknowledged master of empirical studies of the union wage effect. Lewis, *Union Relative Wage Effects: A*

Survey (Chicago: University of Chicago Press, 1986). Some of the important conclusions from these studies are highlighted below.

1. *Measuring Gap versus Gain.* Professor Lewis carefully distinguishes the union "wage gap" from a union "wage gain." The wage gap focuses on the individual worker by estimating the average wage increase a worker would obtain from switching from nonunion to union status, assuming that no one else switches. The wage gain estimates the average wage increase a unionized worker would obtain compared with an economy without any unions. The difference may be captured in the following way: the wage gap reveals the wage loss of remaining nonunion given that others are unionized; the wage gain shows the advantage a unionized worker has in our current partially unionized economy over an economy without monopoly unions. Lewis's best estimate of the wage gap is 15 percent. He insists the wage gain is unmeasurable.

Is the wage gain likely to be lower or higher than the wage gap? This depends greatly on whether wages would generally be lower in an economy without monopoly unions (there being no institution to wrest income from capital) or higher (if unions wrest most of their wage gains from nonunion labor and reduce the overall pie).

2. *Who Gains from Unionism?* As predicted by the internal labor market model (see Wachter and Wright selection in Chapter 1), a major union policy is to prevent management from setting pay on an individual basis, but rather to set pay based on seniority and job category. One effect of this policy is to raise the wage of workers who otherwise would tend to be paid lower amounts. Correspondingly, one would expect unions to have the biggest impact on the pay of the young, the unskilled, and minorities.

In broad brush, these empirical studies reveal that unions increase the wages of young workers (ages 20 to 35) considerably more than the wages of middle-aged workers (ages 36 to 55). Interestingly, the most senior workers (ages 56 to 65) likewise do better with unions than do middle-aged workers. Workers without a high school education receive 27 percent higher wages if they belong to a union, while union representation gives college graduates only a 6 percent increase. The union wage differential for whites is 17 percent, but 25 percent for nonwhites. Gender, on the other hand, runs counter to the expectation that the union impact is largest for lower-paid groups. The union wage differential averages 19 percent for men but only 15 percent for women. See Richard B. Freeman and James L. Medoff, *What Do Unions Do?* (New York: Basic Books, 1984), 48–52.

Perhaps because of the bigger payoff, union membership is higher for blacks and men than for other groups. In 1997, the percentages of employed workers who were union members were 16.4 percent for white men, 21.6 percent for black men, and 13.7 percent for Hispanic men. The corresponding figures for women were 11.3 percent for white women,

16.5 percent for black women, and 11.8 percent for Hispanic women. See Department of Labor, Bureau of Labor Statistics, News Release, "Union Members Summary: Union Members in 1997," Table 1 (Jan. 30, 1998).

3. *Fringe Benefits and Union "Voice."* Unionized workers have substantially more generous fringe benefits than nonunion workers. Thus, the wage differential understates the impact of unions on their members' economic well-being. In a survey using mid–1970s data, unionized employers spent 18 percent of compensation on voluntary fringe benefits, compared with only 12 percent for nonunion employers. See Freeman and Medoff, *What Do Unions Do?*, 62–63.

Two factors cause unionized workers to have greater fringe benefits than nonunion workers. First, unions exercising monopoly power push up fringe benefits just as they push up wages. Second, for a given level of total compensation, unions seek a higher proportion of fringe benefits than nonunion workers receive. This relative preference for fringe benefits cannot be explained by the monopoly model. However, the median voter model of unions suggests that unions try to represent the average or median worker, who is likely to value fringe benefits more highly than a marginal worker will. Freeman and Medoff estimate that the monopoly-power and collective-voice explanations are quantitatively similar. Of the total hourly increase in fringes from unionization, about 55 percent is a willingness to trade wages for fringes, reflecting the collective-voice aspect of unions. About 45 percent comes from higher total compensation, reflecting the monopoly power of unions.

Unions also alter the types of fringe benefits employers provide. Consistent with the median voter model, union fringe benefits generally favor more senior, career workers. Most prominent are the union effects on pensions. Unionized workers are far more likely than nonunion workers to be covered by a pension plan, and pension contributions are a larger share of total compensation for union workers. Union pension plans are predominantly defined-benefit plans, promising a definite payout on retirement (a typical promise might be a yearly payment of 0.02 times years of service times final average salary). Most nonunion pension plans, by contrast, are defined contribution plans, whereby the employer promises to invest a certain amount (say 10 percent of salary) into individual employee accounts for retirement, but makes no promises about how well these investments will do or how much money will be available in retirement. Senior workers generally prefer defined-benefit plans, because they will enjoy any increase in benefits without paying the full cost of extra contributions. Younger, more transient workers would prefer defined-contribution plans, which are more portable.

Like pension benefits, life and health insurance are a greater proportion of total compensation for unionized workers. These benefits, too, are relatively attractive to older, more senior workers. In contrast, unions have little effect on maternity leave, and actually reduce bonuses and sick leave. As Freeman and Medoff explain, unions "discourage bonus payments because they typically are based on employer discretion, and make compensation sensitive to business conditions; sick leave may be lower because of the tendency for unionized plants to work 'by the book,' with sick absences monitored more carefully." Freeman and Medoff, *What Do Unions Do?*, 65–66.

4. *Compensating Wage Differentials.* Compared with otherwise similar nonunion workers, unionized workers endure a more structured work setting, more rigid hours, more employer-set overtime, and a faster work pace. Perhaps 40 percent of the union wage gap compensates workers for these unpleasant working conditions rather than increasing their overall well-being. See Greg J. Duncan and Frank P. Stafford, "Do Union Members Receive Compensating Wage Differentials?" 70 *American Economic Review* 355 (1980).

The interesting question is why unionized plants have these more structured work conditions. One possibility is that employers respond, after unions force up wages, by squeezing greater production from workers. Duncan and Stafford label this the "union-partial-control" hypothesis. Another possibility is that unions tend to take hold where uniform conditions (temperature, level of safety, work pace, length of workday) must apply to all workers. Under this "interdependency" hypothesis, unions do not lead to the onerous conditions but rather are a mechanism to ameliorate the unpleasantness that certain production technologies create.

5. *The Inequality of Earnings.* A major issue in the study of union wage effects is whether unions increase or decrease the overall inequality of earnings. On the one hand, unions exacerbate inequality by increasing wages of unionized workers at the expense of nonunion workers. This is the union wage gap, discussed earlier. On the other hand, unions lessen inequality by (1) compressing earnings within a unionized firm; (2) decreasing wage differences among firms (following the union goal of taking wages out of competition); and (3) increasing the wages of blue-collar workers, who tend to be more unionized, relative to generally higher-paid white-collar workers.

Which of these conflicting effects dominates is an empirical question. It appears that the inequality-reducing impact of unions dominates. Freeman and Medoff, for example, summarize several studies by suggesting that "[o]n the basis of the new empirical research, it appears that trade unionism in the United States reduces wage inequality by around 3 percent." Freeman and Medoff, *What Do Unions Do?*, 93. Similarly, Hirsch and Addison conclude:

> Wage standardization appears to be the dominant union effect on wage dispersion. Unions seek to establish job rather than individual rates of pay within establishments and to acquire a similar wage structure across establishments. This goal apparently derives from the union's representational

nature—survival requires that it responds more to the interests of average workers and majority coalitions than to marginal workers—coupled with its rational attempt to lessen wage competition across establishments.

Hirsch and Addison, *The Economic Analysis of Unions*, 177.

C. Unions as Providers of Collective Goods

In the monopoly model and its efficient contract and median voter variants, the central role of unions is to increase worker compensation by restricting labor supply. Much of the debate within these models is whether unions could do this without loss of efficiency (by simply redistributing rents from firms to workers) or whether unions must inefficiently restrict employment levels.

Another vision of unions suggests that they might actually enhance efficiency. Unions serve as institutions that can solve collective-goods issues in the workplace. By giving workers a "voice" when conditions are bad, unions provide an alternative to the "exit" option of quitting work. In the reading below, Freeman and Medoff give the basic framework for understanding how unions enhance efficiency through voice.

"The Two Faces of Unionism"*
RICHARD B. FREEMAN and JAMES L. MEDOFF

. . .

Unions as collective voice

One key dimension of the new work on trade unionism can best be understood by recognizing that societies have two basic mechanisms for dealing with divergences between desired social conditions and actual conditions. The first is the classic market mechanism of exit and entry, individual mobility: The dissatisfied consumer switches products; the diner whose soup is too salty seeks another restaurant; the unhappy couple divorces. In the labor market, exit is synonymous with quitting, while entry consists of new hires by the firm. By leaving less-desirable jobs for more-desirable jobs, or by refusing bad jobs, individuals penalize the bad employer and reward the good—leading to an overall improvement in the efficiency of the social system. The basic theorem of neoclassical economics is that, under well-specified conditions, the exit and entry of persons (the hallmark of free enterprise) produces a "Pareto-optimum" situation—one in which no individual can be made better off without making someone worse off. Economic analysis can be viewed as a detailed study of the implications of this kind of adjustment and of the extent to which it works out in real economies. As long as the exit-entry market mechanism is viewed as the only efficient adjustment

* 57 *Public Interest* 69 (1979).

mechanism, institutions such as unions must necessarily be viewed as impediments to the optimal operation of a capitalist economy.

There is, however, a second mode of adjustment. This is the political mechanism, which Albert Hirschman term "voice" in his important book, *Exit, Voice, and Loyalty* (Cambridge, Mass.: Harvard University Press, 1970). "Voice" refers to the use of direct communication to bring actual and desired conditions closer together. It means talking about problems: complaining to the store about a poor product rather than taking business elsewhere; telling the chef that the soup had too much salt; discussing marital problems rather than going directly to divorce court. In a political context, "voice" refers to participation in the democratic process, through voting, discussion, bargaining, and the like....

In the job market, voice consists of discussing with an employer conditions that ought to be changed, rather than quitting the job. In modern industrial economies, and particularly in large enterprises, a trade union is the vehicle for collective voice—that is, for providing workers as a group with a means of communicating with management.

Collective rather than individual bargaining with an employer is necessary for effective voice at the workplace for two reasons. First, many important aspects of an industrial setting are "public goods," which affect the well-being (negatively or positively) of every employee. As a result, the incentive for any single person to express his preferences, and invest time and money to change conditions (for the good of all), is reduced. Safety conditions, lighting, heating, the speed of a production line, the firm's policies on layoffs, work-sharing, cyclical-wage adjustment, and promotion, its formal grievance procedure and pension plan—all obviously affect the entire workforce in the same way that defense, sanitation, and fire protection affect the entire citizenry. "Externalities" (things done by one individual or firm that also affect the well-being of another, but for which the individual or firm is not compensated or penalized) and "public goods" at the workplace require collective decision-making. Without a collective organization, the incentive for the individual to take into account the effects of his or her actions on others, or express his or her preferences, or invest time and money in changing conditions, is likely to be too small to spur action. Why not "let Harry do it" and enjoy the benefits at no cost? This classic "free rider" problem lies at the heart of the so-called "union-security" versus "right-to-work" debate.

A second reason collective action is necessary is that workers who are not prepared to exit will be unlikely to reveal their true preferences to their bosses, for fear of some sort of punishment....

The collective nature of trade unionism fundamentally alters the operation of a labor market and, hence, the nature of the labor contract. In a nonunion setting, where exit and entry are the predominant forms of adjustment, the signals and incentive to firms depend on the preferences of the "marginal" worker, the one who will leave (or be attracted) by particular conditions or changes in conditions. The firm responds primarily to the needs of this marginal, generally younger and more mobile worker and can within some bounds ignore the preferences of "infra-marginal," typically older workers who—for reasons of skill, knowledge, rights that cannot be readily transferred to other enterprises, as well as because of other costs associated with changing firms—are effectively immobile. In a unionized setting, by contrast, the union takes account of the preferences of *all* workers to form an average preference that typically determines its position at the bargaining table. Because unions are political institutions with elected leaders, they are likely to be responsive to a different set of preferences from those that dominate in a competitive labor market.

In a modern economy, where workers tend to be attached to firms for eight or more years, and where younger and older workers are likely to have different preferences (for instance, regarding pension or health insurance plans versus take-home pay, or layoff by inverse seniority versus work-sharing or cuts in wage growth), the change from a marginal to an average calculus is likely to lead to a very different labor contract. When issues involve sizable fixed costs or "public goods," a calculus based on the average preference can lead to a contract which, ignoring distributional effects, is socially more desirable than one based on the marginal preference—that is, it may even be economically more "efficient."

As a voice institution, unions also fundamentally alter the social relations of the workplace. Perhaps most important, a union constitutes a source of worker power in a firm, diluting managerial authority and offering members a measure of due process, in particular through the union innovation of a grievance and arbitration system. While 99 percent of major U.S. collective-bargaining contracts provide for the filing of grievances, and 95 percent provide for arbitration of disputes that are not settled between the parties, relatively few nonunion firms have comparable procedures for settling disagreements between workers and supervisors. More broadly, the entire industrial jurisprudence system— by which many workplace decisions are based on negotiated rules (such as seniority) instead of supervisory judgment (or whim) and are subject to challenge through the grievance/arbitration procedure—represents a major change in the power relations within firms. As a result, in unionized firms workers are more willing and able to express discontent and to object to managerial decisions.

Thus, as a collective alternative to individualistic actions in the market, unions are much more than simple monopolies that raise wages and restrict the competitive adjustment process. Given imperfect information and the existence of public goods in industrial settings, and conflicting interests in the workplace and in the political area, unionism provides an alternative mechanism for bringing about change. This is not to deny that unions have monopolistic power nor that they use this power to raise wages for a select part of the workforce. The point is that unionism has two "faces," each of which leads to a different view of the institution: One, which is at the fore in economic analysis, is that of a monopoly; the other is that of "a voice institution," i.e., a sociopolitical institution. To understand fully what unions do in modern industrial economies, it is necessary to examine both faces. . . .

Effects on efficiency

In the monopoly view, unions reduce society's output in three ways. First, union-won wage increases cause a misallocation of resources by inducing organized firms to hire fewer workers, to use more capital per worker, and to hire higher quality workers than is socially efficient. Second, union contract provisions—such as limits on the loads that can be handled by workers, restrictions on tasks performed, featherbedding, and so forth—reduce the output that should be forthcoming from a given amount of capital and labor. Third, strikes called to force management to accept union demands cause a substantial reduction in gross national product.

By contrast, the collective-voice/institutional-response model directs attention to the important ways in which unionism can raise productivity. First of all, unionism should reduce "quits." As workers' voice increases in an establishment, less reliance need be placed on the exit and entry mechanism to obtain desired working conditions. Since hiring and training costs are lowered and the functioning of work groups is less disrupted when "quit" rates are low, unionism can actually raise efficiency.

The fact that senior workers are likely to be relatively more powerful in enterprises where decisions are based on voice instead of exit and entry points to another way in which unions can raise productivity. Under unionism, promotions and other rewards tend to be less dependent in any precise way on individual performance and more dependent on seniority. As a result, in union plants, feelings of rivalry among individuals are likely to be less pronounced than in nonunion plants, and the amount of informal training and assistance that workers are willing to provide one another is greater. (The importance of seniority in firms in Japan, together with the permanent employment guaranteed many workers there, have often been cited as factors increasing the productivity of Japanese enterprises.) It is, of course, also important to recognize that seniority can reduce productivity by placing individuals in jobs for which they are not qualified.

Unionism can also raise efficiency by pressuring management into tightening job-production standards and accountability, in an effort to respond to union demands while maintaining profits. Slichter, Healy, and Livernash wrote in 1960, "The challenge that unions presented to management has, if viewed broadly, created superior and better-balanced management, even though some exceptions must be recognized." Their conclusion means that with a unionized workforce, management is able to extract more output from a given amount of inputs than is management that is not confronted with a union. This appears to occur largely because modern personnel practices are forced on the firm and traditional paternalism is discarded. Management's ability to make such improvements is a function of the union's cooperation, since the union can perform a helpful role in explaining changes in the day-to-day routine....

Explaining managerial opposition

If, in addition to its negative monopoly effects, trade unionism is associated with substantial positive effects on the operation of the economy and on the performance of firms, why do so many U.S. firms oppose unions so vehemently? There are in fact several reasons.

First, the bulk of the economic gains that spring from unionism accrue to workers and not to owners or managers. Managers are unlikely to see any personal benefits in their subordinates' unionization, but are likely to be quite aware of the costs: a diminution of their power, the need to work harder, the loss of operating flexibility, and the like.

Second, though productivity might typically be higher in union than in otherwise comparable nonunion work settings, so too are wages. It would seem, given the objectives and actions of most unions, that the rate of return on capital would be lower under collective bargaining, although there are important exceptions. Thus, there is risk in unionization; the firm may be able to rationalize operations, have good relations with the union, and maintain its profit rate—or it may not. In addition, while the total cost of strikes to society as a whole has been shown to be quite small, the potential cost to a particular firm can be substantial. Since managers—like most other people—dislike taking risks, we would expect opposition to unions even if on average the benefits to firms equal the costs. Moreover, given the wide-ranging differences in the effects of unions on economic performance, at least some managerial opposition surely arises from enterprises in which the expected benefits of collective bargaining are small but the expected costs high. Even the most vocal advocate of the collective-voice/institutional-response view of unionism would admit that, though functional in many industrial settings, unions are not functional in others—and one must expect greater managerial opposition in the latter cases.

Third, management may find unionism expensive, difficult, and very threatening in its initial stages, when modes of operation must be altered if efficiency is to be improved. New and different types of management policies are needed under unionism, and these require either changes in the behavior of current management, or—as appears to be the case in many just-organized firms—a new set of managers.

Finally, U.S. management has generally adopted an ideology of top-down enlightened control, under which unions are seen as both a cause and an effect of managerial failure. In this view, unions interfere with management's efforts to carry out its social function of ensuring that goods and services are produced efficiently. In addition, because unions typically come into existence as a result of management's mistakes in dealing with its workforce, managers frequently resent what unionization implies about their own past performances....

Notes and Questions

1. *Listening to Inframarginal Workers.* One of the key elements of the collective-voice model is that unions become the conduit by which employers can learn and respond to the preferences of their locked-in, inframarginal workers in ways that benefit most workers and the firm. The labor market, by contrast, tends to undervalue the concerns of such workers. See generally Paul C. Weiler, *Governing the Workplace: The Future of Labor and Employment Law* (Cambridge, Mass.: Harvard University Press, 1990), 78. The following stylized example illustrates the point. Suppose a firm is contemplating lowering salaries by $800 in return for an $800 increase in pension contributions. The firm has 1,000 senior workers who have large fixed investments in the firm and thus are unlikely to leave. Each senior worker gains $200 from the proposal, because each would be willing to take up to a $1,000 salary reduction for the $800 increase in the pension fund (tax breaks make the pension attractive to older employees). The firm also has 1,000 junior employees, who are less interested in pensions and would leave if their salary dropped by more than $700 in return for the $800 increase in pension contributions. The increased pension contribution is the efficient strategy in the sense that the $200 net gain to each senior worker outweighs the $100 loss to junior workers. Indeed, a win-win-win solution would have the firm increase its pension contribution by $800 and lower junior salaries by $660 and senior salaries by $960. Nevertheless, a firm that focuses only on the "exit" problem of attracting and keeping workers will reject the pension proposal.

2. *High–Wage Effects and Efficiency Effects.* As Freeman and Medoff emphasize, the empirical challenge in demonstrating the "collective-voice face" of unions is to separate "mere" productivity gains following union wage increases from net efficiency gains. Proponents of the monopoly view acknowledge that, as unions push up wages, firms will use more capital and will hire better workers. Both switches will increase output per worker. Under the monopoly view, however, these switches mitigate but cannot fully counteract the inefficient resource allocation resulting from an inefficient increase in wages. Economy-wide, says the monopoly view, output would increase if union firms used more labor and nonunion firms used more capital.

3. *Measuring Union Productivity Effects.* Freeman and Medoff and several other economists have tried to measure empirically whether unions in fact increase firm productivity as predicted by the collective goods model. The empirical technique is to estimate a production-function regression where one of the explanatory variables is the percentage of the workforce that is unionized:

> The tool used to study the impact of unionism on productivity is the production function, which traditionally makes output per worker depend on capital per worker, other inputs used per worker, and indicators of the quality of the workers (as reflected in their level of schooling, for instance). To determine the effects of unionism on productivity, one adds to the traditional variables a variable giving the fraction of the workforce that is unionized. In statistical analyses the estimated effect of the fraction unionized reflects what unions do to productivity above and beyond changes in the amount of physical inputs used per worker. To isolate the union effect in this framework, one must have good measures of output, capital, and the quality of labor, and one must specify properly the nature of the production relation itself.

> [T]he studies differ in their measures of labor productivity, with some measuring it in dollar units (value added by the firm or the value of shipments) per worker, and others measuring it in physical units (tons, square feet) per worker. The dollar measures of output (price times quantity) have the advantage of including the full spectrum of goods produced by a firm, valued at their market prices. They also have a disadvantage, however: unless the prices charged by union and non-union firms are the same, any finding of higher value added (shipments) per worker in the organized establishments could reflect not the higher physical output per worker but rather a higher price per unit of output. In industries where markets are truly competitive, with a single price for each output, and where unionized and nonunionized firms are equally likely to specialize in high-priced or in low-priced outputs, the possible confusion of price with quantity is small. For industries where these conditions do not hold, one must take great care in estimating a union productivity effect. Physical measures of output alleviate the problem of confusing price differences with output differences, but at the cost of being limited to the few distinct goods that can be so measured. Most modern firms produce a wide variety of products with too many dimensions to be captured by a single physical measure. Because neither measure is perfect, researchers have analyzed both dollar and physical measures of labor productivity.

Freeman and Medoff, *What Do Unions Do?*, 165, 167.

4. *Quit Rates.* One effect of raising wages is that workers will be more reluctant to quit because other jobs are less attractive. Thus, the monopoly model predicts lower quit rates in unionized firms. The collective-goods model predicts that, even controlling for wage rates, unions lower turnover because workers can improve their working lives in ways other than finding a better job at another firm. Empirical studies from numerous countries

confirm the prediction, finding that, controlling for wages as well as other factors, unionized firms have lower quit rates and greater job tenure than comparable nonunion firms. As Mischel and Voos interpret the evidence on turnover, the "exit-voice trade-off at the heart of [the collective-voice model] applies universally to unionism in industrialized countries." See Lawrence R. Mischel and Paula B. Voos, *Unions and Economic Competitiveness* (Armonk, N.Y.: M.E. Sharpe, 1992), 148.

5.   *Studies of the Cement Industry.* One of the key pieces of evidence for the efficiency-enhancing role of unions comes from the cement industry. Cement is an excellent industry to study, because it has both union and nonunion firms in the same region and because cement is a homogeneous product in which physical output can be compared across firms without worrying about variations in quality. Kim Clark, "The Impact of Unionization on Productivity: A Case Study," 33 *Industrial and Labor Relations Review* 451 (1980), studied six cement manufacturing plants that changed union status, and examined the amount of cement produced as a function of the quantity and quality of capital stock, the number of production and supervisory workers, and of course union status. Controlling for these other factors, Clark found that unionized plants produced 6–10 percent more cement per worker than nonunion plants. Clark emphasized that unionization altered the process of management. After unions were introduced, managers initiated staff meetings, on-line time standards for equipment maintenance, and other forms of monitoring and control.

6.   *"It's Hard to Believe."* Judge Richard A. Posner, for one, finds the Freeman/Medoff findings difficult to accept. As he responds, "[a]lthough some empirical support has been marshaled for the productivity enhancement theory of unionization, the theory is extremely hard to accept." Posner, "Some Economics of Labor Law," 51 *University of Chicago Law Review* 988, 1000 (1984). To say that government-protected unions increase productivity, Posner argues, is to ignore a fundamental assumption of economics that employers seek to maximize profits. If union membership really increased employee productivity and efficiency, employers would need no prompting to offer it. If unions did in fact increase productivity, why would employers invest resources in opposing unionization?

7.   *Are Unions Needed for Voice?* In recent years, nonunion firms have increasingly created mechanisms that give their workers voice. One study revealed that in 1992 about 35 percent of private-sector establishments with 50 or more employees used "flexible work organization," which includes teams, job rotation, quality circles, and total quality management. See Paul Osterman, "How Common Is Workplace Transformation, and Who Adopts It?," 47 *Industrial and Labor Relations Review* 173 (1994). While some of the motivation may be to keep employees from organizing a union, much of the motivation seems to be to capture the gains arising from solving collective-goods issues in the workplace. Some have argued that such innovative reorganizations of work are not substitutes for unions. See Eileen Applebaum and Rosemary Batt, *The New American Workplace: Transforming Work Systems in the United States* (Ithaca, N.Y.: ILR Press, 1994), 129.

D. Union Effects on Profitability

One way to explain why employers resist productivity-enhancing unions is to distinguish productivity from profitability. While unions might enhance productivity through collective-voice mechanisms, they could grab those gains and more from employers with their monopoly face, thus reducing overall profitability. As the following readings discuss, unions generally reduce the profitability of firms. Whether that is good or bad depends in large part on where the profits were coming from. In the first excerpt below, Freeman and Medoff emphasize that unions reduce profits primarily in highly concentrated industries where firms would otherwise earn supracompetitive profits. Such a reduction in profits is unlikely to greatly hurt the overall economy. Unions can be seen as relatively benign Robin Hoods, taking from rich industries and giving to their workers.

In the second reading, Barry Hirsch emphasizes that unions sometimes grab the quasi-rents from firms. This source of union gains has more disturbing implications. Quasi-rents arise when a firm makes a large investment that cannot easily be transferred to other uses. Once it is in place, the firm will keep operating with very low profits, because these low returns are better than scrapping the investment entirely. A powerful union, recognizing the vulnerability of such an investment, can come in after the investment is made and appropriate much of the return for its members, without driving the firm out of business. Unfortunately, firms that recognize the possibility of such opportunism will hesitate to make the investment in the first place. Thus, union reductions in firm profits of this type lead to lower investment and long-run growth of the economy.

"But Unionism Lowers Profits"*
RICHARD B. FREEMAN and JAMES L. MEDOFF

Studies of industry or company profitability treat two measures of profits: the "quasi-rent" return on capital, defined as business receipts less variable (usually labor) costs divided by some measure of the value of capital, such as the replacement cost of plant and equipment or the gross book value of total assets; and the "price-cost margin," defined as the excess of prices over variable costs. The quasi-rent/capital measure has the advantage of relating returns directly to capital, but the disadvantage of requiring valid measures of capital. The price-cost margin is widely used in industrial organization to measure the potential effect of market concentration on prices: a sector with monopoly prices will charge an above-normal margin and thus earn higher profits on its investment. As neither of the variables comes from a conceptually correct expected present value analysis, each has been criticized in

* In Freeman and Medoff, *What Do Unions Do?* (New York: Basic Books, 1984), 181–87.

studies of profitability.... Because both contain some information about profitability, we have examined the effect of unionism on both, on the principle that when one cannot measure the theoretically correct concept, one does better to look at several indicators, rather than to debate over which imperfect indicator is "best." ...

The calculations show clear negative union impacts on both the price-cost-margin and the return-to-capital measures of profitability. On the basis of these results, managements of unorganized firms have good reason, in general, to oppose unionization: organization will penalize them on the bottom line.

The magnitude of the reduction in profitability [, ranging from 9 percent to 37 percent,] may strike some readers as suspect, given the estimates of union wage and productivity effects.... If unionism raises wages by 20 percent and if unions raise productivity by 10 to 15 percent, should not one expect (assuming no other variable costs) smaller reductions in profits, on the order of 5 to 10 percent? Is our analysis of profitability consistent with our earlier estimates of union wage and productivity effects?

The figures are consistent. The reason for the large estimated percent of reduction in profitability is that profits are a relatively small component of an industry's income flows, so that percentage changes in costs or in productivity translate into larger percentage changes in profits. Arithmetically, consider what happens to an industry with $1.00 of receipts divided between labor and capital in the proportion of 4 to 1 (labor costs of 80 cents and return-to-capital of 20 cents). An increase in labor costs of 20 percent will raise costs by 16 cents and lower profits 16 cents; but, whereas 16 cents is 20 percent of labor cost, it is 80 percent of profits. In this case, even if unions raise the productivity of capital and labor by 10 percent, so that receipts are 10 cents higher, profits will drop by 6 cents, or 30 percent....

Whose Profits Are Hit Hardest?

It's great that unions lower profits. Big Business has been ripping off the consumer and workers long enough. I'm glad somebody's taking them on for once.–*A radical*

Profits are the golden goose of capitalism. Kill profits and you kill the system. The unions are pricing themselves and American industry out of the market.–*A conservative*

Who is right? Is it good or bad that trade unions reduce profitability in most cases?

The answer depends on the locus of the union impact on profitability. If unions reduce the profitability of industries in which firms have sufficient market power to obtain monopoly-level profits, our radical friend's commentary has some validity. In that case unions are redistributing monopoly profits from capital owners to workers. Indeed, if the industry was charging the prices of a pure monopolist, all of the union effect could come out of the pockets of owners and none out of the pockets of consumers. If, on the other hand, unions reduce profits in competitive settings to levels below the going rate of return, they will drive companies out of business, cause a reduction in the industry's output, and eventually cause a rise in the price consumers pay. In this case, our conservative friend's commentary has validity, for unions will indeed create economic problems of survival for firms and harm consumers.

To see which of the two possible cases best fits U.S. unionism, we have examined the impact of unions on profitability in industries that differ in their level of industrial "concentration," defined as the percentage of an industry's total shipments made by the four largest firms. Concentration is a widely used though imperfect measure of the market power of producers and thus an indicator of where monopoly profits are likely to be found. The impact of unionism on profitability is less likely to be harmful if it occurs in concentrated industries rather than in ones which function under more competitive conditions.

... The results lend considerable support to the radical commentary. Taking the low concentration industries first, we find no substantive difference in profitability between the highly unionized and the less unionized.... These data suggest that unionism has no impact on the profitability of competitive firms. Among highly concentrated industries, by contrast, [there exist] enormous differences in profitability by union density; the highly unionized industries have considerably lower profitability in all calculations [ranging from 17 percent to 26 percent less]. Does this mean that high-concentration high-union industries are doing especially poorly? Because concentrated industries with low unionization have exceedingly high levels of profitability, it does not. Indeed, comparisons of highly unionized concentrated industries and less concentrated industries show basically the same profitability. What unions do is to reduce the exceedingly high levels of profitability in highly concentrated industries toward normal competitive levels. In these calculations, the union profit effect appears to take the form of a reduction of monopoly profits....

"Unionization and Economic Performance"*
BARRY T. HIRSCH

Critical to the assessment of labour unions, performance, and labour law is an understanding of unions' effects on productivity. If collective bargaining in the workplace were systematically to increase productivity

---

* In Fazil Mihlar, ed., *Unions and Right–to–Work Laws* (Vancouver: Fraser Institute, 1997), 35–70.

and to do so to such an extent that it fully offset compensation increases, then a strong argument could be made for policies that facilitate union organizing. A pathbreaking empirical study by Brown and Medoff ["Trade Unions in the Production Process," 86 *Journal of Political Economy* 355–78 (1978)], followed by a body of evidence summarized in Freeman and Medoff's widely read *What Do Unions Do?* (1984), made what at the time appeared to be a persuasive case that collective bargaining in the United States is, on average, associated with substantial improvements in productivity....

The thesis that unions significantly increase productivity has not held up well. Subsequent studies were as likely to find that unions had negative as opposed to positive effects upon productivity. A large enhancement of productivity because of unionization is inconsistent with evidence on profitability and employment. And, increasingly, attention has focused on the dynamic effect of unionization and the apparently negative effects of unions on growth in productivity, sales, and employment....

One issue discussed in this literature concerns the fact that firms facing higher wages must be more productive if they are to survive in the very long run. Hence, the unions' effect upon productivity is not being measured across a representative sample of firms since union firms failing to increase productivity and survive are least likely to be observed. Measurement of union productivity differentials from among a sample of surviving firms may therefore overstate the effect of unions upon the productivity of a representative firm. In fact, union firms are less likely to fail than nonunion firms, although this is because such firms are older and larger and not due to their union status. Once one controls for age and size, union status appears to have surprisingly little effect on firm failure rate, although unionization is associated with slower employment growth. The suggestion here is that unions will push firms to the brink of failure but will not shove them over the cliff....

Despite substantial diversity in the literature about union productivity, several systematic patterns are revealed. First, effects upon productivity tend to be largest in industries where the union wage premium is most pronounced. This pattern is what critics of the production function test predict—that union density coefficients in fact reflect a wage rather than a productivity effect. These results also support a "shock effect" interpretation of unionization, whereby management must respond to an increase in labour costs by organizing more efficiently, reducing slack, and increasing measured productivity. Second, positive effects by unions upon productivity are typically largest where competitive pressure exists and these positive effects are largely restricted to the private, for-profit sectors. Notably absent are positive effects of unions upon productivity in public school construction, public libraries, government bureaus, schools, law enforcement, and hospitals.

This interpretation of the productivity studies has an interesting twist: the evidence suggests that a relatively competitive, cost-conscious economic environment is a necessary condition for a positive effect of unions upon productivity, and that the managerial response should be stronger, the larger the union wage premium or the greater the pressure on profits. Yet it is precisely in such competitive environments that there should be relatively little managerial slack and the least scope for union organizing and wage gains. Therefore, the possibility of a sizable effect by unions upon productivity across the whole economy appears rather limited....

Profitability

Union wage gains lower firm profitability unless offset by productivity enhancements in the workplace or higher prices in the product market. The evidence on productivity reviewed above indicates that unionization does not typically offset compensation increases. A rise in the price of the product sufficient to prevent a loss in profitability is possible only in a regulated industry where firms are "guaranteed" a competitive rate of return. In more competitive settings, where unionized firms compete with nonunion domestic companies and traded goods, there is little if any possibility of passing along increased cost via a rise in prices. Lower profitability will be reflected in decreased current earnings and measured rates of return on capital, and in a lower market valuation of the firm's assets. *Ex-ante* returns on *equity* (risk-adjusted) should not differ between union and nonunion companies, since stock prices adjust to reflect expected earnings.

Profit-maximizing responses by firms to cost differentials should limit the magnitude of differences in profitability between union and nonunion companies in the very long run. Differences in profits will be mitigated through the movement of resources out of union into nonunion sectors—that is, investment in and by union operations will decrease until post-tax (i.e., post-union) rates of return are equivalent to nonunion rates of return or, stated alternatively, union coverage will be restricted to economic sectors realizing above-normal, pre-union rates of returns. Because the quasi-rents accruing to long-lived capital may provide a principal source for union gains and complete long-run adjustments occur slowly, however, we are likely to observe differences in profitability as these adjustments take place.

Empirical evidence shows unambiguously that unionization leads to lower profitability, although studies differ to some degree in their conclusions regarding the magnitude and source of unions gains.... [M]ost studies obtain estimates suggesting that unionized firms have profits that are 10 percent to 20 percent lower than the profits of nonunion firms.

   Economists are understandably skeptical that large profit differentials could survive in a competitive economy, notwithstanding the sizable profit differences between unionized firms and nonunionized firms found in the empirical literature. Yet there are two potentially important econometric biases causing effects of unionization to be understated. First, profit functions are estimated only for *surviving* firms, since those for which the effects of unionization are most deleterious may be less likely to remain in the sample. Second, unions are more likely to be organized where potential profits are higher; hence, the negative effect of unions on profits may be underestimated in empirical work where union density is treated as exogenous. In fact, those studies that attempt to account for the simultaneous determination of union status and profitability obtain larger estimates of unions' effects upon profits....

   More recently, attention has turned to the sources from which unions appropriate rents. Influential early studies concluded that unions reduce profits primarily in highly concentrated industries and that monopoly power provides the primary source for union compensation gains. But that conclusion has not survived further analysis.... Note that these [more recent] studies do not conclude that monopoly rents are not a source for union bargaining power and wage gains. Rather, they find that profits accruing from product-market concentration do not provide such a major source, in part because of the rather tenuous relationship between profitability and concentration. There is no suggestion that unions cannot and do not capture rents; they clearly do so, as can be seen from the close relationship between the unions' wage gains and regulatory rents in the trucking industry, the airlines, and the United States Postal Service.

   What recent studies of profitability do suggest is that many of the gains by unions come from what would otherwise be normal returns to long-lived investments. This has important implications for the effects of labour unions on investment behaviour and long-term growth....

   The area of theoretical and empirical research that has received the most attention in recent years has been the impact of unionization on investments in tangible and intangible capital.... Recent rent-seeking models focus on the fact that unions capture some share of the quasi-rents that make up the normal return to investment in long-lived capital and R & D. In response, firms rationally reduce their investment in vulnerable tangible and intangible capital until returns on investment are equalized across the union (taxed) and nonunion (non-taxed) sectors. Contraction of the union sector, it is argued, has resulted in part from the long-run response by firms to such rent seeking.

   The union tax or rent-seeking framework stands in marked contrast to the traditional economic model of unions. In the standard model, the union's monopoly power in the labour market is viewed as changing relative factor prices through its ability to raise union compensation above competitive levels. In response to a higher wage, union firms move up and along their labour-demand curve by decreasing employment, hiring higher-quality workers, and increasing the ratio of capital to labour. Total investment in innovative activity and labour-saving capital can increase or decrease owing to substitution and scale effects that work in opposing directions.

The traditional model is inadequate for at least two reasons. First, settlements off the labour-demand curve, with lower wages and greater employment than would obtain in the on-the-demand-curve model, are preferred by both the union and management. If settlements are not on the labour-demand curve, the effect of unions on factor mix cannot be predicted in straightforward fashion. A second shortcoming is the traditional model's characterization of union wage increases as an independent increase in the cost of labour relative to capital. In the rent-seeking framework, union wage premiums are viewed as levying a tax on firm earnings, much of which is composed of the returns to capital. The union tax in this view is an outcome made possible both by union power in the labour market and the presence of the firm's quasi-rents. Stated alternatively, wage increases to unions are in part a tax on capital and need not lead firms to shift their factor mix away from labour and toward capital.

Union rent seeking may reduce investment not only in physical capital but also in R & D and other forms of innovative activity. The stock of knowledge and improvements in processes and products emanating from R & D are likely to be relatively long-lived and firm specific. To the extent that returns from innovative activity are appropriable, firms will respond to union power by reducing these investments. Collective-bargaining coverage within a company is most likely to reduce investment in product innovations and relatively factor-neutral process innovations, while having ambiguous effects on innovations in labour-saving processes. Expenditures in R & D also tend to signal—or be statistically prior to—investments in physical capital. Therefore, firms reducing long-range plans for physical capital investment in response to unions' rent-seeking behaviour are likely to reduce investment in R & D. . . .

Despite the very real benefits of collective voice for workers, the positive effects of unions have been overshadowed by union rent-seeking behaviour. Productivity is not higher, on average, in union workplaces. The failure of collective bargaining to enhance productivity significantly results in substantially lower profitability among unionized companies. Because unions appropriate not only a portion of monopoly-related profits but also the quasi-rents that make up the normal return to long-lived capital, unionized companies reduce investment in vulnerable forms of physical and innovative capital. Investment is further reduced since lower profits reduce the size of the internal pool from which investments are partly financed. Slower growth in capital is mirrored by slower growth in sales and employment (and, thus, union membership). The relatively poor performance of union companies gives credence to the proposition that the restructuring in industrial relations and increased resistance to union organizing have been predictable responses on the part of businesses to increased domestic and foreign competition. In the absence of a narrowing in the performance differences between unionized and nonunionized companies, modifications in labour law that substantially enhance union organizing and bargaining strength are likely to reduce economic competitiveness.

Although the evidence indicates clearly that collective bargaining has led to a poor performance in unionized sectors of the economy relative to nonunionized sectors, it is far more difficult to draw inferences about the effects of unions upon economy-wide performance. In fact, a highly competitive economy limits the costs unions can impose since resources flow to those sectors where they obtain the highest return. For example, lower capital investment or employment among unionized firms is in part offset by higher usage elsewhere in the economy. If resources could flow costlessly to alternative uses and if social rates of return were equivalent in nonunion sectors, unions would have little effect on economy-wide efficiency. Increases in unions' power and rent seeking would simply cause the relative size of the union sector to shrink. However, because unions have some degree of monopoly bargaining power, because the shifting of resources from union to nonunion environments occurs slowly, and because social rates of return differ across investment paths, union distortions at the firm level necessarily translate into some degree of inefficiency economy-wide.

Note

1. *Profits and Investment*. Freeman and Medoff support their stylized radical's assessment that unions take from profits rather than consumers, and thus are good for society. Their key bit of evidence is that unionized and nonunionized sectors have similar profit margins in competitive industries, but that unionized sectors have much lower profits in concentrated industries.

Hirsch, writing a dozen years later, suggests that the relationship between concentrated industry and union effects on profitability is more complex. Perhaps most important, unions reduce incentives for firms to invest in long-term capital projects and in research and development.

3

The Changing Face of Industrial Relations: Decline of Private Sector Unionism

One measure of the impact of unions on the national economy is "union density" or the rate of unionization. Because of variations in definitions and data gathering, we include several tables from different sources at the end of the book. (See Appendices A & B.) The downward trend in the unionization rate is clear. In part because of government endorsement of organization and collective bargaining after the enactment of the National Labor Relations Act (NLRA) and during World War II, union membership as a percentage of the nonagricultural workforce grew to a little over 35 percent and fluctuated near that figure until the mid–1950s. Since 1955, the union density rate in private firms has steadily declined, and by 1979 had dropped to 22.3 percent, below the level of the late 1930s (See Appendix A). These percentages change only slightly if the figures include all employees covered by collective bargaining agreements, whether or not they are members of unions. The rate of decline in private-sector unionism has accelerated in recent years, plummeting from about 25 percent in 1973 to 16.5 percent in 1983 and 9.7 percent in 1997 (See Appendix B).

Union decline cuts across all areas of private employment, including traditional areas of union strength such as manufacturing, construction, and transportation. Unions are not keeping pace with the growth of the workforce, especially in service industries. For the period between 1983 and 1995, total employment increased by 21.74 million jobs, but unions actually lost 2.53 million members in private firms. Many of the private-sector unions, including the Service Employees, Automobile Workers, and Steel Workers, have become "general" unions seeking members outside their traditional areas of focus. See Victor G. Devinatz, "From Industrial Unionism to General Unionism: A Historical Transformation," 44 *Labor Law Journal* 252 (1993).

The story in the government sector is different. For the period between 1983 and 1995, union density has remained steady at somewhere between 36 and 38 percent of the government workforce. Jobs in government offices rose by 3.17 million during this period and union membership actually increased by 1.19 million. The fastest-growing unions are in the public sector. The nation's largest labor organization is

85

the National Education Association, a group of public school teachers not currently affiliated with the AFL–CIO; the second largest AFL–CIO affiliate is the American Federation of State, County and Municipal Employees.

Union decline in private firms is indisputable. Not surprisingly, observers differ on the underlying causes. This chapter includes materials on four leading explanations given in the literature. The extent of union organization is a function of both the supply of unionized jobs and the demand for union services. See generally Orley Ashenfelter and John Pencavel, "American Trade Union Growth: 1900–1964," 83 *Quarterly Journal of Economics* 434 (1964). Section A deals with the supply-side claim that union decline is principally a function of structural, geographic, and demographic shifts in the economy that have eroded the union-friendly terrain of manufacturing jobs in the Northeast, Midwest, and Pacific Northwest. Section B discusses explanations on the demand side of the equation—that American workers increasingly do not believe that the benefits of traditional union services are worth the cost of undertaking collective representation. In Sections C and D, we consider explanations that affect both supply and demand. Section C takes up the argument that employer opposition, both lawful and unlawful, has increased the size of the nonunion sector and driven up the costs of unionization. In Section D, we look at the role of enhanced product-market competition as a factor making it increasingly difficult for unions to promote their traditional objectives.

A. Structural Shifts

We begin with an excerpt from the work of Professor Leo Troy of Rutgers University, a leading exponent of the structural-change thesis. Taking issue with what he calls the "unique school" of writers like Freeman and Medoff, Troy argues that lower levels of union density in the United States, compared with Canada and European countries, reflect our relatively smaller government sector and our earlier shift to a services-based economy. Troy's other writings in a similar vein include "Convergence in International Unionism, Etc., the Case of Canada and the U.S.A.," 30 *British Journal of Industrial Relations* 1 (1992), and "Will a More Interventionist NLRA Revive Organized Labor?," 13 *Harvard Journal of Law and Public Policy* 583 (1990).

"Is the U.S. Unique in the Decline of Private Sector Unionism?"*

LEO TROY

. . .

I. *Issues*

Two opposing views have developed to explain the decline of U.S. private sector union membership since 1970 and density since 1953. Succinctly

* 11 *Journal of Labor Research* 111 (1990).

stated, one holds that the decline is unique to this country and attributes it to employer opposition.... Hereinafter, I identify those sharing this view as the "unique school." The other view contends that the decline of membership and density characterizes the economies of Canada and Western Europe as well as the U.S. and attributes it to structural changes in the labor market. The "unique school" rejects structural changes because, its proponents assert, Canada and Western Europe have also "experienced essentially the same structural change [in labor markets] as the United States" and without an accompanying decline in union density....

Two issues divide the two viewpoints: First, have Canada and Western Europe experienced the same structural change in labor markets as the U.S.? Second, has private sector unionism declined in Canada and Western Europe as well as in the U.S.? My answer is "no" to the first and "yes" to the second. Facts on employment contradict the premise that Canada and Western Europe have experienced "essentially the same labor market as the U.S." ...

I give special attention to Canadian unionism in this essay because Freeman and others have made the Canadian experience a litmus test of any challenge to the uniqueness of the decline in private sector union membership and density in America: "A persuasive explanation of the decline in union density in the United States should also explain why density did not decline in Canada in the same time period [1970 to 1985]." ...

II. *Are American and Foreign Labor Markets Essentially the Same?*

The Service Economy.... Data ... show that as late as 1966, public and private services combined still accounted for less than half (49.7 percent) of total employment in Canada. *Thus, Canada trailed the U.S. by more than a decade in the transition to a service dominated labor market, a service labor market which included the public sector.*

All European countries also trailed the U.S. and, except for The Netherlands, for even longer periods than Canada. As of 1985, the Federal Republic of Germany, with Europe's most powerful economy, had not yet made the transition to a service dominated labor market. As of 1985 the Federal Republic's labor market employed 47 percent of all workers in services. A key reason for Germany's continuing lag in transition to a service economy is the manufacturing sector's importance to its export-oriented economy....

Since all advanced capitalist countries lagged the U.S. in the switch to services, should not they also lag the U.S. in the decline of private sector membership and density? Except for The Netherlands, they all do.... Especially surprising is that private sector union density began declining in The Netherlands *before* it did in the U.S., even though it lagged the U.S. by more than a decade in the transition to services. The importance of international trade and competition are probably responsible for The Netherlands' lead among Atlantic Community nations in the decline of private-sector unionism.

The Public Sector: Services and Goods. Another structural difference distinguishing the labor markets of the U.S. and the rest of the Atlantic Community is the relative size of the public sector. Because public services are relatively much larger in Canada and Western Europe than in the U.S., these countries have developed a *different* service sector. Canada and Western Europe committed themselves to welfare state programs sooner and on a larger scale than the U.S. While public policy accelerated the process of transition to a service dominated labor market abroad, market forces generated private services so much more rapidly in the U.S. that the U.S. led in the overall shift to services, private and public combined....

Table 3–1

Labor Market Structure, Canada and the U.S.A., 1975–1985

	1985				1975			
	Canada		U.S.A.		Canada		U.S.A.	
Total Employment	10,159.1	100.0%	100,698	100.0%	8,375.0	100.0%	80,353	100.0%
Services	6,481.7	63.8%	67,422	67.0%	4,889.0	58.4%	49,803	62.0%
Goods	3,677.4	36.2%	33,276	33%	3,486.0	41.6%	30,550	38.0%
Service Employment	6,481.7	100.0%	67,422	100.0%	4,889.0	100.0%	49,803	100.0%
Public Services	2,474.4	38.2%	16,394	24.3%	1,938.8	39.7%	14,685	29.5%
Private Services	4,007.3	61.8%	51,028	75.7%	2,950.2	60.3%	35,118	70.5%
Goods Employment	3,677.4	100.0%	33,276	100.0%	3,486.0	100.0%	30,550	100.0%
Public Goods	558.6	15.2%	1,767	5.3%	557.9	16.0%	1,556	5.1%
Private Goods	3,118.8	84.8%	31,509	94.7%	2,928.1	84.0%	28,994	94.9%
Total Employment	10,159.1	100.0%	100,698	100.0%	8,375.0	100.0%	80,353	100.0%
Public	3,032.9	29.9%	16,394	16.3%	2,496.7	29.8%	14,685	18.3%
Private	7,126.2	70.1%	84,304	83.7%	5,878.3	70.2%	65,668	81.7%

Sources: Canada, Corporations and Labour Unions Return Act (CALURA); U.S., Bureau of Labor Statistics. [*Eds.* All numbers in thousands.]

Table 3–2

Labor Market Structure, Western Europe, 1975–1985

	1975	1985		1975	1985
U.K.	100.0%	100.0%	*Netherlands*	100.0%	100.0%
Goods	49.7%	40.8%	Goods	46.7%	39.4%
Services	50.3%	59.2%	Services	53.3%	60.6%
Germany	100.0%	100.0%	*Norway*	100.0%	100.0%
Goods	58.6%	52.6%	Goods	53.0%	43.5%
Services	41.4%	47.4%	Services	47.0%	56.5%
France	100.0%	100.0%	*Sweden*	100.0%	100.0%
Goods	55.0%	46.1%	Goods	49.6%	41.7%
Services	45.0%	53.9%	Services	50.4%	58.3%
Italy	100.0%	100.0%	*Switzerland*	100.0%	100.0%
Goods	55.9%	50.2%	Goods	55.7%	50.5%
Services	44.1%	49.8%	Services	44.3%	49.5%

Sources: OECD, BLS.

Table 3–3

Public Employment as a Percentage of Total Employment
in Western Europe, 1975 and 1985

	1975	1985
France*	18.7%	27.9%
Germany**	21.9%	23.3%
Italy	20.4%	23.1%
Netherlands	15.5%	19.9%
Sweden	33.2%	33.1%
G.B.***	29.0%	27.0%
Canada	29.8%	29.9%
U.S.	18.3%	16.3%

Sources: European Trade Union Institute, *Privatisation in Western Europe* (Brussels, April 1988), 14–15, Tables 3 and 4; OECD, p. 79; Table 1 of this paper.
* Figures underestimate the public sector.
** Volkswagen and VEBA AG are excluded.
*** Includes British Gas.

Canadian Public Sector. . . . Table [3–1] addresses four issues of labor market structure comparing Canada and the U.S.: (1) the relative size of goods and services employment; (2) the size of public versus private services; (3) the share of public versus private goods employment; and (4) the size of total public and private employment in each country. The results reveal differences between Canada and the U.S. which cannot be reconciled with the claim that both countries have essentially the same labor market structure.

Table [3–1] shows that total services (private and public) are relatively larger in the U.S. than in Canada for both 1975 and 1985. Whether the margin in 1985 is sufficient to disqualify Canada as having "essentially" the same labor market structure as the U.S. is arguable. However, measured by the size of public and private services separately, the disparities are large and increasing. In the public service sector the Canadian lead over the U.S. increased to 1.6 times by 1985, compared to a ratio of 1.3 in 1975. On the other hand, private services in the U.S. exceeded the Canadian by 1.17 times (17 percent) in 1975 and increased the margin to 1.22 (22 percent) by 1985.

Canada also produces a sizable portion of goods in the public domain. By comparison, government production of goods is negligible in the U.S. When public goods production is combined with public services, the overall public sector in Canada is relatively nearly double the size of the American public sector. In contrast, the proportion of private to total employment in the U.S. substantially exceeds that of Canada, and the share grew between 1975 and 1985. Can labor market structures depicted in Table [3–1] be reconciled with the claim of similarity between the two countries? They cannot. Not only do they differ quantitatively, but the disparities reflect the outcomes of two different economic policies, policies that have a great bearing on what happens to unionism as well as to the structure of labor markets. The policy differences are the greater reliance on market forces in the U.S. versus greater government intervention in Canada in the allocation of resources. Market forces played a much larger role in generating the service sector in the U.S., while in Canada it was government policy.

Such significant policy differences spill over to unionism, making the private sector union movement in the U.S. more subject to market forces than the Canadian and, therefore, susceptible to an earlier and larger decline in union density. In Canada, greater government intervention in the product and labor markets sheltered the Canadian union movement from market forces and blunted the impact of competition. Nothing is forever, however, and Canadian private sector unionism has been feeling the impact of competition since approximately the mid–1970s. . . .

Western Europe. Western European countries also lagged the U.S. in switching to a service-dominated labor market (Table [3–2]) and, like Canada, also have much larger public sectors than the U.S. (Table [3–3]), including significant public ownership in industrial enterprises. The size and composition of public sector employment (including both goods and services) reinforce the stability of union membership and density levels in Canada and Western Europe. Indeed, it should come as no surprise that the proportion of public sector membership to total membership exceeds the ratio of public to total employment in all countries, including the U.S. . . .

III. *Structural Shifts Within Manufacturing*

Besides the U.S. lead over Canada and European countries in the switch from goods to services, the U.S. also leads in structural changes within the largest goods industry, manufacturing. The principal change within manufacturing over the last 20 years (or longer), and accelerating during the last decade, has been the substitution of "high tech" for "traditional" manufacturing. The changes in the industrial composition of employment have been accompanied by profound changes in occupational composition. Enormous gains in professional and technical occupations have reduced the relative importance of blue-collar jobs, the bedrock of unionism in manufacturing. . . .

Because the structural changes in manufacturing took place in the epicenter of unionism and because they unfolded more rapidly than the general switch from goods to services, they reduced union ranks more rapidly as well. The impact of these changes may be seen from the record of manufacturing unionism in this country. Between May 1980 and 1988, union membership in manufacturing in the U.S. dwindled from 6,711,00 to 4,516,000, a loss of nearly 2.3 million; employment from the same Bureau of Census survey (published by the BLS) declined 533,000. In other words, manufacturing union membership declined 4.2 times as rapidly as employment, indicating rapid growth in the unorganized high tech and other manufacturing industries. . . .

IV. *Structural Change and the Railways*

Railway transportation provides another example of structural change and its consequences for union membership in the U.S. (and doubtless in Canada and Western Europe as well, albeit to a lesser extent because of government ownership). Unpublished figures that I prepared at the National Bureau of Economic Research many years ago put membership at 1,075,000, employment on Class I Railways at 1,418,000, and density at 76 percent in 1947. Currently, I estimate total railway membership at about 225,000 and a density of over 90 percent of employment. While density rose, membership declined by some 850,000 over the past 40 years. . . .

The decline in membership in railways came about in the face of the most "supportive labor legislation" (to use the euphemism many academics apply to pro-union law) in American labor relations. Membership fell drastically because of structural changes in the labor market—shifts to other forms of transportation and technological change. On the other hand, density climbed because the union shop, the check-off, and the grievance procedures have virtually shut out nonunion employment on the railways. . . .

V. *Exports, Manufacturing, and Structural Change* . . .

The importance of export-oriented manufacturing continues to be a significant factor in the structure of employment. It also contributes to the differences in membership and density trends between the U.S. and Western Europe, especially during the 1980s. For the U.S., it meant fewer members; for Western Europe, it meant stable membership, particularly in Germany. Paradoxically, the revival of U.S. manufacturing exports has not been accompanied by a revival of unionism. Productivity gains and an export mix including more nonunion-made goods are probably responsible.

VI. *Geography and Structural Shift*

Another structural factor affecting the comparability of labor markets is ascertained by asking whether European countries and Canada have a South to which employers can move. Even within the limited geographic opportunities for companies to move from more to less unionized areas, British data indicate such an internal migration, from more to less organized areas of the country. . . . Now that the Canadians have approved the proposed trade agreement with the U.S., it will be interesting to see how many companies in Canada may get the urge to migrate to the American South and Southwest....

. . .

IX. *Trends in Unionism: Canadian Private Sector, 1975–1985*

... [As Table 3–4 indicates,] *in contrast to overall density, Canadian private sector density shrank from 25.7 to 20.7 percent, a decline of nearly one-fifth, over the decade 1975 to 1985.* Density fell in both private goods and private services. In goods, the decline was from 44 to 38 percent; in private services, from 6.5 to 6.3 percent....

Manufacturing and construction offer further evidence of the decline of Canadian private sector membership and density. The two industries form the core of private sector unionism in Canada, as elsewhere, and in both industries membership and density declined markedly....

Table 3–4. Union Membership and Density, Public and Private Sectors, Canada, 1975–1985*

1985

	Public Sector				Private Sector		
	Members (000)	Employ (000)	Density %		Members (000)	Employ (000)	Density %
GOODS	263.1	451.1	58.3%	GOODS	1,241.6	3,226.3	38.5%
SERVICES	1,674.6	2,474.4	67.7%	SERVICES	254.3	4,007.4	6.3%
GOODS	263.1	451.1	58.3%	GOODS	1,241.6	3,226.3	38.5%
Mining	20.9	40.9	51.1%	Mining	57.4	210.7	27.3%
Manufacturing	13.3	24.5	54.3%	Manufacturing	729.8	1,934.4	37.7%
TCOU	228.9	385.7	59.3%	TCOU	224.2	467.6	47.9%
				Construction	228.6	478.2	47.8%
				Agriculture	1.5	135.4	1.1%
SERVICES	1,674.6	2,474.4	67.7%	SERVICES	254.3	4,007.4	6.3%
Education	547.3	758.0	72.2%				
Health	548.5	857.1	64.0%				
Trade	15.6	46.1	33.8%	Trade	167.4	1,798.4	9.3%
FIRE	8.3	30.4	27.3%	FIRE	8.2	578.4	1.4%
Pub Admin.	554.9	782.7	70.9%	Service	78.7	1,630.6	4.8%
Tot/Avg.	1,937.7	2,925.5	66.2%	Tot/Avg.	1,495.9	7,233.7	20.7%
Public and Private Sectors (combined)					3,433.6	10,159.1	33.8%

* Adapted from Troy, Is the U.S. Unique ...?, Table 4.

1975

	Public Sector				Private Sector		
	Members (000)	Employ (000)	Density %		Members (000)	Employ (000)	Density %
GOODS	239.9	408.4	58.7%	GOODS	1,357.9	3,077.7	44.1%
SERVICES	885.2	1,946.2	45.5%	SERVICES	191.9	2,942.9	6.5%
GOODS	239.9	408.4	58.7%	GOODS	1,357.9	3,077.7	44.1%
Mining	16.4	33.2	49.4%	Mining	46.4	170.9	27.2%
Manufacturing	13.1	23.1	56.7%	Manufacturing	826.4	1,824.9	45.3%
TOCU	210.4	352.1	59.8%	TOCU	190.8	426.9	44.7%
				Construction	293.9	518.0	56.7%
				Agriculture	0.4	137.0	0.3%
SERVICES	885.2	1,946.2	45.5%	SERVICES	191.9	2,942.9	6.5%
Education	211.2	621.2	34.0%				
Health	201.5	592.7	34.0%				
Trade	14.1	44.3	31.8	Trade	107.4	1,433.7	7.5%
FIRE	6.4	23.0	27.8	FIRE	6.4	436.1	1.5%
Pub Admin.	452.0	665.0	68.0%	Service	78.1	1,073.1	7.3%
Tot/Avg.	1,125.1	2,354.6	47.8%	Tot/Avg.	1,549.8	6,020.6	25.7%
Public and Private Sectors (combined)					2,674.9	8,375.2	31.9%

Sources: CALURA, adjusted by the author.
FIRE: Finance, Insurance and Real Estate.
TCOU: Transportation, Communication, and Other Utilities.

X. *Public Sector Unionism in Canada*, 1975–1985

Coupled with the decline of private sector unionism in Canada during1975–1985 was the meteoric rise in public sector unionism. Density in Canada's public sector skyrocketed from 48 percent to 66 percent over the decade, and it is probable that I have underestimated the gain....

Public sector membership jumped from 1.1 million members in 1975 to nearly 2 million, an increase of just under 75 percent. Nevertheless, the rate of increase was insufficient to offset the decline in private sector unionism that had set in during the 1970s. As a result, by 1983 the overall density rate peaked.

Because of the divergent behavior of public and private sector unionism in Canada, the composition of Canadian union membership was radically altered in favor of public sector unionism. Indeed, the switch was so extensive that the relative positions of the two branches of the union movement were reversed in the short span of 10 years. In 1975, private sector unionism dominated Canada's union movement with 58 percent of total membership; by 1985, public sector unions dominated with 56 percent of total membership. In contrast to the union movement in Canada, private sector membership continues to dominate the make-up of the American union movement. In 1975, private sector membership comprised just under three-fourths of the total; by 1985, it had dipped to a bit over 71 percent....

The Canadian and American surveys of union membership in 1986 do show that union density among all occupational groups is uniformly higher in Canada than the U.S., including the hard-to-organize professionals, managers, and other white-collar workers. However, the comparisons are misleading, as necessarily are the conclusions drawn from them. Because the public sector employs relatively more white-collar workers than the private sector and because the public sector is more highly unionized in Canada than in the U.S., the overall higher union penetration rate of white-collar occupations is naturally higher in Canada. Similar private/public sector analysis also explains the greater importance of women in the Canadian union movement....

Notes and Questions

1. *Questions of Magnitude.* Professors Freeman and Medoff report that the changing structure of the workforce, in terms of its personal, job, and geographic characteristics, explains "72 percent of the observed decline" in unionization for the 1954–79 period, but argue that such "technocratic explanations" assume that worker preferences do not change over time and cannot account for union successes in the public sector and other countries (notably Canada). See Richard B. Freeman and James L. Medoff, What Do Unions Do? (New York: Basic Books, 1984), 225–28. Looking at a more limited period, Professors Farber and Krueger conclude that "[a]bout 35 percent of the 4.8 point decline in unionization between 1977 and 1984 can be accounted for by structural change in the labor force." Henry S. Farber and Alan B. Krueger, "Union Membership in the United States: The Decline Continues," in Bruce E. Kaufman and Morris M. Kleiner, eds., *Employee Representation: Alternatives and Future Directions* (Madison, Wis.: Industrial Relations Research Association, 1993), 105, 115 (excerpted in section B of this chapter). Thus, these scholars agree with Troy that structural changes explain much of union decline, but insist that other factors are also important.

2. *Danger of Fixed Coefficient Correlations.* Richard B. Freeman revisited the structural-change explanation in "Contraction and Expansion: The Divergence of Private Sector and Public Sector Unionism," 2 *Journal of Economic Perspectives* 63, 76 (Spring 1988). He warns that the structuralist

hypothesis incorrectly assumes that the union share within a sector remains fixed over time, while sectors themselves expand or shrink:

> [The structuralist hypothesis uses] a fixed coefficient model which decomposes the workforce into a number of groups with varying degrees of unionization at some base time, and explores the impact of changes in the relative size of the groups on aggregate union density under the assumption that the density of each group is fixed at its base level.

> Fixed coefficient analyses covering from the 1960s through 1980 attribute 50 percent to 70 percent of the decline in private sector union density to compositional factors with the increase in white collar employment having a particularly sizeable depressant effect on density. While these calculations would appear to go far toward explaining the decline in unionization, I believe the structuralist analysis is misleading and should be rejected. There are three reasons for rejecting it.

> First, the structuralist hypothesis is inconsistent with the rise in union density in other countries (notably Canada), which had structural changes in the work force similar to those in the United States. Second, surveys of worker desires for unionism show that ... groups whose proportion of the workforce has increased (such as women and young workers) have as great or greater desire to unionize as do white prime-age male workers.... Third, I reject the structuralist hypothesis because it assumes that the union share of workers in a sector should remain fixed over time. That assumption is inconsistent with the history of union growth, which is one of expansion into nonunion areas, as occurred in the private sector in the period under study. The claim that public sector workers organized because of pent-up demand for unionism, indeed, implies that unionism "naturally" grows in new sectors over time. Fixed coefficient calculations sidestep the key issue in the decline in U.S. organization, which is why unions failed to organize historically nonunion workers in the private sector while doing so in the public sector and other countries.

3. *Unionism in Other Countries.* We include in Appendix C data on union density rates from an article by Professor Jelle Visser of the University of Amsterdam. The use of cross-national comparisons of unionization as a basis for drawing inferences about the American experience is a hazardous enterprise for at least two reasons. First, as Troy emphasizes, unionization figures from other countries often commingle the private and public sectors, an important source of distortion because of the vastly larger relative size of the government sector in many of these countries. Second, the labor relations systems of these countries differ in material respects that stymie fruitful comparison. For example, the extent of unionization in a country like Germany (which is based on a dual track of centralized multiemployer bargaining structures and statutorily mandated integrative organizations at the level of the firm) may not be very revealing of the prospects for unionization in a country like the United States with different institutional arrangements. See Samuel Estreicher, "Labor Law Reform in a World of

Competitive Product Markets," 69 *Chicago–Kent Law Review* 3, 15–20 (1993) (excerpted in section D of this chapter).

The Canadian experience is more relevant to the U.S. debate. The union density figures (combining public-and private-sector unionism) in Canada are twice as high as our own, and despite a decline in the 1970s, appear in recent years to have leveled off or increased slightly. The extent to which unions have lost their position in private firms during recent decades, despite favorable pro-union laws, is a matter of considerable dispute. Professors Meltz and Verma find that private-sector union density stabilized during the 1980s at 20.7 percent, with unions strengthening their position in growing trade and finance services to compensate for losses in goods-producing industries. See Noah Meltz and Anil Verma, "Developments in Industrial Relations and Human Resources Practices in Canada: An Update from the 1980s," in Richard Locke, Thomas Kochan, and Michael Piore, eds., *Employment Relations in a Changing World Economy* (Cambridge, Mass.: MIT Press, 1995), 17–18. Troy, in the principal reading, generally agrees with these numbers, but projects a continuing decline in union membership, explaining that the higher Canadian unionization rate at present is a function of differences in the timing of structural changes, such as the shift from manufacturing and primary industries to services.

Using data from a 1984 household Survey of Union Membership by Statistics Canada, Professor Riddell pegs the private-sector unionization rate at 29 percent (workers who are union members) and 34 percent (workers covered by collective agreement)—figures considerably higher than the Meltz–Verma or Troy estimates of around 21 percent. See W. Craig Riddell, "Unionization in Canada and the United States: A Tale of Two Countries," in David Card and Richard B. Freeman, eds., *Small Differences That Matter: Labor Market and Income Maintenance in Canada and the United States* (Chicago: University of Chicago Press, 1993), 109, 136 (Table 4.9).

4. *U.S. Public Sector.* The relative success that unions have enjoyed in the government sector is some evidence that U.S. workers in private firms would choose collective representation to the same extent as their colleagues in government offices if they could be sure (1) they would obtain similar benefits from union representation and (2) at the same or lower costs than those borne by unionized government workers. These premises, however, may be questioned. Unions in the government sector rely on an essentially political process for determining wages and benefits that is relatively insulated from market forces. Also, government typically provides services for which private substitutes are nonexistent (as in police and fire protection) or that require additional expenditures without rebates from government taxes (education). Consider Harry H. Wellington and Ralph K. Winter, Jr., "The Limits of Collective Bargaining in Public Employment," 78 *Yale Law Journal* 1107, 1120–21 (1969):

> [M]arket-imposed unemployment is an important restraint on unions in the private sector. In the public sector, the trade-off between benefits and employment seems much less important. Government does not

generally sell a product the demand for which is closely related to price. There usually are no close substitutes for the products and services provided by government and the demand for them is inelastic.... Because much government activity is, and must be, a monopoly, product competition, non-union or otherwise, does not exert a downward pressure on prices and wages. Nor will the existence of a pool of labor ready to work for a wage below union scale attract new capital and create a new, and competitively less expensive, government enterprise.... [I]f the cost of labor increases, the city may reduce the quality of the service it furnishes by reducing employment.... However, the ability of city governments to accomplish such a change is limited not only by union pressure, but also by the pressure of other affected groups in the community. Political considerations, therefore, may cause either no reduction in employment or services, or a reduction in an area other than that in which the union members work.

B. Demand Shifts

Are unions faring badly in private firms because workers in those firms no longer view collective representation as an effective vehicle for advancing their interests? Consider the following excerpt from a study by Professors Farber and Krueger.

"Union Membership in the United States: The Decline Continues"*

HENRY S. FARBER AND ALAN B. KRUEGER

... There is no disagreement about the dimensions of the decline of labor unions. However, there is an ongoing debate about its causes....

A Demand–Supply Framework

[Consider] a model of the determination of the union status of workers that allowed for queues for union jobs. In this model, workers might demand union jobs in the sense that they would prefer a union job (or prefer their job to be unionized) without being willing to invest in organizing a union (either on their current job or on another job). This is because the rights to existing union jobs are not owned either by the workers who organize union jobs or by the workers who currently hold union jobs. Outside of a few craft-based unions, employers are free to hire whomever they see fit to fill vacancies in union jobs. While dues and initiation fees are required of union members, these generally are not sufficient to capitalize the flow of benefits of union employment. The

---

* In Bruce E. Kaufman and Morris M. Kleiner, eds., *Employee Representation: Alternatives and Future Directions* (Madison, Wis.: Industrial Relations Research Association, 1993), 105.

result is that there is likely to be excess demand for existing union jobs while there may be equilibrium in the market for new union jobs. The quantity of union jobs available depends on the costs of organization (supply) and benefits of organization to workers (demand)....

The data requirements for measurement of the demand for and supply of union jobs exceed what are normally available. Ordinarily, data are available on the union status of workers. However, while it is reasonable to assume that all union workers prefer union representation, the queuing model suggests that not all nonunion workers prefer to be nonunion. Nonunion workers fall into two categories: (1) those who prefer nonunion employment, and (2) those who prefer union employment but are not hired by a union employer. The core analyses in this study rely on four surveys that have specific information on the preferences of nonunion workers that can be used to assign them to one of these two categories.

The total demand for union jobs is measured by the fraction of workers who are either union members or would prefer to have union representation. The supply of union jobs relative to demand is measured by the fraction of workers demanding union representation who are actually union members. If there were no queues for union jobs, this fraction would be one. To the extent that there are nonunion workers who prefer union representation, this fraction will be less than one. A direct measure of the size of the queue for union jobs (and, hence, an inverse measure of relative supply) is the fraction of the total work force that demands union representation but are working in nonunion jobs. If there were no queues this fraction would be zero. We focus on this measure of frustrated demand as our (inverse) measure of supply.

To see this more clearly note that a worker is unionized if and only if he/she demands union representation and is hired by a union employer. A probability statement for the likelihood of worker i being unionized is

(1) $Pr(U_i=1) = Pr(U_i=1 \mid D_i=1) \bullet Pr(D_i=1),$

where U_i is a dichotomous variable that equals one if worker i is unionized and zero otherwise, and D_i is a dummy variable that equals one if worker i desires union representation and zero otherwise. The probability that worker i is not unionized is

(2) $Pr(U_i=0) = Pr(D_i=0) + Pr(U_i=0 \mid D_i=1) \bullet Pr(D_i=1).$

This makes clear the two groups that make up the nonunion sector. The first group does not desire union representation, and the second group desires union representation but does not hold union jobs. Finally, note that we can write the probability that i is unionized as

(3) $Pr(U_i=1) = Pr(D_i=1)—Pr(D_i=1, U_i=0).$

The first term represents the demand for union representation, and the second term represents frustrated demand or inverse supply. Thus, the probability that a worker is unionized is equal to the probability that he/she desires union representation *minus* the probability that the worker desires union representation but is not hired by a union employer. . . .

Data

The key information required for our analysis is information on the preferences of nonunion workers for union representation. There have been [four] surveys designed to be broadly representative of the nonunion U.S. labor force that have this information. . . .

The measure of preferences of nonunion workers for union representation is based on the responses to similar questions in all four surveys asking whether the worker would vote for union representation on their current job if an election were held. . . . We interpret the response to these questions as indicating the desire of the worker for union representation *assuming that the worker does not have to bear the cost of organization.* . . .

Analysis of Change in Union Membership in the United States

[Farber and Krueger first provide estimates] from linear-probability and logit models of union membership estimated using the 1977, 1984, and 1991 [Current Population Survey (CPS)] data. The model without controls for labor force structure . . . shows a 4.3 percentage point drop in the union membership rate between 1977 and 1984. There is a further 2.4 percentage point drop between 1984 and 1991. The central point to note is that when controls for labor force structure (sex, marital status, race, age, education, region, industry, occupation, and public sector) are introduced, the differences in unionization rate by year fall somewhat. About 35 percent of the 4.8 point decline in unionization between 1977 and 1984 can be accounted for by structural changes in the labor force. However, only about 7.3 percent of the 2.9 point drop in unionization between 1984 and 1991 is accounted for by structural changes. Overall, about 25 percent of the 7.7 point overall decline between 1977 and 1991 can be accounted for by structural changes in the labor force.

The demand for unionization among nonunion workers fell between 1977 and 1984 but remained relatively steady between 1984 and 1991. . . . The model without controls for labor force experience indicates a significant 5.5 percentage point drop in nonunion-worker demand between 1977 and 1984 . . . , and it shows an insignificant 0.9 percentage point *increase* between 1984 and 1991. . . . Demand remains significantly lower (by 4.7 percentage points) in 1991 than in 1977. . . .

Table 3–5

Analysis of Change in Union Membership
Probabilities
(standard errors)

	Level 1977	Level 1984	Level 1991	Change 77 to 84	Change 84 to 91	Change 77 to 91
$Pr(U=1)$	.253	.206	.177	−.047	−.029	−.076
	(.0019)	(.0010)	(.0010)	(.0022)	(.0014)	(.0022)
$Pr(D=1\|U=0)$	.386	.331	.340	−.055	.009	-.046
	(.0189)	(.0156)	(.0187)	(.0245)	(.0244)	(.0266)
$Pr(D=1,U=0)$	.288	.263	.280	−.0256	.0170	−.0085
	(.0048)	(.0032)	(.0033)	(.00582)	(.0046)	(.0059)
$Pr(D=1)$	.541	.469	.457	−.0725	−.0120	−.0845
	(.0142)	(.0124)	(.0154)	(.0188)	(.0198)	(.0209)

Sources and Definitions:

$Pr(U=1)$: The probability that a worker is a union member. Computed
from weighted tabulations of the CPS....

$Pr(D=1 \mid U=0)$: The probability that a nonunion worker demands union
representation. Computed from tabulations of the "vote" question on the
1977 Quality of Employment Survey (QES), 1984 AFL survey, 1991/92
General Social Survey (GSS), and Farber–Krueger (F–K) surveys....

$Pr(D=1, U=0)$: The probability that a worker demands union representation but is not employed on a union job (frustrated demand). Computed
as $Pr(D=1 \mid U=0) \bullet Pr(U=0)$ from this table.

$Pr(D=1)$: The probability that a worker demands union representation.
This is the sum of the probability that a worker is a union member and
the probability that a worker desires union representation but is not
employed on a union job (union membership plus frustrated demand).
Formally, this is $Pr(U=1) + Pr(D=1, U=0)$ and is computed from this
table....

With these estimates in hand, we are ready to apportion the decline
in unionization to changes in demand and supply. Table [3–5] contains
the levels of key probabilities in 1977, 1984, and 1991 along with
computations of changes from 1977 to 1984, 1984 to 1991, and 1977 to
1991. The first row summarizes the changes in the probability of union
membership while the second row summarizes the change in nonunion-
worker demand for union representation.... The third row of the table
uses these quantities to compute frustrated demand, $Pr(D=1, U=0)$,
which is defined in terms of the measured quantities as

[(4)] $Pr(D_i=1, U_i=0) = Pr(D_i=1 \mid U_i=0) \bullet Pr(U_i=0)$.

Frustrated demand seems to have remained fairly constant at about 28
percent of the work force. Finally, the fourth row of the table contains
estimates of overall demand for union representation computed as the
sum of union membership plus frustrated demand. This is

[(5)] $Pr(D=1) = Pr(U=1) + Pr(D=1, U=0)$.

Total demand has fallen sharply. Fully 54 percent of the work force
demanded union representation in 1977, and this fell to 46 percent by
1991.

[T]he change in union membership is the difference between the change in overall demand and the change in frustrated demand. By definition, the change in union membership in the first row of Table [3–5] is fully accounted for by the change in overall demand in the fourth row and the change in frustrated demand (inverse supply) in the third row.

The results of this decomposition are quite striking. *All* of the 7.6 percentage point drop in the unionization rate between 1977 and 1991 is accounted for by a drop in overall demand for union representation. Since demand fell 8.5 percentage points, relative supply actually increased slightly (though insignificantly). Virtually all of the drop in demand seems to have occurred by 1984 (7.25 points of the 8.45 point overall decline). It is interesting that this drop in demand was offset by a significant 2.56 point reduction in frustrated demand between 1977 and 1984. Thus, the relative supply of union jobs actually increased between 1977 and 1984, and the unionization rate would have been even lower in 1984 without this supply increase. Between 1984 and 1991 demand fell insignificantly, but frustrated demand did increase slightly and significantly. Thus, there does seem to have been a small reduction in relative supply between 1984 and 1991.

Overall, virtually all of the decline in unionization between 1977 and 1991 seems to be due to decline in demand for union representation. There is no evidence that any significant part of the decline in unionization is due to increased employer resistance other than the sort of resistance that would be reflected in lower demand for unionization by workers.

Job Satisfaction and Demand for Unionization Among Nonunion Workers

[U]nderstanding the determinants of nonunion workers' demand for union representation is critical for explaining the decline in union membership in the U.S.... [V]arious aspects of job satisfaction are key determinants of workers' reported desire for union representation....

Table [3–6] summarizes [the] main findings. In each year, nonunion workers are less likely to report that they would vote for a union if they are satisfied with their job overall, satisfied with their pay, or satisfied with their job security. The difference in the proportion who say they would vote for a union between satisfied and unsatisfied workers is quite sizable, and ... the gap is not diminished if demographic, industry, and occupation variables are held constant in a probit model....

Table 3–6

Fraction of Nonunion Workers Who Would Vote for Union

(Representation Broken Down by Year and Job Satisfaction)

	1977 (n=663) Satisfied?		1984 (n=865) Satisfied?		1992 (n=125) Satisfied?	
	No	Yes	No	Yes	No	Yes
Satisfaction with:						
Overall job	.671	.342	.615	.289	.455	.333
Pay	.522	.291	.511	.259	.520	.291
Job Security	.533	.331	.485	.295	.500	.330

Note: Data set for 1977 is QES, data set for 1984 is AFL–CIO survey, and data set for 1992 is Farber–Krueger Survey.

Table [3–7] presents evidence on trends in worker satisfaction between 1977 and 1992. The overall level of satisfaction ... increased slightly for nonunion workers. The 1992 union sample is extremely small, but the results indicate that the overall level of satisfaction for union workers is not terribly different from that for nonunion workers. Different trends between union and nonunion workers emerge when workers are asked to focus specifically on their satisfaction with pay or job security. Between 1977 and 1984 there was a substantial increase in nonunion workers' reported satisfaction with pay and job security. No similar trend is visible for union workers in these years. The [Farber–Krueger] survey indicates that nonunion workers report about an equal level of satisfaction in 1984 and 1992, providing further evidence that nonunion workers are reporting higher levels of satisfaction.

Table 3–7

Job Satisfaction by Union Status

	Nonunion Workers			Union Workers		
	1977	1984	1992	1977	1984	1992
Fraction Satis-fied with:						
Overall	.867	.894	.903	.879	.853	.903
Pay	.587	.745	.758	.748	.770	.871
Job Security	.729	.850	.880	.762	.783	.774
N	663	865	125	298	217	31

Note: Data set for 1977 is QES, data set for 1984 is AFL–CIO survey, and data set for 1992 is Farber–Krueger survey.

[Farber's 1990 study] presents evidence that the increase in reported satisfaction can account for the entire decline in demand for union representation among nonunion workers between 1977 and 1984. Note that this is consistent with the finding in Table [3–7] that the level of satisfaction remained roughly constant between 1984 and 1992 and our earlier finding of hardly any change in the proportion of nonunion workers who desire union representation over this same period.

A critical question is: Why did the proportion of nonunion workers who claim to be satisfied with their pay and job security increase between 1977 and 1984? The increase in reported satisfaction with pay is particularly surprising in view of the fact that real wages were stagnant in this period. These are issues that we leave for further examination. . . .

Notes and Questions

1. *Satisfied Nonunion Workers.* The main conclusion of the Farber–Krueger study is that virtually all of the 1977–1984 decline in demand for union representation can be accounted for by an increase in nonunion workers' job satisfaction, particularly with respect to pay and job security.

2. *Frustrated Demand.* Farber and Krueger acknowledge that "frustrated demand" (the probability that a worker prefers union representation but is not employed on a union job) "remained fairly constant at about 28 percent of the work force" from 1977 to 1991. Based on poll results, Professors Richard Freeman and Joel Rogers maintain that about a third of the nonunion workforce desire union representation:

> [W]e note that four surveys asking this question [about willingness to vote for a union in an NLRB election] since 1977 have shown at least a third of the nonunion workforce (roughly 30 million people in 1991) desire unionization. The Fingerhut/Powers poll asked a variant of this question that tells a similar story: "If a union did try to organize the place where you work, would you be inclined to support the effort or oppose it?" Nearly half (47 percent) of employed nonunion respondents answered affirmatively—which translates into approximately 40 million workers—a larger number than indicated by other surveys. On the other hand, only 28 percent of nonunion workers in Fingerhut/Powers thought a union at their workplace would help, which suggests less substantive support for unions.

Richard B. Freeman and Joel Rogers, "Who Speaks for Us? Employee Representation in a Nonunion Labor Market," in Bruce E. Kaufman and Morris M. Kleiner, eds., *Employee Representation: Alternatives and Future Directions* (Madison, Wis.: Industrial Relations Research Association, 1993), 12, 32.

Do these findings provide clear support for a change in public policy allowing a minority of workers in a nonunion facility to demand union representation and collective bargaining? We could use some answers to the following: Can we assume that the 28–33 percent of nonunion workers desiring union representation are randomly distributed in all workplaces, such that this level of support can be expected at any work site? What do we know about the intensity of the preferences involved? To what extent are the preferences evinced through a survey instrument relatively uninformed choices that quickly change once more detailed information about the expected benefits and costs of a union organization is provided?

3. *Fear of Employer Retaliation?* Contrary to the "employer opposition" thesis, discussed below, Farber and Krueger find "no evidence that any significant part of the decline in unionization is due to increased employer resistance other than the sort of resistance that would be reflected in lower demand for unionization by workers." In a footnote to their essay, the authors concede that their measure of demand for union representation, even though provided by responses to an anonymous survey, will reflect not only "higher wages or better working conditions offered by employers hoping to avoid unionization," but also "fear of job loss by workers as a result of unionization...." "Union Membership in the United States," 118 and n.14.

Both the 1988 Gallup and 1991 Fingerhut/Powers polls, Freeman and Rogers argue, "show that most of the public believes managers actively discourage unionization, judges management action to be unfair, and wants it corrected"; and that "awareness of the personal costs of seeking union organization against management wishes" is likely to "contaminate efforts to infer an intrinsic 'demand for unionism' from questions about voting intentions...." Freeman and Rogers, "Who Speaks for Us?," 31–32. However, their later survey of nonunion workers for the Commission on the Future of Worker–Management Relations (the Dunlop Commission) provides some ammunition for the Farber–Krueger view. Even when asked if they would vote for a union when management was not opposed, "unions win majority support in only one major subgroup—blue-collar workers. By sector, Transportation/Communication workers are the only subgroup that clearly leans in favor of unions." Princeton Survey Research Associates, *Worker Representation and Participation Survey: Report on the Findings*, prepared for Richard B. Freeman and Joel Rogers (Dec. 1994), 37 and Table 17.

4. *Demand for a Different Union "Product."* The Freeman–Rogers survey for the Dunlop Commission raises the interesting question of whether the "product" that unions conventionally offer fits well with what nonmanagerial American workers want from a workplace-based organization:

> In their preferences for how an ideal employee organization should be structured, workers diverge sharply from the union model in some respects—again reflecting their perceptions that management cooperation is essential. By an overwhelming 86% to 9% margin, workers want an organization run jointly by employees and management, rather than an independent, employee-run organization. By a smaller, but still sizable margin of 52% to 34%, workers want an organization to be staffed and funded by the company, rather than independently through employee contributions.

Worker Representation and Participation Survey, 49 and Table 21.

C. Employer Opposition

A dominant view in the literature attributes the decline of private-sector unionism to employer opposition to the rights of workers to form independent organizations and insist on collective bargaining. Harvard professor Paul Weiler, a former chair of the British Columbia Labour Board, is a leading exponent.

"Promises to Keep: Securing Workers' Rights to Self–Organization Under the NLRA"*
PAUL C. WEILER

In their halcyon days of the early 1940's, American unions fared very well under the formal certification procedure of the NLRA; elections involved more than one million eligible voters annually, and trade unions won approximately 80% of those elections. Union success rates were still high in 1950; but ... there has been a steady and stark decline ever since, both in the union victory rate in certification elections (from 74% in 1950 to 48% in 1980) and, even more dramatically, in the percentage of voters included in union victories (from 85% to 37%). The result of these trends is that the number of employees successfully organized each year has dropped from 750,000 to fewer than 200,000. In 1950, new certifications raised the level of union representation in the private sector work force by 1.92%; in 1980, the entire organizational effort of American unions under the NLRA increased union density by a near-infinitesimal 0.24%, a rate just one-eighth that of thirty years earlier (and one that was far outstripped by natural attrition from job loss in unionized firms).

The Pattern of Employer Intimidation

... To a dispassionate observer, the simplest explanation for the drop in the union victory rate would be that it represents a corresponding drop in interest in collective bargaining among American workers. My thesis, however, is that the decline in union success in representation campaigns is in large part attributable to deficiencies in the law: evidence suggests that the current certification procedure does not effectively insulate employees from the kinds of coercive antiunion employer tactics that the NLRA was supposed to eliminate.

It is the time lag between the filing of a representation petition and the vote, usually about two months, that gives the employer the opportunity to attempt to turn its workers against the union. Typically, the firm will mount a vigorous campaign to fend off the threat of collective bargaining. It will emphasize to its workers how risky and troubled life might be in the uncharted world of collective bargaining: the firm might have to tighten up its supervisory and personnel practices and reconsider existing, expensive special benefits; the union would likely demand hefty dues, fines, and assessments, and might take the employees out on a long and costly strike with no guarantee that there would be jobs at the

* 96 *Harvard Law Review* 1769 (1983).

end if replacements had been hired in the meantime; if labor costs and labor unrest became too great, the employer might have to relocate.

The employees might well dismiss this message as mere bluffing were it not that a determined antiunion employer has at its disposal a potent weapon with which to demonstrate its power over the lives of its employees: the dismissal of selected union activists, in violation of section 8(a)(3) of the NLRA. Dismissal has the immediate effect of rendering these union supporters unable to vote—a consequence that by itself might tip the balance in a close election—and also excludes the discharged employees from the plant, the setting in which they could have campaigned most effectively among their fellow employees. Even more importantly, the dismissal of key union adherents gives a chilling edge to the warning that union representation is likely to be more trouble for the employees than it is worth.

Perhaps the most remarkable phenomenon in the representation process in the past quarter-century has been an astronomical increase in unfair labor practices by employers. One would not have anticipated such an increase at this stage in the life of a law like the NLRA. For the half-century before the enactment of the Wagner Act, American industrial employers fought bitterly against unionism, with little legal restraint. In 1935, the legal setting was drastically transformed by the Wagner Act, which many considered the most radical legislation of the New Deal. Not surprisingly, there was massive defiance of the new regime by employers determined not to give up their prerogatives. The discriminatory discharge, the most powerful weapon in the employer's arsenal, was heavily used in the years just after the NLRA's passage: in 1939 alone, the NLRB reinstated 7738 employees who had been illegally fired. One would have assumed, however, that once the basic principle of workers' rights to self-organization had become woven into the social and legal fabric, employer noncompliance would naturally have declined. And indeed, by 1957 only 922 illegally dismissed employees had to be offered reinstatement by the Board.

The 1957 lull in unfair labor practices proved to be the calm before the storm. Contrary to expectations, the rate of employer violation of the NLRA suddenly began a precipitous climb.... From 1957 to 1965, unfair labor practice charges against employers increased by 200%, while the number of certification elections increased by only 50%. By 1980, the annual number of certification elections had declined slightly, but unfair labor practice charges against employers were up another 200% from 1965, and fully 750% from 1957. Worse, employees entitled to reinstatement in 1980 numbered 10,033, a 1000% increase from the low point in 1957.

A rough calculation from the figures ... gives an even more graphic index of the current pathology of the American representation process. In 1980, the NLRB secured reinstatement for more than 10,000 employees who had been discriminatorily discharged. A majority of these workers, though not all, were discharged during representation campaigns. Furthermore, the Board obtained backpay for another 5000 employees who had suffered some form of illegal treatment; many of these employees had also been fired but had settled for monetary relief in lieu of reinstatement. One can surmise as well that an additional but indeterminate number of workers were actually discharged in violation of the law but did not file or were unable to substantiate unfair labor practice complaints. A reasonable estimate, therefore, is that about 10,000 employees were fired in 1980 for involvement in representation campaigns. One would suppose that union supporters are most at risk from such employer reprisal. Unions obtained approximately 200,000 votes in representation elections in 1980. Astoundingly, then, the current odds are about one in twenty that a union supporter will be fired for exercising rights supposedly guaranteed by federal law a half-century ago. Such a widespread pattern of employer intimidation has ramifications that reach far beyond the units in which discharges actually occur. It fosters an environment in which employees will take very seriously even subtle warnings about the consequences of joining a union.

Notes and Questions

1. *Updating the Data.* Weiler's data and conclusions were criticized in Robert J. LaLonde and Bernard D. Meltzer, "Hard Times for Unions: Another Look at the Significance of Employer Illegalities," 58 *University of Chicago Law Review* 953, 990–98 (1991). The Dunlop Commission's *Fact–Finding Report*, issued in May 1994, incorporated some of the criticisms and updated the data. The Commission's tables on trends in unfair labor practices and discriminatory discharges during elections are shown below.

Table 3–8
Unfair Labor Practice Charges Against Employers

Year*	Total Number of 8(a) Charges	% of Charges Found Meritorious	Total Number of 8(a)(3) Charges	Total Number of 8(a)(5) Charges	Backpay Awards (Number/Average Amount)		Employees Offered Reinstatement
1950–54	4,345	32.9	3,036	1,266	2,940	458	2,194
1955–59	5,175	21.8	3,993	1,047	1,627	495	9,437
1960–64	9,067	33.9	6,746	2,279	4,349	444	2,876
1965–69	11,397	37.4	7,657	3,902	9,156	517	4,180
1970–74	16,428	34.6	10,684	5,306	6,407	846	4,317
1975–79	25,199	37.9	15,912	7,420	8,729	1,607	4,817
1980	31,281	42.6	18,315	9,866	15,433	2,050	10,033
1981	31,273	40.2	17,571	9,815	25,793	1,415	6,463
1982	27,749	40.1	14,732	10,898	N/A	N/A	6,332
1983	28,995	42.5	14,866	12,211	17,984	1,713	6,029
1984	24,852	41.1	13,177	10,349	34,863	1,050	5,363
1985	22,545	41.4	11,824	9,186	18,482	2,066	10,905
1986	24,084	42.6	12,714	10,131	17,635	1,937	3,196
1987	22,475	41.4	11,548	9,760	17,175	2,093	4,307
1988	22,266	44.4	11,196	9,501	17,496	1,928	4,179
1989	22,345	45.0	11,567	9,479	18,956	3,007	4,508
1990	24,075	43.9	11,886	10,024	16,082	2,733	4,026

* Numbers represent annual averages.

Source: U.S. Departments of Labor and Commerce, Commission on the Future of Worker–Management Relations, Fact–Finding Report, Exhibit III–3, p. 83 (May 1994).

Table 3–9

Discriminatory Discharges During NLRB Elections[1]

Five Year Period	Reinstatement Offers Arising from Certification Elections[2]	Ratio of Workers Offered Reinstatement to Workers Voting for Unions[3]	% of Elections Producing Reinstatement Offers[4]	% of Workers Involved in Elections Whose Units Voted to Unionize[5]
1951–1955	608	1/689	5%	75%
1956–1960	429	1/584	4%	59%
1961–1965	1019	1/272	8%	56%
1966–1970	1346	1/225	8%	54%
1971–1975	1473	1/171	8%	43%
1976–1980	2238	1/92	14%	37%
1981–1985	2855	1/38	32%	38%
1986–1990	1967	1/48	25%	38%

1 The figures in this Table represent annualized averages for each five year period reported.
2 The figures in this column represent the number of all reinstatement offers recorded by the election campaigns. The figures do not represent all election-time discriminatory discharges, but only those leading to the particular remedy of reinstatement. In other words, they do not account for 1) illegal firings not reported to the NLRB; 2) those reported to the NLRB but not producing an NLRB charge or complaint; 3) those producing a complaint but not a favorable resolution; 4) those resulting [in] a favorable resolution not including reinstatement, such as an award of back pay....
3 This column shows how many workers voted to unionize for every one worker offered reinstatement as a result of an illegal firing during election campaigns. The figures are derived by dividing all workers voting to unionize in NLRB elections by the number of election-time reinstatement offers (column one)....
4 The figures in this column are derived by dividing the number of reinstatement offers arising in the election context (column one) by the number of [representation] elections. The source for the annual number of elections is 16–55 NLRB Annual Report Table 13 ("RC" and "RM" elections only) (1951–1990).
5 This column represents what one might call organized labor's effective yield in NLRB elections. It reveals the percentage of workers in such elections whose group ended up unionizing. The percentages are derived by dividing the number of workers in units that voted to unionize by the total number of workers eligible to vote in NLRB elections. The source for both halves of the equation is 16–55 NLRB Annual Report Table 13 (1953–1990), Table 10 (1952), Table 12 (1951).

Source: U.S. Departments of Labor and Commerce, Commission on the Future of Worker–Management Relations, Fact–Finding Report, Exhibit III–4, pp.84–85 (May 1994).

2. *"Employer Opposition" as an Explanatory Variable.* Some points need to be raised about the employer-opposition thesis. First, a distinction needs be drawn between lawful employer opposition (whether in the form of urging negative votes in NLRB representation elections or plant siting decisions that avoid pro-union locations) and unlawful tactics such as retaliatory discharge that the law has prohibited since the 1930s, however imperfectly. Second, we need to understand to what extent employer opposition is an exogenous, or independent, variable driving down the incidence of unionization and to what extent employer opposition is an endogenous, or dependent,

variable that is largely the product of other forces, such as the emergence of global products and deregulation of certain industries (air, rail, trucking, and telecommunications) that once provided enclaves for unionism. Finally, because employer opposition has to some extent been a constant feature of U.S. labor relations, if the claim is that such opposition explains the current fate of private-sector unions, one needs a dynamic account that tells us why such opposition is now different, more emphatic, or more effective in keeping unions at bay than in the period between the New Deal and the mid–1950s. See, e.g., Samuel Estreicher, "Labor Law Reform in a World of Competitive Product Markets," 69 *Chicago–Kent Law Review* 3, 9–10 (1993).

3. *Employer–Opposition Thesis and Union Organizing Activity.* The employer-opposition explanation also has to be considered in light of the considerable drop-off in union organizational expenditures and the consequent decline in the number of employees involved in NLRB certification elections. The rate of organization (eligible voters in NLRB elections as a percentage of all unorganized workers) has been falling since the early 1950s. Professor Flanagan reports:

> Recent research casts doubt on the idea that declining union election success is the main source of falling union representation.... The percentage of the nonunion labor force involved in certification elections fell from about 2.6 percent in 1950 to about 1 percent in 1980. Most of the decline occurred rather precipitously in the 1950s, but the decrease continued, at a slower rate, throughout the 1970s. The decline after 1950 in the union success rate in those elections that did occur reinforced the effect of reduced organizing activity.

Robert J. Flanagan, "NLRA Litigation and Union Representation," 38 *Stanford Law Review* 957, 983 (1986).

Organizing activity plummeted during the 1980s. Although union victory rates in NLRB elections stayed constant at slightly under 50 percent, the number of elections sought by unions fell from 6,858 in 1980 to 3,561 in 1982 and remained at the 1982 level for the rest of the decade; the number of employees annually involved in NLRB elections dropped from an average of 445,084 for the 1975–1981 period to 199,367 for the 1982–1987 period. For the 1988–1993 period, the average rose slightly to 205,781. See Gary N. Chaison and Joseph B. Rose, "The Macrodeterminants of Union Growth and Decline," in George Strauss, Daniel G. Gallagher, and Jack Fiorito, eds., *The State of the Unions* (Madison, Wis.: Industrial Relations Research Association, 1991), 26–27; Gary N. Chaison and Dileep G. Dhavale, "A Note on the Severity of the Decline in Union Organizing Activity," 43 *Industrial and Labor Relations Review* 366, 369–370 (Table 1) (April 1990); NLRB, *Annual Reports*, 1988–1993.

The extent to which workers were involved in NLRB representation elections even during the 1960s was no more than 0.7 percent of the total workforce. From 1973 on, the rate fell to 0.2 percent of the workforce. Even if unions had won every election sought in 1993, union density in the private sector would still have declined: unions would have added an additional 119,539 employees, while overall the workforce expanded by more than two million workers. In some cases, of course, unions do not seek NLRB elections because they are able to secure voluntary recognition from employers; and conceivably, union success of this magnitude would have encouraged a higher rate of voluntary recognition. It is doubtful, however, that the union density figure could have been substantially improved without much greater union investment in organizing new units.

4. *Employer Opposition and Union Density.* Drawing a contrast between the "high density centralized case" (HDCC) in continental Europe and the "low density decentralized case" (LDDC) in the United States, Professor Joel Rogers of the University of Wisconsin argues that employer opposition is best viewed as a U-shaped function responding to extremes of union density and centralization. Consider the following excerpt from his "Divide and Conquer: Further Reflections on the Distinctive Character of American Labor Laws," 1990 *Wisconsin Law Review* 1, 41–43:

> Imagine the curve now describing moments in political (or political-economic) space. Abstracting from the important complications and exceptions of sectoral arrangements—that is, assuming an even distribution across sectors of the given level of union power—we can hypothesize two different patterns of employer strategy and their variants, along with two distinct equilibria in union-employer dealings. To the left of the vertical line—which might be understood as the line of "social peace," "political exchange," or, for those with a Hegelian bent, "mutual recognition"—employers are essentially hostile to unions. The strategic expression of this hostility takes different forms, depending on the respective strengths of capital and labor. With union strength low, a strategy of rollback, or attempted destruction of unions, is pursued. If union strength nonetheless grows, however, an uneasy peace, our first political equilibrium, may be reached at A, while union advances beyond that point meet with a strategy of increasing resistance. A may be thought of as the political location of the LDDC. It is generally unloved by employers and (always with sectoral exceptions) is held in place by union muscle. A can move uneasily up and down the left side of the line, depending on the shifting strengths of the parties and the (by no means unmixed) incentives to unions of expanding membership in the face of continued resistance. In any case, this should be thought of as a non-cooperative (Nash) equilibrium. Finally, should unions pursue an increase in membership, their efforts may provoke a sharp increase in the intensity and extent of capitalist resistance and conflict. This is the "class warfare" indicated at the bottom of the curve.
>
> At some point, however, if unions succeed in consolidating themselves, employers' incentives shift markedly—first to enforcement and then containment of a compromise with workers. With growing levels of unionization, likely expressed in increased national political activity, as well as increased membership and coordination of the labor movement itself, employers accept the reality of union power. They move from attempting to eliminate its costs to generalizing them. At the same time, they find that an increasingly confident union movement, claiming a

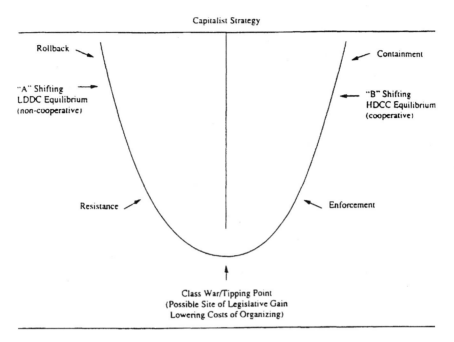

Capitalist Strategy

Rollback

Containment

"A" Shifting
LDDC Equilibrium
(non-cooperative)

"B" Shifting
HDCC Equilibrium
(cooperative)

Resistance

Enforcement

Class War/Tipping Point
(Possible Site of Legislative Gain
Lowering Costs of Organizing)

Union Power (Density/Centralization)

larger share of the population and enjoying greater control over its component parts, is prepared to adopt strategies aimed more squarely at collective gain. The possibility of cooperation between unions and employers becomes mutually apparent. A new equilibrium is reached at B, describing the political location of the HDCC. Unlike its counterpart equilibrium, B is reached with employer assistance; hence its denotation as a cooperative (Stackelberg) equilibrium. It too may shift around a bit, though probably less than A, and less as a direct function of the contests of strength between the parties than of the structure of the rules governing their cooperation, their ability to realize gains through the state, and changes in external economic environment. Considering options further down the curve, while B is preferable (to both parties) to class warfare or the LDDC, and further expansions of union power may be regarded with less unmitigated hostility by employers, anxiety over the political consequences of such expansions recommends an employer strategy of containment, keeping union power within some HDCC limits. As in the case of the LDDC equilibrium, the motives of unions may also come into play here. Given the employer strategy of containment, the costs of further membership expansion and consolidation may not recommend their pursuit, especially in light of the gains already being achieved.

D. Union Wage Policy and Product Market Competition

It may be that the most complete explanation of union decline would combine aspects of the structural-change and employer-opposition accounts. More competitive and often more global product markets may have stiffened the resistance of employers to unions and reduced the potential gains from unionization, thus affecting workers' assessments of the potential rewards and costs of traditional union representation.

We begin with an article by University of Pennsylvania researchers that explores the relationship between the wage premiums paid to union workers (as compared with their nonunion counterparts) and the employment levels of unionized firms. The authors argue that conventional measures of union wage premiums understate their negative effect on employment levels because comparisons are confined to workers and firms in the same industry.

"Evaluating the Evidence on Union Employment and Wages"*

PETER D. LINNEMAN, MICHAEL L. WACHTER, and WILLIAM H. CARTER

... In this study we analyze the pattern of union employment shares and union wage premiums across and within industries for the years 1973–86 to investigate the hypothesis, thus far largely neglected, that the decline in union employment shares is related to shifts in union wages relative to nonunion wages. It is surprising that little attention has been devoted to this explanation, since it is the one that is immediately suggested by the microeconomics model. Perhaps the connection between union employment and relative wages has been dismissed because the literature on union wages has estimated a basically stable aggregate union wage premium since 1973. The large decline in unionization in the face of a stable wage premium apparently challenges any microeconomic explanation of the decline. . . .

We explore two alternative measures of the union wage premium. The first is the traditional measure, calculated by comparing the union wage in an industry with the nonunion wage in the same industry. This measure best captures the direct product market competition of union and nonunion firms in the same industry. On the other hand, the employment losses that have occurred in the union sector of heavily unionized industries have not been primarily captured by the nonunion sector of the same industries. Thus, purely within-industry wage comparisons may be too limited.

* 44 *Industrial & Labor Relations Review* 34 (1990).

The second measure of the union premium, denoted the "opportunity wage index" (OWI), replaces within-industry nonunion wages as the base, by a base group of wages in expanding employment industries. This measure best approximates the rents that union workers receive over alternative employment opportunities. It also may capture changing cost competitiveness across industry lines, which could be relevant to international trade effects. Clearly, there has been a trend toward increasing international competition. Domestic losers in this competition are companies with relatively large cost disadvantages in their domestic wage structure, rather than in their absolute wage or within-industry premium (domestically measured). A third reason for using the OWI measure is that it is attuned to our primary dependent variable, employment shares across-industry....

By focusing on relative wage effects, our study adds important evidence to the recent literature that uncovers a pattern of decline in profits, stock market valuations, and investments at union firms. That literature has not provided direct evidence that the decline in union employment is related to increasing wage premiums; it leaves open the possibility that the poor performance of union firms may be due to adverse shifts in international trade patterns or simply to bad management, with the union connection a coincidence. We believe that our evidence on wage premiums, although not directly related to firm data, suggests that union status is an active, rather than a passive, part of the story of declining profits and valuations.

Changes in the Union Share of Employment

... The substantial decline in union employment in the face of a relatively stable aggregate union wage premium suggests a puzzle, in that traditional price effects do not explain the falling union employment shares....

It is useful to discuss these results in the context of the broad themes of deindustrialization and deunionization. The decline in employment in the goods-producing sectors and the offsetting growth in employment in the service sectors is consistent with a deindustrialization hypothesis. The fact that virtually the entire loss in goods-producing employment is in the union sector, however, requires the inclusion of a deunionization hypothesis as well. Deunionization is supported by the experience of the trades sector, in which union losses were offset by nonunion gains.

The puzzle that is not well explained by either of these hypotheses is the mixed picture in service-producing industries. Although the union sector is losing shares in both retail and wholesale trade, union sectors in services, finance, and government are either growing or at least holding steady. Clearly, something other than single trends away from goods-producing industries and away from unions is at work.

Changes in Union Premiums

The neoclassical model would trace the declining union shares to a rise in the relative wage of union labor. Union wage premiums cause the firm to raise its labor demand curve, hiring fewer workers at higher wage levels. The resulting increase in the marginal costs of the unionized firm over the costs of nonunion competitors (or union competitors who do not pay a wage premium) also results in reduced output, as well as reduced profitability. . . .

In this section, we use the [Current Population Survey] to estimate disaggregated union wage premiums for one-digit industries for the years 1973 to 1986. (These premiums are referred to as "WIN," for *within-industry* premiums.) We also present an alternative measure of industry-specific union-nonunion wage gaps. This alternative premium compares the union wage in each industry to the wage in a base group of expanding sectors of the economy. . . .

The most notable feature of the aggregate wage premium is a slight upward trend from the beginning to the end points of the series for the 1973 to 1986 period. [O]ur wage gap series increases from 15.5% in 1973 to 16.6% in 1986, a 1.1 percentage point increase.

The stability of the aggregate premium, however, masks important trends in the industry-specific union wage premiums. Specifically, sizeable increases in union wage premiums occurred where premiums were already high. The aggregate premium masks these changes because these high-premium sectors have also suffered the largest employment losses, and hence have reduced weights in calculating the aggregate wage premiums. . . .

One–Digit Results . . .

To evaluate the quantitative effects of the changing union wage premiums, we use the estimated equations to simulate the changes in union employment shares between 1973 and 1986. Specifically, we simulate the 1986 employment share implied by the 1973 union premiums. The difference between the actual 1973 employment shares and the simulated 1986 employment shares reflects the changes attributable to union premium changes.

The actual changes in the employment shares for the share-of-economy (EE) and share-of-industry (EI) are shown in columns 1 and 4, respectively, of Table [3–10]. The predicted changes for the OWI specification are shown in columns 2 and 5 for EE and EI, respectively. These simulations indicate that union wage premiums account for 27.8% of the change in economy share employment and for 18.2% of the decline in within-industry employment. The simulations based on the WIN equations indicate that the changes in union wage premiums account for 15.4% and 13.9%, respectively, of the change in these employment shares.

Table 3–10

One–Digit Industry Simulation Results

Industry	Changes in Share Economy			Changes in Share Industry		
	Actual Change	OWI Model Predicted Change	WIN Model Predicted Change	Actual Change	OWI Model Predicted Change	WIN Model Predicted Change
	(1)	(2)	(3)	(4)	(5)	(6)
Government	0.65	−0.08	0.28	9.16	1.99	2.55
Construction	−1.39	0.59	0.41	−15.96	5.69	3.34
Mining	−0.26	−0.13	0.04	−26.47	6.48	1.97
Mfg. Durables	−4.61	−2.34	−1.23	−17.87	−7.42	−3.52
Mfg. Nondurables	−2.47	−0.92	−0.47	−13.84	−4.81	−2.23
Transp. & Utilities	−1.19	−0.44	−0.22	−14.30	−4.13	−2.19
Wholesale Trade	−0.26	−0.03	−0.05	−7.06	−0.82	−1.31
Retail	−0.76	−0.07	−0.22	−7.72	−0.67	−2.05
Finance, Insurance & Real Estate	0.00	0.01	0.02	−1.22	0.14	0.36
Service	1.70	0.19	0.21	3.63	0.70	0.82
Total	−7.96	−3.30	−0.96			
Aggregate (1986 industry share weights)				−6.12	−1.39	−0.56
For Private Sector: Simulated Changes as Percent of Absolute change	27.8	15.4			23.3	13.9

Note: Simulated Changes Are the Difference Between Fitted Values for 1986 Calculated Using the 1986 and 1973 Premiums. . . .

Turning to industry-specific results, the negative trends in manufacturing durables and nondurables, transportation, and wholesale and retail trade are correctly predicted by these simulations, as is the positive trend in services. The negligibility of the change in the union share of finance employment in share-of-economy is also correctly predicted, although the signs are incorrect. . . .

Mining is [a] sector for which the OWI-and WIN-based simulations diverge. In this case, union employment declines, both as share-of-economy and as share-of-industry. This downward trend is correctly predicted by the OWI premium (which increases by 12.2 percentage points over the sample period), whereas the WIN premium (which peaks in 1975) misses the trend in unionized mining employment.

Neither the WIN-based simulation nor the OWI-based simulation accurately tracks the movements of the construction industry. . . . Union employment shares in construction trend downward over the sample period, in spite of a declining union wage. One possible explanation for the puzzling conjunction of declining employment and declining premiums in this sector is that the employment declines reflect lagged responses to the increased wage premiums existing prior to our sample period. Specifically, from 1968 through 1971, unionized construction wages grew faster than the wages of other union workers. Based on this consideration, we are inclined to view these construction sector results as a sampling period problem.

Since the union sector construction share moves in a direction opposite that predicted, it seriously affects the ability of the employment share equations to track other industries. When the model is re-estimated omitting construction and government (for which the coefficient in the WIN model also diverges from the prediction), union wage premiums are much more accurate predictors of employment share changes in the other private sectors. Simulation using these re-estimated equations for 1986 based on 1973 wage premiums accounts for 71% of the share-of-economy employment change and 47% of the share-of-industry employment share change between 1973 and 1986. Similarly, re-estimated WIN equations account for 40% of the share-of-economy and 30% of the share-of-industry. Although we are reluctant to push these results too far, they strongly suggest that the decline in union employment in the face of a stable aggregate wage premium is consistent with the simple neoclassical model. . . .

Conclusion . . .

Our answer to the puzzle is that the constant aggregate union wage premium is a statistical artifact. The already high-premium industries have generally been increasing their wage premiums, and thus losing employment share. Union premiums in services and finance, on the other hand, have held constant or fallen over the same time period. These findings suggest that although unions may have been hurt by exogenous forces causing sectoral output shifts from goods-to service-producing industries, they have been hurt even more by their rising wage premiums. . . .

"Labor Law Reform in a World of Competitive Product Markets"*

SAMUEL ESTREICHER

.   .   .

II. Explaining the Persistence of Employer Opposition

. . . Even if, for the sake of argument, structural factors (narrowly conceived as the changing personal, job, and geographic characteristics of U.S. workers) are discounted as too static an explanation and employer opposition is viewed as the principal cause, we need a dynamic account: what has changed? What explains the resilience, if not rise, of employer opposition, and why has it succeeded in reducing the power of unions and the prevalence of collective bargaining? Blame is often laid at the door of the Reagan administration, which displayed a level of hostility to unions, as demonstrated by its 1981 firing of air traffic controllers for engaging in an illegal strike and some of its appointments to the NLRB.

* 69 *Chicago–Kent Law Review* 3 (1993).

Although the PATCO strike and decisions of the Reagan Labor Board influenced employer behavior at the margin, this point is largely a rhetorical one. Private sector unionism was in decline throughout the 1960s and 1970s. That was why a major campaign for labor law reform was launched during the Carter years (but could not overcome a Senate filibuster). We entered the 1980s at a union-density rate of around 20%. We are now at 13%. At the most, Reagan administration policy arguably accelerated the rate of decline.

Something more fundamental is at work. The labor laws have allowed permanent replacement of strikers at least since 1938 and lawful employer opposition to union organizing drives since 1947 (if not earlier) and have never provided other than mild remedies for employer infractions. The conflicts of interest between labor and management, and hence the incentive to economize on labor costs, have been with us since the very beginning. American managers have never welcomed unions, and yet unions grew from 1935 to 1954 and have declined ever since.

The change in labor-management relations, and the relative position of unions, is essentially due to an unleashing of competitive forces in the markets for American products and services. Given a large domestic market and barriers to entry in many industries, unions for many years were able to pursue traditional high-labor-cost policies across entire product markets and thus grow or at least maintain their positions despite hostile, or at best grudging, managements and a relatively toothless labor law. As we enter an era of intense product market competition, however, the underlying strains in the system are now apparent.

A. *Premises of the U.S. Labor Relations System*

The persistence and growth of employer opposition (and perhaps other causes of union decline) stem from an incompatibility between the premises of our labor relations system and the pressures of competitive product markets. Consider the following features of our system.

First, it is decentralized. Largely because unions seek elections on the basis of the smallest organizing unit, NLRB elections are held at the plant level, usually among a subset of the workers—with craft workers and professionals having the right to opt for separate representation. Multiemployer bargaining units are formed only by consent and in many industries have unravelled. Union organizers like small organizing units, and decentralized structures often ensure a relatively high level of responsiveness to affected employees.

Second, the system is based on an adversarial model of labor-management relations. Admittedly, the system does not "require" adversarial unions or managements. However, an essential premise of the NLRA is that there is a fundamental conflict of interest—a chasm—between labor and management, that is thought to require structural guarantees to keep separate their respective spheres of influence. Thus, employers can play no role in forming labor organizations or providing assistance to them. Similarly, the representatives of management, including supervisors and nonsupervisory personnel having a role in the making or implementation of policy, have no right to form unions and are aligned by the statute against the ranks of the organized, largely blue-collar workers. Also, the scope of mandatory bargaining is defined so as to rigidly separate the domains of labor and management.

Third, unions are multiemployer organizations representing employees of competing firms. This makes it very difficult for any firm to share proprietary information with, or to secure variable labor terms from, the multiemployer union. For example, in the still-unresolved Caterpillar–UAW dispute, at stake is not the rather modest economic differences between the two sides. Rather, the union's concern is its ability to maintain "pattern" bargaining—in this case, to impose on Caterpillar the terms agreed to by its weaker, less export-sensitive competitor, Deere, and also to preserve that strategy for bargaining with the Big Three auto manufacturers.

Finally, unions are institutionally insecure. In the old days, the competition came from rival unions. This has diminished since the 1955 merger of the AFL and CIO (although the demise of manufacturing has spawned a new form of competition among "general" unions for employees in the growing service and public sectors). Today the unions' vulnerability comes from the growing nonunion sector, and the various mechanisms for policing union responsiveness, such as decertification elections, the employers' ability to test majority support by withdrawing recognition, duty of fair representation suits, the rights of nonunion members to seek rebates of union dues used for non-collective-bargaining purposes, and union democracy safeguards. All other things being equal, union leaders would like to maintain (and increase) employment levels. Internal political pressures require them, however, to cater to the preferences of the median voter in the bargaining unit—typically long-service, older workers who are relatively free of the risk of layoff because of seniority rules. Absent a palpable crisis threatening the jobs of those voters, flexibility in bargaining objectives and cooperation with management in reducing labor costs are politically unpopular, as Donald Ephlin, an advocate for greater union-management cooperation, learned during his leadership of the UAW's GM department.

B.   The Illusive Quest: "Taking Wages Out of Competition"

The features I have described are, on one level, desirable and certainly understandable. As a general matter, they help promote independent unions that are responsive to rank-and-file preferences, and reflect individualist values of our political culture. Also, for several decades they coexisted with union growth and strong unionism. This was largely because unions could credibly promise unionized firms that they would, in due course, organize all firms in the relevant product market, and hence ensure that any gains at the bargaining table would be imposed on all competitors. Consumers might lose in such a world, but most importantly the union-represented firm suffered no competitive disadvantage.

This story has changed because American industry and the U.S. place in the world economy have changed. The ability of unions to "take wages out of competition" has declined substantially thanks to the competitive forces unleashed by the emergence of global product markets; the deregulation of previously union-dense industries, such as airlines, trucking, and telecommunications; and technological change altering needs for skilled labor and reducing the advantages of local producers.

U.S. unions can no longer credibly promise employers that they will succeed in imposing the costs of union contracts on their competitors. However, to retain the support of their members and attract new ones, many unions must continue to pursue "wage premium" and "job control" policies that raise labor costs in excess of the productivity gains attributable to unionization. (The studies of Robert Lawrence, now at Harvard's Kennedy School, and Michael Wachter of Wharton and their associates suggest that the union wage premium actually increases as union density declines in some industries.) Share prices usually fall in response to union organizing drives....

A union movement that today represents a little under eleven million private sector workers will continue to be a factor and, it must be noted, unions like the Steelworkers, Autoworkers, and Rubberworkers have reached creative and constructive solutions with managements in some settings to preserve jobs and enhance the firm's market position. But these are the unions whose memberships are dropping the fastest, and they have reached these accommodations against a background of forces that spell a diminishing role for unions. To avoid this fate, there must be a change in union objectives, management responses, and, ultimately, the labor-management climate.

Notes and Questions

1. *Profits Effect.* Professors Blanchflower and Freeman attribute the decline in unionization of the late 1970s and 1980s to the jump in the union-nonunion wage differential from 15 percent to 20–25 percent during this period, observing that in the United States "unionism is associated with markedly lower profitability"—a "profits effect" that is the result of "the large effect of unionism on wages, which exceeds the positive effect of unions on productivity." David G. Blanchflower and Richard B. Freeman, "Unionism in the United States and Other Advanced OECD Countries," in Mario F. Bognanno and Morris M. Kleiner, eds., *Market Institutions and the Future Role of Labor Unions* (Cambridge, Mass.: Blackwell, 1992), 56, 69, 71. The authors add: "[T]he decline in U.S. union density is not an aberration—the

result of Reagan's breaking the air traffic controllers union, of stodgy, incompetent union leadership, or of the decline in manufacturing in the 1980s—but is structurally rooted in what U.S. unions do on the wage front." Id. at 76.

2. *Declining Union Employment Shares and Votes Against Unionization.* As we saw in Chapter 2, employment growth is significantly slower in union plants. See also Jonathan S. Leonard, "Unions and Employment Growth," 31 *Industrial Relations* 80 (Winter 1992). Declining employment prospects in union firms may influence voting behavior in NLRB representation elections. Professor Reder observes: "I suggest that the declining success rate of unions may have been due, in part, to increased awareness among low wage nonunion workers that their long-run employment prospects *in present locations* depended on continuation of sub-union wages and working conditions. To the extent that this was the case, antiunion votes reflected a rational preference for a nonunion status quo, with employer antiunion campaigns serving as a method of spreading information." Melvin W. Reder, "The Rise and Fall of Unions: The Public Sector and the Private," 2 *Journal of Economic Perspectives* 89, 103 (1988) (emphasis in original). For a similar view, see Ethel B. Jones, "Private Sector Union Decline and Structural Employment Change, 1970–1988," 12 *Journal of Labor Research* 257 (1992).

3. *Effects of Deregulation.* In the for-hire sector of the trucking industry, cost pressures due to deregulation narrowed union-nonunion wage differentials. Nevertheless, the unionization rate declined from about 60 percent during the regulatory period to about 25 percent by 1990. See Barry T. Hirsch, "Trucking Deregulation and Labor Earnings: Is the Union Premium a Compensating Differential?," 11 *Journal of Labor Economics* 279, 297–298 (1993).

Professor Card reports that airline workers' relative wages have declined by only 10 percent since deregulation in 1980. This suggests either (1) a modest 10 percent wage premium under regulation or (2) that airline workers are still earning rents, perhaps because the industry has become more concentrated after deregulation. Card discounts the second explanation because airline workers who have lost jobs do not suffer larger wage losses than job losers from other industries. See David Card, *Deregulation and Labor Earnings in the Airline Industry*, NBER Working Paper No. 5687 (July 1996).

4. *Contrary Evidence.* For evidence pointing in the opposite direction from the view taken in the principal readings, see John M. Abowd and Henry S. Farber, *Product Market Competition, Union Organizing Activity, and Employer Resistance*, NBER Working Paper No. 3353 (May 1990). Abowd and Farber find, both before and after 1973, a significant negative trend in union organizing activity and a significant positive trend in employer resistance, after controlling for available "quasi-rents" per worker (defined as the difference per worker between total industry revenues net of raw materials costs and labor costs evaluated at the opportunity wage of the workers).

Part II
Regulation of Labor Relations

In this part of the book, we examine the existing legal framework for regulation of collective bargaining. Chapter 4 considers the principal goals and some of the salient institutional features of U.S. labor law. Chapter 5 explores the growing "law and economics" literature in this area.

4

Goals and Institutional Features of Federal Labor Law

The principal objectives attributed to U.S. labor law are (1) redressing the inequality of bargaining power between workers and their employers and (2) promoting industrial peace. Although some aspects of the scheme can be reconceived in efficiency terms, labor law is not avowedly about promoting an efficient allocation of resources; and efficiency-based accounts will have a difficult time explaining the institutions and processes that the law has put in place.

A. Redistribution

Section 1 of the NLRA speaks of "[t]he inequality of bargaining power between employees who do not possess full freedom of association or actual liberty of contract, and employers who are organized in the corporate or other forms of business association," and the depressing effect such inequality has had on "wage rates and the purchasing power of wage earners in industry." Senator Robert F. Wagner, Jr. of New York and his colleagues believed that labor organization and collective bargaining could, by increasing the returns to labor, boost consumer demand and lift the country out of the 1930s Depression. See Kenneth M. Casebeer, "Holder of the Pen: An Interview with Leon Keyserling on Drafting the Wagner Act," 42 *University of Miami Law Review* 285 (1987). Wagner's economic theory is discussed in the reading that follows.

"Inflation, Unemployment and the Wagner Act: A Critical Reappraisal"*

DANIEL J.B. MITCHELL

. . .

I. *A Historical View of the Wagner Act*

... The macroeconomic motivation behind the Wagner Act is clearly stated in its preamble: "The inequality of bargaining power between employees ... and employers ... burdens and affects the flow of commerce, and tends to aggravate recurrent business depressions, by depressing wage rates and the purchasing power of wage earners...." So central is this economic theme that one searches the preamble in vain to find a corresponding justification based on industrial democracy. The only other justification suggested by the language of the preamble is that the Act will lead to fewer strikes....

The original version of the Wagner bill, submitted as the "Labor Disputes Act" in March 1934, did not in its preamble relate the proposed law to economic recovery. Like the Norris–LaGuardia Act it merely concentrated on the issue of equalizing "the bargaining power of employers and employees." However, Senator Wagner, in introducing the bill, stated that such balancing was "necessary to ensure a wise distribution of wealth ..., to maintain a full flow of purchasing power, and to prevent recurrent depressions." The [National Industrial Recovery Act of 1933 (NIRA)], he indicated, was not having the desired effect of boosting real wages "upon which permanent prosperity must rest." Indeed, he declared, failure to pass the Wagner bill would "jeopardize the whole recovery program."

Senator Wagner's wage-purchasing power justification appears to have been widely accepted. It was noted correctly that the upward pressure on wages induced by the NIRA had been offset by corresponding price boosts. The Wagner bill was intended to tilt the bias toward wages more successfully than had the NIRA. Not surprisingly, the wage-purchasing power theory was supported by organized labor; it was (and

* 38 *Stanford Law Review* 1065, 1073–1076 (1986).

to some extent remains) a traditional justification of the labor movement for raising wages. To the extent the justification was criticized, the criticisms came from employers. . . .

Although the Wagner theory did not seem particularly controversial in Congress, the view that pushing up wages would stimulate output and employment was by no means uniformly accepted in the academic community. Economist Edward Mason of Harvard wrote of the "crudity of the errors" of NIRA administrators who believed in recovery via wage increases. However, empirically oriented economists—as opposed to theoreticians—were more receptive to the NIRA view. A Brookings study published in 1936, while conceding that contemporary economists were split on the wage theory, cautiously indicated that "expansion of purchasing power among the masses is a primary essential to sustained prosperity." On the other hand, the book argued, boosting real wages would not ensure "*permanent* prosperity."

Actually, what strikes the modern reader most is the general absence of economic data in these discussions. It was widely accepted that there had been an increase in profits in the late 1920s and that this had led to a decline in consumption. Information available now (but not necessarily readily obtainable then) indicates that although there was a profit expansion, real consumption also rose steadily during the 1920s. Moreover, from 1929 to 1933, real investment fell absolutely by as much as real consumption even though investment accounted for only 18 percent of real GNP in 1929 while consumption accounted for 68 percent. In a world in which unemployment—the key problem facing the country in the 1930s—went largely unmeasured, it is hardly surprising that the debate on the wage-purchasing power theory was largely nonempirical. Debaters were free to indulge their prejudices without fear of contradiction by statistical analyses.

The role that monetary policy might have played in causing or exacerbating the Depression, or in engineering a recovery from it, was largely neglected. . . .

When the Taft–Hartley bill—which was to amend the Wagner Act substantially—was being debated after World War II, the issue of changing the Wagner preamble arose. The impetus for Taft–Hartley arose out of the postwar wave of strikes, and the strike issue was therefore much more central to the debate than the economic impact of collective bargaining. Although economic issues were discussed, the tenor of the discussions was very different than in 1934–35. . . .

Various reasons can be suggested to explain the shift in Congress away from the view that the Wagner Act was an antidepression measure. First, there was no depression when Taft–Hartley was passed, despite many predictions that one would occur after the end of World War II. The absence of a depression naturally eroded interest in antidepression measures. Second, since inflation was seen as the major problem in the

War's aftermath, concern over its abatement took precedence over worries about a new depression. After relative price stability was fostered by elaborate federal wage-price controls, retail prices rose by 8.5 percent in 1946 and by over 14 percent in 1947. Unions, freed from wage restraints, negotiated large, cross-industry pattern settlements and came to be seen as part of the inflation problem.

In addition to changes in the immediate economic background, there were changes occurring in the way macroeconomic policy was conceived. The Wagner Act's economic rationale—that pushing up wages would boost consumption and economic activity—was a pre-Keynesian notion. The essence of postwar Keynesianism was that government, not unions or businesses, had the major role in economic stabilization. Government was to carry out this responsibility through appropriate macroeconomic policies (the Keynesians emphasized fiscal policy), not by manipulating prices or wages directly....

II. *Analytical Problems With the Wagner Theory*

Since the wage-purchasing power theory was never rigorously stated, critiquing it is difficult....

The essence of the wage-purchasing model is simple. Labor's real share of national income can be defined as the nominal wage (W) times the amount of labor input (L) divided by a price index (P). If it is assumed that workers have a positive marginal propensity to consume out of their wage income, then anything which raises labor's real wage share should also raise real consumption. As consumption rises, the output needed to supply that consumption must also rise and, in turn, the amount of labor employed should increase. All elements of the model appear to reinforce the positive employment effect of the wage increase.

The difficulty with this model is that it omits reference to pricing and production for nonconsumption goods. Note that labor's share is expressed in real terms (WL/P). If P rises due to the increase in labor costs, the positive impact of a nominal wage increase will tend to be offset. Furthermore, if increasing labor's share in national income squeezes the nonwage (profit) share, there could be negative effects on investment. An adequate model of the wage-purchasing power theory must account for these pricing and investment relationships. Such a model is substantially more complicated than the simple view represented in the Wagner Act's preamble.

Whether an augmented model which took account of pricing and investment relations would produce a positive employment impact following a nominal wage boost is unclear. Unconstrained by other considerations, such a model might well suggest that wage boosts would be offset by price boosts on the basis of a simple markup theory of pricing. Indeed, under the NIRA during the years 1933–35, wages and prices rose at parallel rates, leaving the real wage unchanged. This lack of growth in real wages coincided with a lack of productivity improvement. From 1935 to 1940, after passage of the Wagner Act and before World War II began to affect output, real wages rose at about two percent per annum, roughly paralleling the growth of productivity. In short, pricing during the post–1933 period seemed to be based on a markup over unit labor costs. Real wages rose when productivity rose and failed to rise when productivity was flat.

Given this markup behavior, it is difficult to put much faith in a wage-led recovery story. Indeed, about half the real wage increase after 1935 occurred from 1935 to 1937, a period which ended in recession. Of course, these observations do not prove that the wage boosts did not have a net positive effect. One might argue that without union pressure, real wages might not have "captured" the productivity improvement and consumption might therefore have been depressed, causing the economy to slip backward even after 1937. These conclusions, however, do not leap out from the data.

Perhaps a greater cause for skepticism is the omission—even in the augmented model—of a financial monetary sector. If wage boosts lead to price boosts—even price boosts that are insufficient to prevent real wage growth—the real value of the money supply would decrease. Such a development could lead to an increase in real interest rates and a decrease in investment and—through multiplier effects—to reductions in other forms of economic activity. Again, it cannot be stated with absolute assurance that a wage increase must lead to decreased output and employment, even with a monetary effect included. Nevertheless, adding a monetary constraint does suggest that unless the monetary authorities accommodate the resulting inflation, real output and employment are likely to be retarded.

The outcome of a sudden boost in wages can be analyzed using a contemporary multiple equation econometric model. As is always the case, the results of such an experiment do not necessarily provide an accurate prediction of what would happen in the real world. Such models have built-in assumptions which may or may not be valid. Nevertheless, use of such a model will at least illustrate the modern consensus view of economists concerning the results of a sudden burst of wage push inflation.

One such model is the DRI annual scenario model, which contains 191 equations focusing on the national income accounts and other commonly forecasted variables, such as unemployment and inflation. The model was used to simulate the effects of a 10 percent increase in wage push in 1985. Since, in the model, wage increases feed into prices and back into wages, the immediate effect was an increase in wages by a little more than 11 percent above what would otherwise have been predicted. Inflation—as measured by the GNP deflator—rose by about six and one-half percentage points. Real consumption expenditures rose slightly but overall real GNP declined by about 0.7 percent in the first year. This drop was due to a decrease in real investment triggered by falling real profits and rising interest rates. Finally, unemployment tended to rise, partly due to the employment drop and partly because the model assumes that higher real wages attract a greater supply of job seekers.

As noted, the above simulation does not disprove the Wagner Act's wage-purchasing power theory. Indeed, although most economic indicators in the model continue to deteriorate after the initial shock, some do not. However, even given the limitations in the model, the Wagner Act's economic assumptions can no longer be accepted uncritically. The most dramatic effect is a burst of inflation from the cost-push pressures of the initial wage shock. Such a result would undoubtedly goad the monetary authorities into taking restrictive—i.e., demand-depressing—measures. With the greater willingness in 1985 as opposed to 1935 to use macroeconomic policy, especially monetary policy, in pursuit of economic objectives, the view that wage boosts are inevitably beneficial can no longer be the assumption underlying national labor relations policy. . . .

Notes and Questions

1. *A Process–Based Approach to Redistributing Wealth.* The NLRA is principally a procedural measure. The statute assumes that inequality of bargaining power can be corrected by protecting workers' ability to obtain collective representation. There is, notably, no provision for government to set the terms of the labor contract, and no provision on the continental European model to extend labor agreements to unorganized sectors of an industry. Senator Wagner initially omitted a good faith bargaining provision from his bill, fearing it would be vulnerable to the charge that he was seeking a form of compulsory arbitration of labor disputes. See James A. Gross, *The Making of the National Labor Relations Board: A Study in Economics, Politics and the Law, vol. 1, 1933–1937* (Albany, N.Y.: State University of New York Press, 1974), 137. The bill as it emerged out of the SenateLabor Committee (and was enacted into law) required employers to bargain with unions in good faith, but the committee took pains to

> dispel any false impression that this bill is designed to compel the making of agreements or to permit governmental supervision of their terms. It must be stressed that the duty to bargain collectively does not carry with it the duty to reach an agreement, because the essence of collective bargaining is that either party shall be free to decide whether proposals made to it are satisfactory.

S. Rep. No. 573, 74th Cong., 1st Sess. (1935), reprinted in 2 *Legislative History of the National Labor Relations Act of 1935* (1985), 2312.

The legislative commitment to voluntarism became even clearer after Congress enacted Section 8(d) of the NLRA as part of the Taft–Hartley amendments of 1947, which declares that the bargaining obligation "does not compel either party to require the making of a concession."

2. *Search for Macroeconomic Justifications.* For Professor Kaufman, the demand-stimulation rationales of the National Industrial Recovery Act of 1933 (NIRA) and of Section 1 of the NLRA were essential to public acceptance of these laws and their early success in promoting unionism:

> [T]he NIRA was crucial to revitalizing the labor movement because it wrapped unions in the flag and made collective bargaining an instrument for promoting economic recovery and thus the general welfare of society.
>
> ... [T]he hard facts are that in 1935 it was the prospect of ending the Depression, not bringing democracy to the workplace, that made enactment of the Wagner Act possible.

Bruce E. Kaufman, "Why the Wagner Act?: Reestablishing Contact with Its Original Purpose," in David Lewin, Bruce E. Kaufman, and Donna Sockell, eds., *Advances in Industrial and Labor Relations*, vol. 7 (Greenwich, Conn.: JAI Press, 1996), 51, 59.

In Kaufman's view, the demise of this "public interest" justification for the NLRA requires a reassessment of labor law (64–65):

> Is there still a rationale for the NLRA when it is premised on an inequality of power in the wage determination process that may have been substantially reduced or eliminated by full employment demand management policies?
>
> When the federal government is able to keep the economy much closer to full employment, does the industry-wide collective bargaining facilitated by the Wagner Act change from a social virtue because it protects wages and labor standards from destructive competition to a social evil because it promotes cost-push inflation and various inefficiencies on the supply side?
>
> Does it make sense to continue the ban on nonunion forms of employee representation when the original purpose of doing so—facilitating collective bargaining and taking wages out of competition—may have either been made redundant by Keynesian full employment policies or impossible to achieve by the globalization of markets?

3. *Redistribution Through Labor Law: The Affirmative Case.* In an influential essay, "In Defense of the Contract at Will," 51 *University of Chicago Law Review* 947, 976 (1984) (excerpted in chapter 7), Professor Richard Epstein of the University of Chicago argues against legal intervention to influence how the surplus generated by firm-specific investments of workers and firms ends up being distributed:

> ... The whole question of inequality of bargaining power arises in the bounded context of how much of a *supra*competitive wage the worker will obtain. At the very worst, the worker will get the amount that is offered in some alternate employment where he has built up no specific capital. To try to formulate and administer a set of legal rules that will allow some trier of fact to measure the size of the surplus embedded in the ongoing transaction, and to allocate half (or more) of it to the worker, cannot be done at any social cost that is less than the expected

size of the surplus, if it can be done at all. The entire enterprise is fraught with the possibility of real error, as real resources would have to be expended solely to make transfer payments that can in no way enhance productive efforts.

Responding to Epstein's position, Georgetown law professor Michael Gottesman presents the affirmative case for redistribution through the labor laws in the excerpt that follows.

"Whither Goest Labor Law: Law and Economics in the Workplace"*

MICHAEL H. GOTTESMAN

I see two possible justifications . . . for legal intervention on behalf of all employees—whether that intervention takes the form of direct statutory conferral of benefits or strengthening of the right to collective bargaining. One, which is consistent with Epstein's assumption that inefficiency is the sole justification for intervention in the market, asserts that individual employees want, but cannot negotiate efficiently for, employment benefits that possess the characteristic of a "public good," i.e., benefits that cannot be furnished to one employee without simultaneously being provided to all. The other approach is operative if society determines not to accept efficiency as the sole justification for legal intervention and instead elects to intervene for the purpose of redistributing wealth. . . .

The [latter] justification for rejecting Epstein's market thesis will be applicable if a societal determination is made to use the law to redistribute wealth from capitalists to workers. The case for redistributing wealth from shareholders to workers can be made on two levels. First, even if such redistribution does not maximize overall social wealth, a majority in a society controlling its legislative agenda is entitled to determine that the greater marginal utility of money to the less privileged justifies more equitable allocation of resources even if the loss to total societal wealth exceeds in absolute dollars the gain to the poor. Second, wholly apart from considerations of marginal utility, perceptions of historical injustice may persuade some that redistribution from capital to labor is warranted. In that view, the present distribution of wealth is not a pre-ordained "right" but merely represents the consequence of the rather arbitrary decision made in the nineteenth century to treat suppliers of capital but not suppliers of labor as "owners" of the enterprise. That legal ordering was not inevitable; it was merely conventional. Employees can reasonably argue that they make the greater contribution to the enterprise, committing not only their labor but the bulk of their waking lives, and indeed their bodies as well. Society might choose not to accept the disparities visited by the law of the past and commit present bargaining to a market in which each side must deal from the historically determined status quo.

* 100 *Yale Law Journal* 2767, 2786–88, 2790–93 (1991).

To argue that a desire for redistribution of wealth justifies intervention into the labor market requires taking on Epstein's assertion that wealth redistribution can be accomplished more efficiently through tax and welfare laws than through labor laws. There are two rejoinders to Epstein. First, ... there is a great difference in the culture of our society between a recipient of a transfer payment and one who has earned a benefit through working. The latter is perceived as an achiever, the former a failure. This difference is important to the psychological well-being of the recipient, but even more critically it is likely to affect whether society chooses to bestow the benefit at all. There may be little societal impetus to make increased transfer payments to the poor, yet much greater disposition to provide increased rewards for work....

Second, and more fundamentally, many of the benefits society might wish for moral or aesthetic reasons to assure that employees enjoy (e.g., self-esteem, intellectual satisfaction, bodily integrity) are not monetary in nature and thus not easily deliverable through transfer payments. Providing such opportunities is costly and may reduce the employer's profits; the employer will not be disposed to provide them to those lacking the power to extract them in bargaining. These are goals that many employees cannot secure for themselves in the market.

There is a school of economics that treats all interests as commodifiable; that school would point out that there is some price at which a worker would forgo each of the interests I have described. Nonetheless, there are several reasons why society might choose to disregard the equation. From an aesthetic standpoint, it might prefer that employees retain their limbs rather than sell them for a price they found acceptable. Society might also be concerned that there will be costs that others, not the employee, must bear because of his handicap. Finally, employees would put widely varying price tags on these interests, as they are highly subjective; it would thus be difficult and expensive for the law to redistribute the "wealth" associated with these interests through monetary transfer payments.

This recitation suggests two ways in which the nonmonetary character of benefits points to intervention through the labor law. First, it is likelier that there will be a societal consensus to tackle a particular workplace problem such as safety and health than a consensus to redistribute wealth in the abstract. Second, it is more efficient to decide just once what should be spent to reduce workplace accidents than to arrive on a case-by-case basis at a "price" to pay to each employee losing a limb in lieu of avoiding those accidents. In the real world, the nonmonetary interests we have been discussing likely will be protected through the labor laws or not at all.

But, it may be argued, what I have said to this point does not refute Epstein's assertion that if we wish to redistribute wealth we can do it through transfer payments; if we provide monetary transfers through the tax system, employees could afford to sacrifice wages to purchase these nonmonetary benefits (the transferred money would replace the wages sacrificed). Indeed, the argument might go, that is the preferable approach, for it allows each employee to decide whether the benefit is worth the purchase price, rather than having the government make a paternalistic decision that binds all. Ultimately, the response to this argument is the same as that presented earlier within the efficiency model: the "public goods" character of most of the interests in question precludes their purchase by individual employees. Thus, a model that would redistribute wealth, just as a model that would accept the present allocation of wealth, points ultimately to either collective bargaining or government dictation as the means for ordering "public goods" in the workplace. Tax laws might generate the revenues, but we need labor laws to achieve their optimal distribution.

4. *Redistribution and Decline of Union Density.* Irrespective of the merits of promoting redistribution through collective bargaining, is this still a viable goal when unions represent less than 10 percent of workers in private firms? See Samuel Estreicher, "Labor Law Reform in a World of Competitive Product Markets," 69 *Chicago–Kent Law Review* 3 (1993) (arguing that unions cannot effectively pursue traditional wage premium and job control policies because they can no longer impose uniform terms across product markets); Joel Rogers, "Divide and Conquer: Further Reflections on the Distinctive Character of American Labor Laws," 1990 *Wisconsin Law Review* 1, 85 (positing an "optimal density level beyond which it is irrational for unions to continue bargaining" because density determines whether they will be able to take wages out of competition).

Wage differentials increased dramatically during the 1980s. Some labor economists have estimated that 20 percent of this increase came about because of the drop in union density, since unions were too weak to effectively reduce wage inequality. See Richard B. Freeman and Lawrence F. Katz, "Rising Wage Inequality: The United States vs. Other Advanced Countries," in Richard B. Freeman, ed., *Working Under Different Rules* (New York: Russell Sage Foundation, 1994), 48. See Chapter 2 of this volume for a discussion of the effect of unions on inequality.

B. Routinization of Industrial Conflict

Prominent among the purposes listed in § 1 of the NLRA is the prevention of industrial strife. Indeed, some academics have criticized the labor laws for routinizing conflict and hence robbing the labor movement of the 1930s of what they believed was its radical potential to transform society. See, e.g., Karl E. Klare, "Judicial Deradicalization of the Wagner Act and the Origins of Modern Legal Consciousness, 1937–1941," 62 *Minnesota Law Review* 265 (1978). We include an excerpt from Cornell law professor Katherine Stone's article which argues that labor law has been dominated by a philosophy (in her view, really a mythology) of "industrial pluralism" that has served as a "vehicle for the manipulation of employee discontent and for the legitimation of existing inequalities of power in the workplace."

"The Post–War Paradigm in American Labor Law"*

KATHERINE VAN WEZEL STONE

. . .

Industrial pluralism is the view that collective bargaining is self-government by management and labor: management and labor are considered to be equal parties who jointly determine the conditions of the sale of labor power. The collective bargaining process is said to function like a legislature in which management and labor, both sides representing their separate constituencies, engage in debate and compromise, and together legislate the rules under which the workplace will be governed. The set of rules that results is alternatively called a statute or a constitution—the basic industrial pluralist metaphors for the collective bargaining agreement. . . .

IV. *The Premise of Joint Sovereignty*

In order to understand the current doctrinal confusion in labor law, it is first necessary to understand the ways in which the theory is flawed and the reasons why courts and commentators refuse to acknowledge its impending demise. Central to the industrial pluralist view of the NLRA—as merely establishing a democratic framework within which labor relations occur rather than as endowing substantive rights—is the proposition that labor and management jointly determine workplace conditions by negotiating a collective bargaining agreement. Through private negotiations, labor and capital compromise their own self-interest and arrive at mutually agreeable terms for their services. Government intervention is limited to facilitating the negotiations; it does not dictate the terms that result.

This view of industrial relations assumes that labor and management come to the bargaining table not only in an adversarial position, but also out of mutual need and with comparable power. The fact of negotiations alone, however, does not ensure that one party has not dictated terms to the other. Labor and management have different powers at the bargaining table, powers partially determined by the law itself. These disparities affect the extent to which the agreement can be said to have been "jointly" settled. In addition, the agenda of the negotiations—that is, what issues are put up for discussion—is constrained by practical and legal barriers. . . .

Joint sovereignty, if it is to mean anything at all, must mean a redefinition of the incidents of ownership, which entails both an attack on private property and a rejection of technological determinism. It must involve a relinquishment by management of what it has heretofore

---

* 90 *Yale Law Journal* 1509 (1981).

regarded as its exclusive decisionmaking prerogatives, even in such "vital" areas as investment decisions. Giving unions a voice in matters like wages and hours is of limited value if they have no say in matters that affect the competitive position of the firm, for that is what ensures the firm's ability to pay any wage at all. For the union to participate meaningfully in any matter that concerns workers, it must address issues that lie at the core of entrepreneurial control. A form of collective bargaining that gave unions an equal voice in such matters would be true joint sovereignty. Such a form, however, would deprive management of many of the incidents of private ownership, a result that neither management nor the industrial pluralists intended. Joint sovereignty must also acknowledge the possibility that unions do influence the operation of the business, and thereby reject the view that industrial conditions are the inevitable and necessary result of large-scale organizations as such. Otherwise there would be no point in permitting the union to have input into decisions—the decisions would be predetermined.

V.   *The Premise of Neutral Adjudication*

A second premise of the industrial pluralist ideology is that impartial arbitration of breach of contract disputes is possible. This premise is implicit in the metaphor of industrial life as a mini-democracy. The analogy of an arbitrator to a judge subsumes the notion that a judge can decide a case in an apolitical way, above the conflict of forces that went into making the laws. . . .

Although the pluralists insist on the possibility of neutral arbitration, their description of the arbitrator's role and methodology appears strange. Any normal picture of judicial neutrality is abandoned altogether. They insist that arbitration is superior to a court for resolving day-to-day labor disputes because the judicial method is too rigid and therefore inappropriate in an industrial setting. They posit a "common law of the shop which implements and furnishes the context of agreement." This common law differs from that applied by a judge: it is made up of the "practices, assumptions, understandings, and aspirations of the going industrial concern."

The pluralists themselves suggest an answer. They state that the apparent surface-level calm of industrial life may mask deep tensions that threaten to explode. An individual grievance that appears slight may spark a great upheaval in the shop. According to Shulman: "[T]he frequent instances of stoppage of work in a department or a whole plant because of a disciplinary penalty imposed on a single employee indicates that what is involved is not merely the case of an individual but a group dispute." . . .

This then is the special expertise of arbitrators which Douglas referred to in the *Steelworker Trilogy*. It is an expertise that enables the arbitrator to sense undercurrents of discontent beneath an individual grievance. Similarly, the flexibility that the pluralists claim makes arbitration superior to judicial resolution of these disputes is not only flexibility of procedure or of remedies, but also flexibility of outcomes. The pluralists suggest that arbitrators should tailor outcomes to alleviate tensions when underlying conditions are about to explode. This may be why "the arbitration hearing has been called the psychiatrist's couch of industrial relations." . . .

If the pluralists' arbitrator in practice does not even try to be a neutral interpreter of the collective agreement, then a different view of the role of arbitration in the shop emerges. No longer is arbitration a judicial process of law application. It becomes an element in the existing conflicts between management and the union. This is because all changes in plant conditions affect the relative balance of power between management and labor. In a situation of constant conflict, there is no possibility of neutral intervention. The resolution of each dispute becomes part of the background against which future disputes arise and are resolved. Arbitrators function in this power contest as active interveners in plant life in order to ensure the smooth continuity of operations and the diffusion of tensions, so as to help to preserve industrial order. But, as with any form of social order, it is important to see who benefits from industrial orderliness, and at whose expense it is achieved. It is in disorder that workers experience and exercise their power in the production process. The entire history of the labor movement is a history of workers creating "disorder"—strikes, disruptions of production, picketing—in order to achieve unionization and to better their working conditions. Like the law of gravity, the collective power of workers is only evident when the everyday structures collapse. Only in the midst of "disorder" do workers have the leverage to press for their demands. Thus by intervening to preserve order, arbitrators are not only nonneutral, they are acting consistently on the side of management.

VII. *The Locus of Struggle*

 . . . The starting point for any new approach is a more accurate description of the industrial world and a more viable analysis of the impediments to democracy built into it. Any new theory must also take a position on the question of whether the wage contract is a purely private concern or a concern of society as a whole. Industrial pluralism mandates legal arrangements that force workers to fight the daily struggles in the workplace in an invisible, privatized forum, where each dispute is framed in an individuated, minute, economistic form. The alternative is to define labor issues as a matter of public concern, and to submit resolution of these issues to the political process.

This approach would enable workers to struggle in the arena in which their strength is greatest—the national political arena. At the level of national economic and political institutions, they could utilize their collective strength and define their problems in such a way that genuine solutions would be possible. It is at that level that major decisions about investment policy, both private and public, are made. In the arena of national politics, the numerical strength of the working class and its commonality of interests around these problems would make it a potent force. By keeping labor disputes out of the political arena, however, industrial pluralism fosters the illusion, so central to pluralist theory in general, that there is no class conflict in America.

Notes and Questions

1. *Industrial Peace as a Statutory Objective.* By providing an administrative procedure in lieu of strikes over recognitional disputes, and by encouraging the use of grievance arbitration, the NLRA helps reduce some of the causes of industrial conflict. In another sense, however, the statute recognizes the central role of the strike and other forms of conflict as a legitimate part of the process of collective bargaining. The NLRA, unlike the Railway Labor Act of 1926, creates no obligation to maintain agreements as such, and does not require the parties to await an agency's declaration of impasse before they can resort to self-help and contracts may be changed. Moreover, unlike the laws governing public-sector labor relations, which generally outlaw resort to strikes and lockouts, the NLRA does not provide for compulsory interest arbitration as the mechanism for resolving impasse.

2. *Is Routinization of Conflict Bad for Labor?* Professor Stone questions both the general tendency of the law to channel grievance disputes away from the NLRB and the courts into contractual processes and the specific rules crafted by arbitrators (such as the "work now, grieve later" rule). Unions, however, typically favor use of grievance arbitration and rarely have negotiated express exclusions from the arbitral rules Stone criticizes, which suggests that the system generally reflects the preferences of union negotiators. If default rules were changed, and workers were given the initial entitlement to refuse disputed work assignments or engage in work stoppages mid-term contract disputes, would they simply trade these entitlements back to employers as soon as contracts were open for renegotiation? See Stewart J. Schwab, "Collective Bargaining and the Coase Theorem," 72 *Cornell Law Review* 245 (1987), and materials in chapter 5 of this volume.

3. *Critical Legal Studies.* For other examples of labor law scholarship from the "critical legal studies" perspective, see Karl E. Klare, "Workplace Democracy & Market Reconstruction: An Agenda for Legal Reform," 38 *Catholic University Law Review* 1 (1988); Jack M. Beerman and Joseph W. Singer, "Baseline Questions in Legal Reasoning: The Example of Property in Jobs," 23 *Georgia Law Review* 911 (1989); James B. Atleson, *Values and Assumptions in American Labor Law* (Amherst: University of Massachusetts Press, 1983); and "Forum on 'Critical Labor Law Theory,'" 4 *Industrial Relations Law Journal* 449–506 (1981) (contributions by Karl Klare, Staughton Lynd, Melvyn Dubofsky, and Duncan Kennedy).

C. Institutional Features

In this section, we examine how the statutory objectives have been addressed in three controversial areas of labor law doctrine: (1) the "company union" prohibition in Section 8(a)(2) of the NLRA; (2) the scope of mandatory bargaining; and (3) the hiring of permanent replacements for economic strikers. The rules in these areas are shaped by the adversarial premises of the NLRA and raise questions over whether the labor laws, as originally conceived, fit well with modern workplace conditions and worker preferences. With collective bargaining viewed principally as a mechanism for bolstering labor's bargaining position in the distributional contest, the law insists that worker organizations be free of employer influence, represent narrowly defined interests, and seek leverage through alliances with other groups and sustained work stoppages. This conception, in turn, requires limits on the bargaining subjects that may be coercively influenced through collective pressure. The third area considers the role of labor market forces in influencing collective bargaining outcomes through employer countermeasures to strikes.

1.   Adversarialism

"Employee Involvement and the 'Company Union' Prohibition: The Case for Partial Repeal of the Section 8(a)(2) of the NLRA"*

SAMUEL ESTREICHER

. . .

I.   *Origin of the "Company Union" Prohibition*

Those who drafted the NLRA, principally Senator Robert F. Wagner of New York, offered two distinct explanations for section 8(a)(2). The first—what we might call the "employer coercion" rationale—was that the provision would remove an effective management device for beating down unions even where the employees plainly preferred independent representation. In the period between the enactment of the National Industrial Recovery Act of 1933 (NIRA), which announced in section 7(a) that employees had a right to organize and engage in collective bargaining, and the 1935 *Schechter Poultry* decision that declared the NIRA unconstitutional, employee representation plans mushroomed as companies sought to fend off union organizing drives. For many companies, the in-house representation plans were part of an arsenal of tactics that also included use of spies, professional strikebreakers, and mass discharges of union supporters. Because of his service on the National Labor Board (one of a number of agencies formed to mediate labor-management disputes during the NIRA period), Senator Wagner personally confronted a number of notorious cases in which employers openly defied the NIRA. These companies insisted that they would deal with their employees as a group only through the vehicle of the employer-sanctioned representation plan—even when the independent union enjoyed the overwhelming support of the workers....

* 69 *New York University Law Review* 125 (1994).

Despite this history, the employer-coercion explanation does not explain the full breadth of the section 8(a)(2) prohibition because other aspects of the 1935 legislation directly addressed the coercive tactics that often accompanied the installation of employee representation plans during the NIRA period. In place of the powerless NIRA labor boards, Congress established the NLRB, an independent federal agency with authority to conduct elections and issue judicially enforceable orders against employers who refused to comply with the law. The statute clearly commanded that employers had to recognize and negotiate exclusively with the majority representative of the workers and could not discharge or otherwise discriminate against union supporters. Hence, even without section 8(a)(2), a company union could not be erected to block an independent union that the workers desired.

But, for Senator Wagner, there was a second, broader objective— what we might call the "false consciousness" rationale for section 8(a)(2). Wagner believed that employers must be removed from the process altogether in order to preserve the preconditions for genuine employee free choice. Company-supported systems, he argued, were inherently flawed vehicles for workplace representation. Representatives could not effectively advance worker interests because they could not form alliances with national labor organizations. In addition, Wagner viewed these plans as inherently deceptive because the representatives were beholden to the employer, who would thus be able "to exercise a compelling force over the collective activities of his workers."

For employees, the upshot of the statutory scheme is that it compels them to choose between relying on individual bargains or opting for collective bargaining by independent organizations. For employers, the statute essentially requires a unilateral mode of decisionmaking when dealing with employees as a group. Sophisticated, typically large, companies have established modern personnel or human relations offices to fashion policies and procedures which anticipate employee preferences and concerns. Employers may use one-way communication devices, such as employee polls and focus groups, to solicit reactions to proposed changes in compensation and working conditions. Employers can (and are often well-advised to) listen to, and take into account, employee reactions. But what the statute does not permit, the NLRB emphasized in its December 1992 ruling in *Electromation, Inc.*, [309 N.L.R.B. 990 (1992), enforced, 35 F.3d 1148 (7th Cir. 1994)], is any form of employer-supported vehicle for bilateral communication in which employers respond to employee proposals on wages, hours, and working conditions.

II. *Changes in the American Workplace*

A. *Central Assumptions of Section 8(a)(2)*

The model of the NLRA rested on two key assumptions about worker preferences and the nature of the American workplace. The first was that workers, if given freedom of choice, would resoundingly prefer representation by independent unions. . . .

The second, perhaps even more important, premise of section 8(a)(2) was that the organization of work in mass production industries relied on minute specialization of tasks repetitively performed by workers and on hierarchical structures of authority that required little or no input from production workers other than obedience to management commands. Influenced by Frederick W. Taylor's principles of "scientific management," American manufacturers strove to replicate Henry Ford's early success in standardizing the production of automobiles, by removing "brain work" from the realm of the production worker. In this "Taylorist" world, the management unilateralism required by section 8(a)(2) reflected governing conceptions in the management community of the efficient utilization of front-line workers.

B. *Erosion of the Assumptions Underlying Section 8(a)(2)*

The last two decades have witnessed a substantial erosion in both the position of unions in private industries and in management adherence to the "Taylorist" model. Because section 8(a)(2) no longer fits well what workers want and how work is organized, Congress should significantly relax the statutory prohibition as part of a comprehensive reform of American labor law.

Unions in private firms have been in a state of decline since the mid–1950s, with the union-density rate today under thirteen percent of nonagricultural workers. . . . Thus, for the vast majority of American workers who for whatever reason do not want, or will not choose, to be represented by unions, we have a labor law that—in the name of employee free choice—confines employees to the choice between management unilateralism and a single alternative that they are unlikely to select.

Changes in the design and organization of work have also eroded the second premise behind section 8(a)(2). Competitive pressures on U.S. firms from a variety of sources—the emergence of international product markets, deregulation of air and truck transport and telecommunications, technological advances that reduce the advantages of local firms, and capital market forces that require enhancement of shareholder values—are undermining Taylorist conceptions of how best to utilize front-line workers.

U.S. firms understand that they have to eliminate unnecessary costs, while at the same time reengineering their production and service operations in order to achieve and maintain a reputation in the marketplace for high-quality, specialized products and services. Increasingly, employers need "smart" workers who can operate computer controls and understand entire processes involved in making a product or delivering a service, in order to take full advantage of systems that enable operators to monitor quality and communicate with engineers, parts suppliers, and other support personnel. To meet customer demands more effectively and reduce capital requirements, firms are utilizing general purpose, multifunctional or programmable equipment to facilitate the ability to switch to new product designs—technology that requires workers to develop problem-solving and "debugging" capabilities, once the preserve solely of engineers, in order to improve equipment performance over time. In addition, workers who acquire such skills are increasingly able to take on tasks that under the Taylorist model required small armies of industrial engineers and supervisory personnel, thus enabling "lean production" firms to shed substantial layers of supervisors and other "indirect" workers.

C. *On–Line and Off–Line Employee Involvement Initiatives*

This ongoing transformation of the workplace requires a high level of commitment and understanding from front-line workers that is inconsistent with the unilateral style of the Taylorist school of management. Workers cannot be treated as passive recipients of management dictates if they are at the same time expected to learn new tasks and skills, rotate among work assignments, interact with engineers, customers, and suppliers, and supervise themselves. Employers are now experimenting with a variety of approaches for producing a high-commitment workforce. Some take the form of Japanese-style "quality circles," problem-solving teams, or cross-functional teams that bring together workers and managers to solve operational problems and develop improvements in work design and processes. In these systems, employee involvement takes place "off-line" because the systems are parallel to the production or service delivery processes with which the workers are normally engaged, and hence leave undisturbed the pre-existing organization of work.

Increasingly, leading companies such as Ford, Motorola, Texas Instruments, General Foods, Procter & Gamble, General Electric, TRW, Inc., and Eastman Kodak, to name but a few, have moved to "on-line" systems that seek to integrate employee involvement with actual production or service delivery processes, and thus transform the organization of work.... Many of these firms have also sought to delegate responsibilities by training front-line workers to function as "self-directed work teams" responsible for task assignments, scheduling of work, maintaining and improving performance levels, cost and quality controls, and safety—all with a minimum of supervision.

These developments certainly have not taken hold in all U.S. companies, and indeed the shift towards self-directed teams is still at an early stage. Even within the same company some divisions and even buildings utilize traditional processes alongside those employing team-based systems. But considerable diffusion of these new approaches has already occurred. MIT Professor Paul Osterman's survey of work sites with fifty or more employees reveals that over half use teams to some extent, and 40.5% involve at least half of their nonsupervisory front-line workforce in teams.

III. *Potential Impact of Section 8(a)(2) on Employee Involvement*

There is considerable concern in many, although not all, management circles that these workplace innovations may run afoul of section 8(a)(2), at least under conventional interpretations....

In part to allay concerns in the management community that section 8(a)(2) might be invoked to strike down employee involvement initiatives, the Bush Administration's Labor Board announced it would utilize a pending case involving an Elkhart, Indiana unit of Electromation, Inc., a manufacturer of electrical components and related products, as a vehicle for clarifying the status of such programs under the NLRA. On September 5, 1991, departing from its usual practice, the Board held an oral argument eliciting the participation of labor and management groups and attracting considerable public attention.

Electromation, Inc. involved an off-line system of employer-initiated committees that plainly dealt with section 2(5) subjects. Responding to employee dissatisfaction with unilateral changes in its existing attendance bonus and wage policies—and well before any union appeared on the scene—Electromation formed employee "Action Committees" for dealings with management over absenteeism, pay progression, attendance bonus, and no-smoking policies. The committees consisted of six employees who volunteered to sit along with one or two management officials. There was no evidence that the employer initially was aware of an incipient Teamster union organizing drive. After the union surfaced and demanded recognition, management informed the employees that it would no longer participate on the committees, but that the employees could continue to meet if they so desired. On these facts, the Board in December 1992 found a violation of section 8(a)(2) because the committees were a company-dominated bilateral mechanism for dealings with employees....

IV. *The Case for Partial Repeal of Section 8(a)(2)*

As interpreted by the Board—an interpretation that is largely faithful to the congressional intent in 1935—section 8(a)(2) is thus likely to present significant obstacles for certain types of employee involvement programs in nonunion firms. Paradoxically, it is precisely those features that we otherwise might most want to encourage in the nonunion sector—management "give and take," some sort of selection procedure to ensure representativeness, wide-ranging discussion extending into matters of pay and working conditions—that are most likely to trigger regulatory difficulties....

In my view, a substantial modification of section 8(a)(2) is called for as part of a broader package of reforms of the labor laws. I propose limiting section 2(5)'s definition of "labor organization" to entities that "bargain with" their employer over terms and conditions of employment.... Under this proposed standard, Electromation's "Action Committees" would have been lawful because there was no evidence in that case that the employees in that plant believed, reasonably or otherwise, that the committees were acting as a collective bargaining agency.

Under my proposal, employees would retain their section 7 rights to engage in concerted activity for self-representation and "other mutual aid and protection," and, most importantly, their section 9 right to petition for independent unions. No agreement with an employer-dominated structure would bar an NLRB election. An employer's antiunion campaign, including retaliatory discharges, would still be reached under section 8(a)(3). Moreover, timing would be important; employers would not be permitted to install employee committees as a purely strategic device to win over workers in the midst of an NLRB representation election....

"Democracy and Domination in the Law of Workplace Cooperation: From Bureaucracy to Flexible Production"*

MARK BARENBERG

. . .

V. *Flexible Work Organizations in the 1990s: New Possibilities for Productivity, Democracy, and Domination*

. . .

C. *The Perils of the Team Workplace: New Processes of Domination*

The very features of team-based organization that promise to enhance efficiency and self-governance also generate new potential for management illegitimately to coerce workers, distort their communication, and manipulate their subjective experience. Before examining this potential, it is useful to identify the social and psychological dynamics of self-managing teams that distinguish them from work groups under mass production.

1. *Social and Psychological Dynamics of Self–Managing Teams.* Members of a self-managing team would face hierarchical constraints even in the most democratic imaginable enterprise. The firm's organizational chart may accurately depict a "web" or "network" of teams aligned in horizontal equality, but overall organizational goals still constrain team autonomy in an effectively "hierarchical" way....

* 94 *Columbia Law Review* 758 (1994).

Work teams' greater discretion and responsibility systematically produce a higher level (or, perhaps more accurately, a different kind) of anxiety than that experienced by workers doing routinized tasks....

Team responsibilities not only enhance stress, but also place great interpersonal emotional demands on team members. Self-managing teams generally fulfill their productive and self-governance potential only if they are more than an interdependent work group anointed with a "team" label. Unlocking that potential generally requires the formal development of deliberative and problem-solving skills, including the capacity for ongoing reflexive learning and improvement of team process-es. One of the team facilitator's key tasks is to help the team become increasingly self-evaluating and self-revising—a difficult task made only incrementally easier when workplace information-technology provides automatic feedback on team performance. Management wraps much team-building activity in the rhetoric of "trust" and "consensus." But team meetings and problem-solving can easily become ineffective, demo-ralizing exercises if members are not also trained to voice disagreement and frustration over perceived obstacles to fulfilling (or effectively defin-ing) team goals and strategies. That is, work teams' effectiveness often turns on their members' development of interpersonal skills in self-assertion—in overcoming the (further) anxiety that many experience in confrontations within small face-to-face groups. If the well-functioning self-managing team *is* a cell of deliberative democracy, that deliberation does not take the form of a communitarian convergence of opinion and feeling. Such convergence is too frequently a recipe for suppression of disagreement, confusion, or anger that impedes both self-development and effective collaborative work. Participants in team workplaces widely observe that interpersonal skill-development in self-managing teams heightens their intersubjective attunement and effectiveness in their nonwork lives as well....

2. *Structural Coercion: The Instrumental Abuse of Team Relations.* The team system has the potential concurrently to intensify structural coercion of workers and to make that coercion more subtle and covert compared to old-style company unionism. Enough reliable case studies in North America, Japan, and elsewhere have documented such heightened coercion—undermining both workers' free choice of governance modes and their self-transformative work activity—to warrant legal attention.

a. *The Team Leader Turned Intimidator.* As the above discussion of team psychodynamics shows, the team facilitator/leader plays a poten-tially powerful role in the work lives of team members—more powerful than the role of employee representative in the lives of a company-unionized workforce. Three features of work teams—their heightened formalization, discretion, and interpersonal exposure—account for the team leader's great *instrumental* power. These features give the team leader access to more information about team members' work performance and union sympathies. That greater access has several sources: the probing discussions that the team leader orchestrates in team meetings; the leader's presence in (or rotation through) the work process itself; and the enhanced opportunity, discussed presently, for "cronyism" that allows team leaders to use some team members as informants.

In addition to greater information-extraction, the team leader may have a larger arsenal of instrumental incentives with which to threaten or bribe individual team members. If the authority "flexibly" to allocate tasks and rewards is vested in the team leader, the team system recreates the potential for the kind of abuse of discretion that was rampant in the "foremen's empire" of the era before industrial unionism....

b. *From Mutual Learning to Mutual Coercion in the Panoptic Workplace.* Whereas the informal sanctions within shopfloor groups may restrict work pace under mass production, and the collaborative camaraderie of self-managing teams may yield as a byproduct (or render unnecessary) mutual monitoring in textbook flexible organizations, the peer pressure within pathological teams may reach the unmistakable pitch of coercion. A team facilitator/leader determined to use the team apparatus as an anti-union tool can deploy discretionary incentives not only directly to penalize pro-union workers, but to turn his loyal favorites against their pro-union peers. The instrumental pressures available to team members include, at a minimum, the withholding of daily cooperation and social recognition. When the organization authorizes team members (under the guidance of team leaders) to evaluate, reward, and discipline peers, instrumental anti-unionism among team members can be devastating.

Three broader features of "lean" organizations—in which teams are generally embedded—encourage such mutual coercion in the work process itself and further detract from the goals of self-governance in team decision-making. First, the norm of no-slack production removes certain buffers that otherwise enable workers to vary their pace of work to satisfy their individual needs or preferences. Such buffers include informal stockpiles of finished work; backup workers to fill the temporary gaps left by sick, injured, or exhausted workers; easier jobs into which older workers can transfer or younger workers can rotate for breathing spells; and the informational buffer of shopfloor know-how that the team structure disimpacts. The logic of lean production is to allocate tasks in order to strive for sixty minutes of high-effort work per hour by all workers with zero buffers of back-up workers, intermediate or final output, or inventory.

Second, lean organization relies heavily on the "principle of visualization." Workers' performance data [are] publicly displayed and formally discussed. Spatial layout leaves work stations open to the view of co-workers and managers. A more novel feature of the new "panoptic" workplace is the so-called *andon* board. It displays the rate of production—often using red, yellow, and green lights—at each stage in the work flow among teams. Management seeks organizational design that achieves neither red, indicating that an emergency stop or slowdown in production is required, nor green, indicating smooth flow, but yellow lights. Yellow lights warn of production stress and therefore, unlike green lights, ensure the absence of buffers or slack time.

Third, team organizations generally base pay and nonpecuniary recognition in large part on group performance. These three features together create strong incentives—internalized by individual workers or conveyed through peer pressure—for team members to work even when sick or injured in order not to overload peers or diminish group performance. There is substantial evidence that systemic speed-up—"exploring the limits of human capacity"—itself enhances the likelihood of physical injury, stress, or debilitating work pace. There is also a tendency for team workplaces gradually to reduce the time devoted to deliberative problem-solving as the stress of lean production cumulates....

3. *Distorted Deliberation: The Manipulation of Team Communication.* The potential for instrumental distortion of communication in the team system can be summarized briefly. If management is committed to avoiding unionization or undermining an existing union, team facilitators/leaders play the central role traditionally assigned to supervisors in anti-union campaigns. Upper management, human-resource staff, and experienced anti-union consultants coach leaders on day-to-day strategies for small-group or one-on-one solicitation against unionization. The leaders may control the agenda and procedure of team meetings in a way that subtly or overtly diverts the substance and outcomes of group discussion. Managers instruct leaders to raise topics and guide discussions to flush out and isolate pro-union workers, and to signal to undecided workers that the leader considers complainers and malcontents to be misfits or "losers" who are disloyal to both team and organization. Leaders may enlist team-member loyalists in turn to convey the same message. While these practices amount to the direct structural coercion discussed above, they also have distinctly deliberation-distorting effects. They chill pro-union speech and concurrently amplify anti-union viewpoints expressed through formal organizational channels and resources of communication....

Notes and Questions

1. *Section 8(a)(2) and Redistributive Unionism.* Is the principal purpose of Section 8(a)(2) to promote a particular form of employee organization

capable of waging redistributive battle? Employees at a work site could, of course, form their own independent unions. This will be difficult in many settings, however, because employees may lack the expertise and time to organize entirely on their own, and individual employees face reduced incentives to produce "collective goods" like representation. Since the employer is denied any role in the representational process, the organizing task is left to the national labor unions. Even where "independent local unions" have been established—often having had their origin in a management-initiated process—they ultimately seek to join the AFL–CIO affiliate. See Sanford Jacoby and Anil Verma, "Enterprise Unions in the United States," in Mario F. Bognanno and Morris M. Kleiner, eds., *Labor Market Institutions and the Future Role of Unions* (Cambridge, Mass.: Blackwell, 1992), 137–58; see also Sanford Jacoby, "Current Prospects for Employee Representation in the U.S.: Old Wine in New Bottles?," 16 *Journal of Labor Research* 387 (Summer 1995). If unions can no longer function effectively as agents of wealth redistribution, does it make sense to retain a prohibition that is rooted in such a conception of the union's role?

2. *Section 8(a)(2) and Freedom of Choice.* Supporters of the Section 8(a)(2) prohibition argue that excluding any employer role in the representational process is a critical precondition to employee freedom of choice because of the effects of (1) employer favoritism and (2) employer co-optation. The first explanation assumes that employees will not be able to assess appropriately the costs and benefits of outside representation if the employer can put in place an internal process of bilateral dealings. The second explanation assumes that such an internal process will provide an opportunity for identifying employees with organizing skills and oppositional tendencies not available under conventional management techniques. On the other side of the coin, when employers establish an internal process they also help solve for employees the collective-goods problem identified in the previous note. See, for example, the role of company unions in the formation of the Steelworkers Union, as recounted in Raymond L. Hogler, "Worker Participation, Employer Anti–Unionism, and Labor Law: The Case of the Steel Industry, 1918–1937," 7 *Hofstra Labor Law Journal* 1, 26–36 (1989); Irving Bernstein, *Turbulent Years: A History of the American Worker, 1933–1941* (Boston: Houghton Mifflin, 1970), 455–68. Is it clear the net result of these countervailing effects will always be detrimental to independent representation if that is what the employees truly want?

3. *Adversarialism and Alignment.* The conception of the labor-management relationship underlying Section 8(a)(2)—that the relationship is principally one of conflict of interest—also helps explain other aspects of the statutory scheme. Thus, for example, supervisory and managerial employees are denied organizing rights because they are aligned with management as agents of capital, and bargaining obligations (as discussed in the next reading) are narrowly defined to preserve mutually exclusive spheres of influence belonging to management and labor.

2. Scope of Bargaining

"The Scope of the Duty to Bargain Concerning Business Transformations"*

MICHAEL C. HARPER

The Importance of Defining the Scope of the Duty to Bargain

This [essay] focuses on the extent to which an employer does or should have an obligation to bargain with an exclusive representative of its employees over significant business decisions that will affect the jobs of these employees. In order to analyze this problem intelligently, however, one must understand clearly the legal consequences of classifying a topic within the scope of obligatory bargaining. . . .

Five such consequences should be noted. The most obvious and probably least controversial consequence is that placing a topic within the mandatory scope means that the NLRB will require the party who would control the topic unilaterally absent bargaining obligations to bargain about decisions concerning the topic with a sincere desire to reach an agreement. The "controlling" party—who on decisions to transfer a business is, of course, almost always the employer—need not make any particular concessions on the topic to the "noncontrolling" party, but must discuss and explore alternatives thoroughly, with an authentic interest in reaching some mutually acceptable compromise. Failure to do so is an illegal action, an unfair labor practice under the NLRA, and the Board will remedy it not only by ordering further bargaining, but also in some cases by ordering the undoing of any action taken without adequate bargaining.

Second, and perhaps more important, the Board will permit the party who, absent bargaining would not control a decision that requires bargaining, to use economic leverage to attempt to compel the controlling party to compromise. This economic leverage can be exerted by refusing to reach an agreement on other mandatory bargaining topics unless the other party compromises on the disputed topic. The leverage can also be exerted by some commonly employed means of industrial coercion, such as strikes or lockouts. In a somewhat controversial decision almost thirty years ago, the Supreme Court in *NLRB v. Wooster Div. of Borg–Warner Corp.*, [356 U.S. 342 (1958)], held that employers, and by implication unions, may not use economic leverage to compel the other party to compromise on topics about which the other party is not required to bargain. Since this decision, the definition of mandatory bargaining topics thus has determined not only the topics over which the Board will compel bargaining, but also the topics over which the Board will permit noncontrolling parties to attempt to compel compromise.

* In Samuel Estreicher and Daniel G. Collins, eds., *Labor Law and Business Change: Theoretical and Transactional Perspectives* (Westport, Conn.: Quorum Books, 1988).

The third notable consequence of including a topic within the mandatory scope derives from the Board's general and judicially approved policy of offering more protection to employees striking in protest of unfair labor practices than to employees striking merely over economic issues. The Board requires employers to reinstate unfair labor practice strikers, but not economic strikers, to their former positions even if this requires the discharge of permanent replacements. This distinction means that when an employer refuses to bargain in good faith on a mandatory topic of bargaining, the employees not only may invoke the legal assistance of the Board, but also may engage in collective and coercive action themselves with the assurance that they will be able to reclaim their jobs after the action.

Fourth, the Act prohibits either party without the consent of the other party from modifying collectively bargained agreements until their expiration dates. In *Allied Chemical Workers v. Pittsburgh Plate Glass Co.*, [404 U.S. 157 (1971)], the Court held that the prohibition attaches only to modifications concerning mandatory topics of bargaining.

The fifth and final consequence of defining a topic to be within the mandatory scope ... was also established by a Supreme Court decision, or at least by a broad interpretation of it. In *NLRB v. Katz*, [369 U.S. 736 (1962)], the Court held that even a party generally willing to negotiate in good faith on a topic commits an unfair labor practice if it implements a change concerning a topic without first bargaining to impasse with the other party over that change. The *Katz* Court, of course, made it clear that the rule against unilateral action that it announced applies only to mandatory topics of bargaining....

A Coherent and Principled Definition of the Scope of Mandatory Bargaining

[*Editors' Note:* In lieu of the Supreme Court's muddled efforts to define the scope of mandatory bargaining, the author offers what he terms the "product market principle."]

[A]ny decision determining what products are created and sold, in what quantities, for which markets, and at what prices should not be subject to the influence of collective and coercive employee economic power. Any decision that need not determine such product market policies if adequate resources are reallocated to the needs of employees, however, should be subject to the influence of the collective action of employees.

This principle is based on two important policy considerations, one central to the NLRA and one central to the organization of our society and not compromised by the Act. A fundamental tenet of the Act is the authorization of collective employee action to attempt to influence the share of resources of a business enterprise that are allocated to the needs of labor. The Act assists employees not by giving priority to any particular set of needs, but by protecting whatever economic power that the employees can aggregate to satisfy their own preferences as they perceive them. A statute that establishes a system of free contracting between employers and collectivities of employees should not be read to authorize an agency or the courts to determine how or at what level employees can ask to be compensated by a different allocation of company resources.

While the Act thus contemplates the use of collective employee power to influence the level and form of the allocation of resources to meet employee needs, it does not seem in any way to compromise the means by which our society makes decisions about the goods and services that are made available for its consumption. In the public sector, of course, those decisions are made by managers under the supervision of elected officials, who presumably want to be responsive to citizens as voters. In the private sector, those decisions are made by managers under the supervision of shareholder representatives, who presumably seek to be responsive to citizens as consumers. Private companies, of course, attempt to modify the desires of consumers, just as politicians attempt to modify the desires of voters; however, product market manipulations should be addressed by public representatives through regulatory legislation, not by employees through collective bargaining.

The product market principle is thus cogent as well as coherent. Collective bargaining should be concerned with the division of economic resources between capital and labor, not the allocation of products to consumers. Any increase in the relative labor costs of one business of course affects distributional efficiencies in the economy by increasing the relative price of that business's products. This much indirect distortion of product markets must be accepted if the NLRA is to offer any protection to collective bargaining. Direct distortion of product markets, however, need not be accepted and protected. . . .

A New Frontier for Bargaining

The product market principle also can at least help illuminate questions concerning an employer's obligation to bargain about perhaps the most intriguing proposals to transform business operations: proposals to grant employees ownership or participation in the management of the enterprise. There is little law on bargaining obligations concerning such proposals, no doubt in part because these proposals generally have been pressed in recent concession bargaining for which the scope of the objects of legitimate union coercive power has not required definition.

Proposals to increase the control and investment of employees in the enterprises for which they labor can be divided into four categories for consideration of bargaining obligations: representation on boards of directors or other high corporate policy-making committees; participation in collective decision making about plant operations; ownership and control of the voting rights of corporate stock; and rights to timely notice of planned liquidation and to the opportunity to purchase corporate assets before the implementation of such plans.

The first category—employee representation on corporate boards—has of course achieved particular prominence in this present era of economic transformation and dislocation. One might argue that proposals to place at least union officials on corporate boards ought not to be even permissible, let alone mandatory, bargaining items because union representation on corporate boards would lead inevitably to the violation of some law. Some have suggested that placing a union official on a corporate board (1) could eventuate in a violation of federal antitrust laws, especially Section 8 of the Clayton Act, which proscribes interlocking directorates between competitive corporations; (2) could constitute employer interference with the union's autonomy in violation of Section 8(a)(2) of the NLRA; or (3) could result in the union board member violating either his corporate fiduciary duty or his duty of fair representation to unit employees under the NLRA or his fiduciary duty to union members under Section 501 of the Landrum–Griffin Act.

All of these problems of potential illegality are surmountable....

No matter how potential conflict of interest and Section 8(a)(2) problems are avoided, employers should not be obligated to bargain about union proposals to place any employee representative in any high corporate post, including a seat on the board, that has responsibility for making decisions that are themselves outside the mandatory scope of bargaining, whether these decisions be the selection of an employer's collective-bargaining team or the definition of a product line. Decisions that should not be influenced by collective employee power ought not to be influenced by an employee whose decision-making influence has been secured through the exercise of such power. This seems true even if the employee's influence on such decisions is limited to his or her power to persuade after consultation and does not include a voting right. Employers who wish to secure wage concessions by offering unions board representation can do so through voluntary negotiation without treating board representation as a mandatory topic over which unions can exert economic pressure.

Of course, this analysis does not preclude mandatory bargaining over proposals fitting in the second category listed above—proposals to make more democratic decision making about production operations. Although management might resist, or indeed advance, such proposals for reasons other than a desire to reduce labor costs ... , even the present NLRB might view employee-participation proposals as appropriate for bargaining because they primarily concern labor costs and labor relations....

The third category of worker-control proposals—measures to facilitate employee ownership in the enterprise that employs them—requires a somewhat different analysis. Requests of unions, as well as managements, that employees who are represented be compensated by a particular negotiable instrument of value should not be outside the scope of mandatory bargaining simply because the instrument happens to be stock in the employees' company. As the Board recognized thirty years ago in a decision holding that a company must bargain about a plan to subsidize its employees' purchase of the company's own stock, shares of company stock are as much "emoluments of value" as rights in pension or insurance plans.

Control by employees of common stock in the corporation that employs them, however, may have much different implications than the control of rights in pension or insurance plans, if enough voting stock is controlled to enable the employees to influence corporate decision making. Should unions be able to insist that management bargain about a proposal to place employees in a collective role of controlling shareholders in the company, perhaps through the creation of an Employee Stock Ownership Plan (ESOP) with pass-through voting rights? The issue may seem fanciful because management cannot commit incumbent shareholders either to the dilution of their equity through the authorization of new stock or to the sale of the incumbents' own stock. There are, however, several realistic scenarios for union bargainers proposing employee control of management through ownership: the employees' company might be a wholly or primarily owned subsidiary of a larger corporation with whose management the union could bargain; the employees already might be majority owners in the enterprise, again perhaps through an ESOP *without* pass-through voting rights; or incumbent stockholders might otherwise have authorized management to issue sufficient new voting stock and to take other steps necessary to pass control to the employees. At least, the employees could negotiate with management to solicit shareholders' proxies to obtain such authorization, just as they could negotiate for the solicitation of proxies to place employee representatives on the board of directors.

A strong argument can be made that employees ought not to be able to use collective economic leverage to compel management to bargain about facilitating employee control of the enterprise through stock ownership because such control would enable employees to use collective power to achieve full control over matters that ought not themselves be topics of mandatory bargaining. Achieving control of a board of directors through stock ownership, however, is fundamentally different from achieving direct employee representation on the board of directors. Control of a large block of common voting stock would enable employees to achieve control of the corporation as stockholders, rather than as employees. The difference is of more than formal importance. Control over the destiny of a corporation, as any equity market analyst knows, is part of the wealth of the corporation. When employees seek to secure that wealth, they seek to obtain a particular form of compensation and a particular allocation of corporate resources.

Making the collective employee purchase of a corporation's equity a mandatory topic nonetheless presents a close issue in my mind. Employees may seek to control the destiny of their corporation not simply to secure the best return on their investment capital, but also to provide the best security for their human capital. Collectively bargained employee ownership of enterprises therefore is somewhat in tension with the present social policy in favor of consumer control of product market decisions. On balance, however, I would favor making employee purchases of controlling equity interests mandatory, even without special legislation, because the board of directors' mandate to represent the interest of shareholders as such would remain formally unchanged; the representatives of employee stockholders would have to be much more sensitive than union officials to consumer demand in the product market. . . .

Notes and Questions

1. *Does the Mandatory–Permissive Distinction Promote Bargaining?* The underlying rationale for the mandatory-permissive line drawn in the *Borg-Warner* decision is that (1) collective bargaining is likely to work best, and presumably agreements are more likely to occur, if the duty to bargain and right to insist are limited to "core" subjects of wages, hours, and working conditions; and (2) strong parties should not be able, by economic pressure, to influence decisions that are within the other side's sphere of control. Critics argue that the mandatory-permissive distinction encourages deception and stymies bargaining. See, e.g., Archibald Cox, "Labor Decisions of the Supreme Court at the October Term, 1957," 44 *Virginia Law Review* 1057, 1083–84 (1958); William B. Gould IV, *Agenda for Reform: The Future of Employment Relationships and the Law* (Cambridge, Mass.: MIT Press, 1993), 172.

2. *Alternatives to Borg–Warner.* Consider the following alternatives to the current division between mandatory and permissive topics of bargaining:

(1) The parties have a duty to bargain over "all subjects." See Gould, *Agenda for Reform: The Future of Employment Relationships and the Law*, 172. Stanford law professor (and former NLRB chair) Gould's proposal does not make clear whether bargaining would be required over all lawful subjects or only those subjects that in some way affect working conditions or job security.

(2) The parties have a duty to bargain over Section 8(d) subjects ("wages, hours, and other terms and conditions of employment"), but also a right to insist on all lawful subjects, subject to an overall duty to bargain in good faith. This was Justice Harlan's position, dissenting in *Borg-Warner*. Some limits would have to be recognized on the employer's right to insist, say, that workers be represented by an entity other than the union representative certified by the NLRB. Other subjects, like interest arbitration, could

be insisted upon but could not be implemented without an agreement. See Samuel Estreicher, "Labor Law Reform in a World of Competitive Product Markets," 69 *Chicago-Kent Law Review* 3, 39–40 and n.134 (1993).

(3) The duty to bargain and the right (of noncontrolling parties) to insist are limited to Section 8(d) subjects, but the parties would have a duty to "meet and confer" over permissive subjects. The duty to meet and confer may involve some sharing of information, but disagreements over permissive subjects would not forestall a declaration of impasse over Section 8(d) subjects. This model has been used in some public-sector labor relations statutes. See Janice R. Bellace, "Mandating Employee Information and Consultation Rights," *Proceedings of the 43rd Annual Meeting of the Industrial Relations Research Association* (Madison, Wis.: IRRA, 1990), 137–44.

3. Strikes

"Replacing Economic Strikers: The Law and Economics Approach"*

GEORGE M. COHEN AND MICHAEL L. WACHTER

The Internal Labor Market Model

The distinction recognized in the economics literature between the external and the internal labor markets is critical to our analysis. In the external market, jobless workers seeking to join the labor force, or employed workers seeking to change jobs, search among different firms for the best array of wages and working conditions. Meanwhile, firms with job vacancies search among workers for those best able to fill the job at the lowest wage. . . .

In the internal labor market (ILM), on the other hand, high transaction costs exist. The distinguishing characteristic of the ILM is that firms and workers incur substantial sunk (irretrievable) investments in the training of workers. Because these investments are firm-specific, that is, are not portable across firms, job immobility results. If workers switch jobs or firms discharge workers, the sunk investments are lost. This immobility thus creates a bilateral monopoly: in the ILM neither workers nor firms can make relatively cheap substitutions for each other.

As a consequence of the need for firm-specific training, the potential for inefficiency exists in ILMs. For ILMs to be efficient, the firm and the worker need to be able to make whatever firm-specific investments are cost-justified. But such investments raise the potential for opportunistic behavior by creating a surplus, the size of which reflects the greater productivity of the specifically trained worker compared to the worker from the external market. If only one party invests in the specific

---

* In Bruno Stein, ed., *Proceedings of New York University's 43rd Annual Conference on Labor* (Boston, Mass.: Little, Brown, 1990).

training, the other party can threaten to [terminate] the relationship unless it receives a greater proportion of the surplus. Investment in such rent-seeking behavior reduces the size of the surplus from the relationship and hence is inefficient.

Mackay Radio

The central focus of this paper involves the superior ability of the efficiency model of labor law to explain *NLRB v. Mackay Radio & Telegraph Co.*, [304 U.S. 33 (1938)], and its progeny. In *Mackay Radio*, the Supreme Court held that an employer has the right to replace workers striking for economic (as opposed to unfair labor practice) reasons with new workers and the right to give those replacement workers the first claim to jobs even after the strike is resolved. . . .

The line drawn by *Mackay Radio* is consistent with the efficiency model . . . because the rule helps deter opportunistic behavior by both sides in the ILM. Recall that in the ILM, sunk, firm-specific investments by both parties create the potential for opportunistic behavior. Suppose that a strike occurs because a firm with monopsony power in the ILM has demanded that the workers agree to lower future wage rates, that is, a lower expected return on their sunk investments. If the firm's product market conditions have not changed, then such a demand by the firm is an opportunistic threat rather than an efficient adjustment as long as the prevailing wage rates represent a competitive return on workers' investments. In this case, striking workers would have little to fear from replacement workers, because these replacements would not accept jobs that offer a stream of future wages below competitive levels. Alternatively, any replacement workers who accepted jobs would be reluctant to make sunk investments in a firm that had developed a reputation for opportunistic behavior. . . .

On the other hand, suppose that the union is striking to achieve or to preserve a monopoly wage premium or a monopoly return on workers' investments. In this case, the right to hire replacement workers is an important weapon. The higher the premium, the greater the attractiveness of those jobs to replacement workers. Replacements would find such jobs better than those they could obtain elsewhere; moreover, the age premium would compensate them for the risk and nonpecuniary costs associated with acting as replacement workers.

Limitations of the Mackay Radio Doctrine

. . . In *NLRB v. Erie Resistor Co.*, [373 U.S. 221 (1963)], the Court held that although the firm could offer replacement workers permanent employment, it could not offer them superseniority for working during the strike. Absent such a limitation, the potential for opportunistic behavior by the firm would be great. Indeed, without such a restriction, the efficient division of *Mackay Radio* would be undermined.

Central to the efficiency of *Mackay Radio* is that a firm that opportunistically pays below-competitive wages would not be able to hire permanent replacements because the job offers would be unattractive. But without *Erie Resistor*, such a firm would be able to attract permanent replacement workers by offering them greater long-term rewards than those offered the strikers. If, however, the firm is limited to offering replacements the below-competitive wage that the strikers have already rejected, the efficiency of *Mackay Radio* is preserved.

Moreover, if a firm could offer replacements a supercompetitive wage short term, it could secure *temporary* replacements who would work only long enough to defeat the strike. An opportunistic firm could use such a scheme to induce its strikers to have to return to work under the old, below-competitive terms. The strikers would return to their old jobs instead of seeking new ones because of their firm-specific investments. *Erie Resistor* deters such behavior.

A second, related limitation on the *Mackay Radio* doctrine is that after replaced striking workers have communicated an unconditional request for reinstatement, they are entitled to reinstatement in the same or substantially equivalent employment as these jobs open up. This rule is also important to protect efficient ILM contracting, because it limits the ability of a firm that has won or is winning a strike by successfully hiring permanent replacements from using that victory to act opportunistically.

The ability of the firm to hire permanent replacements usually implies that the firm is on its way to winning the strike. In such circumstances, some or all of the striking workers may ask for reinstatement in order to protect their past firm-specific investments. Although the firm was presumably not acting opportunistically when the strike began—that is why it was able to hire permanent replacements—the firm may now decide to use its impending strike victory to act opportunistically at the strike's conclusion. The striking workers who seek reinstatement are those most likely to be in the recoupment phase of their firm-specific investments. A firm that has already recouped its investment could increase its share of the ILM surplus by denying such workers reinstatement....

"Collective Bargaining or 'Collective Begging?': Reflections on Antistrikebreaker Legislation"*
SAMUEL ESTREICHER

. . .

III. *A Collective Process–Based Theory for Reform of Mackay Radio*

[W]e need a theory of the role of the strike and strike replacements in the process of collective bargaining that accords with the central premises of the NLRA.

* 93 *Michigan Law Review* 577 (1994).

A. *Central Premises of the NLRA*

I take the premises of the NLRA to be the following:

First, workers have a right to opt for collective representation in setting the terms and conditions of employment.

Second, the law protects the freedom of workers meaningfully to decide whether to be represented on a collective basis, but it is otherwise indifferent to the extent of unionization or the extent of coverage of union contracts. Absent from our law is the provision of German law permitting extension by administrative fiat of collective bargaining agreements to nonunion firms. The NLRA, including the 1947 Taft–Hartley amendments, and in particular section 7's recognition of the employee's "right to refrain" from union activities, reflects a public policy that does not seek to promote the spread of unions where it is not otherwise sought by the affected employees.

Third, the NLRA assumes there is a problem of inequality of bargaining power when individual workers negotiate terms of employment with firms. Congress, in the language of section 1, sought to redress "[t]he inequality of bargaining power between employees who do not possess full freedom of association or actual liberty of contract, and employers." The import of this latter assumption is that for workers who have opted for collective representation, the statute seeks to promote a process by which the workers acting as a group negotiate terms with their employer, even if the employer would prefer to deal with its employees on some other basis.

Fourth, again within the domain of the statutory scheme as it presently stands, the problem of inequality of bargaining power is thought to be corrected by the ability of workers to invoke the collective representation option and the statutory protection of their declared preference for collective bargaining. Unlike the Fair Labor Standards Act of 1938 or the laws common in European countries, the NLRA does not stipulate the minimum terms under which workers may be employed. Nor, as we have seen, is it a law requiring the parties to reach any particular outcome or any agreement at all.

Rather, the NLRA is an essentially *proceduralist* statute that facilitates collective bargaining without nullifying the influence of market forces. The parties at the table are not insulated from the forces of competition, whether between firms in the product market or between union and nonunion workers in the labor market.

Some may argue that the purpose of the NLRA is to eliminate competition in the labor market—"to take wages out of competition." That is certainly an objective of unions, and where such competition is eliminated, unions are at their strongest point. It is also true that, as a general matter, unions enjoy an immunity from the antitrust laws in pursuing that objective. The NLRA, however, aids that objective only in the very limited sense of providing a collective representation option and insisting on good-faith collective bargaining once that option has been exercised. The NLRA does not itself eliminate or seek to eliminate labor-market competition.

B. *Unraveling the Paradox of Mackay Radio*

... Consistent with the premises outlined above, the only justification, in my view, for allowing employers to hire permanent replacements in the course of a strike is that the statute does not eliminate the role of labor-market competition—of competition among workers—in the setting of the terms and conditions of employment. Hence, the risk of permanent replacement serves as a market-based check on unreasonable union demands at the bargaining table.

There are, of course, other checks on union demands, notably the limited ability of many workers, even when aided by union strike funds and state laws extending unemployment benefits, to pay for the necessities of life without working. The NLRA does not, however, insulate workers from labor-market competition even if their union were willing to invest its entire strike treasury on a particular dispute, or if all strikers were able to secure temporary employment elsewhere, to facilitate a strike of indefinite duration.

But that is only half of the story. It is also a central premise of the statute that when workers have opted for collective representation, the terms of the labor contract are to be determined by what workers organized *collectively* will accept, not by what individual workers are willing to accept. Collective bargaining is not quite the same thing as "collective begging," a term of derision used by advocates of *Mackay Radio*'s repeal. Thus, we also have to ask whether there is a corresponding collective-labor check on unreasonable management demands. Given the congressional judgment, it is not a sufficient answer to say that such a check comes from the willingness of *individual* replacement workers to brave the picket line and work on the terms of management's final offer to the union. The very inequality of individual worker bargaining power that led Congress to enact a collective representation option cannot help but influence the reservation wage of individual replacement workers and hence the content of management's final offer to the union.

Mackay Radio seems, on one level, to permit this paradoxical result. On another level, if we consider the union density levels of the 1940s and 1950s, it is possible to argue that firms could often expect that at the end of a strike, replacement workers would either support the preexisting union or enlist the services of another labor organization. It is this prospect of continuing union organization at strike's end that, in my view, provides the necessary moderating influence of a *collective* employee check on management demands at the bargaining table. That check acts to ensure that management, too, faces the right incentives from the standpoint of the statute. . . .

Whatever the causes of the decline in union density, under present conditions *Mackay Radio* threatens to unravel the statutory scheme [because employers face a substantially lower risk of continuing organization at the conclusion of the strike]. This is particularly true given the existing rules that allow representational issues to be decided during the course of a strike. Those rules empower employers to treat a strike, not simply as a dispute resolution mechanism consistent with a continuation of the bargaining relationship at strike's end, but as an occasion for eliminating that relationship.

C.   *The Proposal*

This state of affairs requires legislative action. How should the law be changed?

1.   *The Case Against a Per Se Ban on Permanent Replacements*

One option is the current legislative initiative to overturn *Mackay Radio*. A per se prohibition on the hiring of permanent replacements would, in my view, substantially diminish the influence of labor-market competition in the setting of terms and conditions of employment in the union sector. If an employer cannot maintain operations by other means or withdraw its capital by relocating operations elsewhere, such a prohibition effectively insulates labor demands from market checks. Collective bargaining should not be an endurance contest. If the employer has met its bargaining obligations and is fully prepared to continue to deal collectively with its employees at strike's end, and if sufficient time has passed for the informational and signaling benefits of the conflict to manifest themselves, there has to be a mechanism for testing the reasonableness of the union's demands in the marketplace. The ability to hire replacements willing to work on the basis of the firm's final offer to the union provides that check. . . .

When the firm is unable to continue operations by other means, the firm should not be locked into an acceptance of the union's demands; rather, it should be able to force a marketplace test of the union's bargaining position. If the employer makes known at the outset its intention to hire permanent replacements, it can minimize the need for an endurance contest and avoidable job loss for strikers, as well as induce an earlier moderation of the union's demands.

2.   *Requiring a Prior Showing of Business Necessity*

The objective of labor law reform in this area should be to devise a means of minimizing the strategic use of *Mackay Radio*—that is, when firms permanently replace strikers for the purpose of ousting the union and deterring future unionization rather than in the interest of maintaining operations in the face of a strike—while preserving the beneficial check on union demands for employers who cannot maintain operations without hiring replacements. This statement of the objective suggests that all that is needed is a rejection of the irrebuttable presumption in the *Mackay Radio* opinion that permanent replacements are always needed to maintain operations.

Under this view, the firm would have to make an affirmative showing that it could not maintain operations with temporary help before resorting to permanent replacements. A firm that can attract temporary replacements on the terms of its final offer to the union has no need for permanent replacements and should not be allowed to inflict permanent job loss without economic justification. . . .

In my view, a prior showing of business necessity should be required only if an administrative mechanism is available for obtaining a prompt declaratory ruling, keying the availability of temporary replacements to objective indicators, such as unemployment rates in the particular locality or industry. Uncertainty is unfair to workers who should not have to bet their jobs on the hope that the Labor Board will at some point in the distant future treat them as "unfair labor practice strikers" entitled to displace their replacements. Employers, too, should be able to respond to union demands with a minimum of legal uncertainty. . . .

Moreover, while such a showing would be based in part on unemployment rates in particular industries and regions, it would also have to take account of the educational, skill, and motivational requirements of the positions in question. . . . In many industries, job requirements . . . require better educated workers who are willing to cross-train and able to function effectively in a team-based system. The availability of such workers is not likely to be fully captured by unemployment statistics, and extensive reliance on temporary help is likely to be inconsistent with the high level of commitment to firm objectives required of front-line workers in this new environment.

If both of these qualifications—prompt determinations and true measures of the availability of temporary help—are accepted, any prior showing of business necessity will have "bite" only for unskilled, high-turnover positions and, for other positions, only in areas where there is a high rate of unemployment of educated, skilled workers.

3. *A Six–Month Moratorium Period on Job Loss Due to the Hiring of Permanent Replacements*

Even when the employer is able to obtain a declaratory ruling that temporary workers are not available in sufficient number and quality to meet its requirements—or if the administrative difficulties of providing such a ruling argue against requiring a showing of business necessity—there remains a need for a substantial moratorium period during which the process of collective bargaining has a chance to work free of labor-market pressures. I favor the approach that was Ontario law until very recently—requiring reinstatement of strikers who announce their intention to return to work at any point within the first *six months* of a strike.

A clearly defined period of immunity from permanent replacement is desirable. It encourages the parties to continue talking even though a strike has occurred, yet it preserves the corrective influence of the prospect of permanent replacements. Moreover, it helps avoid mistakes; workers are not rashly betting their jobs. By striking, workers indicate the intensity of their preferences and test the employer's resolve and ability to operate without them. After six months, any useful information of this type has already been imparted; workers who persist in their demands do so at peril of losing their jobs if they misjudge their bargaining position.

Advocates of a flat-out repeal of *Mackay Radio* criticize this six-month moratorium approach for allowing employers bent on ousting the union to prolong disputes beyond the sixth month. Six months is, however, a long time in the life of any company to endure the disruption of a strike—particularly during a period when firms maintain "just-in-time" inventory levels.... If the strike nevertheless persists, we have a fundamental dispute over terms to be resolved in the marketplace. A rule barring the hiring of permanent replacements in such circumstances may strengthen the union's position in a particular dispute; it does not, however, improve the economic position of the union-represented firm or the relationship between the parties....

Notes and Questions

1. *Law and Economics Literature on Striker Replacements.* For other analyses of striker replacement laws from a law and economics perspective, see Leonard Bierman and Rafael Gely, "Striker Replacements: A Law, Economics, and Negotiations Approach," 68 *Southern California Law Review* 363 (1995); and William R. Corbett, "Taking the Employer's Gun and Bargaining About Returning It: A Reply to 'A Law, Economics, and Negotiations Approach to Striker Replacement Law,'" 56 *Ohio State Law Journal* 1511 (1995).

2. *"Joint Costs" Theory of Strikes.* The "joint costs" theory of strikes in the economic literature argues that strikes will be used less by the parties when the joint costs to both parties are high relative to the cost of other mechanisms for resolving their differences. See Melvin W. Reder and George R. Neumann, "Conflict and Contract: The Case of Strikes," 88 *Journal of Political Economy* 867 (1980); John Keenan, "Pareto Optimality and the Economics of Strike Duration," 1 *Journal of Labor Research* 77 (1980). This theory offers no clear prediction, however, as to the likely effects of legislation that would curb the use of strikebreakers. Such a law would make strikes more costly to firms (by increasing output losses) and less costly to workers (by reducing the risk of job loss). It will improve labor's bargaining

power and may affect relative wages. But, in theory, strike incidence and duration should not be affected where a policy change leaves undisturbed the joint costs to both parties of a strike. See Morley Gunderson and Angelo Melino, "The Effects of Public Policy on Strike Duration," 8 *Journal of Labor Economics* 295, 297–98 (1990).

In practice, the effects of such laws may be quite different. The Canadian experience here may be instructive. An empirical study conducted by University of Toronto researchers finds that the impact of anti-"scab" legislation in Canada has been to increase, rather than decrease, both the incidence and duration of strikes:

> Certainly the most controversial policy variable is the anti-scab legislation, which prohibits the use of replacement workers during a strike. Such legislation exists only for 13 percent of our contracts, essentially in Quebec since 1977. Somewhat surprisingly, our results indicate that the legislation is associated with statistically significant and quantitatively large increases in both strike incidence and duration and hence overall strike activity. This is surprising because the legislation was introduced in part to curb picket line violence and animosity that otherwise could convert a peaceful, short-duration strike into a violent, long-duration one as picketers were confronted with replacement workers. As well, prohibitions on replacement workers should increase the cost of the strike to employers by removing their option of carrying on production by using replacement workers (albeit this may also reduce the cost to striking workers as they are under less threat of being permanently replaced and it may reduce costly picket line violence).

Morley Gunderson, Angelo Melino, and Frank Reid, "The Effects of Canadian Labour Relations Legislation on Strike Incidence and Duration," 41 *Labor Law Journal* 512, 517 (1990). See also Peter C. Cramton and Joseph S. Tracy, *The Use of Replacement Workers in Union Contract Negotiations: The U.S. Experience, 1980–1989*, NBER Working Paper No. 5106 (May 1995). Professors Kennan and Wilson argue that these findings are due to the fact that

> removing the firm's option to hire replacement workers increases the union's uncertainty about the firm's reservation value. In the case of screening and signaling models, this greater uncertainty generates strikes that will be longer on average, although also wage settlements will be higher.

John Kennan and Robert Wilson, *Strategic Bargaining Models and Interpretation of Strike Data*, Stanford Center on Conflict and Negotiation, Working Paper No. 5 (Dec. 1988), 35. For a contrary view, see John W. Budd, *Canadian Strike Replacement Legislation and Collective Bargaining: Lessons for the United States*, University of Minnesota Industrial Relations Center, Working Paper No. 93–08 (1993), 21–22.

These results are not necessarily inconsistent with other studies finding that U.S. strikes where permanent replacements have been hired tend to be longer than strikes where firms attempt to maintain operations by other means. See John F. Schnell and Cynthia L. Gramm, "The Empirical Relations Between Employers' Striker Replacement Strategies and Strike Duration," 47 *Industrial and Labor Relations Review* 189 (1994). It is not clear whether use of replacements prolongs strikes, or whether firms use or threaten to use replacements where they anticipate a long, intractable dispute. Because these studies do not control for all of the relevant characteristics of the parties contributing to the nature of the dispute between them, the correlations found between strike duration and use of replacements may simply "reflect a tendency on the part of employers expecting or actually experiencing long strikes to announce the intention to hire, or actually hire, permanent replacements." Id. at 203.

3. *Striker Replacement Laws in Other Countries.*

a. *Great Britain.* Among decentralized bargaining systems somewhat similar to the United States, there is considerable variation in the rules governing strikes. Great Britain's law is not materially different with respect to the reinstatement of economic strikers. The Industrial Relations Act of 1971 provided limited protection against selective dismissal or selective rehiring that discriminated against union activists. The Employment Protection (Consolidation) Act of 1978 slightly expanded the protection against selective dismissal:

> It was only if the employer selectively dismissed or selectively re-engaged (for any reason—not just union membership or activities as before) any of those who had participated in the action that a complaint of unfair dismissal could be made. But even in such a case a dismissal would not necessarily be unfair for the complaint would have to be determined on established principles. And even if this were to lead to a holding of unfair dismissal, it is almost inconceivable that an employee would be successfully reinstated into his employment by a tribunal.

K.D. Ewing, *The Right to Strike* (New York: Oxford University Press, 1991), 42.

With the return of the Conservative Party to power, the Employment Act of 1982 substantially diluted the prohibition of selective dismissal by allowing employers to selectively re-engage striking workers after a period of three months had elapsed from the dismissal of the workforce, and allowing employers to dismiss only those who were on strike on the date of their dismissal, without dismissing those who had returned to work during the strike. Id. at 44–45, 57–59. The Employment Act of 1990 further narrowed the protection against selective rehiring where the workers are striking without the authorization of their union. See Sheldon Leader, *Freedom of Association: A Study in Labor Law and Political Theory* (New Haven, Conn.: Yale University Press, 1992), 194.

b. *Japan.* Japanese law appears to bar permanent replacements; see Kazuo Sugeno, *Japanese Labor Law* (Seattle: University of Washington Press, 1992), 542. But the labor relations system is based on enterprise unionism and other collaborative features that place strikes by Japanese workers, in terms of their incidence and average duration, at the low end internationally—see Tadashi Hanami, "Conflict Resolution in Industrial

Relations," in Tadashi Hanami and Roger Blanpain, eds., *Industrial Conflict Resolution in Market Economies* (Boston, Mass.: Kluwer, 1989), 210–11 & Table 3—and certainly in comparison with the United States—see Masanori Hashimoto, *The Japanese Labor Market in a Comparative Perspective with the United States* (Kalamazoo, Mich.: W.E. Upjohn Institute, 1990), 54–57 & Figs. 3.7 and 3.8.

   c. *Canada.* Several provinces and the federal labour code (as interpreted) bar use of permanent replacements; Quebec also prohibits use of temporary help to perform struck work. See Manitoba Labour Relations Act Sec.12; P.E.I. Rev. Stat. ch. L–1 (1974), amended by ch. 39, 1987 P.E.I. Acts 1665; Quebec Labour Code §§ 109.1–109.4; on the federal Canada Labour Code, see Canadian Air Line Pilots' Assn. and Eastern Provincial Airways Ltd., 5 C.L.B.R. (NS) 368 (1983). From 1993 to 1995, Ontario had a law similar to Quebec's. However, with the return of the Conservative party to power, Ontario law reverted to its pre–1993 position in limiting the job protections of employees engaged in a lawful strike to those who have made an unconditional application to return to work within six months of its commencement. See Labour Relations Act of 1995, § 80, 1st Sess., 36th Legis., Ont., 44 Eliz. II, 1995.

4. *Striker Replacement and Firm–Specific Investments by Striking Workers.* Consider Professor Estreicher's criticism of the Cohen–Wachter thesis in "Collective Bargaining or 'Collective Begging?,' " 600 n. 97:

> [The Cohen–Wachter position] is problematic on a number of grounds. First, they have no explanation for the role of unions and collective bargaining in firms not characterized by [internal labor markets (ILM)]. Second, even for ILM-type firms, they substantially overstate the role of reputation costs, particularly for firms that have changed location or operations and perhaps have less need for firm-specific worker investments in the future. Third, they fail to take into account the possibility that what may look like cheating on relational contracts for the strikers may be a good deal for a different group of workers—replacements and cross-overs—because when the latter group obtains employment during a strike, changes in product markets, changes in labor market supply or in the skills needed for these jobs may have altered that group's marginal productivity calculus. Finally, and most importantly, the Cohen–Wachter analysis—though purporting to provide a positive theory of the NLRA—does not give due recognition to the congressional intention to provide a *collective* employee check on management demands at the bargaining table.

5

The Law and Economics of Federal Labor Laws

Chapter 4 analyzed the variety of goals underlying the federal labor laws. An efficient allocation of labor resources was—at best—only one of those goals. Still, in recent years scholars have spent considerable effort analyzing the degree to which the labor laws can (best) be understood as an effort to enhance efficiency in labor markets. Even more controversially, several scholars have normatively declared that the labor laws should be interpreted so as to enhance efficiency.

Analogous claims have been made that the common law can best be understood as a set of rules that enhance efficiency. See generally Richard A. Posner, *Economic Analysis of Law*, 5th ed. (New York: Aspen Publishers, 1998). A central question with this thesis is how judges, who speak in the language of rights and justice, could create a common law that promotes efficiency. The most promising explanation is that litigants, through their decisions whether to settle cases, tend to relitigate inefficient rules more often than efficient rules, and thus, over time, the stock of efficient rules grows. However difficult the economic analysis of the common law has been, most observers find it harder to make the case that the rules in a statutory field such as labor law are or should be based on efficiency.

In the first reading, Keith Hylton examines the process by which labor-law rules achieve efficiency. He distinguishes statutory law, which he argues may or may not be efficient, from case law, which tends toward efficiency. Hylton recognizes that the initial Wagner Act passed by Congress did not promote efficiency, but he argues that later labor-law doctrines as shaped by the National Labor Relations Board (NLRB, or the Board) have evolved toward efficiency. This evolution occurs because the NLRB process, which focuses on case-by-case adjudication rather than rulemaking, is broadly similar to common law adjudication and thus has a similar tendency to reach efficient rules.

In the second reading, Stewart Schwab applies the Coase Theorem to collective bargaining. The Coase Theorem derives from an article by Nobel Prize winner Ronald Coase, "The Problem of Social Cost," 3 *Journal of Legal Studies* 1 (1960). The Theorem asserts that when bargaining costs are low, efficient or wealth-maximizing outcomes occur regardless of initial legal entitlements, because parties will bargain around inefficient legal rules. Applying the Coase Theorem to collective bargaining, Schwab argues that efficiency can result regardless of the initial set of labor laws, so long as the parties, through collective bargaining, can contract around the laws at low cost. To the extent that the Coase Theorem applies, Schwab concludes, the only appropriate arguments in these cases concern the distribution of wealth rather than efficiency.

In the third reading, Douglas Leslie examines whether NLRB rules on appropriate bargaining units make sense under various economic models of unions. The NLRB uses a multifactor test to decide whether a group of workers is appropriate for a union: these factors include the similarity of compensation, the functional integration of the firm, the centralization of labor policies, and geographical cohesion. Leslie argues that the price-theory model of unions (what we called the monopoly face in Chapter 2) cannot explain the Board's test. A relational contract model of unions does a little better, but most consistent with the Board's test is a collective-goods model of unions. The Board's test thus implicitly attempts to create a bargaining unit that furthers the ability of a union to help solve collective-goods problems in the workplace.

In the fourth reading, Michael Wachter and George Cohen argue that the labor-law rules governing bargaining over plant relocation decisions promote efficiency.

"Efficiency and Labor Law"*

KEITH N. HYLTON

I. *Introduction*

... The notion that the New Deal labor legislation which set the initial conditions for today's federal labor law may have been largely inefficient is one that I find uncontroversial. The New Deal legislation was a reaction to the Depression. We are slowly discovering that some of the legislation of that period, such as federal deposit insurance, may have been ill-advised in many respects. It would not be surprising to discover that federal labor legislation suffers from mistakes of the same order as those in the banking legislation of the New Deal period. However, I implicitly argue that the problems are not so great that we need to wipe the slate clean and start over again, as some commentators have suggested.

In this article, I examine the economic efficiency of labor law. My claim is that much of labor law seems to be efficient—in a sense that will be made precise below. I approach this issue by examining the process by which labor law develops and some important areas of labor law doctrine. The central question addressed is whether the process by which

* 87 *Northwestern University Law Review* 471 (1993).

labor law develops differs substantially from the common law process. I demonstrate that there are differences that have implications for the efficiency of labor law. But the differences do not seem to be so great as to make the efficiency thesis inapplicable to labor law. . . .

.   .   .

IV.   *Could Labor Law Be Doctrinally Efficient?*

In this part, I reexamine the traditional position in the law and economics literature that case law tends toward efficiency, while statutory law is inefficient. I also argue that the common law efficiency hypothesis is applicable to labor law.

A.   *Doctrinal Efficiency and the Statutory Versus Common Law Distinction*

One branch of the law and economics literature has distinguished statutory and case law, arguing that the former may or may not be efficient, while the latter tends toward efficiency. . . .

Two general reasons can be given for the distinction between the efficiency characteristics of statutory and case law rules. One is that statutes, unlike court judgments, are the result of majority voting, and there is a large body of literature making the point that voting can produce irrational results, in the sense of being inconsistent with standards of rational decisionmaking. The second reason for the distinction between statutory and common law is that statutes are thought to be generated by a process which can easily be exploited by informed, organized special interest groups. Provided the majority of voters are uninformed, interest groups can use the legislative process to transfer wealth to themselves. They are able to do this because intelligent voting, unlike intelligent consuming, generally requires vast amounts of information.

Because participation in the legislative process requires information, a type of collective action problem is observed. No voter is sufficiently concerned about a typical issue to inform himself about all of the relevant facts. The informational gap can be exploited by well-organized parties. For example, a statute whose main effect is to provide a competitive advantage to one set of firms may be promoted under the guise that it will help clean up the environment.

One problem with differentiating between statutory and common law is that there may be no easy distinction between the two. Much of what is referred to as statutory law is the result of judicial interpretation of statutes. Indeed, the gap-filling function of interpretation produces a body of law that may grow in scope to a point at which the statute becomes relatively unimportant in comparison.

It is an oversimplification to say that the standard economic criticism of statutory law applies to statutes alone. The literature recognizes the difficulty in distinguishing statutory and case law. A better description of the critique would suggest, roughly, that as the statutory component of any body of law becomes more important, or assumes a larger share of the relevant doctrine, the less likely it is that the doctrine in a given area can be explained on efficiency grounds. . . .

B.   *The Development of Efficient Legal Doctrine*

How is it that case law tends toward doctrinal efficiency? One of the arguments suggesting that common law tends toward efficiency is based on a negative inference: it seems unlikely that the common law could be used to subsidize or transfer wealth to a given type of litigant. One obvious reason is that common law rules seldom identify the type of litigant. The rules are typically stated in a form that grants A a right against B or all others, whether or not A happens to be of a certain economic class. More importantly, the common law process seems to be less vulnerable to exploitation than is the legislative process since it is difficult to trace the wealth effect of common law rules. Because it is hard to trace the wealth effect, it is unlikely that any party could use the process to create a subsidy for himself.

A second reason for the relative difficulty in exploiting the common law process to subsidize a particular interest group is that it is unlikely that any party can simply have its way with case law. Holmes made this clear in his discussion of the evolution of common law. The common law process gives judges few if any opportunities to create subsidies for a particular interest group. Holmes suggested that judges are bound by precedent, and where the law or the facts are unclear the question is generally submitted to the jury, not simply decided by the judge. In Holmes's model, the jury serves as a source of information. . . .

Another factor which makes it unlikely that the common law process can be used to create subsidies for a particular class of litigants is that the parties themselves will tend to litigate a certain dispute or to pursue the dispute to the appellate level only in cases in which the facts concerning legal compliance are ambiguous or the legal standard itself is unclear. In any dispute in which the legal standard and the facts concerning compliance are clear, the incentive to settle will dominate. Rubin, Priest, and Landes and Posner have presented models of common law evolution which emphasize the incentives of litigants. Efficiency in these models results largely from the behavior of litigants.

Inefficient legal rules create asymmetric stakes, or at least increase the stakes of litigation, and for this reason, tend to generate litigation. Thus, one class of parties who may have an incentive to litigate even though the rule is crystal clear will be those parties affected by inefficient legal rules. Over time, inefficient legal rules will be the subject of litigated disputes, and these rules will be overturned more often than will efficient legal rules. . . .

C. *Does Labor Law Tend Toward Doctrinal Efficiency?*

... Labor law doctrine is developed in both the NLRB and the federal courts. The Board has jurisdiction over disputes concerning representation matters and unfair labor practices. Board orders are "appealed," through efforts to seek enforcement, to the federal appellate courts. The labor statutes grant federal trial courts jurisdiction over disputes concerning the enforcement of collective bargaining agreements, that is, section 301 disputes.

Labor law disputes that generally are decided in the federal courts fall within the system described by the evolutionary model of the common law. Disputes concerning compliance with a collective bargaining agreement often require courts to interpret the provisions of the agreement. Although the collective bargaining agreement resembles something more than a contract, it is hard to see how disputes concerning compliance with such an agreement can escape an analysis using methods developed in contract cases. In section 301 litigation, courts interpret terms with respect to which one of the parties has superior information in favor of the relatively uninformed party. This is a traditional approach of contract law that is justifiable on efficiency grounds. Allowing a party with superior information regarding certain terms of a contract to impose his desired interpretation after the contract has been signed gives that party the power to change the terms of the contract ex post. Unless there is some effort to control or deter such activity, the contracting process will become more expensive as parties attempt to weed out every ambiguous term, and the increased costs of contracting will make some potentially wealth-enhancing contracts unprofitable for all parties.

One could argue that, in terms of the process, the contract interpretation cases in labor law enjoy an advantage over many other legal areas in which contract interpretation is required, such as the interpretation of insurance contracts. Arbitrators, who presumably have experience and enjoy at least some respect from both parties to the conflict, generally decide such contract interpretation cases. The deference given by federal courts to the decisions of arbitrators restricts the ability of courts to impose interpretations that are far outside of the reasonable expectations of the involved parties. Thus, the treatment of section 301 disputes is quite consistent with the efficiency theorists' notions of the common law process. Disputes that do not reach arbitration may reach the federal courts, where the terms of a collective bargaining agreement, specifically the agreement to submit disputes to arbitration, are likely to be read in favor of the relatively uninformed party. Disputes that do reach arbitration are treated deferentially in the federal courts. If arbitrators, because of their experience or information concerning the disputed issues, are capable of finding and specifying joint-wealth maximizing agreements, the regime under which section 301 disputes are decided should generate doctrinally efficient rules.

Consider a dispute over a decision by a firm to close down a plant or to subcontract work to another firm. Recent models of the bargaining process suggest that the arbitrator's role in this type of dispute is to distinguish efforts to opportunistically reduce the firm-specific rents earned by employees from sincere efforts to reduce production costs in order to stay afloat. However, this is bound to be a complicated determination, hardly one that an uninformed jury could be trusted to decide correctly. It is quite possible that the grievance procedures encouraged by the NLRA are far superior to the mechanisms provided by traditional courts. One could argue, however, that the problem with leaving things in the hands of a single arbitrator is that the decisions will depend on the preferences or mood of each individual arbitrator, which may vary more than the preferences of a typical jury. This would suggest that the process by which labor law doctrine develops generates more uncertainty than the case law process. On the other hand, review by appellate courts of arbitrators' decisions allows the system to generate doctrinal rules that define standards; the rules have the effect of limiting the discretion of the arbitrator in the same sense that appellate decisions limit the discretion of the jury in the common law process.

There are two important areas in which the development of labor law differs from that of ordinary case law in ways that have implications for the doctrinal efficiency thesis. The first is the Board itself, composed of members appointed to five year terms by the President. The President's ability to significantly alter the composition of the Board in the course of a single term generates a serious compliance problem: there is little to guarantee that Board members will respect the decisions of previous Boards. The greater likelihood that rules developed by an earlier Board will not be respected by future Boards generates litigation. The Board is, in fact, notorious for reversing itself on certain politically controversial issues when a new party comes into power and has the opportunity to control it. Though it is impossible to measure the effects, the compliance problem probably generates an enormous amount of litigation by putting a cloud of uncertainty over even the clearest doctrinal rules.

The second sense in which the labor process diverges from the common law process is the point at which the decision to litigate is made in unfair labor practice cases. Whether an unfair labor practice charge will lead to a complaint filed with the NLRB is almost entirely within the discretion of the General Counsel. This obviously differs from the common law process because in the courts, the individual plaintiff decides whether to bring suit after weighing the costs and possible rewards. The General Counsel may not file a complaint in every case in which the complainant would prefer to see one filed. And although the dearth of commentary suggests that the practice is rare, the General Counsel may proceed with litigation even when the complainant would prefer to settle. In any event, the private incentives that are important in generating doctrinal efficiency in the common law process are not at work in the same manner in unfair labor practice disputes. There is at least the possibility that enforcement could be undermined through political influence or bribery. This is not generally a problem in the common law process.

In unfair labor practice disputes, the forces that push legal doctrine toward efficiency are, it seems, not as strong or as reliable as those identified by the efficiency theorists examining the common law process. The instability of the Board generates rent-seeking litigation, and the decision to pursue an unfair labor dispute is, in part, in the hands of a government official rather than a private plaintiff. On the other hand, federal appellate courts review unfair labor practice decisions in which the Board seeks enforcement through a court order. Judicial review, though, may prevent private parties from using the process in order to transfer wealth. Therefore, it is at least possible that the forces tending toward efficiency may predominate even in the area of unfair labor practice disputes. Several commentators have noted that although the Board has the power to fashion rules directly, it relies on adjudication. The Board's reliance on adjudication, while it has been criticized because of the frequency of reversals, is an important feature that makes the process by which federal labor law develops similar to the common law process. Because the Board relies on adjudication rather than rulemaking, it essentially takes the sort of passive role toward generating law that common law courts have traditionally accepted. The benefits of such an approach ... have been underestimated in the labor law literature. An active approach such as rulemaking may generate greater clarity, but it is more vulnerable to being exploited by special interest groups. Furthermore, the clarity of rulemaking is only a short-run clarity because the Board could always decide to change the rule in the future. Under this theory, a significantly larger proportion of the rules developed by the SEC, which takes an active approach toward rulemaking, is likely to be inefficient than of those generated by the NLRB....

Notes and Questions

1. *Common Law Rules and the Haves and Have–Nots.* In describing the common law push toward efficient rules, Hylton emphasizes that the incentives of litigants to challenge rules often play a larger role than the preferences of judges. In general, litigants are more likely to litigate inefficient rules than efficient rules, because the stakes are larger. Thus, even if judges have no preference for efficient rules and only randomly deviate from precedent, the law can evolve toward efficiency. See Richard A. Posner, *Economic Analysis of Law*, 5th ed. (New York: Aspen Publishers, 1998), § 21.5.

The law evolves toward efficiency in these models, however, only when both sides have repeat players who have an incentive to change unfavorable precedents, with the side burdened by an inefficient rule having a greater incentive to litigate. Several authors have emphasized that when only one side (the "haves," to use Marc Galanter's famous terminology) is a repeat player, the law will tend to favor that side over the "have-nots," which may not be the efficient result. See Marc S. Galanter, "Why the 'Haves' Come Out Ahead: Speculations on the Limits of Legal Change," 9 *Law and Society Review* 95 (1974); Paul H. Rubin, *Business Firms and the Common Law: The Evolution of Efficient Rules* (New York: Praeger, 1983). The repeat-player concern may be less of a problem in labor law than in other areas, for unions and large employers would seem to have equal long-term stakes in labor law doctrine that favors their respective interests.

2. *Interpreting Rent–Seeking Statutes*. Professor Hylton argues that labor law will evolve toward efficiency because of the case-by-case resolution of disputes, even if the underlying statute is initially inefficient. A number of scholars have debated the more general issue of how courts should interpret statutes that are the product of deal-making between special interest groups. Under the so-called public-choice perspective, statutes do not represent a coherent set of collective choices, but rather a set of outcomes resulting from deal-making between special interest groups and the legislature. One implication is that standard statutory interpretation that attempts to find the public policy behind a statute is not possible, since courts cannot predict how a whole legislative body would have decided an issue it did not consider. Frank H. Easterbrook, "Statutes' Domains," 50 *University of Chicago Law Review* 533, 547 (1983). Judge Easterbrook urges courts to interpret statutes as if they were a contract between these interest groups and the legislature, and enforce them as such, even if it means that the public interest is not served. Frank H. Easterbrook, "The Supreme Court, 1983 Term—Foreword," 98 *Harvard Law Review* 4, 18 (1984). Professor Macey accepts Judge Easterbrook's public-choice framework, but rejects the notion that courts should be an agent in promoting the "rent-seeking" deal-making of special interest groups. Instead, he argues that courts should actively interpret statutes to limit the benefits to special interest groups, and transform the statute into one that promotes the public interest. Jonathan R. Macey, "Promoting Public–Regarding Legislation Through Statutory Interpretation: An Interest Group Model," 86 *Columbia Law Review* 223, 250–56 (1986).

"Collective Bargaining and the Coase Theorem"*
STEWART J. SCHWAB

The dominant vision of labor law scholars is that management and labor are involved in an incessant tug-of-war. The major goal of labor law is to reduce the conflict, and thus promote "industrial peace." In creating new rules, the National Labor Relations Board (the Board) and reviewing courts typically justify their decisions by appealing to industrial peace or related national goals, rather than the partisan interests of

* 72 *Cornell Law Review* 245 (1987).

management or labor. The Board exists to regulate the inevitable warfare which underlies the labor market.

This vision of warfare and the need for Leviathan differs dramatically from the basic law and economics vision of parties bargaining peacefully over a contract. Like "industrial peace" ... for labor lawyers, "efficiency" is the ever-present term for law and economics scholars. But law and economics scholars have a much rosier view of parties' ability to achieve efficient bargains without intrusive government regulation. They see legal rules as the starting point for bargaining, but believe the parties will reach an efficient bargain regardless of where the law places the parties initially.

The law and economics perspective has important implications for labor law. This article explores how far the Coase Theorem—the centerpiece of law and economics scholarship—can be pushed in labor law. My thesis is that the Coase Theorem applies to a large and important class of labor law issues. In this class, arguments based on industrial peace are misplaced, because the law cannot promote industrial peace when the Coase Theorem applies....

I. *Industrial Peace and Efficiency* ...

The term "industrial peace," unfortunately, has become a buzz word for any argument relying on the national interest distinct from the narrow aims of labor or management. As a result, the term has become so vague and overused in labor law that it provides little guidance to disputants or decision makers. This article suggests that industrial peace can be equated with the economic notion of efficiency. Efficiency occurs when resources flow to their most valued uses, so that society obtains the maximum output from its resources: in short, an efficient system maximizes the overall social pie....

Congress's decision to use collective bargaining as the method of achieving industrial peace has important consequences. This article stresses the limited role of legal rules in furthering industrial peace. Because collective bargaining allows private parties to contract around legal rules, decision makers cannot promote the system's efficiency, or industrial peace, by adopting a particular rule.

[To illustrate his argument, Schwab discusses the *Milwaukee Spring* cases, where the National Labor Relations Board had to decide whether a firm could transfer work from its unionized plant to a nonunionized plant during the term of the collective bargaining agreement, when the agreement was silent on the precise question. In *Milwaukee Spring I*, 265 N.L.R.B. 206 (1982), the Board held that the transfer violated the Act. The Board reversed itself upon rehearing in *Milwaukee Spring II*, 268 N.L.R.B. 601 (1984), aff'd sub nom. UAW v. NLRB, 765 F.2d 175 (D.C. Cir. 1985).]

II. *Collective Bargaining Under the Coase Theorem*

. . .

A. *Effect of Milwaukee I and II on Efficiency*

... The protagonists confront two separate issues: whether to include a
go clause or a stay clause in the contract; and what wage to pay. To
benefit, bargainers must resolve both issues. The costless Coase Theorem predicts that rational bargainers will resolve the first issue by
putting the highest-valued clause in the contract because this maximizes
the total value of the bargain. The parties will reach this solution
regardless of their initial entitlements. The Theorem does not firmly
predict how the parties will resolve the second issue—dividing the
surplus created by the bargain.

The Coasean result occurs in the following manner. The union
enters negotiations with labor for sale. In addition, under *Milwaukee I*
the company cannot transfer work to avoid the contract wage unless the
agreement includes an express go clause. The union can sell this *Milwaukee I* right to the company, but recall that the company values this
right less than the union does. Suppose the parties tentatively agree on a
wage rate of $8 an hour. The company then offers to raise the wage to
$8.50 in exchange for a go clause. The union will reject this offer because
it will not trade its implicit stay clause for less than a $2 an hour
increase in wages. Only a wage above $10 would induce the union to
move from $8 and its implicit *Milwaukee I* stay clause. The company
similarly will reject any counteroffer by the union because the largest
wage increase the company will accept for a go clause is $1 an hour.
Therefore, the company will prefer the original $8 an hour to $10 an
hour with a right-to-go clause. In effect, when bargaining under *Milwaukee I* (which presumes a stay clause), once the parties tentatively agree
on a wage, no other contract can benefit both parties. In sum, given the
assumed preferences of the parties and the rule established in *Milwaukee I*, the Coase Theorem predicts that the contract will include a stay
clause and have a wage somewhere between $8 and $10 an hour.

Alternatively, suppose the parties bargain under *Milwaukee II*.
Under this rule, the company can move unless the contract specifies
otherwise. Again, suppose the parties tentatively agree on a wage of $8
an hour, with an implicit go clause. The union would accept a wage as
low as $6 accompanied by a stay clause. The company would accept a
stay clause if wages were below $7. Room for trade exists. Suppose the
union suggests lowering the wage to $6.50 in exchange for a stay clause.
The company will accept this proposal (perhaps haggling to reduce the
wage to $6), and the contract will contain an explicit stay clause. Thus,
under both *Milwaukee I* and *II* the contract will require the company to
stay during the contract term.

Nothing inherent in work relocation makes a stay clause more or less efficient than a go clause. By definition, the efficient outcome depends solely on the relative valuations of labor and management. In the above example, the stay clause is efficient because the union values it more than the company values a go clause. If relative preferences of the company and the union are reversed, so that the company values a go clause more highly, the Coasean prediction is also reversed. Under either *Milwaukee I* or *II*, the contract would allow the company to move during the contract term, the now-efficient outcome.

The Coase Theorem thus predicts that, in the absence of transaction costs, *Milwaukee I* or *II* cannot affect job security or the mobility of capital during the contract term. Instead, the parties' preferences determine the contract terms. Recall that, in justifying *Milwaukee I*, the Board proclaimed that the result promoted industrial peace by fostering contract stability. If contract stability means that the company should not be able to transfer work during the contract term, the Coase Theorem demonstrates that the Board's decision is irrelevant. Regardless of the Board's holding, the company will stay only if the union values a stay clause more than the company values mobility....

B. *Distributional Impact of Milwaukee I and II*

If law has such a limited effect, one may wonder why the parties feel so strongly about the choice of legal rules and why the decision generates such controversy. So far, I have suggested that the Board rule cannot affect the long-run efficiency of the collective bargaining agreement. The rule will, however, have a short-run and possibly a long-run distributional effect.

In the short run, a shift in the legal rule creates windfall gains and losses to parties in the midst of a contract. This applies to both the litigated contract and other contracts with similar clauses interpreted in light of the new rule. For example, when *Milwaukee II* overruled *Milwaukee I*, employers under existing contracts without express relocation clauses became better off and employees became worse off. Employers who had not bargained for an express relocation clause were suddenly free to transfer work during the contract term with no simultaneous adjustment of the wage. Conversely, workers no longer were protected by an implicit stay clause. The Board rule thus directly affected the distribution of welfare in the short run.

The more difficult question is whether a Board decision changing the legal rule permanently alters the distribution of wealth. Recall the bargaining example discussed above. Under *Milwaukee I*, the union had two things to sell: labor and its security entitlement. The example suggested that the final contract might include an $8 wage and a stay clause. Under *Milwaukee II*, the union has only its labor to sell and must bargain for job security. In that situation, I suggested that the final contract might include a $6.50 wage and an explicit stay clause. Because *Milwaukee II* gives the company more bargaining chips, the parties might settle upon a lower wage than under *Milwaukee I*, even if the stay clause will appear in the contract under either Board rule. Professor Coase asserted in his original article that entitlements affect the distribution of welfare between the parties, at least in a tort setting. That analysis might suggest that wages will be lower under *Milwaukee II* because the union must "buy" the company's right to leave by agreeing to lower wages.

Later analysts, however, have suggested that in a contract setting where all terms are negotiable, initial entitlements should not affect distribution. When a legal rule regulates only one term of a multifaceted bargain and allows parties voluntarily to reassign the entitlement, the law's power over the distribution of wealth between the parties is limited. For example, if the parties previously relied on silence in the contract, presuming that courts would construe it in a particular way, then the parties can simply include an express clause in their next contract if the law changes its interpretation of silence. This reestablishes the original allocation of entitlements and leaves the distribution of wealth undisturbed....

Ultimately, whether the assignment of entitlements affects the long-run relative welfare of unions and firms is not the primary focus of the Coase Theorem. The Theorem is primarily a prediction that unions and firms will negotiate an efficient bargain regardless of the assignment of entitlements. The Theorem does not predict whether initial entitlements alter the distribution of the surplus from bargains. Until empirical studies reveal more about actual bargaining results, one should remain somewhat agnostic about the long-run distributive effects of initial entitlements.

III. *Criticisms of the Coase Model*

... This section outlines the major criticisms of the Coase Theorem and assesses their force in the context of labor negotiations.

I stress at the outset that my point is not that the Coase Theorem applies in all circumstances, but only that it may be more valid in labor negotiations than in many other contexts. Two characteristics of collective bargaining distinguish it from many other bargaining situations to which Coasean analysis has been applied. First, the extensive government regulation of labor negotiations—capsulized in the duty to bargain in "good faith"—may minimize the transaction costs of bargaining. Second, the parties in collective bargaining have little alternative to bargaining with one another. Once the Board has certified a union as the bargaining representative, a company cannot simply leave if negotiations become difficult. Although individual employees can quit work, they cannot negotiate with the employer, either individually or in small groups.

A. *Transaction Costs*

The most fundamental criticism of the Coase Theorem is that the assumption of zero transaction costs is inaccurate in most settings. As Coase himself emphasized, initial entitlements can affect final results if bargaining is costly. When transaction costs exceed the gains from trade, bargainers will not trade resources to their most valued use.

Obviously the Coasean assumption of zero transaction costs is stylized, but the Coasean prediction will often remain accurate with a less extreme assumption. Specifically, transaction costs will not impede efficient bargaining whenever the difference in values that the union and company place on an item exceeds the costs of bargaining over the item. For example, under the *Milwaukee I* and *II* scenarios discussed earlier, the company valued a go clause at $1 an hour while the union valued the stay clause at $2 an hour, an aggregate difference of $600,000 over the life of the contract. As long as the costs of bargaining over a stay/go clause are less than $600,000, an efficient bargain will result, and the contract will have a stay clause.

Bargaining costs are likely to be lower in labor negotiations than in many other settings. The largest impediment to reaching an efficient agreement, according to many scholars, is coordinating the desires of multiple parties. The common example used for this proposition is that of homeowners bargaining with a factory over air or water pollution. In a typical labor negotiation, only two parties bargain. Thus, the most substantial transaction cost is absent when a union and a company bargain.

Other features of labor negotiations reinforce the proposition that transaction costs are low in collective bargaining. First, the specific term at issue (in *Milwaukee I* and *II*, the stay/go clause) is but one item of many on the bargaining table. Once the parties are assembled, the marginal cost of discussing an additional item is small. Second, in many cases the parties have established a stable, long-term relationship. Accumulated good will discourages the parties from bargaining too aggressively over one item in one contract. The parties may value long-term cooperation more highly than any individual contract term. Third, the representatives of the union and the company are typically experienced, skilled negotiators, able to recognize and react swiftly to cues that agreement or compromise is possible.

B. *Strategic Behavior*

I have argued that the one-on-one bargaining of labor negotiations lowers transaction costs. This bilateral monopoly can, however, create incentives for strategic behavior that may produce an inefficient contract. In a competitive market, an equilibrium price is set by the bargaining of many individual parties. In a bilateral monopoly, no clear price exists, enabling a party through threats or lies to capture for itself most of the gains from trade. To gain a larger share, one party may threaten destructive behavior. As long as the other side recognizes the threat, however, the parties can negotiate based on the fear of destructive behavior without anyone having to carry out the threat. Thus, bluffs and threats by themselves do not cause inefficiency. Only when strategic behavior actually prevents trade will it prevent efficient contracts.

Inefficiency does occur, however, when one side cannot back down after its bluff is called, and the parties fail to transfer the item to its most valued use. Indeed, commentators often cite labor strikes as an example of strategic behavior leading to inefficient bargaining. For example, suppose *Milwaukee II* controls (that is, silent agreements are presumed to include a go clause), but the union values a stay clause more than the company values the right to go. The Coase Theorem predicts that the company will trade the *Milwaukee II* right to the union. Suppose the company takes a tough bargaining stance, however, insisting on the rock-bottom wage of $4.01 in exchange for its right to a go clause. The union may call the company's bluff by striking. A strike is usually inefficient because employees on the picket line would prefer to be working for a wage/stay clause package that the company is willing to pay. For a time, at least, the parties are avoiding an efficient bargain by struggling to divide the spoils of a surplus-creating agreement.

Even when a strike occurs, the Coasean prediction of efficient bargains may be accurate. If the parties resolve the strike by including the most valued clause in the contract, efficiency will result despite the strategic behavior. For example, in *Milwaukee I* and *II*, the Coasean prediction of efficiency occurs when the parties agree to a stay clause, whether or not the union "wins" the strike. Suppose, as in the initial *Milwaukee I* and *II* example, the union values the stay clause more than the firm values the go clause. If the firm bluffs that it will never accept a stay clause, the union may counteroffer with a rock-bottom wage. As a result, the strike is averted but the firm gains nearly the entire surplus from the trade. Alternatively, if the union strikes and prevails, the firm will agree to a stay clause and also pay high wages. In each scenario, the stay clause exists, fulfilling the Coasean prediction. Only if the initial bluff ("I will never agree to a stay clause") is called, and the parties cannot transform the issue into a tradeoff with other items ("I will agree to a stay clause only in return for a rock-bottom wage"), will strategic behavior prevent the parties from agreeing on the higher-valued stay clause.

Despite the obvious presence of strikes, labor negotiations may have fewer problems with strategic behavior than do many other bargaining situations under bilateral monopoly. A major purpose of labor law is to prevent the breakdown of negotiations and encourage agreement. Unlike most other bargainers, labor negotiators are under a statutory duty to bargain in good faith. The parties cannot burn bridges or engage in other absolutist tactics, but must remain flexible. One can question the effectiveness of the Board in mandating good faith negotiations, but even the Board's incomplete supervision of the good faith requirement may make strategic behavior less problematic in labor negotiations than in other bilateral monopoly contexts.

In addition to the short-term inefficiency caused by threats, strategic considerations can create inefficiencies by inducing negotiators to lie, even if lying shrinks the overall size of the pie. To create the maximum surplus, parties must reveal their true preferences to ensure that every item goes to the party who values it the most. But if one party convincingly underrepresents the value it attaches to an item, it may capture a larger share of the surplus. Returning to the *Milwaukee II* example, suppose the union convinces the company that it would trade, at most, $1.50 in wage reduction for a stay clause. In fact, the union is willing to accept a $2 wage reduction to obtain a stay clause. Having been duped, the company is unlikely to demand $1.75 for its go clause, even though the union would, if pressed, accept such a demand. In general, then, a trade-off exists between revealing true preferences to create maximum societal surplus, and lying in order to grab the largest possible portion of the surplus. If parties follow the latter strategy, they may contradict the Coasean prediction that parties always reach efficient bargains.

The critical question, though, is whether the choice of legal rule affects parties' incentive to lie. Professor Leslie suggests Board rules might have this effect. For example, under *Milwaukee I* the union has an initial entitlement to a stay clause. It may be able to understate its valuation of a stay clause and still retain it. Under *Milwaukee II* the union must purchase a stay clause and in the process may be forced to reveal its true valuation of job security. If job security is a factor throughout the contract, the union may be forced to forgo a stay clause in order to preserve the strategic advantage of understating its preferences on job security. Under this "preference exposure theory," the Board rule may affect efficiency.

Two factors mitigate the problem of strategic lying in labor negotiations. First, labor law attempts to minimize strategic tactics by prohibiting lying during contract negotiations. Second, tradeoff between maximum surplus and maximum share occurs only when the parties bargain over items that they can divide between them. In labor negotiations, many contract terms are either/or choices. For example, in *Milwaukee II*, if the union understates its preferences so that a go clause appears more valuable than a stay clause, it has destroyed any incentive to bargain. No surplus is created, mooting the fight over dividing it . . . .

C. *The Invariance Thesis*

The Coase Theorem, as I have described it, predicts not only that bargainers will reach an efficient result (the efficiency thesis), but also that bargainers will reach the same efficient result (the invariance thesis), regardless of the distribution of initial entitlements....

The invariance thesis is subject to two basic attacks....

1. *Long-Run Effects of Legal Rules*

[Schwab argues that the Coase Theorem, as applied to labor relations, is as valid in the long run as in the short run.]

2. *Wealth Effects and Backward Steps*

The second criticism of the invariance thesis emphasizes that legal rules influence the parties' valuations of contract clauses. If so, the legal rule affects which clause is the most highly valued, or efficient, clause. When the legal rule changes, the efficient outcome changes. In support of this criticism, Professor Kelman argues that initial legal entitlements affect the values that bargainers place on goods because people treat "opportunity cost" income differently from "received" or "realized" income. If Kelman's armchair psychology is correct, a union with an implicit stay clause under *Milwaukee I* will demand more from the company to waive its right than it will be willing to pay the company to obtain a stay clause under *Milwaukee II*. Thus, Board decisions may affect the parties' valuation of the stay or go clause and ultimately influence the percentage of stay or go clauses in contracts.

The standard response to this argument is that, to the extent Kelman is correct, he has identified wealth effects.... After reducing Kelman's argument to an observation about wealth effects, his critics note that wealth effects are often insignificant.

Even when wealth effects are significant, the invariance thesis may hold if the entitlement, as often occurs in labor law, is an either/or choice. For example, in the *Milwaukee I* and *II* situation, the contract either gives the company the right to go or requires it to stay; the company cannot go a little way. In an either/or situation, wealth effects must substantially change the parties' valuations before a switch in legal rule alters the most valued or efficient outcome....

Beyond wealth effects, Kelman's argument is troubling in another way. His assertion that a union demands more to relinquish a right than it will pay to obtain a right sounds similar to the rallying cry of many unions, "No Backward Steps." Under this strategy, once the union receives an entitlement, it will not relinquish it even in return for higher wages.... If the union follows a "no backward steps" policy, a change in the legal rule might affect the outcome of contract negotiations. The invariance thesis of the Coase Theorem would then be wrong.

Whatever its strength in the abstract, the practical force of the "no backward steps" argument is limited. First, this strategy may be a bargaining tactic rather than an ultimatum. The union's supposed intransigence may simply represent a gambit intended to obtain a higher price for waiving its legal right. Second, the union may not consider agreeing to a pro-management relocation clause under *Milwaukee I* a backward step. The only thing traded away is an implicit, unwritten right to a stay clause. Prior contracts may have consistently given the firm these rights. Prior contracts, rather than initial legal entitlements, may be the benchmark for determining whether union negotiators have made backward steps. Third, the union can emphasize the gains in higher wages or other benefits in return for not insisting on its legal entitlement. The more these factors reduce the vitality of the "no backward steps" strategy, the less likely the strategy is to change the union's valuation when legal rules change. If the union does not reevaluate terms after legal rules change, the invariance thesis holds.

D. *Imperfect Information Problems*

Many formulations of the Coase Theorem require that bargainers have perfect information, including knowledge of available alternatives, prices, and, most critically, of each other's preferences. . . .

Perfect information, however, is an unnecessary assumption that makes the Coasean prediction uninteresting. If each side knew how much the other valued each item, bargaining would be infinitely simpler. Searching and signaling about synergies would evaporate. Parties would know almost automatically what clauses to put in the contract. Parties would only bargain over dividing the surplus from trade, and bluffing and lying would be impossible. The central Coasean prediction that parties search for and achieve an efficient bargain (i.e., the bargain that awards each item to the person who values it most highly) would become tediously pro forma. As long as the parties have sufficient information about alternatives to make informed choices, the Coase Theorem predicts that the parties will find the highest valued use for each item.

In general, the labor laws are designed to alleviate the problem of inadequate information. When a firm justifies its bargaining position during negotiations by claiming an inability to pay, it may be required to substantiate its claim through financial disclosures. This rule stems from labor law's explicit requirement of good faith bargaining. Whether a union negotiating nonmonetary items, such as a work transfer clause, can demand information on costs and profits is less clear.

Nevertheless, lack of information may impede efficient labor negotiations. One complication from imperfect information arises when one side's valuation depends on the other side's behavior. In the *Milwaukee I* and *II* context, for example, the union may be less able than the company to assess the likelihood that the company will find more attractive opportunities elsewhere during the three-year contract. This informational asymmetry may prevent the parties from agreeing on the most efficient clause. Suppose, for a given likelihood that outside opportunities will arise during the three-year contract, a union values job protection more than the company values flexibility. In such a case, the efficient contract would contain a stay clause. Because the union cannot independently assess the likelihood of leaving, however, it must evaluate the stay clause based on the company's behavior. The union knows that a company will accede to a minimal wage reduction for a stay clause only when the company is unlikely to leave. In such a situation, the union may discount the value of such a stay clause and reject it. Such an outcome undermines the Coasean prediction that parties will always make efficient contracts.

This asymmetrical information problem can be overstated, however. The critical question is whether the placement of the legal entitlement exacerbates the problem. In the *Milwaukee I* and *II* situation, the value each party places on a stay/go clause depends on its assessment of the economic health of the industry. The union's assessment may depend on signals it receives from management. But whether the parties negotiate under the shadow of *Milwaukee I* or *II* should not affect their valuations. If not, the invariance thesis that the legal rule does not affect whether a contract will contain a stay or go clause remains accurate, even though the parties have different amounts of information.

. . .

V. *Proper Arguments in These Cases*

Despite these criticisms of the Coase Theorem as applied to collective bargaining, this article's central argument remains viable. In cases like *Milwaukee I* and *II*, ... the power of the law to affect collective bargaining contracts is constricted by the parties' ability to bargain around Board rules. Therefore, decision makers should not justify their result by citing national policy arguments such as industrial peace. Instead, arguments justifying the distributional consequences of the decision are appropriate. As discussed earlier, legal rules in this area have short-run and perhaps long-run distributional consequences.

One legitimate argument would emphasize equalizing the bargaining strength of labor and management....

Decisions under the Act also have recognized a distributional goal that systematically favors management. The protection of "management rights" is never explicitly stated in the Act, but is universally acknowledged by the Board and courts.... Under Coasean analysis, "inherent management rights" is a relevant rationale for setting initial presumptions. The rationale is not based on a societal efficiency goal over which the law has no power, and thus offers a justification that honestly recognizes the consequences of the decision....

Notes and Questions

1. *Collective Bargaining Around Legal Presumptions.* Schwab's central claim is that parties to collective bargaining contracts can bargain around inefficient legal rules, as long as the rules are not mandatory and the problems of inadequate information and strategic bargaining are surmountable. In what types of cases is this most and least plausible? Schwab argues that an easy case is bargaining over the *Weingarten* presumption. That doctrine allows workers to have a union representative present at investigatory interviews that might lead to discipline. It is merely a presumption because the collective bargaining contract can waive this right. For a more difficult example, consider the work now/grieve later presumption that dominates labor arbitration, discussed in Katherine Van Wezel Stone, "The Postwar Paradigm of American Labor Law," 90 *Yale Law Journal* 1509 (1981) (excerpted in chapter 4). Could a union obtain a contractual clause allowing its members to walk off the job whenever it had a grievance (i.e., grieve now/work later)? If not, is the reason some impediment to bargaining or simply that the cost to employers of such a rule exceeds the gains to workers (i.e., workers are not willing to accept the wage reductions necessary to make such a rule worthwhile to employers)?

2. *Inefficiency of Yellow–Dog Contracts.* In a "yellow-dog" contract, a worker promises never to join a labor union while an employee of the firm. Until the Norris–LaGuardia Act of 1932 prohibited them, yellow-dog contracts were a prominent anti-union weapon, particularly after the Supreme Court held in *Hitchman Coal & Coke v. Mitchell*, 245 U.S. 229 (1917), that courts could enjoin a union organization drive on the grounds that it tortiously interfered with yellow-dog contracts. Richard Epstein has defended the yellow-dog contract on freedom-of-contract grounds. See Epstein, "A Common Law for Labor Relations: A Critique of the New Deal Labor Legislation," 92 *Yale Law Journal* 1357, 1370–75 (1983).

Keith Hylton has questioned the efficiency of yellow-dog contracts, arguing that "strategic coercion" can cause parties to agree to a yellow-dog contract even when it does not maximize the joint surplus of employer and employees. Hylton, "A Theory of Minimum Contract Terms, with Implications for Labor Law," 74 *Texas Law Review* 1741 (1996). Suppose workers as a group are willing to pay for the freedom to join a union. Still, it may be in each worker's individual interest to sign a yellow-dog contract for some compensation. If the majority of other workers refuse the contract, the individual worker benefits from a union and keeps the compensation. If the majority of other workers sign yellow-dog contracts, it would be a futile gesture for the individual worker to refuse to sign. Hylton defends the Norris-Laguardia Act's ban on the yellow-dog contract because it eliminates this strategic coercion.

"Labor Bargaining Units"*
DOUGLAS L. LESLIE

. . .

II. *Determinants of Labor Bargaining Units*
Employee elections conducted by the [National Labor Relations] Board

* 70 *Virginia Law Review* 353 (1984).

are the most important mechanism by which a union secures representation rights for a group of employees. The National Labor Relations Act directs the Board to conduct elections in appropriate bargaining units upon the request of a union. The Board looks at many facts to decide if a proposed unit is appropriate. When a union wins an election, however, the Act does not require the union and the firm to confine their collective bargaining to the unit in which the election was conducted. A negotiating unit may evolve that is larger or smaller than the election unit, and unions are not limited to negotiating for goods that have an impact only on employees within the unit. A bargaining agreement often affects employees outside the unit. . . .

A plausible surmise is that managers want to minimize the union's power and the costs of collective bargaining, and that they take bargaining unit positions accordingly. On this view, keeping the union out of the firm is the preferred outcome if it can be accomplished at reasonable cost. For managers, the best Board ruling usually is one that designates as the only appropriate unit one that is too large for a union to organize. . . .

B. *Theories of Optimal Bargaining Units*

1. *Unit Determinations in a Price Theory Model*

It is hard to imagine any place for a normative theory of bargaining units in a price theory model because the optimal amount of union monopoly power over wages in a competitive labor market is presumably zero, and the optimal bargaining unit is none at all. Even in an imperfect labor market involving monopsony power, where unionization might be a second-best alternative to wage competition, bargaining unit manipulation is too rough a guide to ensure that union power will be adequate to push wages to a competitive level, yet sufficiently weak so as not to push wages beyond that level. All the same, the single most important factor used by the Board in making unit determinations is that unionization is to be encouraged, despite the obvious difficulty in squaring that factor with the price theory model of unionization. . . .

After the general policy favoring unionization, the facts cited most often by the Board in passing on bargaining units are similarity of wage rates, manner of determining wage rates, hours of work, and other compensation benefits. One can group these under the term "compensation similarities." [Assume that a] union is seeking a bargaining unit of meat clerks, which the managers oppose by arguing that because of the compensation similarities the only appropriate unit includes all of the store's clerks at this location.

It is not clear how the facts cut on the bargaining unit issue. Either similarities or differences could be thought to predominate, and the

Board could approve the unit or not by emphasizing or characterizing particular facts. More important, none of the facts seem relevant if the policy is to designate the unit that optimizes the union's monopoly power over wages. According to the price theory model, the union could produce monopoly wage gains for meat clerks without affecting the wages of other clerks. Over the long run, the store may reduce the number of meat clerks, or competition may force the store out of business, but the clerks' compensation similarities do not affect these possibilities. . . .

Another factor sometimes relied on by the Board is whether the firm is "functionally integrated." The Board examines the firm's organization of production to determine if there is a continuous flow process. For the Board, such a process is one factor favoring a broad unit and disfavoring a narrow unit. The significance of functional integration appears only to be that groups of the firm's employees will be able to shut down the entire firm (one location) independently of one another. A multiplicity of unions, in separate units, each with the capability of shutting down the firm creates no more union monopoly power than does a single, location-wide unit with the same capability. Functional integration could bear indirectly on the need for demand coordination by identifying the groups of employees who are likely to have monopoly power and by channeling them into the same union. Beyond this point, the functional integration factor pours little content into the concept of optimal monopoly power.

Although functional integration may have an indirect connection to optimizing union monopoly power, the firm's organizational and supervisory structure and the frequency of employee interchange and contact lack even this connection. Whether the firm's managers determine labor relations policies at the local level or at a regional headquarters does not affect a union's monopoly power over wages; it only affects the traveling costs of collective bargaining. That employees are regularly in contact with one another and that managers often transfer employees from one job to another have no effect on a union's monopoly power. . . .

In short, the Board's bargaining unit factors are not coherent in a price theory model of unionization. Some of the factors, notably the presumption in favor of unionization, promote union monopoly power over wages. Others, such as the firm's functional integration, are either irrelevant or they diminish the union's power. The most important policy arguments to emerge from the analysis are those relating to gain-spreading and demand coordination. Some of the Board's unit factors can be tied to those arguments but other factors cannot. There is no reason to assume that the Board has had these policies in mind.

2. *Unit Determinations in a Relational Contract Market*

The relational contract model, like the price theory model, offers some insights into Board bargaining unit determinations. The Board's factors, however, no more appear to be directed at promoting the policies suggested by this model than they do those suggested by the price theory model. The statutory bargaining unit presumption favoring unionization promotes explicit relational contracting, which has the potential to reduce friction by substituting a single bilateral monopoly for many bilateral monopolies and to encourage employee cooperativeness in acquiring and transmitting firm-specific skills. The presumption does not discriminate, however, between firms on the basis of whether firm-specific skills predominate. The presumption favoring unionization also does not carry with it a rationale for refusing a union its proposed unit. One argument for denying a proposed less-than-location-wide unit is that there may be economies of scale in relational contracting. If a bargaining unit covers only a few employees, they may be unwilling to bear the contracting costs of collecting adequate information and negotiating a comprehensive agreement. A presumption favoring a single-location unit might help to alleviate this problem. If employees favor a unit smaller than location-wide, it may mean that they are willing to bear these contracting costs, or it may mean that their purpose in unionizing is wage monopolization.

In a relational contract model, firm-specific skills predominate, and wage differentials and customary rules tend to stabilize over time. The workforce tends to coalesce into "relative groups"—employees with common wage rates and working conditions. Employees in a relative group are conscious of sharing an identity of interests, among which are common expectations of how managers will treat them vis-à-vis other relative groups. The approval of a single-location unit, or the insistence by the Board on such a unit, will put several relative groups together in a single unit. It is unclear how this will affect the ability of managers to secure consent to changes in established wage differentials and customary work rules. The problem resembles the need for demand coordination in a price theory model. Relative groups will resolve their conflicts within the union rather than in a series of separate negotiations with managers. It is unclear, however, whether this will lead to more or less resistance to change.

Board use of compensation similarities as a factor in determining unit appropriateness could tend to make bargaining units correspond to relative groups, but the nature of the similarities is critical if this is to be the Board's purpose. [C]ompensation similarities are matters of characterization and emphasis. . . .

The Board's use of functional integration as a unit factor has an effect in a relational contract model similar to its effect in a price theory model. Functional integration means that two or more groups have power to shut down the firm. In the price theory model, the plausible concern was demand coordination; in the relational contract model it is similar. Assume that one relative group, with power to shut down the firm by a strike, unionizes, while another relative group remains nonunion. Should the unionized group seek to alter historical wage differentials, managers will have difficulty maintaining the cooperativeness of nonunion employees. This problem may be more serious when two unions separately represent two relative groups, each with the power to close down the firm. The two unions may play "leap-frog" with wage differentials and make inconsistent demands with respect to customary work rules. Forcing the two relative groups into a single bargaining unit tends to promote more comprehensive relational contracting and to encourage settlement within the union of conflicts between groups. Leaving these conflicts unsettled is more serious if the firm is functionally integrated and if more than one group can shut down the firm in support of its demands. The critical question is whether conflicts between relative groups settle more easily within a single union or through negotiation between unions....

Analyzing bargaining units in a relational contract model does not share the deep contradiction of a similar inquiry in a price theory model. All the same, the analysis is unsatisfying, not because the model is inaccurate, but because the effects of unionization are so uncertain. Unionization may facilitate comprehensive relational contracting with its attendant advantages, but the effects of alternative bargaining structures are unclear. In any event, there is no reason to conclude that the Board has developed its bargaining unit criteria to promote policies that presuppose a relational contract market. Thus, although some of the Board's factors are likely to influence bargaining by clustering or separating relative groups, this does not appear to have been a conscious choice by the Board.

3. *Idealized Outputs of Collective Goods*

In the previous sections I explored whether the attributes of the labor market, as described by two models, suggest theories of optimal bargaining units. I now consider whether there is an output of collective goods that is on quality or quantity grounds superior to some other output and, if so, whether the Board's bargaining unit criteria tend to promote superior outputs. The central argument is that a union producing collective goods for its members is in some, but not all, respects like a city producing public goods for its citizens. I begin by discussing certain features of the production of public goods in order to show why the coercive power of the state is thought necessary and to show what is meant by an optimal level of public goods production.

a. *Optimal Level of Public Goods*

A city chooses which public goods to produce at what levels of production. It is the nature of a public good that it is too expensive to exclude people from enjoying the good once it is produced. An individual faced with a choice of producing a public good will, ignoring free-rider problems, produce the good when the benefits he would receive outweigh his costs of production. A second individual, now benefited by production of this public good, will make a similar individualized calculation to decide whether to pay the costs of increasing production. If many enjoy the good, the ultimate level of production resulting from these individualized calculations is likely to be far less than the level that a government that summed the value of the good for all the beneficiaries and adjusted the level of production accordingly would produce. There might be various notions of what constitutes optimal production by the government, depending on one's normative perspective. By optimal production, I mean that which duplicates the result that would occur if purely voluntary cooperation were costless, preferences were honestly revealed, and contributions to costs (taxes) were made according to benefits received.

If the government's coercive power does not reach all those who benefit from a public good's production, or if it reaches and taxes some who do not benefit, the optimal level of production will not be reached. Failure to sweep in all the beneficiaries results in underproduction, and it allows some people to enjoy the benefits of the public good for free. When the government taxes nonbeneficiaries, public goods are overproduced and beneficiaries do not shoulder the full costs....

b. *Optimality of Collective Goods in Choosing Bargaining Units*

It is possible to talk in terms of an optimal provision of public goods, and this notion of optimality is relevant to bargaining units. The argument grows from an analysis of the "publicness" of public goods—that is, the degree to which the members of a group share the costs and the benefits of the goods; its shortcoming is that it tells us nothing about the normative qualities of any particular public good. In this theory, there are advantages in having three groups be coextensive: those who decide which public good will be produced and at what level; those who will benefit from the public good; and those who will pay the direct and indirect costs of producing the good (in other words, those who prefer that the good not be produced). I refer to this as "coextensive grouping." Coextensive grouping minimizes positive and negative externalities and improves the chances that the collective good will neither be overproduced nor underproduced. It also minimizes the probability that production of the good will result in an unintended wealth redistribution. Coextensive grouping is the ideal for optimal production, but the costs of separate governments for each public good and the costs of setting individualized taxes for everyone receiving a benefit or suffering a detriment, no matter how small, are likely to be too high. A citizen might agree to a taxing and decision scheme spread across time and across groups if he thought that he would be extra-benefited by the production of some goods and under-benefited by the production of others, that these effects would fall randomly, and that overall there would be an excess of benefits over costs to him.

A union produces collective goods for workers, just as a city produces public goods for its citizens, but unions differ from cities in several critical ways. There is an important distinction between cities and unions with respect to overproduction. When the taxed group is larger than the group that benefits from a public good, there will be a tendency to overproduce the public good. It is unclear that this is so when a union produces public goods by striking a firm. Suppose a union's bargaining demand is for a guarantee against discharge without just cause. The value of this guarantee over the life of the agreement is $500 to each of the ten employees in the negotiating unit. A strike over this demand will shut down the firm, and the predicted cost of the strike is $400 in lost wages per employee. Twenty employees outside the unit (who will not enjoy the guarantee even if the strike is successful) will also be put out of work by the strike. It is true that the wages lost by the twenty nonunit employees are costs of producing the collective good, but there is no reason to believe that the failure of the union to internalize these costs leads the union to strike if it otherwise would not do so. It does not matter to purely self-interested union members whether twenty (or 1000) other workers are affected by the strike, unless that fact happens to put additional pressure on the managers to capitulate to the union's demands.

Another respect in which cities and unions differ is that although the residents of a city may be under the coercive control of several governments, there is no formal equivalent of these separate governments regarding workers. Several unions may have bargaining rights at a firm, but only one union will represent any particular employee. Perfectly coextensive grouping at the workplace would require a separate formal bargaining unit for each collective good. Current law does not permit such a scheme. To do so would cause a host of problems in any event.

Because of the ways in which unions must charge for collective goods, workers will want to overconsume them. Cities spread the costs of producing public goods in a variety of ways, depending on the good. Unions tend only to charge per capita taxes. Because unions produce collective goods primarily by exercising collective voice and by using or threatening to use monopoly power, employees pay production costs in the form of dues and in the losses from strife (strikes, for example). Dues are usually uniform across the membership. Although a union may calculate dues amounts by hours worked, it will not assess dues according to the benefit a particular worker receives from the array of collective goods. Strikes and other forms of strife also approximate a per capita tax, and, as with any per capita tax, the impact on a particular worker depends on such individual characteristics as family obligations and savings. A union could charge for some goods according to the benefit derived by an individual employee. It could, for example, charge for use of the grievance and arbitration procedure, but unions rarely do this. As a result, employees will want to overconsume the good and the union will look for another way to limit consumption. . . .

c. *Relationship Between the Norms of the Collective Goods Model and NLRB Factors*

The collective goods model suggests a logic to some of the Board's bargaining unit criteria. The model suggests a rationale for the labor statute's pro-union presumption, because without unions, the model says, many workplace collective goods would not be produced at all. The election procedures also fit the model. They permit employees to act on their estimate of whether the costs of producing workplace collective goods outweigh their predicted benefits. One might dispense with the unit appropriateness requirement on the ground that the goods produced in a suboptimal unit are better than no collective goods at all. One might retain the requirement, however, because an underinclusive bargaining unit may preclude the unionization later of a more optimal unit.

The ideal bargaining unit policy in a collective goods model would have the Board look at the range of collective goods likely to result from unionization of a firm and approve proposed units that best approximate coextensive grouping. Coextensive grouping facilitates preference revelation, minimizes externalities, and prevents unintended wealth redistributions. Unfortunately, this approach may be impractical. It is difficult to predict which collective goods an organized unit is likely to produce and whether the goods will affect nonunit employees. It is especially difficult to assess the relative importance of particular goods when they point to inconsistent groupings. . . .

Although the Board gives no reason for considering compensation similarities, their use fits the collective goods model well. When these similarities are present, employees are more likely to share preferences for particular collective goods. Even when similarly situated employees do not have identical preferences, the similarities may make it easier to discover strategic overstatement and understatement of preferences. Considering similarities in determining bargaining units may reduce externalities. For example, unionized employees may force a firm to change its method for determining a wage rate, even though the firm's nonunion workers prefer that the method not be changed. The effect on the nonunion employees is a negative externality, a cost of collective action not considered by the union. Similarities are thus a rough guide to the impact unit, and it is because preferences do differ that it is important for those who will be affected by the collective goods to have a voice in their production.

The Board's use of geographical separation as a bargaining unit factor probably has a similar effect. Wide geographical separation makes it less likely that there will be externalities in collective goods production. This is so whether wages, hours, and working conditions would, absent unionization, be dictated by local labor markets or by relational contract considerations. Put more simply, where employees are widely separated, it is unlikely that a collective good produced by a union at one location will affect employees at another. When employees are widely separated, moreover, it may be difficult to communicate preferences....

On the bargaining unit question, the collective goods model is more satisfying than the price theory or relational contracts models because coextensive grouping, although too costly in its idealized form, suggests a basis for bargaining unit policy. Some of the Board's unit factors square well with this model. Others do not. It bears repeating that the collective goods model is not a description of labor markets, but is a model for analyzing features of the collectivization process. Because it does not purport to say anything about the normative qualities of particular collective goods that a union chooses to produce, nor anything about the fairness of the means a union adopts, the model is limited....

Notes and Questions

1. *Bargaining Units as Cartel Behavior*. Richard Posner disputes Leslie's analysis that the rules governing bargaining units enhance the collective-voice aspects of unions. To the contrary, says Posner, NLRB rules enhance the inefficient cartel power of unions:

> The design of the electoral unit in representation election—the bargaining unit as it is called—is critical.... Consistently with the law's policy of promoting worker cartels, the Board generally certifies the smallest rather than largest possible unit. Transaction costs among workers are lower the fewer the workers and the more harmonious their interests ..., while the benefits of unionization are greater the smaller the unit is relative to the total employment of the firm.... Of course, the unit must be important enough to the work of the firm to be able to make a credible threat to strike, but if the unit really is distinct, this condition can be satisfied even though the unit is small.

Richard A. Posner, *Economic Analysis of Law*, 5th ed. (New York: Aspen, 1998), 355.

2. *Narrow Unit Myopia*. Narrow units can be problematic, even if they promote union organization and reduce intra-group conflict. Narrow units, almost by definition, do not reflect the interests of the entire workforce. Unions representing the interests of a craft group or of production workers become a faction because they do not internalize the perspective of other worker groups affected by their policies.

"The Law and Economics of Collective Bargaining: An Introduction and Application to the Problems of Subcontracting, Partial Closure, and Relocation"*

MICHAEL L. WACHTER and GEORGE M. COHEN

. . .

II.   The Firm's Adaptation to a Decline in Product Market Conditions: An Internal Labor Market Approach

This part applies the internal labor market model to a problem that has become increasingly important in labor law: the need for a firm to respond to a decline in the product market through subcontracting, partial closure, or work relocation. In the internal labor market model, the firm's adaptation to changing market conditions raises the inherent dilemma of efficient labor contracting. . . . The allocation of responsibilities that is most efficient is one that gives the firm the entitlement to decide on the scale and scope of operations in the depressed product market. That entitlement recognizes the firm's cost advantage in gathering and adjusting to new product market information. At the same time, the efficient entitlement must also restrict the firm's ability to act strategically.

The "sunk-cost-loss rule," defined and explained in this part, accomplishes the above task. The economic literature on efficient labor market contracts suggests that the sunk-cost-loss rule is one of the efficient, implicit contractual terms found throughout internal labor markets in both union and nonunion sectors. The rule can be interpreted as one that the parties themselves would write in a low-transaction cost setting. The rule permits changes that are consistent with joint profit maximization, while preventing moves that are profitable to the firm only because of strategic gains at the expense of the workers.

This article maintains that the labor law rules governing subcontracting, partial closure, and work relocation are compatible with the sunk-cost-loss rule. Although it has not been explicitly stated by either the Board or the courts, the rule explains the economic intuition underlying recent legal decisions. Because the economic rule indicates a common (if unrecognized) thread among recent major court and Board decisions, a fuller understanding of it can better focus the legal analysis of new cases.

A.   The Sunk–Cost–Loss Rule

The sunk-cost-loss rule is a rule of thumb that assigns to firms the entitlement to respond to changes in product market conditions, while at the same time limiting the channels through which the firm can adjust

---

* 136 *University of Pennsylvania Law Review* 1349 (1988).

to these changes. Under the sunk-cost-loss rule, the firm has broad power to determine the scale and scope of its operations. The entitlement is intermediate, rather than absolute, because the firm must accept a sunk cost loss in the process of reducing its total labor costs, or wage bill.

The sunk cost loss suffered by the firm is the loss of expected profits accruing to the firm's sunk investments in labor (through specific training and monitoring) and in physical capital. The sunk-cost-loss rule deters strategic behavior by both parties. The firm is less likely to act strategically, by expropriating the workers' deferred compensation, if in order to cut its wage bill the firm must simultaneously suffer lost expected profits. In addition, workers are less likely to retaliate strategically by increasing monitoring costs because the sunk cost loss incurred by the firm provides objective evidence to the workers that supports the firm's claim of a product market decline.

Ideally, workers would be able to verify a firm's sunk cost losses by observing the reduced profits and output associated with a decline in the firm's product market. But these changes may be difficult to measure directly. What can be verified are the sunk cost losses associated with investments in the firm's inputs, which, when combined with the firm's production technology, create the output. The two main categories of inputs are labor, or total hours (H), and capital (K). Thus, proxy variables representing H and K enable workers and adjudicative bodies to test for lost profits without the need to examine the firm's balance sheet.

A major variant of the sunk-cost-loss rule is the W * H test. The W * H test requires the firm to reduce its wage bill (W * H) through a reduction in total hours (H) rather than the wage rate (W).The firm can cut W without incurring a sunk cost loss; therefore, allowing the firm to make unilateral changes in W would not deter strategic behavior.

When a firm suffers a decline in the demand for its product, it must retrench by cutting either output or marginal costs, or some combination of the two. If marginal costs were reduced through a reduction in wage rates, profits and output could remain unchanged and the firm would incur no sunk cost loss. If the firm had the entitlement to cut wages, therefore, it would have an incentive to fabricate or overstate the decline in the demand for its product and could actually increase its profits. Thus, the firm could behave strategically by seizing the deferred compensation owed to its workers. Of course, the firm would not lower wages below the opportunity wage (OW), net of the costs of finding a new job, because the workers would then quit, but the firm would have an incentive to lower W to just above OW.

If output were reduced, in contrast, then hours of work and profits would decrease from previous levels and the firm would incur a sunk cost loss. Since any overstatement of the degree of product market decline would cause the firm to reduce its output and profits below profit-maximizing levels, the firm is deterred from engaging in strategic overstatement of a decline in its product market. In this sense, the sunk-cost-loss rule has important self-enforcing qualities.

But a further restriction is needed.... [T]he firm may employ experienced workers who are in the recoupment phase of their investment in training and monitoring.... And the firm may also employ workers on whom the firm is recouping past investments.... Given an unrestricted entitlement to decrease total H, the firm ... could reduce its average wage rate, thus disguising a reduction in W by using its entitlement to set H.

To avoid this potential for strategic behavior in adjusting H, the sunk-cost-loss rule forces the firm to follow a previously agreed upon schedule, typically based on seniority, which provides an ordering of layoffs. A seniority schedule requires the firm to lay off those workers in whom the firm is investing or recouping before it can lay off those workers who themselves are recouping. Thus, a seniority schedule effectively means that the firm increases its average wage as it makes layoffs. Such seniority provisions control recalls as well as layoffs: if the firm were to lay off senior workers owed deferred compensation, they would have to be recalled first if the firm increased its output in a future period....

As the next section demonstrates, the W * H test combined with the seniority schedule successfully distinguishes on-site subcontracting (an impermissible cut in W) from partial closure (a permissible cut in total H). In certain complex cases, however, the seniority schedule provides an incomplete buffer because it does not apply across all relevant workers. These cases involve shifting work to an off-site subcontractor or relocating work to a different plant. Because the seniority schedule across plants is often incomplete, the firm may be able to disguise strategic cuts in W. That is, all workers, including those owed the most deferred compensation ..., might be laid off at one plant, while workers on whom the firm is recouping ... were retained at a second plant or by a subcontractor. The self-enforcing properties of the W * H test are thus reduced in multiplant cases in which the different plants are not connected by cross-plant seniority provisions.

In these cases, a second test, the K test, is used to supplement the W * H test. The K test focuses on physical capital (K) inputs, such as plant and equipment. Under the K test, a firm is presumed to have incurred a sufficient sunk cost loss when it loses the value of the capital stock used by the workers in the affected plant. The K test imposes a second buffer, similar to that created by the seniority schedule: the firm must lose the plant-specific value of its physical capital, that is, the quasi-rents from this capital, before it can cut its labor costs.

The K test has self-enforcing properties similar to the W * H test. In a conjectural setting, workers agree to deferred compensation while the firm agrees to post a bond not only in the form of its investment and return on junior workers in the plant, but also in the value of the firm's physical capital used in the plant. The contract is self-enforcing to the extent that the buffers represented by both the junior workers and the physical capital are greater than the deferred compensation owed to the senior workers.

When a decline in the product market begins, the firm starts discharging its junior workers as, at the same time, the economic value of the firm's capital investment begins to decline. By the time the product market has declined enough to lead to an H cut affecting workers in the [their recoupment] stage, the junior workers will have already been laid off and the capital equipment will typically have a much reduced value; this means the buffers will have vanished. Hence the W * H and K tests would be satisfied when the firm has no junior workers remaining in the idled plant and the remaining K equipment is not transferred to the new plant, but is idled. Alternatively stated, relocation or off-site subcontracting is more likely to be strategic to the extent that workers junior to the senior worker at the first plant are retained at the subcontractor's plant or transferred to the firm's second plant and capital equipment is transferred or sold for close to its use value in the closed plant.

B. *The Sunk–Cost–Loss Rule and the Protection of Default Entitlements*

The sunk-cost-loss rule is an economic rule, not a legal rule. Fashioning labor law principles from the sunk-cost-loss rule requires integrating the rule into the framework of default entitlement settings developed in the previous part. Three cases must be differentiated: conjectural cases; nonconjectural cases covered by the contract; and nonconjectural cases not covered by the contract. The sunk-cost-loss rule provides the legal default setting only for the third case: a nonconjectural situation in which the collective agreement is either silent or ambiguous.

The sunk-cost-loss rule plays no direct role in conjectural cases because no sunk cost loss has yet occurred, and, in any case, there is less need to restrict the use of bargaining rules. In the conjectural stage, there is no issue of whether a product market decline has occurred; both parties agree that they are bargaining over future contingencies. Consequently, the firm has less asymmetric information that it can use strategically. Additionally, the sunk-cost-loss rule does not affect cases in which the collective agreement contains explicit allowances of or restrictions on the firm's means of adapting to product market conditions. The parties may explicitly adopt or override the sunk-cost-loss rule in the collective agreement. If the parties write explicit contingent agreements in the conjectural stage, then, in the nonconjectural stage, the Board and the courts protect with property rules the specific contingent entitlements "contained in" the collective bargaining agreement. The contract terms must, however, be sufficiently specific in defining the relevant contingency and the permitted response to ensure that the terms show a conscious attempt by the parties to create contingent entitlements. . . .

III. *An Application of the Sunk–Cost–Loss Rule to Leading Labor Law Cases*

. . .

1. *Fibreboard*

Fibreboard Paper Products Corp. v. NLRB[, 379 U.S. 203 (1964).]. A firm decided to subcontract for plant maintenance work upon expiration of its collective bargaining agreement, which provided for automatic renewal absent notice to modify or terminate the contract. The union workers had performed the maintenance work for over twenty years. The firm claimed that the maintenance work had become too costly and that an independent contractor could do the work more cheaply. The firm did not consult or bargain with the union about its decision to subcontract nor did it give the contractually required notice.

The Supreme Court held that the firm committed an unfair labor practice by not bargaining over the subcontracting decision, which the Court deemed a mandatory subject of bargaining. . . .

In an influential concurrence, Justice Stewart accepted this economic interpretation of the firm's subcontracting decision. According to Justice Stewart, "All that is involved is the substitution of one group of workers for another to perform the same task in the same plant under the ultimate control of the same employer." Nevertheless, Justice Stewart attempted to limit some of the broad language in the majority opinion. He argued that mandatory bargaining rules should not be applied to managerial decisions that "lie at the core of entrepreneurial control," including decisions concerning "what shall be produced, how capital shall be invested in fixed assets, or what the basic scope of the enterprise shall be."

In the context of the internal labor market model presented in the last two parts, both opinions in *Fibreboard* are consistent with the sunk-cost-loss rule. The economic effect of the subcontracting in *Fibreboard* is a cut in the wage rate (W) without a reduction in total hours (H). Although the firm reduces the hours of work of its own workers, it maintains H and hence its total output and revenue by buying labor services through a subcontractor. In addition, although the firm does not change the wage rate it pays to its remaining workers, substituting the lower wage employees of a subcontractor to do the "same work under similar conditions of employment" effectively reduces the firm's average W across total H. By reducing the average wage rate and maintaining total hours (including those of the subcontractor), a firm engaged in such subcontracting violates the W * H test and therefore the sunk-cost-loss rule.

The critical point is that the subcontracting firm can cut labor costs without incurring any sunk cost losses. Because the potential for strategic behavior in such a situation is great, the parties in a low transaction cost setting would not assign to the firm the unilateral right to engage in *Fibreboard*-type subcontracting. Thus, the default setting implied by the sunk-cost-loss rule would be a bargaining rule and not a property rule entitlement allowing the firm to subcontract in this way.

Justice Stewart's concurrence, however, implicitly recognizes that subcontracting can be a nonstrategic means of adjustment and that, consistent with the sunk-cost-loss rule, there may be situations in which a firm contemplating subcontracting to reduce its labor costs could be deterred from behaving strategically. For example, if the subcontracting results in a change "in the basic scope of the enterprise" (a reduction in H in our terminology), the firm might incur a sunk cost loss large enough to verify that the subcontracting was efficient rather than strategic. Similarly, if a change in "invest[ment] in fixed assets" accompanies the subcontracting, the firm may suffer a substantial sunk cost loss from outdated physical capital that the firm abandons or sells at a value substantially below replacement cost. In contrast, if a firm were allowed to replace senior workers at its plant with junior workers of the subcontractor, or transfer all of its physical capital to the subcontractor, there would be neither a change in basic direction nor an investment in fixed assets and thus no sunk cost loss. Presumably Justice Stewart would have construed this type of subcontracting as a mandatory subject of bargaining.

2. *First National Maintenance*

The second Supreme Court case [*First National Maintenance Corp. v. NLRB*, 452 U.S. 666 (1981),] confirmed the Court's implied willingness to allow a firm to act unilaterally in response to market declines when the firm incurs a sunk cost loss. First National Maintenance, which performed maintenance services for other businesses, laid off all the workers assigned to a nursing home when First National terminated its maintenance contract with the home. The cancellation of the contract resulted not directly from labor costs, but from a dispute over the amount of the fee to be paid above labor costs. Although the newly elected bargaining representative requested bargaining over First National's decision to terminate the nursing home contract, First National refused.

The Supreme Court held that First National did not have to bargain over the "decision" to terminate the maintenance contract with the nursing home and to lay off the workers employed under that contract. In making this determination, the Court found controlling the fact that the firm's decision "involv[ed] a change in the scope and direction of the enterprise." On the other hand, the Court ruled that the firm had to bargain over the "effects" of the partial closing.

Thus, the Court gave the firm an entitlement protected by a property rule to lay off workers when it partially closed its operations. Largely adopting Justice Stewart's analysis in *Fibreboard*, the Court formulated the following balancing test: "bargaining over management decisions that have a substantial impact on the continued availability of employment should be required only if the benefit, for labor-management relations and the collective-bargaining process, outweighs the burden placed on the conduct of the business."

In applying this test, the Court can be viewed as having implicitly analyzed the costs of bargaining rules compared with those of property rules in nonconjectural cases. The Court discussed three ways in which property rule entitlements were relatively less costly than bargaining rules. First, the Court recognized the potential for strategic behavior by the union under a bargaining rule: "Labeling this type of decision mandatory could afford a union a powerful tool for achieving delay, a power that might be used to thwart management's intentions in a manner unrelated to any feasible solution the union might propose." Second, the Court acknowledged management's "need for speed, flexibility, and secrecy in meeting business opportunities and exigencies," which mandatory bargaining and its informational requirements would render difficult. Finally, the Court noted the remaining protections available to the union under a property rule, such as effects bargaining, mandatory bargaining in the conjectural stage, and prohibition of decisions based on antiunion animus.

Given this implicit balancing of property rules versus bargaining rules, the Court attempted to distinguish the partial closure situation in *First National Maintenance* from the subcontracting decision in *Fibreboard*. The Court argued that the "decision to halt work at this specific location represented a significant change in petitioner's operations, a change not unlike opening a new line of business or going out of business entirely." The Court contrasted such a decision with a decision "to replace the discharged employees or to move that operation elsewhere;" the Court, however, did not explain satisfactorily the basis for its distinction....

The sunk-cost-loss rule articulates the distinction that provides a principled rationale for the Court's ruling in *First National Maintenance*. The economic effect of a partial closure is to cut the level of employment, and therefore the level of production. This drop in production makes the partial closure similar to "going out of business" and not similar to "replacing discharged employees." Both subcontracting and partial closure reduce the wage bill ($W * H$), but *Fibreboard*-type subcontracting does it by reducing the wage rate (W), while partial closure does it by reducing the size of the labor force (H) in accordance with the seniority schedule. Thus, only partial closure satisfies the W * H test. . . .

Notes and Questions

1. *Bargaining Rules vs. Consent*. Consider, as Wachter and Cohen do, the situation where the employer has engaged in strategic behavior to defeat deferred-compensation investments by senior workers in high-cost plants. Why do the authors assume that a bargaining duty is sufficient in this situation, rather than a rule that would require the union's consent? Note that in the Wachter–Cohen account of internal labor markets, if workers' firm-specific investments are subject to expropriation by the employer's strategic behavior, unions will seek to compensate for this risk by insisting on high present wages in lieu of a deferred-compensation system which might have yielded a more efficient utilization of firm resources.

2. *Self–Policing Claims and the W * H Test*. Under Wachter and Cohen's "sunk-cost-loss" rule, a firm can change the scale and scope of operations without bargaining so long as the change forces the firm to lose its fixed investments. Often the issue arises when the firm wants to cut labor costs because of bad business conditions, and must decide between wage cuts and layoffs. According to the W*H variant of the sunk-cost-loss rule, the firm must bargain before reducing wages but can unilaterally reduce hours. The reason is that the firm's decision to lay off workers is self-policing: the firm loses its sunk investments and cannot make profits if it lays off workers when times are good. Stated more colorfully, the firm shoots itself in the foot when it lays off workers when times are good. On the other hand, a union rightfully is suspicious of the firm's claim that bad business conditions require wage cuts, because wage cuts increase firm profits even when times are good. The test mandates bargaining in such situations.

3. *Plant Closing Literature*. For other law-and-economics articles that examine bargaining over plant closings, see Armen A. Alchian, "Decision Sharing and Expropriable Specific Quasi–Rents: A Theory of *First National Maintenance v. NLRB*," 1 *Supreme Court Economic Review* 235 (1982); Benjamin Duke, "Note, Regulating the Internal Labor Market: An Informa-tion–Forcing Approach to Decision Bargaining Over Partial Relocations," 93 *Columbia Law Review* 932 (1993); and Jeffrey D. Hedlund, "Note, An Economic Case for Mandatory Bargaining over Partial Termination and Plant Relocation Decisions," 95 *Yale Law Journal* 949 (1986).

Part III

Legal Regulation of Employment Contracts

For much of this century, labor unions were thought to be the primary means for improving working conditions and benefits of workers. The core problem with the "unregulated" labor market, under this view, was the inequality of bargaining power between individual workers and employers. The policy solution was to enhance, within certain limits, worker bargaining power by fostering and controlling collective action. Labor law can be seen as a regulation of the *process* by which actual workplace conditions and benefits are determined. With strong unions, it was commonly thought, government did not need to specify the substantive terms of the labor market.

Today, with the power of private-sector unions at a low ebb, collective bargaining is no longer seen as the primary solution to labor market problems. Instead, substantive government regulation of the workplace has come to the fore. This substantive or direct regulation of the workplace is now called employment law, as distinct from labor law, which regulates labor unions and collective bargaining.

Part III provides an introduction to the leading issues in employment law. We begin, in Chapter 6, with the basic justifications for legal intervention in the employment market. Chapter 7 turns to legal regulation of termination of workers. Chapter 8 surveys two areas where employment law has been particularly important—minimum wage legislation and the regulation of pensions.

197

6

Mandating Minimum Terms

An "unregulated" labor market may create outcomes that policy makers find unacceptable. Some workers become unemployed; others earn too little to sustain a decent living for themselves or their dependents; others have no savings for retirement; others are maimed or killed while working. The law has intervened to ameliorate these outcomes, usually by mandating that employers provide certain minimum benefits and working conditions to their workers. For example, employers must contribute to unemployment insurance, pay at least a minimum wage, follow funding and disclosure requirements if they want favorable tax treatment for their pension programs, and meet detailed regulations governing workplace health and safety. Often these regulations are justified on the ground that individual workers have too little bargaining power and therefore need government protection from employers who would otherwise exploit them.

Advocates of these employment laws must counter what Steven Willborn calls the "standard economic objection" to legal interference with private contracts. The standard economic objection is that free contracting through well-functioning markets maximizes overall welfare, and regulation harms all parties to the contract. The "standard" way of countering this objection is to identify some failure or imperfection in the labor market, and argue that government regulation works better than the imperfect market in serving the needs of workers. It is important to recognize that this is a two-part argument: (1) the market solution reaches undesirable results; and (2) government intervention will improve results. Advocates of employment laws who simply point out a market failure, without recognizing that government intervention may create problems of its own outweighing any attendant benefits, succumb to the "Nirvana fallacy" of assuming that government intervention will always provide optimal solutions.

In our first reading, Professor Willborn articulates the standard economic objection and catalogs ways in which labor markets fail—and thereby ways in which the standard economic objection can be overcome. In the second reading, Stewart Schwab argues that unequal bargaining power is an incoherent justification for employment regulation. In the third reading, Lawrence Summers examines what form government intervention should take. In particular, he compares regulations that mandate that employers provide certain benefits with government programs that provide those benefits directly.

"Individual Employment Rights and the Standard Economic Objection: Theory and Empiricism"*

STEVEN L. WILLBORN

In the abstract, effective minimal terms provide a benefit to workers and impose a cost on employers. All other things being equal, when a minimal term is added to the wage package, both the wage cost to the employer and the effective wages of the workers go up. Minimal terms, at least in the short run, are the equivalent of a wage increase.

. . . One part of the standard objection to minimal terms . . . is that minimal terms do not confer any benefits on workers as a class. Any benefits received by one set of workers are paid for (and often more than paid for) by other workers in unemployment.

The effects of minimal terms . . ., however, are not stable. The excess supply of labor creates competition between workers for the available jobs and, as a result, tends to force the wage level back down to equilibrium. Whether the wage actually moves back to (or at least closer to) the equilibrium level depends on whether the employer can avoid the minimal term which effectively raised the wage level by making a compensating change in another part of the wage package. That is, an employer may be able to avoid a minimal term by offsetting the effective wage increase caused by the minimal term with an effective wage decrease in another part of the wage package. For example, a minimal term requiring employers to pay workers for maternity or paternity leave would be avoidable if employers reduced the wages of workers by an amount equivalent to the cost of the required leave program. Some minimal terms may not be avoidable. Minimum wage laws, for example, effectively apply only to low-wage, low-benefit jobs, so offsetting the wage increase by an effective wage decrease in another part of the wage package may not be possible. Most minimal terms, however, should be avoidable, at least in the long run. Even if employers cannot make compensating changes immediately, as in the maternity or paternity leave example, they should be able to do so in the long run, for example, by reducing the rate of increase in wages. When minimal terms are avoidable through compensating changes, wages and quantity of labor should tend to move back to equilibrium. . . .

A corollary of this objection is that when wages and quantity of labor move back to equilibrium in reaction to a minimal term, both employers and workers are worse off than they would have been if the minimal term had never been imposed. Using the maternity or paternity leave example again, if the wages and quantity of labor move back to equilibrium, the overall wage package is worth the same as the overall wage package before the minimal term was imposed, but its components

* 67 *Nebraska Law Review* 101 (1988).

are different. Before the minimal term, the package provided no maternity or paternity leave, but a higher wage; after the minimal term was
imposed, the package provided maternity or paternity leave, but a lower
wage. By hypothesis, the ex post position leaves the parties worse off. In
a world with perfect competition, if the parties had wanted that wage
package, they would have bargained for it ex ante. Since they did not,
imposition of the minimal term frustrates the wage package preferred by
the parties. . . .

. . .

III. *Justifications for Minimal Terms Within the Price Theory Model*

. . . This section considers circumstances in which minimal terms might
not be subject to the standard objection but, rather, may enhance
efficiency or lead to a more desirable distribution of resources.

A. *Efficiency Justifications*

1. *Collective Terms*

Some terms of employment are collective in nature; that is, if they are
supplied to one worker, they must also be supplied to other workers.
Terms may be collective by their very nature or they may be collective
for practical reasons. Health and safety terms, for example, are often
collective by their very nature. If an employer supplies clean air or good
lighting to one worker, other workers are usually able to share in the
benefits. More often, however, terms are collective for practical reasons.
When workers work together closely, an eight-hour day for one worker
may mean an eight-hour day for other workers. When one worker
demands and receives a new vending machine in the cafeteria, it is likely
that other workers will be allowed to use it. When an employer establishes a disciplinary system for a few workers, it may be efficient to use
it for all workers.

     Collective terms are likely to be underproduced. That is, the terms
will often not be offered even though the cost to the employer of
providing the terms is less than the value the workers place on the
benefits of the terms. To illustrate why this is the case, consider an
employer who employs ten workers and who could install Equipment A
at a cost of one, which would clean the air in the plant a bit, or
Equipment B at a cost of twenty, which could clean the air in the plant
quite a bit. Assume that each worker would value the cleaner air
produced by Equipment A at two and the cleaner air produced by
Equipment B at five (i.e., each worker would be willing to accept a
reduction in pay of two and five, respectively, in return for the cleaner
air). From an efficiency standpoint, the employer should install Equipment B. At a marginal cost of nineteen, the employer can produce
cleaner air with a marginal value of thirty; both the employer and the
workers would be better off if the employer installed Equipment B and

reduced the workers' aggregate wages by an amount between twenty and twenty-nine.

Because of strategic behavior and information imperfections, however, Equipment B will not always be installed and, indeed, even Equipment A may not be installed in some instances. Consider the calculations of each individual worker who is deciding whether to accept lower wages for cleaner air. Clearly the best outcome for an individual worker would be to refuse to accept lower wages, but to have the equipment installed because other workers accepted lower wages. In that situation, the worker would be a free rider; she could share in the benefits of the clean air, but would not have to pay for it. If all of the workers engaged in this type of strategic behavior, neither Equipment A nor Equipment B would be installed. . . .

Minimal terms, however, are not a very fine-tuned method of breaking the roadblock. Minimal terms generally apply to broad classes of employers. As a result, even when they require collective terms, minimal terms may not be efficient with respect to *every* employer to which they apply. If a minimal term required all employers to provide Equipment B, for example, the minimal term would be inefficient for employers with six or fewer workers, but efficient for employers with seven or more workers. Despite this, minimal terms would be justified if the efficiencies created by them outweigh the inefficiencies. In the example, a minimal term requiring Equipment B would be justified if the efficiency gains of workers employed by large employers outweighed the efficiency losses of workers employed by small employers.

Viewed in this way, minimal terms which require collective terms are more likely to be necessary in a labor market in which there is a low level of unionization. Collective bargaining is another, but a finer-tuned, mechanism for breaking the roadblock that results in an underproduction of collective terms. Collective bargaining enables the union, an entity with better access to worker preferences than the employer, to assess those preferences and then to demand the minimal term if it is efficient or to demand instead higher wages if the minimal term is not efficient. Thus, minimal terms may be less necessary when a large portion of the workforce is unionized because the extent of the inefficiencies caused by the roadblock should be less in that type of labor market. . . . [Editors' note: See the Freeman–Medoff article in chapter 2 for a more detailed discussion of the role of unions in supplying collective goods in the workplace.]

2. *Imperfect Information*

. . . The conventional argument from imperfect information is that workers cannot enter into optimal employment contracts if they do not have all of the information necessary to evaluate their options. . . .

Imperfect information does not justify intervention, however, merely because individual workers make mistakes. Intervention is justified only if the labor market fails to produce optimal terms because workers make decisions based on imperfect information. Even if many workers make mistakes because of imperfect information, optimal terms may be produced. If some workers seek optimal terms and if employers both wish to attract those workers and cannot distinguish between them and the workers making mistakes, the market should produce optimal terms. In essence, those workers who demand optimal terms protect other workers from the consequences of their limited information. On the other hand, if insufficient numbers of workers seek optimal terms, or if employers do not wish to attract those workers, or if employers can distinguish between those workers and workers with imperfect information, the labor market may fail to produce optimal terms.

Intervention in the labor market is justified, then, if the labor market fails to produce optimal terms because workers make decisions on the basis of imperfect information. This provides only a weak justification for minimal terms, however, because there are other, less intrusive options for remedying this type of information failure. Ensuring that workers receive fuller information ... would remedy the information failure and lead to a more fine-tuned result than simply requiring the [term]. It would permit those workers who prefer higher wages even when they have knowledge of the true value of the [term], to continue to receive higher wages.

Another type of information failure provides a stronger justification for minimal terms. If there is information failure not because of limited information, but because workers cannot rationally evaluate the available information, the less intrusive remedial option of providing information may not be effective. Minimal terms may be required to correct the suboptimal choices made by workers.

Information overload and cognitive dissonance are two reasons workers may not be able to effectively evaluate the information necessary to make a choice. Evidence from outside the employment context suggests that there is a point at which additional information becomes dysfunctional; that is, the additional information does not contribute to a better decision because the people to whom it is provided are "overloaded" and simply cannot process it. . . .

Cognitive dissonance may also interfere with the ability of workers to evaluate additional information. Stated generally, cognitive dissonance means that people are uncomfortable when they simultaneously hold two conflicting ideas. People prefer to view themselves as smart and if new information indicates that a prior belief was in error, the new information tends to undermine the preferred self-image. As a consequence, people tend to reject, ignore or accommodate information that conflicts with prior beliefs.

Cognitive dissonance may also justify minimal terms. To illustrate, consider workers who when they first choose a job, choose an industry that is hazardous, but necessarily hazardous because no safety equipment is available to correct the hazards. Over time, cognitive dissonance may lead the workers to believe that the job is really fairly safe. (Smart workers would not work at a hazardous job, therefore the workers must either view themselves as not smart or their jobs as not hazardous. Viewing the jobs as safe is less threatening to the workers' self-image.) If cost-effective safety equipment then becomes available, the workers will not purchase the equipment (by accepting a reduction in their wages). Because of cognitive dissonance, they have come to believe that their jobs are safe even without the equipment. As a result, they are unable to evaluate fairly the value of the newly available equipment. A minimal term which required the equipment to be installed would be necessary to achieve the efficient outcome. . . .

3. External Costs

Minimal terms may also be justified when employment terms impose costs on third parties, that is, when there are "external" costs that are not weighed by employers and workers when they negotiate the employment contract.

Consider an employer that hires a worker who smokes. In a price theory world, the employer would pay the worker less than a worker who does not smoke by an amount equal to the extra costs imposed on the employer by smoking. Thus, if smokers are absent from work more often than non-smokers, the employer should pay a lower wage to a worker who smokes to compensate for the costs to the employer of the extra absences. Considering only the employer and the smoking worker, the price theory world would optimally balance the desire of workers to smoke and the employment costs associated with smoking. A worker would smoke if she valued smoking more than the decrease in pay caused by her smoking. An employer would hire smokers if they would agree to work for an amount sufficiently less than non-smokers to compensate the employer for its increased costs.

Some of the costs of smoking in the workplace, however, may be external, that is, they may be imposed on parties other than the employer and the smoking worker. Fellow workers, health and life insurance companies, social welfare agencies, and others may all bear some of the costs of smoking. To the extent this occurs, the efficient result may not be achieved. The costs of smoking are actually higher than the amount by which the employer reduces the pay of smokers; the employer reduces the pay only enough to recapture *its* losses, not enough to recapture *all* losses associated with smoking. As a result, some workers will continue to smoke even though they would not if they had to accept a reduction in pay sufficient to cover all of the costs of smoking. There will be "too much" smoking in the workplace.

Minimal terms can be used to correct for this type of overproduction. The test of efficiency is what the market would have produced if *all* the costs of workplace smoking were considered. A minimal term which prohibited workplace smoking, or which taxed employers or workers for workplace smoking, would reduce the amount of workplace smoking and may produce an amount of smoking which more closely approximates the efficient ideal.

Minimal terms, of course, may overcorrect. A minimal term which prohibited smoking would be likely to produce "too little" workplace smoking because it would prohibit smoking by workers who would smoke even if they had to absorb all the costs. Even in this situation, however, the minimal term may be justified. If the "too low" amount of smoking with the minimal term was closer to the efficient ideal than the "too high" amount of smoking without the minimal term, the minimal term would be justifiable on efficiency grounds. . . .

B.   *Distributional Justifications*

Minimal terms are popular politically because the common perception is that they benefit workers at the expense of employers. When the government requires employers to provide maternity benefits or health insurance, the perception is that *employers* will pay for the benefits, that there will be a reduction in employer profits and a corresponding increase in worker compensation.

The standard objection casts doubt on this type of distributional justification for minimal terms. . . .

Whether the common perception or the standard objection better describes the distributional effects of minimal terms depends on the rigidity of the relevant labor market. To the extent employers in the relevant market have the unfettered ability to respond to minimal terms by lowering wages and/or reducing employment levels, the costs of minimal terms can be transferred to workers. The standard objection, then, better describes that type of flexible labor market.

Other labor markets, however, may be more rigid. Certain employers, for example, may not be able to respond to minimal terms by lowering wages because of minimum wage laws or because of individual or collective contracts requiring a certain level of wages. Indeed, only in very rare circumstances will employers be able to transfer all the costs of minimal terms to workers through lower wages. If unemployment effects are not considered, employers will have to absorb some of the cost of minimal terms in the vast majority of cases. Similarly, certain employers may not be able to reduce employment levels because of plant closing notification laws or because they have made long-term investments in specialized types of equipment. In these more rigid labor markets, then, employers may have to absorb some of the costs of minimal terms, at least in the short run. Thus, the common perception may be accurate—

minimal terms may cause a redistribution from employers to workers. . . .

Notes and Questions

1. *Paternalism and Inadequate Information.* Suppose the labor market
responds to the preferences of workers and provides every benefit they are
willing to pay for and no benefit they are unwilling to pay for. This result
might still be termed a market failure if the worker preferences are faulty.
Advocates of regulation to correct this market failure immediately face
charges of paternalism—how can the advocates know what workers want
better than the workers themselves? One response is to argue that workers
are misguided or irrational in, say, failing to value safety. In other words, the
regulation advocate knows better than the worker what is good for the
worker.

Usually, however, the regulation advocate seeks to dismiss the paternalism charge by pointing instead to a public goods problem, an information
problem, or some other nonpaternalistic market failure. These other market
failures allow the advocate to assert that if workers understood the true
trade-offs between wages and safety, they would opt for safety.

Cass Sunstein has examined the information problems facing workers
and others. Information is a public good, in the sense that once one worker
has the information, others can use it at little or no extra cost. Individual
firms or workers cannot easily capture the benefits outsiders get from
information, and thus are unlikely to produce an optimal amount. As
Sunstein explains, the usual remedy for information problems is for the
government to produce and disclose (or mandate that employers produce and
disclose) information, thus allowing the now informed workers to decide how
to react. But if nearly all workers, when fully informed, would demand safety
even recognizing how much it would lower wages, it may be more efficient
for the government to mandate safety directly. Cass R. Sunstein, *After the
Rights Revolution: Reconceiving the Regulatory State* (Cambridge, Mass:
Harvard University Press, 1990), 52–53.

2. *Errors in Calculating Low–Probability Events.* In addition to the general
public-goods problem that may lead labor markets to underproduce information about safety, a further problem is that workers may be unable to
evaluate the information rationally. This is particularly true for information
about long-term, low-probability health risks at the workplace. Sunstein,
summarizing the psychology literature, emphasizes the problems individuals
face in evaluating low-probability events. He refers here to the concept of
"regression to the mean"—that if random factors contribute to an outcome,
unusually high or low outcomes (the classic example beings parents' height)
are likely to be followed by more moderate outcomes (children of tall parents
are likely to be tall, but not as tall as their parents):

> Disclosure remedies are especially troublesome in view of the enormous
> difficulties people face in dealing with low-probability events. People
> tend to rely on heuristics that lead to systemic errors in assessing

probability, by misunderstanding the phenomenon of regression to the mean, giving too much weight to recent catastrophes, or starting from a general initial expectation that is insufficiently adjusted to take account of the particular problem at hand. The result is that popular understandings of the risks posed by low-probability events are seriously distorted. There is also evidence that the provision of information is unhelpful when views about risk are deeply ingrained. People may be accustomed to believing that a risk is low, or want to believe that they are not subject to danger; it is difficult to dislodge that belief. If people seek to reduce cognitive dissonance, information campaigns may not alter beliefs at all.

Sunstein, *After the Rights Revolution*, 53.

3. *Behavioral Decision Theory and Employment Regulation*. In support of safety regulation, Sunstein emphasizes that people have difficulty assessing low-probability events, which could include the likelihood of being arbitrarily dismissed or contracting cancer from benzene exposure at work. Sunstein cites the classic work on behavioral decision theory, Daniel Kahneman, Paul Slovic, and Amos Tversky, eds., *Judgment Under Uncertainty: Heuristics and Biases* (Cambridge: Cambridge University Press, 1982). Sunstein is a careful contributor to the literature applying insights from this branch of psychology to law. Nevertheless, casual citation of the literature is becoming endemic. It is worth parsing the issues.

One of the major insights of behavioral decision theory is that people use two important heuristics, or mental shortcuts, in estimating the likelihood of bad events. When using the *availability heuristic*, people estimate frequency by how quickly examples come to mind. Often this approach is a helpful mental shortcut, but can lead people astray when memorable events are relatively uncommon. For example, workers might overestimate the safety risks of ladders if they can easily recall a worker who was injured falling off a ladder.

Another important heuristic is *representativeness*. Here, people estimate the likelihood that an event is part of a larger class based on whether the event's characteristics are salient features of the category. In doing so, people typically ignore whether the event is a large or small part of the population (i.e., they ignore the base rate).

Availability and representative heuristics are both in play when people are asked to estimate the probability of being killed by venomous or nonvenomous animal bites or stings. The actual numbers are that 48 people die annually from venomous animals and 129 from nonvenomous animals. In a survey, respondents estimated that 350 people died from venomous animals and 174 from nonvenomous animals. Because examples of each type of death are readily available, the availability heuristic leads people to overestimate both dangers. But people overestimate venomous deaths to a far larger extent, and indeed believe they are the greater danger. This is because venom is representative of a central danger of animal bites, even though the base rate of nonvenomous bites from dogs and cats far exceeds the bites of venomous animals.

Good data do not exist on how workers use heuristics. The psychological model would suggest, however, that the availability and representativeness heuristics would cause some workplace dangers to be overestimated relative to others. Workers might overestimate the dangers of cancer from chemical exposure compared to death from driving automobiles at work. Cancer is a classic or "representative" consequence of toxic chemical exposure, while workers might ignore the ubiquity of driving. In fact, "40 percent of recent workplace fatalities were from transportation accidents and about 20 percent from assaults and other violent acts." John F. Burton, Jr. and James R. Chelius, "Workplace Safety and Health Regulations: Rationale and Results," in Bruce E. Kaufman, ed., *Government Regulation of the Employment Relationship* (Madison, Wis.: Industrial Relations Research Association, 1997) 277. Workplace driving accidents rarely make news, however, and so the availability heuristic will also underplay their significance.

Another problem with estimating risk comes not from mental shortcuts, sometimes called "cold" cognition, but from "hot" cognition problems such as *cognitive dissonance*. People do not like to hold inconsistent beliefs, because it creates internal dissonance. To alleviate the dissonance, they try to shape their beliefs into consistent patterns. The classic reference here is Leon Festinger, *A Theory of Cognitive Dissonance* (Evanston, Ill.: Row, Peterson 1957). As an example, Festinger pointed out that smokers estimate the risks of smoking to be much lower than nonsmokers do. Workplace applications are easy to imagine. A worker might believe that he would not endanger his life for a low-paying job. Recognizing that his job exposes him to benzene, the worker might underestimate the dangers of benzene in order to avoid internal dissonance.

Whatever estimate a person makes of the risk of a bad event, whether through heuristics or cognitive dissonance or other mental processes, behavioral decision theory also shows that he or she often reacts to the risk in nonobvious but predictable ways. For example, the "psycho-physics of chance," as Kahneman and Tversky labeled it, shows that people do not react in a linear way to perceptions of risk. An example from workplace safety could occur when workers place little value on reducing a risk from 40 percent to 35 percent but place great value on reducing the same risk from 5 percent to 0 percent.

In summary, behaviorial decision theory provides a variety of models showing how workers might misperceive risk or react to risk in nonoptimal ways. Such a showing does not, by itself, indicate that the government should mandate higher levels of safety than the labor market would itself provide. Workers can exaggerate as well as underestimate workplace risks, as the heuristics and biases sketched above indicate.

Additionally, behavioral decision theory suggests that experts have their own psychological biases. Most prominently, experts often are too confident about their ability to accurately predict risk. Lawyers, for example, often are too confident that they can precisely predict the outcome of cases, insisting, for example, that a case has a 40 percent chance of being won when all that can reasonably be known is that the probability is between 20 percent and

60 percent. (Unlike most other experts, weather forecasters are not subject to this overconfidence bias because they receive continuous feedback on the accuracy of their predictions.) The overconfidence bias suggests caution before we rely on experts to set labor standards on the grounds that workers misperceive risk. Lay people often are better at knowing they don't know, and thus suffer less from overconfidence bias.

4. *Cognitive Dissonance and Compensating Risk Differentials.* Professor Willborn asserts that workers may deceive themselves, through a process of cognitive dissonance, into believing their jobs are safe. If workers believe their jobs are safe, even when dangerous, they will not demand higher pay. Mandatory safety standards might alleviate the cognitive dissonance problems. Empirical evidence suggests, however, that workers do receive compensating wage differentials for unsafe work, and thus casts doubt on the cognitive dissonance theory. Whether this extra pay fully compensates workers for dangerous work is more difficult to answer, as Professor Viscusi explains:

> In my study of workers' subjective risk perceptions, I found that workers who believed that they were exposed to dangerous or unhealthy conditions received over $900 annually (1980 prices) in hazard pay. It is especially noteworthy that an almost identical figure was obtained when I used an objective industry injury risk measure as the risk variable. The similarity of the finds using subjective and objective measures of risk lends strong empirical support to the validity of the risk premium analysis.
>
> Unfortunately, these results do not enable us to conclude that markets work perfectly. Is the premium less or more than would prevail if workers and employers were fully cognizant of the risks? The size of the premium only implies that compensating differentials are one element of market behavior. A more meaningful index is the wage premium per unit of risk. If it is very likely that a worker will be killed or injured, a $900 risk premium can be seen as a signal that the compensating differential process is deficient. The average blue-collar worker, however, faces an annual occupational death risk of only about 1/10,000 and a less than 1/25 risk of an injury severe enough to cause him to miss a day or more of work. Consequently, the observed premium per unit of risk is quite substantial, with the implicit value of life being on the order of $2 million or more for many workers.
>
> The safety incentives created by market mechanisms are much stronger than those created by OSHA standards; a conservative estimate of the total job risk premiums for the entire private sector is $69 billion, or almost 3,000 times the total annual penalties now levied by OSHA. Whereas OSHA penalties are only 34 cents per worker, market risk premiums per worker are $925 annually. This figure would be even higher if we added in the premiums that are displaced by the workers' compensation system, which provides an additional $11.8 billion in compensation to workers.

W. Kip Viscusi, *Risk by Choice: Regulating Health and Safety in the Workplace* (Cambridge, Mass.: Harvard University Press, 1983), 43–44.

5. *Relative Preferences and Arms Races.* The standard market model assumes that workers try to maximize their own utility subject to a budget constraint, regardless of what other workers do. Some commentators have explored the implications of recognizing that workers compete against each other and place great value on their relative rankings. This introduces a type of externality. If worker A earns an extra $10,000 by working in a dangerous workplace, this pushes down the relative ranking of worker B. In deciding where to work, worker A does not consider the harmful effects on B, thus creating the externality. The situation results in an arms race. Each worker individually might prefer safety to the extra pay, as long as others did not opt for extra pay. But if some workers try to get ahead by accepting dangerous jobs, other workers are forced to join the arms race (or rat race, if you will), in an attempt to maintain their relative positions. The result is dangerous work with insufficient aggregate pay. Richard McAdams, building on the classic work of Robert Frank, *Choosing the Right Pond: Human Behavior and the Quest for Status* (New York: Oxford University Press, 1985), explains basic labor regulation such as OSHA as in part a legislative attempt to solve the arms-race dilemma:

> Frank argues that workers competing for relative income may jointly sacrifice safety for higher nominal income either to gain or avoid losing relative income, only to find that the parallel sacrifices of other workers cancel out the desired relative effects. Under conditions of this "prisoner's dilemma," government regulations mandating minimum safety standards may limit the investment wasted in acquiring or maintaining relative income. Frank proposes the following example. A and B are two workers each facing a choice between a job at a "clean" mine for $150 a week and a job at a "dusty" mine for $200 a week. A and B each have a relative preference for greater income than the other. In such circumstances, "the payoff to each from working in a given mine will depend in a clear way on the mine chosen by the other."
>
> Assume that, in the absence of concern about relative position, A and B would each choose to work in the clean mine, valuing its healthier conditions at more than $50 a week. Given a sufficiently strong concern with relative income, however, each would rank his choices accordingly: (1) work in dirty mine while the other works in clean mine (gaining the most in relative position); (2) both work in clean mine; (3) both work in dirty mine; (4) work in clean mine while the other works in dirty mine (losing the most in relative position). Under these circumstances, each worker will choose to work in the dirty mine to avoid outcome (4) and to have a chance at outcome (1). Their joint decisions would produce outcome (3), in which the higher absolute income produces no relative advantage for either. Not only do A and B each rank outcome (3) lower than outcome (2), but moving from (2) to (3) means that each has given up the health advantages of the cleaner mine with no compensating

gain. Consequently, a collective rule mandating a minimum level of the nonpositional good of long term health, requiring that all mines be "clean," would prevent this misallocation of resources into individual competition for relative position and make both workers better off. Thus, certain occupational health and safety regulations might be Pareto efficient in providing a minimum level of health or safety if individuals' desires for relative wealth otherwise cause them to underinvest in such goods.

Richard McAdams, "Relative Preferences," 102 *Yale Law Journal* 1, 21 (1992).

Can the primary explanation for OSHA, and other major mandates in the workplace, be that it stops workers from competing with each other in certain dimensions, such as their health and safety? Can such a rationale be maintained with the increase in global markets? OSHA and other federal legislation solve the prisoner's dilemma for American workers, but workers from other countries can still get ahead by agreeing to dangerous work. Or does the entire relative-preference framework break down when considering the global economy, in that American workers do not care whether foreign workers rank above or below them in living standards, but only care whether American workers are doing well? To use Robert Frank's metaphor, are American and foreign workers in the same pond? By extension, are workers in different cities or employed by different firms in the same pond?

6. *Public–Choice Explanations for Mandated Terms.* The so-called public-choice explanation for governmentally mandated terms suggests that benefiting workers, whether well or poorly achieved, is not the only goal of employment legislation. Much employment legislation imposes large costs on employers, but some employers can respond to the mandates more cheaply than others can. These employers may actually support the mandates, because it gives them a competitive advantage that translates into higher profits. If that is so, these firms are willing to "buy" this legislation through campaign contributions and other methods. Economists Ann Bartel and Lacy Glenn Thomas argue that some firms increased profits after OSHA mandates were imposed on their industry. Although the "direct effects" of complying with OSHA regulations apply across the board to all affected firms in an industry, two types of "indirect" effects fall differentially on firms, creating a relative competitive advantage for some. First, some firms have greater unit costs in complying with the regulations. Generally, firms experience large economies of scale in complying with OSHA regulations, so that the compliance burden falls hardest on smaller firms. Second, the Labor Department does not enforce OSHA equally on all types of firms. Bartel and Thomas also found that OSHA was enforced more intensely (per worker) against small, nonunion, and Sun Belt firms. See Bartel and Thomas, "Predation Through Regulation: The Wage and Profit Effects of the Occupational Safety and Health Administration and the Environmental Protection Agency," 30 *Journal of Law & Economics* 239 (1987).

"The Law and Economics Approach to Workplace Regulation"*

STEWART J. SCHWAB

Outside the law-and-economics camp, many scholars justify employment laws as correcting unfair employment relationships caused by workers' lack of bargaining power. Because individual workers lack bargaining power, the justification runs, they are exploited by employers. Government steps in (whether through the courts, the state legislatures, or Congress) to correct this exploitation. Protecting the weaker party to the employment contract becomes the prime positive explanation for employment law.

Law-and-economics scholars are deeply skeptical of rationalizations based on unequal bargaining power. Those rationalizations fail miserably as a positive explanation, for they cannot explain the many legal doctrines favoring employers regardless of their superior bargaining power (e.g., the right to fire employees at will; the right to give no pension to part-time workers). But even as a normative critique of an employment-law doctrine that favors employers, unequal bargaining power is unpersuasive because the concept is so malleable as to be devoid of content. Duncan Kennedy, a prominent critical-legal-studies scholar and hardly an L & E enthusiast, disentangles at least five different ideas within the general concept of unequal bargaining power. ["Distributive and Paternalist Motives in Contract and Tort Law, with Special Reference to Compulsory Terms and Unequal Bargaining Power," 41 *Maryland Law Review* 563 (1982).] As applied to compulsory employment-law terms, these would include (1) the subject is public rather than private; (2) the employer drafted the terms and offered them to workers on a take-it-or-leave-it basis; (3) the employer has monopoly power or is bigger than an individual worker; (4) work is a necessity for workers, making them vulnerable to exploitation; and (5) a shortage of work enables employers to exploit workers. None of these tests, explains Kennedy, captures when a mandatory minimum employment term would benefit workers. For example, the big-employer criticism and the take-it-or-leave-it criticism lose their sting when employment-term bargaining is compared to bargaining in a grocery store. No individual customer can bargain with the manager of a big grocery store over price or other terms. This does not make the customer a victim of unequal bargaining power, however, because the customer can shop at rival stores if the terms are not attractive. . . .

Freed and Polsby have attacked the monopoly-power variant of unequal bargaining power as applied to employment law. True, a monopsonist employer creates a type of market failure, in that it refuses to hire

---

* In Bruce E. Kaufman, ed., *Government Regulation of the Employment Relationship* (Madison, Wis.: Industrial Relations Research Association, 1997).

some workers even though they would willingly work at a wage that would reap extra profits for the monopsonist, but for the fact that the monopsonist must raise wages for other workers. Still, say Freed and Polsby, even a monopsonist will offer an employment benefit if workers value the benefit more highly than it costs the monopsonist to provide— if only to wring even more profits from the workers. [Mayer G. Freed and Daniel D. Polsby, "Just Cause For Termination Rules and Economic Efficiency," 38 *Emory Law Journal* 1097 (1989) (excerpted in Chapter 7).].

The law-and-economics position does not suggest that a properly limited concept of unequal bargaining power is meaningless. Indeed, relative bargaining power determines how the parties to a bargain will share the surplus from trade. If employees have little bargaining power, the employer will gain most of the surplus. For example, suppose workers value a particular safety measure at $5 and an employer can provide it at a cost of $4. If the safety measure is provided, the joint gain to the parties is $1. If the employer has great bargaining power, almost all of that $1 surplus will go to the employer. It will offer safety and lower the wage by $4.99. If the employer has less bargaining power, the wage may fall by only $4.50 or less.

The important law-and-economics point is that unequal bargaining power does not determine whether particular items are traded to their highest valued use. To continue the example above, the degree of bargaining inequality does not affect whether the safety measure will be provided; it only influences how the parties will divide the gains from providing safety. Even an employer monopsonist with complete bargaining power wants to provide a safety measure if workers are willing and able to pay for it. In our example, providing the safety gives the monopsonist another dollar of profit.

The efficient result will occur regardless of bargaining power, unless transaction costs prevent the parties from making the deal. Transactions costs include many things, such as strategic behavior, holdouts, or asymmetric information. These are all worthy of serious study. But unequal bargaining power is not a form of transaction costs that will prevent a joint-welfare-enhancing contract from being consummated.

Unequal bargaining power can reduce the overall compensation package to workers. This is the central inefficiency that arises from a monopsony employer. Reduced compensation, in turn, will affect how workers value certain items. To continue the example, workers paid $15 (per hour) may be willing to pay $6 (per month) on a particular safety measure, while workers paid $5 may only be willing to pay $3. In the latter case, the safety measure is no longer efficient and freely bargaining parties will not agree to it. But all this says is that poor workers value things differently than rich workers, and bargaining power influences whether a worker is poor or rich. Unequal bargaining power does not prevent efficient trades over particular items from occurring. Additionally, mandating safety to workers with low bargaining power will not improve their welfare. If the policymaker wishes the workers were richer and so would value safety more highly, the policymaker should attack the monopsony position.

Notes and Questions

1. *Unequal Bargaining Power vs. Exploitation.* In an exchange with Morgan Reynolds, Bruce Kaufman debated the usefulness of unequal bargaining power in understanding labor markets. Reynolds argued that "the belief in labor's exploitation in a free market economy is illogical and lacks a serious empirical foundation." Morgan O. Reynolds, "The Myth of Labor's Inequality of Bargaining Power," 12 *Journal of Labor Research* 167, 168 (1991). Kaufman responded by distinguishing exploitation from lack of bargaining power. He defines exploitation as occurring whenever workers are paid less than the marginal revenue product of labor. This can occur when one large firm has a dominant, monopsony position in a local labor market. In that situation, even the last (or marginal) worker is producing more value to the employer than he gets in compensation. Kaufman says unequal bargaining power exists when firms can push wages and working conditions below the full employment, competitive level. Exploitation and unequal bargaining power can go together. But in times of massive unemployment, asserts Kaufman, inequality of bargaining power may exist (wages and working conditions are pushed below the full employment level), even if no exploitation exists (the persons able to find work are paid their marginal product):

> Consider Depression-era migrant farmer-workers, such as those depicted in John Steinbeck's *The Grapes of Wrath....* The California labor market for fruit pickers during the Depression was a close approximation of a perfectly competitive market, in that there were many buyers and sellers and a relatively unobstructed mobility of labor. Did the individual fruit picker have an equality of bargaining power vis-à-vis the individual grower? I do not think so. When a grower drove into a labor camp to hire workers, the competition among the unemployed resulted in a bidding down of wages and the level of working conditions. For the sake of argument, assume that the wage fell far enough to restore a balance between the supply and demand of labor. According to Reynolds, at this new equilibrium an equality of bargaining power would once again exist since there is zero exploitation of labor as workers receive a wage equal to their marginal revenue product (even if it was only five cents per hour). According to my definition, however, those workers would still suffer from an inequality of bargaining power, since the wage was much below that which would have been paid if full employment prevailed. Which is the more useful perspective? I believe that mine is, because it captures the reality that the lack of alternative jobs forced workers to accept wages and working conditions that were much below what would have prevailed in a full employment economy.

Bruce E. Kaufman, "Labor's Inequality of Bargaining Power: Myth or Reality?," 12 *Journal of Labor Research* 151, 153–54 (1991).

Reynolds responded by arguing that widespread unemployment has nothing to do with unequal bargaining power:

> Widespread unemployment implies nothing about "bargaining power." Economic analysis of large amounts of unsold labor services is no different than analysis of a glut in any other commodity—prices are too high to clear the markets. Prices demanded by sellers are higher than the community can afford under prevailing conditions. If such discoordination persists for an extended period of time (e.g., one year or more), then the labor idleness in a world of scarcity must reflect "withheld" labor supplies, usually subsidized by public and private transfers, as well as labor prices that are inflexible downward for a variety of market and non-market reasons. In no sense is widespread unemployment evidence for an entrepreneurial monopoly on demand. "Jobs" remain abundant. Labor services, especially at the bottom of the skill ladder where idleness is greatest, are simply overpriced. To argue otherwise abandons economic reasoning.
>
>   Kaufman also claimed that under widespread unemployment, workers "no longer have alternative jobs to choose from." But all unemployment is by choice. . . . It all boils down to a question of price. Kaufman's statement would be analytically correct if he wrote that many workers under conditions of widespread unemployment have no alternative job opportunities *at their current pay rate or higher*. Productive labor services, just like other goods, can always be sold (rented) but not always at ever-higher prices ("decent, American" wages).

Reynolds, "The Myth of Labor's Inequality of Bargaining Power," 12 *Journal of Labor Research* 176 (1991).

2. *Monopsonists and the Efficient Mix of Benefits*. Under one meaning of unequal bargaining power, workers are weakest when a single, large monopsonist employer dominates the labor market. Such a firm effectively controls the wage, and presumably controls benefits and working conditions as well. One might think that legislation mandating minimal benefits is easily justified here: the government must mandate a basic level of safety in the mill, for example, because the mill will never offer it otherwise.

Schwab concedes that monopsony is a market imperfection that causes underemployment. Still, he argues that monopsony is not the type of market imperfection that can be improved by mandating minimum terms for specific parts of the package of compensation and working conditions, while allowing parties to bargain freely over other parts of the compensation package. Even monopsonists have an economic incentive to provide all benefits that workers are willing to pay for. In other words, monopsony power can lower the overall compensation package but will not impede the efficient mix of items in the compensation package.

To illustrate, suppose that a monopsonist mill is thinking about installing ventilators, which would cost it the equivalent of 75 cents in wages. The same number of workers currently employed by the mill would be willing to work for a $1 lower wage, as long as ventilators were provided. (Implicitly, workers are willing to pay up to $1 for ventilators.) The employer, even with extreme bargaining power, has a financial incentive to provide the ventilators, if only to reduce the wages by $1, spend 75 cents on ventilators, and capture the extra 25 cents in profit. Thus, even a monopsonistic employer will provide benefits that workers value, in the sense that the workers would prefer the benefit even when wages are reduced by the cost of providing the benefit.

"Some Simple Economics of Mandated Benefits"*
LAWRENCE H. SUMMERS

When it has been decided that universal access to a good is to be provided, governments in some cases provide it directly, as with public education and old-age benefits almost everywhere and health benefits in many countries. In other cases, governments mandate that employers provide benefits to workers or that persons obtain benefits directly themselves. Requirements that employers keep workplaces safe and provide Workman's Compensation Insurance represent a clear example. Unemployment insurance provides an interesting middle ground. While in most European countries it is financed from general revenues, in the United States, employers are required to pay for the benefits their workers receive, because unemployment insurance taxes are experience rated, albeit imperfectly.

As a general proposition, liberals rank alternative strategies in the order of public provision, mandated benefits, then no action for addressing social concerns. Conservatives have exactly the opposite preferences, ranking the alternatives no action, mandated benefits, and then public provision. With these preference patterns, it is little wonder that governments frequently turn to mandated benefits as a tool of social policy. Mandated benefits raise a host of questions, however: What determines the choices governments make? Are there differences in the real effects of mandated benefits and tax financed programs? Are there efficiency arguments for the use of mandated benefits? ...

I. *Efficiency Arguments for Mandating Employee Benefits*

...When is there ever a case for mandating benefits or publicly providing goods that employers could provide their workers? Most obviously, there is the paternalism, or "merit goods," argument that individuals value certain services too little....

There are at least two further rationales for mandating benefits that do not assume individual irrationality. First, there may be positive externalities associated with the good—externalities that cannot be

* 79 *American Economic Review (Papers & Proceedings)* 177 (1989).

captured by either the provider or the recipient. The most obvious example is health insurance. Society cares about preventing the spread of contagious diseases more than any individual does or would take account of. Further, people prefer for their friends and relatives to remain healthy, yet they cannot individually subsidize health insurance for all other consumers.

Much more important is the externality that arises from society's unwillingness or inability to deny care completely to those in desperate need, even if they cannot pay. The Congressional Budget Office estimates that there are 23 million American employees without health insurance. Health insurance for this group would cost about $25 billion. Currently, these uninsured employees incur $15 billion in health care costs for which they do not pay. The costs are borne in part by physicians and other providers of health care, but most of the cost is passed on to other consumers in the form of higher insurance and medical costs.

The externality here is quite large. About 60 percent of the benefit of employer-provided health insurance accrues ultimately to neither employer nor employee. Even with the current tax subsidy to employer-provided health insurance, there might be a further case for government action. . . .

Externality arguments can be used to justify other mandated benefits. Since unemployment insurance is only partially experience rated, layoffs at one firm raise taxes at others, creating an efficiency case for policies that would interfere with the private layoff decision. Mandatory plant closing notification is one such policy. There is an externality case for it also insofar as layoffs have adverse consequences for communities. The externality case for parental leave is more difficult to make, though even here there is the question of whether the benefits to the child of parental leave provide some justification for public policy intervention.

There is a second, perhaps stronger, argument for government intervention in the market for fringe benefits based on adverse selection considerations, as discussed for example in Michael Rothschild and Joseph Stiglitz (1976). If employees have more information about whether they will need parental leave or face high medical bills than their employers do, then employers that provide these benefits will receive disproportionately more applications from employees who require benefits and so will lose money. The market thus discourages provision of any fringe benefits.

Suppose, for example, that for the 10 percent of the population that knows it has health problems, health insurance is worth $300 and costs $270 to provide, and for the 90 percent of the population without preexisting conditions, health insurance is worth $100 and costs $90 to provide. Assume that individuals know whether they have problems or not, but employers cannot tell healthy from unhealthy individuals. Now consider what happens if employers do not offer health insurance. Any employer offering health insurance and a salary reduction of less than $100 would attract both classes of workers and would lose money, since the average cost of insurance would be $.9·90 + .1·270 = $108. Firms could offer insurance and reduce wages by between $270 and $300. This would attract only unhealthy individuals. Even leaving aside the consideration that for productivity reasons, firms might not prefer a personnel policy that was most likely to attract unhealthy workers, it is clear that the market solution will not provide universal insurance even though all individuals are willing to pay more than it costs to insure themselves.

The same argument holds in the case of other employee benefits. Workers know much better than their employers whether they are likely to go on parental leave or become disabled. They probably also know something about whether they are likely to become enmeshed in employment disputes. This suggests that there are efficiency arguments for limited employers' ability to fire workers at will.

These two considerations suggest that it may be optimal for the government to intervene in the provision of goods that some employers provide their workers. In the next section, I take up the question of the form of government provision.

II. *Mandated Benefits or Public Provision*

It is often asserted that mandated benefits are just hidden taxes with the same efficiency and incidence implications as taxes, so that the choice between public provision and mandated benefits should depend only on the relative efficiency with which employers and the government can provide a service. I challenge the equivalence of these methods of provision below. But even granting the equivalence, there should be at least some presumption in favor of mandated benefits. Mandated benefits preserve employers' ability to tailor arrangements to their workers and to offer more than minimum packages. This avoids what might be called the "government provision trap" discussed in the context of higher education by Sam Peltzman (1973). Suppose that the government provides universal free health care of modest quality. This will be more attractive to many than paying the costs of high-quality care themselves, even though if they had to pay for all their care they would have selected high-rather than low-quality care.

Another argument in favor of mandated benefits rather than public provision is that mandated provision avoids the deadweight loss of tax-financed provision. . . .

[Such distortions caused by the tax system suggest] that there are substantial efficiency gains to accomplishing social objectives in other than government taxation and provision. There is also the consideration that at the present time in the United States, the nature of budgetary

bargaining makes it difficult to find funds even for programs that are
very widely regarded as having substantial benefit-cost ratios.

Mandated benefits do not give rise to deadweight losses as large as
those that arise from government tax collections. Suppose that the
government required that all employers provide a certain benefit, say a
leave policy, that cost employers $.10 per employee hour to provide.
What would happen? Consider first employers whose employees previously valued the benefit at more than $.10 per hour and so had a leave
package greater than $.10 per hour. They would not be affected at all by
the government mandate, since they were previously in compliance with
the law. For employees who valued the benefit at less than $.10 an hour,
they would then receive the plan, at the cost of $.10.

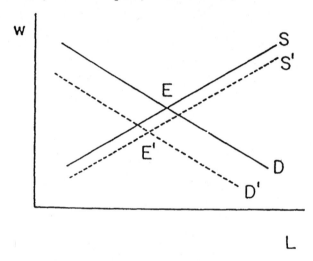

Figure 6–1 Effect of Mandated Benefits

What would happen to the wages of those receiving the benefit?
Figure 6–1 illustrates the answer. Requiring employers to pay for employee leaves shifts their demand curve downwards by $.10. Guarantee-
ing the benefit to employees shifts their supply curve downward by an
amount equal to the value of the benefit. A new equilibrium level of
employment and wages is reached, with lower wages and employment,
but in general employment will be reduced by less than it would be with
a $.10 tax.

Two special cases are instructive. First, suppose that the mandated
benefit is worthless to employees. In this very special case, the change in
employment and wages corresponds exactly to what would be expected
from a $.10 tax on employers. Since the mandated benefit is worthless to
employees, it is just like a tax from the point of view of both employers
and employees. Second, consider the case where employees' valuation of
the policy is arbitrarily close to $.10. In this case, the mandated benefit

does not affect the level of employment, the employer's total employee costs, or the employees' utility.

The general point should be clear from this example. In terms of their allocational effects on employment, mandated benefits represent a tax at a rate equal to the *difference* between the employer's cost of providing the benefit and the employees' valuation of it, *not* at a rate equal to the cost to the employer of providing the benefit.

With this in mind, contrast the effects of mandating benefits with the effects of taxing all employers and using the proceeds to finance a public parental leave program. In the latter case, employers would abandon their plans, and the government would end up paying for all parental leave. This would mean far more tax distortions than in the mandated benefits case for two reasons. First, employers and employees who were unaffected by the mandated benefit program would be taxed for the parental leave program. This creates a larger deadweight loss. Second, for those employers and employees who are affected, the tax levied is equal to the full cost of parental leave, not the difference between the employers' cost and the workers' benefit.

Where is the efficiency difference between the two approaches coming from? To see the answer, suppose that the public parental leave program was exactly tied to the number of hours an employee worked in the past and to his or her wage. In this case, with rational employees, the program would not be distortionary because the extra parental leave one would get by working more hours would offset the extra tax payments. Mandated benefits have effects paralleling benefit tax-financed public programs. Without close links between taxes and benefits, that tend to be lacking in public programs, large distortions can result.

Exactly the same analysis could be carried out with respect to health insurance, but one extra complication must be recognized. Workers do not get more health insurance if they work more hours. Hence, mandating employer health insurance should not affect employees' decisions about working a marginal hour. A public program could achieve the same effect if it was financed by a lump sum tax on employees rather than on payroll or income, but such taxes are not normally contemplated. In the case of health insurance, a lump sum tax is the appropriate benefit tax, since benefits do not rise with income. If labor force participation is very inelastic, but hours of work are quite elastic, then a mandated benefit program will involve less distortion than a tax-financed benefit program, given the government's normal tax instruments.

This analysis suggests at least two possible advantages of mandated benefits over public provision of benefits. First, mandated benefits are likely to afford workers more choice. Second, they are likely to involve fewer distortions of economic activity. Why then should not all social objectives be sought through mandated benefits? I take this question up in the next section.

III.   *Some Potential Problems with Mandated Benefits*

The most obvious problem with mandated benefits is that they only help those with jobs. Beyond the 25 million employed Americans without health insurance, another 13 million nonemployed Americans do not have health insurance. Mandated benefit programs obviously do not reach these people. There is certainly a case for public provision in situations where there is no employer who can be required to provide benefits.

A more fundamental problem comes when there are wage rigidities. Suppose, for example, that there is a binding minimum wage. In this case, wages cannot fall to offset employers' cost of providing a mandated benefit, so it is likely to create unemployment. This is a common objection to proposals for mandated health insurance, given that a large fraction of employees who are without health insurance are paid low wages. It is not clear whether this should be regarded as a problem with mandated benefits or minimum wages. Note that a payroll tax on employers directed at financing health insurance benefits publicly would have exactly the same employment displacement effects as a mandated health insurance program.

A different type of wage rigidity involves a requirement that firms pay different workers the same wage even though the cost of providing benefits differs. For example, the cost of health insurance is greater for older than for younger workers and the expected cost of parental leave is greater for women than men. If wages could freely adjust, these differences in expected benefit costs would be offset by differences in wages. If such differences are precluded, however, there will be efficiency consequences as employers seek to hire workers with lower benefit costs. It is thus possible that mandated benefit programs can work against the interest of those who most require the benefit being offered. Publicly provided benefits do not drive a wedge between the marginal costs of hiring different workers and so do not give rise to a distortion of this kind.

Another objection to mandated benefits is that they reduce the scope for government redistribution. Consider the example of old-age benefits. Many of the arguments I have discussed could be used to support a proposal to privatize Social Security. The principal problem with this proposal is that it would make the redistribution of lifetime income that is inherent in the operation of the current Social Security system impossible. Assuming perfectly flexible markets, wages for each type of worker would fall by the amount of benefits they could expect to receive from a mandated pension; there would be no transfer from poor to rich [sic]. If the government sought to prevent redistribution by preventing wage adjustments, unemployment among those most in need would result. The nonredistributive character of mandated benefit programs is a direct consequence of the fact that, as with benefit taxes, workers pay directly for the benefits they receive.

A different sort of objection to mandated benefits as a tool of social policy follows along the lines of the traditional conservative position that "the only good tax is a bad tax." If policymakers fail to recognize the costs of mandated benefits because they do not appear in the government budget, then mandated benefit programs could lead to excessive spending on social programs. There is no sense in which benefits become "free" just because the government mandates that employers offer them to workers. As with value-added taxes, it can plausibly be argued that mandated benefits fuel the growth of government because their costs are relatively invisible and their distortionary effects are relatively minor.

IV. *Conclusions*

The thrust of this analysis is that mandated benefits are like public programs financed through benefit taxes, thus saving many of the inefficiencies of government provision of public goods. There is an additional difference, however, in that mandated benefits typically allow more choice to employers and employees than public provision. From this perspective it is not surprising that conservatives tend to prefer mandated benefits to public provision, as evidenced, for example, in proposals to privatize Social Security or in proposals in the 1970s to mandate employer health insurance as the "conservative" alternative to national health insurance. Nor is it surprising that liberals tend to prefer mandated benefits to no public action, but have some preference for public provision over mandated benefits....

Notes and Questions

1. *Adverse Selection and Lemons.* Summers suggests that one of the main rationales for government regulation of fringe benefits is to overcome the adverse selection problem. The problem is one of asymmetric information that arises when workers know better than employers how likely they are to use a certain benefit. This can arise for many benefits, ranging from health insurance to maternity leave to children's school tuition benefits. If a firm lowers wages by the average cost of these benefits for all workers, workers who expect to underutilize the benefit will tend to go elsewhere while workers who find the benefit particularly valuable will be attracted to that firm. This raises the cost of providing the benefit, requiring the firm to lower the wage even further, which causes moderate users to drop out, which raises the cost still higher. Depending on the particular supply and demand curves, the benefit may not be offered at all even if every worker would be willing to pay an actuarially fair price for it. A government mandate requiring all firms to provide the benefit is one way to break the cycle.

This adverse-selection problem was first analyzed by economist George Akerlof in an influential article, "The Market for Lemons: Quality Uncertainty and the Market Mechanism," 84 *Quarterly Journal of Economics* 488 (1970). He gave the example of the used-car market, in which sellers have better information than buyers do on whether the car is a lemon. Buyers make their offers based on the average quality of a used car, which causes high-quality sellers to drop out of the market, which lowers the average quality of a used car, which causes more sellers to drop out, and so on. Akerlof suggested that mandatory Social Security coverage could be explained through a lemons model, by requiring the good risks (people who will not live long in retirement) to stay in the market. The lemons model has been applied to many situations. For an application of the model to mandatory just cause, see the Kamiat article in Chapter 7.

2. *Deadweight Losses from Taxes.* Consider an employer payroll tax where the government throws away the money raised (or spends it on national defense, or foreign aid, or aiding the homeless, or on any program where benefits do not vary with how much tax an individual paid). As we saw in the supply and demand model of Chapter 1, this tax will shift down the employer's demand for workers, causing lower wages, employment, and profits. The result is not just a transfer in revenue from employers and workers to the government and its beneficiaries. The fall in total wages and profits exceeds the tax collected. This gap is termed the "deadweight loss" of taxes. It arises because the tax on work (but not on nonwork) reduces the incentive of workers to work. Only if the supply curve were completely vertical (inelastic), implying that workers work the same amount regardless of their wage, would a payroll tax avoid these deadweight losses. The deadweight losses are often labeled "distortionary" because of their effect in altering the trade-off for workers between work and leisure.

In another part of the article, Summers refers to empirical estimates of the deadweight losses caused by taxes. They are large. For every $1 increase in the payroll tax, these studies estimated that wages and profits fell by $1.07 to $1.33. In other words, in the process of transferring $1 from employers and their workers to government, another 7–33 cents is lost.

Summers's main argument is that mandating employer-provided benefits reduces these deadweight losses. To the extent that workers value the benefits they get from working, they will continue to work even after the mandated program is put in place. This reduces the effective payroll tax, thereby reducing the amount of deadweight losses from the program.

3. *European Government Provision versus American Employer Mandates.* In Europe, most of the social safety net is provided by government, whereas in America important social insurance comes from employment. For example, in America most people receive health insurance and pension benefits through their employer. Summers suggests that the American approach causes smaller deadweight loss. On the other hand, more people slip through the social safety net in America.

7

Employment at Will

Most employees in the United States work in the private nonunion sector. With rare exceptions, these employees are employed at will, which means they can be fired, without notice, for any reason or no reason. Employment at will has significant implications for other parts of the employment relationship as well. For instance, an at-will employee can be fired for refusing to work overtime or for refusing a drug test, because these are acceptable "bad" reasons for firing an at-will employee.

Many exceptions have arisen to the basic employment-at-will doctrine. Most important are the statutory prohibitions against firing on the basis of race, sex, religion, age, disability, and certain other protected classifications. For framework discussions on these limitations on the employment contract, see John J. Donohue III, *Foundations of Employment Discrimination Law* (New York: Oxford University Press, 1997); Stewart J. Schwab, "Employment Discrimination," in *Encyclopedia of Law and Economics* (Northampton: Edward Elgar Publishing, 2000). The common law has created exceptions to the at-will rule as well, requiring good faith and fair dealing in certain employment relationships, and prohibiting certain discharges that are against public policy. But only one state, Montana, has abandoned employment at will as the basic legal regime for individual private employment contracts. The lack of legal protection contrasts sharply with the unionized sector, where virtually all collective bargaining contracts forbid employers from firing employees without just cause.

Is employment at will a defensible policy? In the first reading below, Richard Epstein vigorously argues that employment at will protects both employees and employers from the potential exploitation created by long-term employment contracts. In the second reading, Mayer Freed and Daniel Polsby reject any comparison with the just-cause standard of the unionized sector. In the third reading, Stewart Schwab finds greater justification for courts to scrutinize firings for fairness, especially when employees are at the beginning or end of their career. The notes explore other justifications for just cause. In the fourth reading, J. Hoult Verkerke presents the empirical results of a survey of actual employment contracts. Verkerke argues that these empirical results strongly support at-will employment as the appropriate default rule for employment contracts.

"In Defense of the Contract at Will"*

RICHARD A. EPSTEIN

There is ... today a widely held view that the contract at will has outlived its usefulness. But this view is mistaken. The contract at will is not ideal for every employment relation. No court or legislature should ever command its use. Nonetheless, there are two ways in which the contract at will should be respected: one deals with entitlements against regulation and the other with presumptions in the event of contractual silence.

First, the parties should be permitted as of right to adopt this form of contract if they so desire. The principle behind this conclusion is that freedom of contract tends both to advance individual autonomy and to promote the efficient operation of labor markets.

Second, the contract at will should be respected as a rule of construction in response to the perennial question of gaps in contract language: what term should be implied in the absence of explicit agreement on the question of duration or grounds for termination? The applicable standard asks two familiar questions: what rule tends to lend predictability to litigation and to advance the joint interests of the parties? On both these points I hope to show that the contract at will represents in most contexts the efficient solution to the employment relation. To be sure, the stakes are lower where the outright prohibition is no longer in the offing. No rule of construction ever has the power of a rule of regulation, since the parties by negotiation can reverse what the law otherwise commands. Nonetheless, bad rules of contract construction have costs that should not be understated, here or elsewhere. The rule of construction is normally chosen because it reflects the dominant practice in a given class of cases and because that practice is itself regarded as making good sense for the standard transactions it governs. It is of course freely waivable by a joint expression of contrary intention. When the law introduces a just-cause requirement, it flies in the face of ordinary understandings and thus rests upon an assumption that just-cause arrangements are in the broad run of cases either more frequent or desirable than the contract at will, though neither is the case. Where this rule of construction is used, therefore, contracting-out will have to take place in the very large number of cases where the parties desire to conform to the norm by entering into a contract at will. Furthermore, it may be difficult to waive the for-cause requirement in fact, even if waiver is formally allowable as a matter of law, because of high standards for "informed" waiver that cannot be met after the fact. By degrees, the original presumption against the contract at will could so gain in strength that a requirement that is waivable in theory could easily become conclusive in fact....

* 51 *University of Chicago Law Review* 947 (1984).

In this area of private-contracting autonomy, there are some exceptions, arising out of the infrequent cases in which discharge of the contract at will is inconsistent with the performance of some public duty or with the protection of some public right. Just as a contract to commit murder should not be enforceable, neither should one to pollute illegally or to commit perjury.[11] But these cases, however difficult in their own right, in no way require abandoning the basic common law presumption in favor of contracts at will. . . .

I. *The Fairness of the Contract at Will*

The first way to argue for the contract at will is to insist upon the importance of freedom of contract as an end in itself. Freedom of contract is an aspect of individual liberty, every bit as much as freedom of speech, or freedom in the selection of marriage partners or in the adoption of religious beliefs or affiliations. . . . If government regulation is inappropriate for personal, religious, or political activities, then what makes it intrinsically desirable for employment relations? . . .

II. *The Utility of the Contract at Will*

[T]he commonplace belief today (at least outside the actual world of business) is that the contract at will is so unfair and one-sided that it cannot be the outcome of a rational set of bargaining processes any more than, to take the extreme case, a contract for total slavery. . . .

In order to rebut this charge, it is necessary to do more than insist that individuals as a general matter know how to govern their own lives. It is also necessary to display the structural strengths of the contract at will that explain why rational people would enter into such a contract, if not all the time, then at least most of it. . . .

The issue for the parties, properly framed, is not how to minimize employer abuse, but rather how to maximize the gain from the relationship, which in part depends upon minimizing the sum of employer and employee abuse. Viewed in this way the private-contracting problem is far more complex. How does each party create incentives for the proper behavior of the other? How does each side insure against certain risks? How do both sides minimize the administrative costs of their contracting practices? . . .

A. *At–Will Arrangements in Partnerships*

[In this section, Epstein discusses partnerships "in which the problem of bilateral control exists, but where the overtones of inequality of bargain-

---

11. This problem has arisen where employees at will have refused to perjure themselves on behalf of the employer . . . or where workers have been dismissed because they have filed workers' compensation claims. It seems clear that any contract to commit perjury should simply be treated as illegal. The workers' compensation case is more difficult both because there is less justification for the coercive character of compensation, since no third-party interests are at stake, and because in all events the worker is entitled to file his claim and will do so if its value exceeds the gains he expects from the employment contract. . . .

ing power are absent." Partnership law gives a strong presumption that partners can dissolve the partnership at any time for any reason. This unqualified right to withdraw, argues Epstein, protects a hardworking partner from abuse by fellow partners, because the threat to withdraw becomes more credible as the hardworking partner is taken advantage of by others.]

B. *Employment at Will*

1. *Monitoring Behavior.* Begin for the moment with the fears of the firm, for it is the firm's right to maintain at-will power that is now being called into question. In all too many cases, the firm must contend with the recurrent problem of employee theft and with the related problems of unauthorized use of firm equipment and employee kickback arrangements. As the analysis of partnerships shows, however, the proper concerns of the firm are not limited to obvious forms of criminal misconduct. The employee on a fixed wage can, at the margin, capture only a portion of the gain from his labor, and therefore has a tendency to reduce output. The employee who receives a commission equal to half the firm's profit attributable to his labor may work hard, but probably not quite as hard as he would if he received the entire profit from the completed sale, an arrangement that would solve the agency-cost problem only by undoing the firm. . . .

The problem of management then is to identify the forms of social control that are best able to minimize these agency costs. . . .

Internal auditors may help control some forms of abuse, and simple observation by co-workers may well monitor employee activities. (There are some very subtle trade-offs to be considered when the firm decides whether to use partitions or separate offices for its employees.) Promotions, bonuses, and wages are also critical in shaping the level of employee performance. But the carrot cannot be used to the exclusion of the stick. In order to maintain internal discipline, the firm may have to resort to sanctions against individual employees. It is far easier to use those powers that can be unilaterally exercised: to fire, to demote, to withhold wages, or to reprimand. These devices can visit very powerful losses upon individual employees without the need to resort to legal action, and they permit the firm to monitor employee performance continually in order to identify both strong and weak workers and to compensate them accordingly. The principles here are constant, whether we speak of senior officials or lowly subordinates, and it is for just this reason that the contract at will is found at all levels in private markets. . . .

Thus far, the analysis generally has focused on the position of the employer. Yet for the contract at will to be adopted ex ante, it must work for the benefit of workers as well. And indeed it does, for the contract at will also contains powerful limitations on employers' abuses of power. To see the importance of the contract at will to the employee, it is useful to distinguish between two cases. In the first, the employer pays a fixed sum of money to the worker and is then free to demand of the employee whatever services he wants for some fixed period of time. In the second case, there is no fixed period of employment. The employer is free to demand whatever he wants of the employee, who in turn is free to withdraw for good reason, bad reason, or no reason at all.

The first arrangement invites abuse by the employer, who can now make enormous demands upon the worker without having to take into account either the worker's disutility during the period of service or the value of the worker's labor at contract termination. A fixed-period contract that leaves the worker's obligations unspecified thereby creates a sharp tension between the parties, since the employer receives all the marginal benefits and the employee bears all the marginal costs.

Matters are very different where the employer makes increased demands under a contract at will. Now the worker can quit whenever the net value of the employment contract turns negative. As with the employer's power to fire or demote, the threat to quit (or at a lower level to come late or leave early) is one that can be exercised without resort to litigation. Furthermore, that threat turns out to be most effective when the employer's opportunistic behavior is the greatest because the situation is one in which the worker has least to lose. To be sure, the worker will not necessarily make a threat whenever the employer insists that the worker accept a less favorable set of contractual terms, for sometimes the changes may be accepted as an uneventful adjustment in the total compensation level attributable to a change in the market price of labor. This point counts, however, only as an additional strength of the contract at will, which allows for small adjustments in both directions in ongoing contractual arrangements with a minimum of bother and confusion.

The case for the contract at will is further strengthened by another feature common to contracts of this sort. The employer is often required either to give notice or to pay damages in lieu of notice; damages are traditionally equal to the wages that the employee would have earned during the notice period. These provisions for "severance pay" provide the worker with some protection against casual or hasty discharges, but they do not interfere with the powerful efficiency characteristics of the contract at will. First, lump-sum transfers do not require the introduction of any "for cause" requirement, which could be the source of expensive litigation. Second, because the sums are definite, they can be easily computed, so that administrative costs are minimized. Third, because the payments are unconditional, they do not create perverse incentives for the employee or heavy monitoring costs for the employer: the terminated employee will not be tempted to avoid gainful employment in order to run up his damages for wrongful discharge; the employer, for his part, will not have to monitor the post-termination behavior of the employee in order to guard against that very risk. Thus, provisions for severance pay can be used to give employees added protection against arbitrary discharge without sacrificing the advantages of a clean break between the parties.

2. *Reputational Losses.* Another reason why employees are often willing to enter into at-will employment contracts stems from the asymmetry of reputational losses. Any party who cheats may well obtain a bad reputation that will induce others to avoid dealing with him. The size of these losses tends to differ systematically between employers and employees— to the advantage of the employee. Thus in the usual situation there are many workers and a single employer. The disparity in number is apt to be greatest in large industrial concerns, where the at-will contract is commonly, if mistakenly, thought to be most unsatisfactory because of the supposed inequality of bargaining power. The employer who decides to act for bad reason or no reason at all may not face any legal liability under the classical common law rule. But he faces very powerful adverse economic consequences. If co-workers perceive the dismissal as arbitrary, they will take fresh stock of their own prospects, for they can no longer be certain that their faithful performance will ensure their security and advancement. The uncertain prospects created by arbitrary employer behavior are functionally indistinguishable from a reduction in wages unilaterally imposed by the employer. At the margin some workers will look elsewhere, and typically the best workers will have the greatest opportunities. By the same token the large employer has more to gain if he dismisses undesirable employees, for this ordinarily acts as an implicit increase in wages to the other employees, who are no longer burdened with uncooperative or obtuse co-workers....

3. *Risk Diversification and Imperfect Information....* The contract at will is designed in part to offset the concentration of individual investment in a single job by allowing diversification among employers over time. The employee is not locked into an unfortunate contract if he finds better opportunities elsewhere or if he detects some weakness in the internal structure of the firm....

4. *Administrative Costs.* There is one last way in which the contract at will has an enormous advantage over its rivals. It is very cheap to administer. Any effort to use a for-cause rule will in principle allow all, or at least a substantial fraction of, dismissals to generate litigation....

5. *Bilateral Monopoly and Inequality of Bargaining Power.* The reason why these contracts at will are effective is precisely that the employer must always pay an implicit price when he exercises his right to fire. He no longer has the right to compel the employee's service, as the employee can enter the market to find another job. The costs of the employer's decision therefore are borne in large measure by the employer himself, creating an implicit system of coinsurance between employer and employee against employer abuse. Nor, it must be stressed, are the costs to

the employer light. It is true that employees who work within a firm acquire specific knowledge about its operation and upon dismissal can transfer only a portion of that knowledge to the new job. Nonetheless, the problem is roughly symmetrical, as the employer must find, select, and train a replacement worker who may not turn out to be better than the first employee. Workers are not fungible, and sorting them out may be difficult: resumes can be misleading, if not fraudulent; references may be only too eager to unload an unsuitable employee; training is expensive; and the new worker may not like the job or may be forced to move out of town. In any case, firms must bear the costs of voluntary turnover by workers who quit, which gives them a frequent reminder of the need to avoid self-inflicted losses. The institutional stability of employment contracts at will can now be explained in part by their legal fragility. The right to fire is exercised only infrequently because the threat of firing is effective.

Thus far the account of inequality of bargaining power has been wholly negative. But the description of the employment relationship does suggest one way in which inequality can arise, even within the framework of generally competitive markets. In the course of an ongoing relationship between employee and employer, each side gains from the contract more than it could obtain by returning to the open market. The surplus that is created must be divided between the parties. In principle, either the worker or the employer could receive the entire surplus without inducing the other party, who still receives a competitive return, to sever the relationship. A fortiori any solution that divides the surplus between the parties should be stable as well. The contract at will thus creates a bilateral monopoly, but only to the extent of the surplus.

The question of inequality of bargaining power can now be helpfully restated: which side will appropriate most of the surplus in any negotiations between them? Unlike the typical formulations of the problem, this leaves the set of possible solutions strictly bounded because the employee cannot be driven below the competitive wage and the employer cannot be driven to a wage above the sum of the competitive wage plus the full amount of the surplus. An employer can therefore be said to possess an inequality of bargaining power when he is able to appropriate more than half the surplus, while the employee can be said to possess inequality of bargaining power if he can appropriate more than half the surplus. To take an example, assume the employer is prepared to pay 20, while the worker is willing to work for 10. The agreed wage therefore could fall anywhere between those two numbers. If the employer is systematically able to appropriate more than 5 of this surplus, by keeping the wage level below 15, then he has unequal bargaining power, though still within the framework of overall competitive markets.

The existence of some surplus should be pervasive in all labor markets, given that labor is not perfectly fungible. In practice, the size of the surplus on average should be relatively small at the time of contract formation. Because the parties have not built up much specific capital in the relationship, quitting or firing will cause relatively small dislocations. As time passes, however, the gains to both sides from continuing the employment relationship are apt to increase, so that both sides have more to lose from separation. The bilateral monopoly problem now assumes greater significance. The increased size of the surplus can easily make wages somewhat indeterminate (which is why workers are commonly nervous about asking for a raise, and employers are nervous about refusing it). As the stakes become larger, the amount of resources spent in obtaining a larger portion of the surplus should increase. A contractual breakdown should nonetheless be an infrequent occurrence, as both sides have strong incentives to keep the relationship viable. The costs of negotiation tend to be reduced because each side is familiar with the other. The scope for bluffing is somewhat limited by each party's knowledge of the preferences of the other side. Finally, there are strong reasons for each side to avoid squeezing the last drop out of a relationship: miscalculation of the reserve price of the other party (i.e., the minimum he will accept or the maximum he will pay) could lead to a severance of the relationship and thus to a loss of the entire surplus.

It still remains to be determined which side is likely to appropriate most of this contract-specific surplus. One might guess that the employer will be able to achieve this objective, perhaps because his experience in repeat transactions with many workers fosters greater skills in negotiation. In addition, the employer may know in general the market wages available to beginning workers, as these typically will be public knowledge. Yet a number of considerations suggest the opposite conclusion. First, the employer often bargains through subordinate managers and thus faces an agency-cost problem avoided by the worker who bargains on his own account. Second, the worker's opportunity cost for his time will often be lower than the employer's, so that the increased time he can spend on the transaction may offset the employer's greater skill, if any, per unit of time. Third, the worker may be able to learn something about the employer's reservation price (i.e., the maximum wage he would be willing to pay) because the employer must reveal some information about his willingness to pay in negotiations with other long-term workers. Finally, it is not clear that the employer gains any real advantage because of his greater relative wealth, if any. To be sure, the wealthy employer can hold out for a larger share of the surplus because he has less, proportionally, to lose. Yet by the same token the employer's resolve may be weaker because he has less to gain by holding out.

This modest catalogue of considerations shows how difficult it is to determine the exact division of the surplus, although my suspicion is that in the broad run of cases it will tend to be evenly divided. But even if this guess is wrong, there is no reason for the law to interfere in the bargaining process. The whole question of inequality of bargaining power arises in the bounded context of how much of a *supra*competitive wage the worker will obtain. At the very worst, the worker will get the amount that is offered in some alternate employment where he has built up no specific capital. To try to formulate and administer a set of legal rules that will allow some trier of fact to measure the size of the surplus embedded in the ongoing transaction, and to allocate half (or more) of it to the worker, cannot be done at any social cost that is less than the expected size of the surplus itself, it if can be done at all. The entire exercise is fraught with the possibility of real error, as real resources would have to be expended solely to make transfer payments that can in no way enhance productive efforts. The existence of this transactional surplus does not negate the fact that markets are still competitive before prospective employers and employees enter into any transaction at all.

The size of the surplus, and thus the scope of any inequality problem, can be reduced more effectively by adopting legal rules that remove or minimize legal impediments to labor mobility. The contract at will, by allowing either side to sever relationships without legal impediment, tends to reduce rigidities in markets and thus to act as a counterweight to the bilateral monopoly problem that emerges even in voluntary markets. The complex rules that give workers "property" rights in their jobs tend to increase the size of any possible surplus and exacerbate the basic problem. The identification of a transaction-specific surplus, then, adds to our understanding of long-term employment relationships, but it affords no warrant for upsetting the contract at will on supposed grounds of public policy. . . .

III. *Distributional Concerns*

. . . The proposed reforms in the at-will doctrine cannot hope to transfer wealth systematically from rich to poor on the model of comprehensive systems of taxation or welfare benefits. . . . The proposed rules cover the whole range from senior executives to manual labor. . . . Those who tend to slack off seem on balance to be most vulnerable to dismissal under the at-will rule; yet it is very hard to imagine why some special concession should be made in their favor at the expense of their more diligent fellow workers. . . .

IV. *Exceptions to the Contract at Will*

An examination of the contracting objectives of parties explains why contracts at will are common. The same set of considerations, however, also helps explain why contracts at will are not found in all employment contexts, but are instead sometimes displaced by more elaborate contractual mechanisms. The central point is that the contract at will works only where performance on both sides takes place in lockstep progression. This condition will be satisfied where neither side has performed or where the worker's past performance has been matched by appropriate payment from the employer. In these cases the contract at will provides both employer and employee with a simple, informal "bond" against the future misfeasance of the other side: fire or quit. Where the sequence of performance requires one side to perform in full before the other side begins performance, this bonding mechanism will break down because there are no longer two unperformed promises of roughly equal value to stand as security for each other. That is why an employee will have to resort to legal action if the employer simply refuses to pay wages for work that has already been done. It is also why a contract at will cannot handle the question of compensation for job-related personal injuries, for after injury the value of the right to quit no longer balances off the right to fire.

Notes and Questions

1. *Notice Requirements in Employment Contracts.* Epstein argues that at-will contracts protect workers by allowing them immediately to quit, for any reason, if the employer is exploiting them. This protection is symmetric to the employer's right to fire at any time for any reason. Epstein contrasts this right to quit with a definite-term contract in which the employee promises to stay, and the employer promises to retain the employee, for a certain length of time.

Epstein's symmetric term contract, which he argues is less protective of workers than an at-will contract, is similar to the traditional employment contract under English common law. There, both worker and employer were required to give reasonable notice before ending the relationship. The length of reasonable notice varied with the type of employment, reflecting the social differentiation between manual laborers and other workers. For white-collar workers, the length of notice ranged from one month to one year. For manual laborers the length could be as little as a week, an hour, or, in some cases, a minute. Under the Contracts of Employment Act of 1963, Parliament supplemented the common law by imposing statutory minimum notice periods based on the employee's tenure at the firm, in addition to the general requirement of reasonable notice. The scale ranged from one week's notice after two years of tenure to four weeks' notice after four years of tenure. See Paul Davies and Mark Freedland, *Labour Law: Text and Materials*, 2nd ed. (London: Weidenfeld and Nicolson, 1984), 432–34; Jay M. Feinman, "The Development of the Employment at Will Rule," 20 *American Journal of Legal History* 118, 122 (1976); Dorothy Knight Waddy, *Dix on Contracts of Employment*, 3rd ed. (London: Butterworth, 1968).

Parliament broke the symmetry between employers and employees in required notice in 1978, in the Employment Protection Consolidation Act. Employees were now required to give only one week's notice before quitting, regardless of how long they had worked for the employer. Employers, however, had to give one week's notice to employees after four weeks of service, and an additional week of notice for every year of service over two years, up to a maximum of twelve weeks' notice. The remedy for failure to notify was payment for the period of required notice; employers could also make payments in lieu of notice. In addition to these notice requirements before quits or dismissals, since the Industrial Relations Act of 1971, British employees have the right not to be "unfairly dismissed." Payment in lieu of notice does not foreclose an employee's action for unfair dismissal if otherwise warranted. For an assessment of unfair dismissal law in Britain and other major countries, see Samuel Estreicher, "Unjust Dismissal Law: Some Cautionary Notes," 33 *American Journal of Comparative Law* 310 (1985).

Thus, Epstein's feared alternative to at-will contracts—a definite term or notice contract binding on both employer and employee—is a straw person. It is no longer the British model, and is not the proposal of American scholars who criticize the at-will doctrine. No critic of at-will proposes returning to the older English common law requirement of symmetric notice by employer and employee. Rather, advocates of just cause contemplate a system where employees can quit at any time (or, in Britain, after a week's notice), but the employer cannot dismiss without cause (and, in Britain, must give reasonable notice as well).

2. *Binding Employees and Employers to Their Relationship.* Some legal systems do significantly bind employees to their jobs. In the Netherlands, for instance, employees, as well as employers, must get a permit from the Regional Labor Market Agency (Regionaal Bestuur voor de Arbeidsvoorziening, or RBA) in order to unilaterally terminate an employment relationship. Without a permit, any notice given is void and the employment relationship is not terminated. In order to get a permit, the requesting party must show good reason why the employment should be terminated. The other party is given the opportunity to be heard before the RBA makes its final decision. In practice, employers rarely hold employees to this requirement. It is not uncommon, however, for the RBA to refuse employer requests for termination permits. See Ernst P. Jansen, *Labor Law in the Netherlands* (Boston: Kluwer, 1994), 39–50.

3. *Promoters of Just Cause.* Numerous scholars have advocated a mandatory just-cause scheme. The seminal article is Lawrence E. Blades, "Employment at Will vs. Individual Freedom: On Limiting the Abusive Exercise of Employer Power," 67 *Columbia Law Review* 1404 (1967), advocating a tort theory. Others have urged that the legal system should give workers a property interest in their jobs. See William B. Gould IV, "The Idea of the Job as Property in Contemporary America: The Legal and Collective Bargaining Framework," 1986 *BYU Law Review* 885. Others make a comparative point, noting that virtually all other industrialized countries give remedies to a worker who is terminated without cause. See, e.g., Clyde W. Summers, "Individual Protection Against Unjust Dismissal: Time for a Statute," 62 *Virginia Law Review* 481 (1976).

4. *Montana and Just Cause.* Within the United States, Montana is the only state where the baseline rule is not employment at will. By statute, a Montana employer may not dismiss a worker with more than twelve months' tenure without good cause. Montana Wrongful Discharge from Employment Act of 1987, Montana Code Annotated §§ 39–901 to 39-2–914. The statute allows workers to recover lost wages and fringe benefits for four years, but prohibits recovery for pain and suffering, emotional distress, or compensato-

ry damages. Punitive damages are allowed only if the employer engages in actual fraud or malice.

In 1991, the National Conference of Commissioners on Uniform State Laws adopted a Model Employment Termination Act, broadly similar to the Montana statute. No state has yet adopted legislation along these lines.

"Just Cause for Termination Rules and Economic Efficiency"*

MAYER G. FREED and DANIEL D. POLSBY

Introduction

... Supporters of the abandonment of the common law presumption of employment at will claim that a system of mandatory tenure would promote economic efficiency, that is, maximize societal wealth. This assertion, however, confronts an immediate problem. In the private sector and in the absence of unions, employment is almost always at will—in other words, it can be unilaterally terminated by either the employer or the employee for good reason, bad reason or no reason at all. This is true, moreover, even though common law employment at will is merely a presumption and can be overcome by agreement. Why, then, does the at-will employment arrangement persist through so many different businesses, regions, and circumstances? Such robustness evidently requires an explanation. The simplest explanation is that giving the employer legally unconstrained discretion over the composition of its workforce is generally the "efficient" solution as between employers and employees. Contracting parties, in full possession of their faculties and their own interests, would not voluntarily move from this apportionment of legal rights and liabilities because ex hypothesis employers systematically value discretion to fire employees more highly than workers value the substantive right to work and the associated procedural apparatus that might protect them from arbitrary firing....

The efficiency of at-will employment may not account for its persistence; something else may explain its persistence. Some market failure that regularly operates to give the employer both the power and the desire to claim, even if inefficiently, the right to dismiss employees for reasons to which they would not, ex ante, have agreed instead may explain the efficiency of at-will employment.

I. *Monopoly*

The most commonly encountered market failure idea is the inequality of bargaining power that supposedly subsists between employer and employee. This notion of inequality of bargaining power pervades discussions about regulation of the employment relationship. It is an intuitive

* 38 *Emory Law Journal* 1097 (1989).

idea, but one that deserves a careful explication. Two entirely different ideas seem to be embedded in the term "inequality of bargaining power." First, the term suggests that employees, because they have less money than employers, are at a disadvantage in bargaining for terms and conditions of employment. Second, the term implies that employers exercise monopoly power in the labor market.

Inequality of bargaining power in the first sense is not a market failure at all. On the contrary, inequality of bargaining power is consistent with the hypothesis that at-will employment is efficient. Inequality of bargaining power in the second sense—the employer as monopolist— would be a market failure, except that (1) employers are rarely monopolists, and (2) even if they were, one could not possibly account for the prevalence of at-will employment by reference to that monopoly.

Suppose the proposition is true that employers as a class are wealthier than employees. What follows is an "inequality of bargaining power" only in the sense that employers systematically could outbid employees for resources in the open market. What does this inequality imply about the employment relationship?

Conceive of a "job" as an amount of time held by employees, which they can spend on themselves or in the service of employers. With their superior bargaining power, employers are able to "outbid" employees for their time. In other words, because employees need money more than employers do, employees will surrender their "leisure" time, the time that employees "purchase" from themselves, in order to do work for the richer class of employers. By the same token, rich employers will be in a position to outbid employees for terms of employment, such as the tenure property, that are valuable to them.

If this is the sense in which inequality of bargaining power is thought to exist between employers and employees, it demonstrates not market failure but market success. A market is successful when it moves resources from lower-value to higher-value uses.

The claim that employers exercise monopoly power over employees is a legitimate claim of market failure. This analysis assumes that employers are usually job monopolists, exercising some degree of "power," with respect to actual or potential employees.

For the sake of understanding the implications of this "power," consider a literal monopoly situation. In this imaginary world of complete monopoly, only one employer exists and many potential employees are jockeying for job offers. In this world, individuals must work on the employer's terms or not at all. Unless some other employer is offering some sort of competition for employees' services, or threatening to offer competition, the monopoly employer can hire all of its necessary labor for any wage higher than an employee's next best option, to wit, starvation. It is difficult to imagine an employment monopoly anything like the one described without also concluding that the government is the employer. No such monopoly could last for long without plenty of legal protection; individuals would have to be strictly forbidden to employ others or, for that matter, to be self-employed. . . .

But even if it were not contrary to facts, the "monopoly" explanation for the prevalence of at-will arrangements would still be wrong. . . . The theory of monopoly does not predict that the employer would demand that the employee forgo just cause protection. It predicts only that, regardless of how the compensation is structured, the package will be worth less than the market wage. Whether an employee works for a monopolist employer or not, he must ultimately expect to forgo cash wages to the extent that the employer can compensate itself for the costs of the noncash elements of its labor costs, such as tenure protection, pension plans, or medical insurance.

Suppose that a monopolist employer pays each of its workers forty and the competitive wage is fifty. In order to attribute the absence of tenure protection in the private nonunion sector to the theory of monopoly (and conversely, in order to attribute the presence of tenure protection in the union sector to the countervailing economic power of unions), one must believe that employees are unwilling to pay for tenure protection when their wages are forty but suddenly become willing to pay for it when their wages jump to fifty.

Such a guess may have a sort of superficial attraction because people often buy certain "luxuries" when their wages are high that they will not buy when their wages are low—caviar, BMWs, and possibly tenure protection. But the wages of employees in the "at-will" sector are scattered in range, and some wages are very high indeed. If tenure is a luxury that an employee will not buy when he or she is making forty but will buy when he or she is making fifty, should not employees at will who are already making fifty but whose competitive wage is sixty buy it? It is extremely unlikely that virtually all at-will employees, regardless of the absolute level of their incomes, perpetually are one dollar short of the intersection between the supply and the demand curve for unjust dismissal protection. The assumption that tenure protection is a just-out-of-reach luxury good for everyone, regardless of income, is wildly implausible. Such an assumption cannot explain the prevalence of the at-will arrangement in the nonunion sector or its absence in the union sector.

Finally, if monopoly is the problem, mandatory tenure is an utterly futile solution. An employer, faced with a legal requirement that it offer its employees tenure protection, predictably would institute an offsetting wage reduction as a quid pro quo, so that its total labor costs would not change. Monopoly power can be defeated only be regulating it directly, or breaking it up. Attempting to defeat monopoly by contractual terms is well-nigh ridiculous.

II. *Paternalism*

Other market failure arguments on behalf of mandatory tenure systems are essentially paternalistic. One target of paternalistic concern is the class of employees who, contrary to their own best interests, fail to secure protection against unjust dismissal from employment because they do not correctly perceive their own best interests. The second target is the class of employers who insist on arbitrarily dismissing employees when the ability to fire employees only for just cause would be in the employers' best interests. . . .

A. *Paternalism on Behalf of Employees*
1. *Perceptual Distortion*

On the day a person shakes hands with a new employer, it may well be that he or she has given less than careful thought to the possibility of future termination without just cause. The efficiency presumption might be wrong if employees underestimate the value of job security when they accept new jobs. Misperception, rather than efficiency, could account for the fact that private sector employment contracts seldom specify dismissal only for just cause. Of course, even if prospective employees do not give much thought to the possibility of being fired "arbitrarily," employees do not necessarily underestimate the probability of being fired. On the contrary, employees may give little thought to the matter of arbitrary firing because they perceive correctly that the probability of being fired arbitrarily is quite low.

If the claim is that the probability of being fired arbitrarily is high, and that employees fail to perceive this high probability, it must first be established that the probability is high. . . .

[Using estimates of Professor Cornelius Peck on the number of wrongful discharges,] the probability of an employee who is not protected by some form of just cause regime being dismissed or disciplined in one year for reasons that, applying the union just cause standard, an arbitrator would overturn, is .0154%. The probability of an employee being dismissed or disciplined under circumstances that would allow his grievance to be settled is .5769%. All of these probabilities are low enough that a person who disregarded them would not be acting unreasonably.

Evidence regarding the question of systematic perceptual distortion suggests that employees must, if anything, overestimate the value of job security. A recent and growing body of literature addresses the perceptual distortions experienced by individuals in the face of low probability events. Kahneman and Tversky report that people tend either to ignore or to overestimate the probable occurrence of a low probability future event. . . .

What do these findings suggest regarding job security? Based on Professor Peck's numbers, arbitrary firing is a low probability event.

Kahneman and Tversky imply that, in the face of such a low probability loss, employees tend to be risk averse. In other words, employees would prefer a certain loss now (a smaller paycheck) to the larger contingent loss (their jobs) that would occur if they were arbitrarily fired. Employees would be willing to pay more for job security than rational and risk-neutral employees "ought" to pay for the present value of job security. In light of these findings, to suggest that systematic employee misperceptions could account for the absence of tenure arrangements is surely a mistake.

2.　*Public Goods*

Public goods are defined by two properties. The first property is that consumption of the good by one person does not affect the ability of others to consume the good ("jointness of consumption"). The second property is that the good, once created, is or can be consumed by everyone. The creator of the good cannot exclude "free riders" who benefit by the existence of the public good but did not help pay for the good ("non-excludability"). If these qualities are present, the presumption does not exist that a free market will provide the efficient amount of the good if left to its own devices. . . .

The argument that universal just cause guarantees are undiscovered public goods is a dubious proposition. First, tenure guarantees have not been proved to contain the properties of jointness of consumption or non-excludability. Second, even if this first hurdle is cleared, ample reason exists to doubt the argument that tenure's aggregate utility to workers exceeds its costs of production.

a.　*Non–Excludability*

An arrangement by which an employee is protected against discharge, other than for just cause, does not appear to be a non-excludable good. "Non-excludability" means unacceptably high costs of exclusion such that no one is excluded. Why just cause protection is so costly for an employee to procure appears unexplainable.

Suppose an employee values a guarantee of just cause for dismissal more highly than other compensation terms, and no structural impediment prevents him from getting such a guarantee. In the employee's contract negotiations with the employer, the employee is not trying to secure tenure protections for the entire workforce; the other employees will not be free riders on the employee's tenure protection.

If the public goods barrier explains why just cause guarantees seldom emerge from individual bargaining, some less obvious costs must exist for any arrangement in which only one employee has tenure protection. Further, these costs must be great enough that few employees would ever voluntarily incur them.

Two examples illustrate these less obvious costs. First, an employer might be reluctant to promise to be "fair" to one employee without also promising to be "fair" to all employees on the ground that other employees would resent different treatment. . . .

The employee envy example assumes that employees without job security become less productive when some of their fellow workers obtain guarantees against unjust dismissal. This effect of lessened productivity must be present even though the less secure employees, all things being equal, will receive higher cash wages than the more secure employee. Whether lowered productivity occurs or not is questionable. Even if giving job protection to employees who value tenure makes them more productive, which is unlikely, workforce efficiency should not be undermined by employees having the option of taking tenure's value in cash or cash's value in tenure.

A second example of less obvious exclusion costs depends on economies of scale that the employer might be faced with in supplying the tenure good. . . . Suppose an employer would experience large start-up costs in establishing just cause "machinery." This might be the case, for example, if the employer established a new bureaucracy to monitor personnel decisions. To set up such a bureaucracy for just one or two employees would be silly. Indeed, if any employees were excluded from participation in an existing monitoring system, such exclusion would be costly to employees who were included. Each additional person included in the system and charged by the employer for inclusion would lower the per capita costs of buying just cause protection; each person excluded would raise those per capita costs.

In a true public goods situation, members of the public cannot be excluded from enjoyment of the good even if they have not paid for the good. . . . It is easy to exclude those employees who have not paid for their tenure rights. If tenure is a non-excludable good only because of the fixed costs of its creation, any proposal to overcome the public goods barrier by legal compulsion must not permit employees to waive their tenure rights. . . . But if even one employee is allowed to sell back his or her tenure, the per capita costs to the employees who keep their tenure will be forced up. This could lead another employee to sell his or her tenure back because tenure would not be worth the increased price to him or her. Again, this would raise the price higher and produce more sales of tenure back until the whole system would collapse. Consequently, if abandonment of employment at will is advocated on the ground that tenure is a public good in the terms just outlined, then the right to be dismissed only for just cause is inalienable. In other words, this right must be immune from modification by contract.

b. *Aggregate Utility to Workers*

. . . Even if tenure rules are considered to be public goods, the aggregate utility of workers must be larger than the price charged by employers for unjust dismissal protection. This difference is required in order to argue that the law should intervene and create tenure for at-will workers where the market has failed to provide tenure for them. . . .

Workers' behavior in the union sector has been proffered as evidence that the aggregate utility of unjust dismissal protection exceeds the price employers would have to demand in order to provide job protection and recoup their costs. Protection against unjust dismissal is a standard benefit in collective bargaining agreements. Under the theory that unions create public goods, unions will seek contract terms in accordance with the preferences of their inframarginal majority of workers. This behavior indicates that employees will purchase unjust dismissal protection whenever a mechanism (a union or other device) exists that can overcome the public goods/free rider problem by allowing employees to aggregate their preferences. The union then distributes the cost of unjust dismissal protection across the entire bargaining unit. . . .

But ample reason exists to arouse skepticism regarding the correctness of the analogy between the union experience and the ordinary buyer-seller relationship. American labor unions are not purely voluntary associations like retail co-ops, in which employees band together to obtain group discounts for certain goods. Labor unions are compulsory associations, vested with some of the coercive powers of the state. It is possible, therefore, that a bargain struck between a union and an employer will have different characteristics than a bargain struck between a retail co-op and its suppliers. In the situation of a retail co-op, dissenting members can abstain from consuming the benefit (for example, by refraining from buying Belgian endive or anything else the board of managers purchased cheaply), or can exit freely from the co-op relationship.

If tenure, or any other contract guarantee for which the union might bargain, is assumed to be a fixed-cost non-excludable good, employers will demand a price for that good that is higher than any individual employee could or would pay. The costs to the employer in fulfilling a contract promise will be substantial, but will diminish per capita if spread across a larger group of beneficiaries. For example, suppose it would cost an employer $10,000 to deliver X—something demanded by an employee. If 100 employees want X, and the cost of X remains at $10,000, then the per worker cost of delivering X goes down to $100. If the employer has 100 workers and a minority of 49 workers would purchase X for only $50 or less, then the other 51 workers, who also want X but are willing to pay more than $50 in order to obtain X, would have to pay at least $196 per worker ($10,000 divided by 51, rounded off). If all 51 are willing to pay $196, they would presumably be able to get X through a consensual transaction with the employer. The transaction would not automatically occur, however, because the costs of determining the group to whom the employer's offer could be made would vary.

The labor statutes give the 51 who are willing to pay more money a tempting alternative. The 51 workers constitute a majority of the employees and thus they can unionize. Unionization will give them the power to conscript the reluctant 49 workers, driving down the per capita price of X to $100. The $4900 discount to the 51 workers entails no loss for the employer, who will still realize a $10,000 benefit in return for providing X. The only losers are the 49 workers, who must pay $100 per worker ($4900 total) for something that they value at only $50 per worker ($2450 total)....

It is apparent that no one has any reliable evidence regarding the aggregate utility of tenure to workers. Some unreliable evidence exists, however, which will next be discussed. This evidence has been extrapolated from estimates made by Professor Peck, a leading advocate of the at-will employment reform, of the number of employees in the at-will sector who are dismissed or disciplined without just cause.

From Professor Peck's raw numbers, assuming that every settled case would result in reinstatement of the grieving employee, the probability that any particular employee would need this job protection in a given year has been calculated. Using that probability figure, the economic value that a rational employee would assign, or the "premium" he or she would pay, for one year's worth of protection against unjust dismissal can be approximated.

For purposes of this exercise, start with an annual salary of $21,000, which was the average salary of employees in 1987 in the United States. Assume that the duration of unemployment, if it occurs, will be 26 weeks, which is longer than average. [Accounting for unemployment compensation benefits, the] total loss for him or her will be $6704. To calculate the expected value of this loss, this number must be discounted by the probability of its occurrence—that the person will be fired without just cause. Using Professor Peck's figure (the highest we have seen), the likelihood of being fired without just cause is .5769%. Multiply $6704 by .005769 and the person loses $38.68 per year, or 74 cents per week, or a little less than two cents per hour. Of course, lost income is not the sole loss suffered by a terminated employee. Search costs for new employment and psychic costs of various kinds must be taken into account. In order to do so, assume these costs equal the lost income. Based on these assumptions, the person loses $1.48 per week....

c. *Costs of Producing the Tenure Good*

It is improbable that an average employer would not pay approximately two cents per employee per hour to retain the ability to terminate its workers' employment without the necessity of justifying its decisions to the authorities. If employers would willingly pay this amount, then the public goods story, giving it the benefit of all its doubts, is definitely wrong.

The most obvious costs of an unjust dismissal system are administration expenses. Other than costs that will be borne by the public, such as paying for courts to adjudicate cases, and employees' costs of challenging their dismissals, such as legal fees, employers must pay for attorneys and arbitrators. Additionally, employers will have a substantially increased administrative burden because they will have to keep records to document the bases for any dismissals.

Less obvious costs also exist that must be taken into account, which exceed the added overhead of unjust dismissal rules. These costs are borne by the enterprise as a consequence of forgoing decisions to fire employees because of the existence of unjust dismissal rules....

B.   *Paternalism on Behalf of Employers*

[In this section, Freed and Polsby reject three arguments that a law mandating just cause might benefit the employer. The first argument is that supervisors enjoying their own power sometimes fire productive workers contrary to the firm's interests. A mandatory just-cause regime would reduce such inefficient terminations. Freed and Polsby concede that such "agency" problems can produce unjust dismissals, but argue that "[f]or mandatory tenure rules to be effective in eliminating agency costs, the persons reviewing dismissal decisions must be better than the employer at recognizing mistakes, conversion, or sabotage. Alternatively, the mandatory tenure system must be a cheaper monitoring tool than the system utilized by the employer while being equally as effective. It is improbable that either of these conditions will be met very often. On the whole, employers are more likely to understand their own interests better than outsiders, whose jobs are economically unrelated to the business enterprise."

The second argument is that job security increases job satisfaction and thereby improves employee performance, benefitting both employer and employee. Freed and Polsby insist that "[l]ittle support exists for the theory that job security causes higher productivity. In reality, the contrary is probably true.... [M]otivation results chiefly from intrinsic factors such as responsibility, recognition, involvement in decision-making, or a sense of achievement or self-esteem. Thus, job security, which is an extrinsic factor, cannot be relied on to motivate employees to increase their productivity."

The third argument is that job tenure increases the incentive to cooperate. As Freed and Polsby explain, "[a]n experienced worker with practical skills to teach needs an incentive to share his knowledge with an oncoming generation of lower paid and possibly more energetic competitors. One such incentive might be to guarantee that the older worker will not be thanked for his cooperative behavior by being laid off from the job that his junior colleague has now been taught to do." This argument, say Freed and Polsby, "undoubtedly has considerable validity.

Many employers have assented to, even insisted on, some type of tenure for their employees.... However, merely observing that the rule of due process works well for some employers is not a convincing argument for imposing the rule of due process on other employers who have not embraced it. It is not intuitively obvious that good policy for large, national companies is good policy for small, local businesses."]

Notes and Questions

1. *Worker Overestimates of Legal Protection.* Freed and Polsby argue that arbitrary dismissal is a low-probability event that workers probably overestimate, but give no data on worker estimates. Professor Pauline Kim, in a careful survey of Missouri workers applying for unemployment insurance, found that workers greatly overestimate the legal protections of terminated workers. For example, one of several hypothetical questions she asked was whether a supervisor could lawfully fire a worker by falsely accusing the worker of dishonesty because he dislikes the employee personally. Eighty-nine percent of workers thought such a firing was unlawful, even though Missouri law clearly finds it lawful. Kim concludes that "[t]he results strongly indicate that the assumption of full information implicit in the market-based defense of the at-will rule is a flawed one." Pauline T. Kim, "Bargaining with Imperfect Information: A Study of Worker Perceptions of Legal Protection in an At–Will World," 83 *Cornell Law Review* 105, 155 (1997). Kim reports a more extensive three-state survey of worker knowledge of legal protections in "Norms, Learning, and Law: Exploring the Influences on Workers' Legal Knowledge," 1999 *University of Illinois Law Review* 447.

2. *Estimating the Cost of Wrongful–Discharge Law.* Epstein argues on theoretical grounds that the at-will relationship is more efficient than one requiring just cause. Freed and Polsby give some empirical evidence, but the principal thrust of their article is to refute generalized efficiency claims of those claiming that just cause would create more motivated and less fearful workers. The extent of any efficiency loss away from the at-will rule is an empirical question.

James Dertouzos and colleagues at the RAND Corporation have made the most serious attempts to date to quantify the costs of abandoning at-will employment. See James N. Dertouzos, Elaine Holland, and Patricia Ebener, *The Legal and Economic Consequences of Wrongful Termination* (Santa Monica, Calif.: RAND, 1988); James N. Dertouzos and Lynn A. Karoly, *Labor-Market Responses to Employer Liability* (Santa Monica, Calif.: RAND, 1992).

In their 1988 study, Dertouzos and colleagues estimated the "direct" costs of wrongful-discharge law. They first studied California cases in detail, because California has been the trend setter in developing causes of action for wrongful termination and is the only state with enough wrongful-termination jury verdicts to permit empirical research. Using court documents and follow-up questionnaires in 120 California jury trials in which plaintiffs alleged wrongful termination, Dertouzos calculated employer costs, including adverse judgments, settlements, and attorneys' fees. Dertouzos then looked at the frequency of wrongful-termination trials in other states. He calculated that the number of trials for wrongful termination in all states recognizing the covenant of good faith and fair dealing, one of the most important exceptions to at-will employment, amounted to 8.8 trials per million workers. Using the California costs per case, Dertouzos calculated that direct employer costs from adverse judgments and legal fees were $2.56 per worker per year. Including the amount paid to settle cases, which occurs twenty times more frequently than court judgments, the total direct costs of wrongful-discharge litigation amounted to $12.25 per worker per year. With involuntary terminations ranging from 6 to 12 percent of the labor force, the direct employer cost per termination is at most $200 per worker per year in states recognizing these types of wrongful-termination suits. Dertouzos et al., *Legal and Economic Consequences*, 47–48.

In their 1992 study, Dertouzos and Karoly attempted to measure the "indirect" costs of wrongful-termination law, which they found to be up to 100 times greater than the direct costs, equivalent to a 10 percent tax on payroll. These indirect costs include such actions as not terminating bad workers, giving large severance pay to terminated workers to avoid wrongful-termination lawsuits, and adding management layers to centralize and monitor hiring and firing decisions. As the costs of discharging workers increase, employers will be reluctant to hire new workers.

This huge estimate of the indirect costs of wrongful-discharge litigation has been widely cited and has important implications for public policy. The costs are of the same order of magnitude as the entire Social Security program. The methodology Dertouzos and Karoly used to derive this estimate is complex but worth unraveling.

Dertouzos and Karoly's strategy was to develop a statistical model to explain the number of jobs in each state, to see whether wrongful-termination laws were a significant variable in explaining employment (the hypothesis being that such laws reduced employment). They analyzed the period 1980–87, when wrongful-discharge law was changing rapidly. Dertouzos and Karoly ran a regression accounting for total employment in a state as a function of economic strength measured in various ways, as well as the wrongful-discharge law of the state. Regression analysis calculates the set of numbers (coefficients) that, when multiplied by each explanatory variable, comes closest to the values of the dependent variable. A positive coefficient for a particular variable indicates that the variable increases employment, while a negative coefficient indicates that the variable lowers employment.

When Dertouzos and Karoly used actual state law as one of the variables to explain the number of jobs, the positive coefficient suggested that states recognizing a tort exception actually had 1.3 percent more employment than they otherwise would. States recognizing contract exceptions appeared to have smaller, but still positive, increases in employment. Dertouzos and Karoly, *Labor-Market Responses*, 76, Table C3.

At first glance, these results appear to show that wrongful-discharge laws increase total employment. Dertouzos and Karoly reject this quick interpretation, however. They assert that a simultaneous-equations problem makes such an interpretation erroneous. Even if wrongful-discharge law decreases employment in a state, Dertouzos and Karoly suggest, states with a booming economy and rising employment are more likely to adopt a wrongful-discharge law in the first place. It's a chicken-and-egg problem of which came first: the increase in jobs or the wrongful-discharge law. A single regression cannot separate these conflicting causal influences.

To overcome this statistical problem, Dertouzos and Karoly relied on a more complex, two-stage procedure. In the first stage, Dertouzos and Karoly attempted to find variables (called instrumental variables) that affect the adoption of wrongful-discharge laws but do not otherwise affect employment. They used variables such as the number of lawyers in the state, and whether the state has a right-to-work law or a Republican governor. With these instrumental variables, they estimated the probability that a certain state will have a specific wrongful-discharge exception in each year. See Dertouzos and Karoly, *Labor-Market Responses*, 18–21. In the second stage, Dertouzos and Karoly inserted these probabilities (as opposed to the states' actual laws on wrongful discharge) along with their measures of state economic strength as independent variables in the main regression which estimates employment levels for each state. Since these predicted probabilities, in contrast to the wrongful-discharge exceptions themselves, are a function only of variables that are not influenced by the employment level, they are not subject to the reverse causality problem. In econometrics, such a two-step procedure is called an instrumental-variable technique.

With this two-stage method, Dertouzos and Karoly determined that a state with exceptions had significantly lower employment levels than it otherwise would. For example, employment fell almost 3 percent after a state recognized tort damages for wrongful termination. A state's recognition of contract exceptions to at-will employment caused a smaller, but statistically significant, drop of 1.8 percent. Dertouzos and Karoly, *Labor-Market Responses*, 50, Table 5.2.

The last step was to estimate the financial cost of this employment decline. Relying on other scholars' estimates of labor elasticities, Dertouzos and Karoly determined that it would take a 10 percent increase in wages to cause employment in a state to fall by 3 percent. This 10 percent increase in labor costs, then, is the measure of the indirect costs of the exception to at-will employment. Dertouzos and Karoly, *Labor-Market Responses*, 63. These estimates are incremental, meaning that if a state recognizes more than one exception at the same time, the resulting drop in employment, and corresponding rise in costs, will be even bigger. This 10 percent figure is a staggering sum. Such an increase would make wrongful-termination law more costly than unemployment insurance and worker's compensation insurance combined, and would rival the payroll tax imposed by the Social Security system.

How should policymakers react to empirical estimates based on such complex methodology? On the one hand, employment-termination law is an area fraught with conflicting ideology. Using data rather than polemics to resolve issues is to be applauded. Once one turns to data, a sophisticated approach is preferable to a naive approach that gives a misleading interpretation of the empirical relationships. On the other hand, policymakers should be skeptical of results whereby fancy statistical procedures reverse the conclusions given by simpler tabulations of data. A kernel of truth exists in the aphorism that the data will confess to anything if a statistician tortures it enough. In resolving these conflicting concerns in the present case, it is important to recognize that the two-stage instrumental variables procedure employed by Dertouzos and Karoly is widely used by econometricians to analyze problems of this sort. But further study by other researchers with other data sets may be needed before policymakers can be confident that the costs of wrongful-termination law approach 10 percent.

"Life–Cycle Justice: Accommodating Just Cause and Employment at Will"*
STEWART J. SCHWAB

Current termination law does have an underlying coherence.... The current intermediate position of the common law balances two conflicting problems. A career-employment relationship faces two types of opportunism: opportunistic firings by an unfettered employer and shirking by employees with job security. An extreme legal rule can handle either problem alone, but only by ignoring the other. Thus, a legal presumption of employment at will handles the shirking problem well but gives no protection against opportunistic firings. A just-cause regime has the opposite virtue and flaw. The legal challenge is to find an intermediate rule that provides the optimal check against both dangers.

The common law has groped towards such a rule by recognizing that the relative magnitudes of the two problems vary over the life cycle of the worker. The danger of employer opportunism is greatest for late-career workers, and it is also a problem for some beginning-career employees. By contrast, the greater problem at mid-career is shirking. In response, the courts have begun to offer contract protections for workers at the beginning and end of the life cycle, while maintaining a presumption of at-will employment for mid-career employees. In arguing for the wisdom of this approach, I, like the courts, refrain from making a categorical statement that at-will or just-cause employment should never—or should always—be the governing presumption....

I. *Employment as a Relational Contract*

. . .

A. *The Specific Human–Capital Story*
The key feature of the career employment relationship is that both sides are locked into it. The easiest explanation for lock-in comes from a

* 92 *Michigan Law Review* 8 (1993).

human-capital story that emphasizes "asset specificity." Under the basic human-capital model, workers become more productive as they learn the ways of the firm. Because the gains exceed the costs of training, these firm-specific skills are worth learning. In contrast to general skills, however, these skills are not useful to other firms.

The issue becomes whether the employer and employee can decide how to share the costs and benefits so that this desirable training will occur. This issue can be resolved in a number of ways. One possibility is for the employer to pay for the firm-specific training and to receive the benefits of the greater productivity by paying the worker throughout his work life a wage equal to the wage he could get outside the firm. The problem is that the worker has no incentive to stay with the firm because he earns no more than he could get elsewhere, and so the employer risks losing the employee before it can recoup its training investment. Another possible resolution is for the worker to pay for the training, perhaps by accepting a lower wage during the training period, and for the employer to pay the worker a higher wage once trained. The mirror image of the earlier problem occurs in this situation: the firm has an incentive to underpay the worker once he is trained, and the worker has no recourse—because the training is worthless elsewhere—as long as he is paid at least the outside wage.

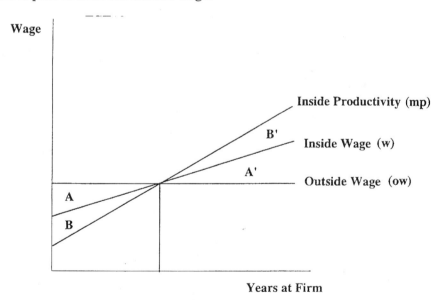

Figure 7–1. Human–Capital Story: Sharing
Throughout Life Cycle

The best solution is for the employer and worker to share both the costs and benefits of firm-specific training. Figure 7–1 gives a stylized view of the situation. The outside wage is constant, equaling productivity based on general skills. In the training period at the firm, the worker accepts less than the outside wage, thereby paying for some of the training, but the employer pays him more than his productivity during the training period, thereby paying for some of the training. After training, the worker receives more than the outside wage, thereby reaping some of the benefits of training, but the employer does not pay the worker for his full productivity, thereby allowing the employer to reap some of the benefits of training. The worker will agree to this arrangement if the higher post-training wages, when appropriately discounted, are at least as large as the lower training wages—that is, if A' is at least as large as A. The employer will agree as long as the gains to it (B') are at least as large as its training costs (B). . . .

A critical part of this simple human-capital story is the self-enforcing feature of the relationship. Because the parties share the costs and benefits of training throughout the employee's work life, both parties want to continue the relationship. The employer pays employees less than their full value later in their career. This protects employees from discharge because a discharge would harm the employer as well. The late-career wage exceeds, however, the outside wage the employee could receive, thereby discouraging the employee from quitting.

B. *The Efficiency–Wage Story and the Potential for Opportunism*

Gary Becker's human-capital theory explained why wages rise with seniority, but puzzles arose that caused commentators to question the theory that workers would receive less than their value late in their career. One such puzzle was mandatory retirement, which covered some thirty-five percent of the workforce before it was prohibited in 1986 by amendments to the Age Discrimination in Employment Act (ADEA). Why would an employer, who is paying older workers less than they are worth, demand that such workers retire? A related puzzle is the presence of actuarially unfair pensions, which even after the 1986 ADEA amendments lawfully encourage older workers to retire. The present value of many pensions declines if older workers keep working. Again, why would an employer establish pension plans that encourage retirement if, as the human-capital model suggests, the employer makes money on older workers? A final puzzle stems from studies that suggest that workers' pay relative to others in their job grade increases with seniority but their relative productivity does not. This evidence conflicts with Becker's hypothesis that productivity increases faster than wages. These puzzles suggest that employers want to end the relationship with late-career workers at some point, probably because employers perceive their wages as exceeding current productivity.

To explain the puzzles, economists have developed an efficiency-wage model. The basic insight behind efficiency-wage models is that workers often work harder when the job pays more. High "efficiency wages" increase worker effort by making the job more valuable to the worker. Because workers want to keep the valuable job, they will work hard to avoid being dismissed. In effect, high wages increase the penalty for being dismissed—a dismissed worker forgoes the large payout. Because workers labor harder than otherwise, the firm can afford the higher compensation. An early version of the model assumed that a firm employing this strategy raised wages by a constant amount throughout a worker's life cycle. One problem with the early, flat-wage version of the model is that workers nearing retirement would care less about losing their high-wage job and would therefore be less deterred from shirking.

Later versions of efficiency-wage models suggest that compensation will rise over a worker's career to induce effort throughout. The implicit contract promises large payouts for senior workers, but it promises this reward only for hard-working employees. The firm recognizes that day-to-day monitoring of a worker's effort may be difficult, but over a period of years the firm hopes to spot and weed out shirkers. The threat of being fired before the large payoff keeps employees working hard. Because employees work harder than otherwise, the firm can afford the higher compensation. Large law firms epitomize this model. . . .

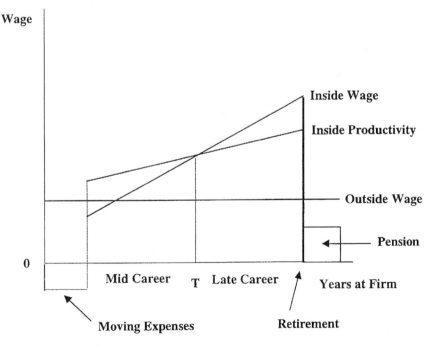

Figure 7–2. Efficiency–Wage Story: Opportunism Possible

Figure 7–2 grafts the efficiency-wage story to the human-capital model. As in the human-capital story, the outside wage is flat and equal to outside productivity. The inside wage may be initially lower than the outside wage, but then rises. Inside productivity rises as job-specific training occurs. Inside productivity is above outside productivity at all stages, even before much training, to emphasize the efficiency-wage story that harder work results in greater productivity throughout. Figure 7–2 adds two other wrinkles that will become important later. First, because I will specifically address the case law of employees who change employers, Figure 7–2 includes a preemployment "moving" period. In this stage, an employee quits the outside job and incurs moving expenses, thus having a negative wage. Figure 7–2 also explicitly illustrates a postretirement pension.

The critical point of the expanded story is that the implicit contract is not always self-enforcing. As Figure 7–2 illustrates, after point T, firms pay late-career employees more than they currently produce. At this point, late-career employees become vulnerable to opportunistic firing because the general self-interest check on arbitrary firings does not exist; firing such a worker does not hurt the employer but is instead in its immediate economic interest. One can see a role for law in improving this situation. By policing against opportunism, the law can make the employment relationship more secure for and valuable to both sides. To understand fully the role law can play, we must examine the concept of opportunism more closely. . . .

C. *Potential for Opportunism*

In the absence of enforceable, detailed contracts that regulate behavior, parties to a long-term relationship become vulnerable to opportunism. They cannot easily leave the relationship because they would have to repeat the investments or forgo their value. The existence of "sunk costs" for one party creates a potential for opportunistic behavior by the other side. A firm can pay workers less than they are worth or treat them more harshly than the initial agreement contemplated, knowing they cannot easily move. The employees can produce less than their skills allow, knowing the employer cannot easily replace them.

The law can sometimes help monitor opportunistic behavior, thereby increasing the parties' overall gains from the relationship. If the law can enforce promises not to exploit the other side's vulnerability, the parties can more confidently invest and the relationship will be more rewarding to both sides. The law has limits, however, because the contractual language often will be general and vague, as we have seen. More importantly, because both employer and employee are investing, both can be exploited. A legal rule favoring one side would leave much opportunism by the other unchecked. To curb opportunism adequately, courts must engage in difficult, case-by-case assessments or create more flexible presumptions. As we will see, courts have responded by adopting presumptions that vary with an employee's life cycle.

1. *Employer Vulnerability to Shirking*

As the human-capital model indicates, employers make heavy investments in recruiting and training workers. To ensure an adequate return on their investment, employers want workers to stay and produce for them after training. Some scholars focus on employer recruitment and training costs in emphasizing employer vulnerability to employees quitting, but this is not the true problem of opportunism. The basic human-capital model suggests that employers can adopt delayed-payment schemes to discourage quitting, thus making the contract self-enforcing. Late-vesting pensions and seniority-based wages can tell workers: "If you stick around, you will do well."

The greater risk to employers comes from employee shirking. The efficiency-wage model highlights the shirking problem. Even if pensions and seniority wages discourage workers from quitting, an employer still faces problems when workers stay. Workers often do not work as hard as they would under a fully specified and monitored contract. Economists label this behavior shirking. A fully specified optimal contract would designate an optimal level of effort. Workers would agree to exert this effort because they prefer the higher wages that accompany it to an easier work life; the employer would agree because the greater productivity is worth the higher wages. Once hired, however, an employee may shirk from this optimal effort if employers have difficulty monitoring or replacing workers. Indeed, it is irrational for workers to work up to "optimal" levels if they prefer coasting a little. Workers know that the employer will have to spend money to catch shirkers and that, if it fires a shirker, the employer will have to recruit and train a replacement. As long as workers perform better than a rookie would—considering the costs of monitoring, recruiting, and training—the firm must accept less than optimal efforts from its workers. . . .

2. *Employee Vulnerability*

As both the human-capital and efficiency-wage models emphasize, employees invest heavily as they pursue a career with a single employer. First, they obtain training that is more useful for their own employer than it would be elsewhere—what economists term job-specific human capital. Second, they join the company's career path. This path, as we have seen, ties pay, promotions, and benefits to seniority and generally forbids lateral entry. A major cost of pursuing a career with one firm is that one forgoes other ladders and must start over at the bottom if one leaves the firm. Additionally, as they plan for a lifetime with an employer, workers put down roots, establish networks of friends in the workplace and the community, buy homes within commuting distance of the job, and build emotional ties to the community.

Losing these investments, roots, and ties can be devastating. Many studies document how even impersonal plant closings lead to increases in "cardiovascular deaths, suicides, mental breakdowns, alcoholism, ulcers, diabetes, spouse and child abuse, impaired social relationships, and various other diseases and abnormal conditions." Being singled out and fired may be even more devastating.

Because of these tremendous costs, no employee wants to lose his job involuntarily. Further, these investments, roots, and ties are sunk costs that trap the worker in his current firm, inhibiting him from departing voluntarily. Even if the career does not proceed as anticipated, the employee is reluctant to quit because the job remains preferable to alternative jobs. Such trapped workers are vulnerable to opportunism. The employer might pay them less than the implicit contract requires or work them harder, knowing they cannot easily quit. By itself, this potential for opportunism does not justify a just-cause standard. Employers want such exploited workers to stay, not to leave. Only when conditions become so intolerable that the employee prefers to quit for another job might termination law come into play. In the economist's framework, this situation occurs when the employer has appropriated all the gains from the relationship, making the career no longer better than alternative jobs. Lawyers label these intolerable conditions a constructive discharge.

Defenders of at will contend that employer self-interest protects productive employees from discharge. An employer hurts itself by arbitrarily terminating a productive worker or by causing him to quit because it wastes the recruiting and training investment in the employee. To avoid its own sunk-cost losses, an employer wants to keep good workers and fire only workers who fall below the standard of new entrants. Figure 7–1 illustrates this self-enforcing feature. After the training period, workers' productivity exceeds their wages, and the employer would lose this gain by firing such workers. . . .

III.   *Legal Supervision of Opportunistic Firings*

A.   *Ad Hoc Judicial Scrutiny of Employer Opportunism*

. . . A party to a long-term relationship is most vulnerable to opportunism when the party has substantially performed while the other side has not. The other side, having received most of its benefit, has an incentive to terminate the relationship to avoid paying out its side of the bargain. Contract doctrine generally imposes a duty of good faith upon parties, in part to protect against such opportunistic behavior. Section 1–203 of the Uniform Commercial Code (U.C.C.), for example, mandates good faith in commercial transactions. While good faith defies simple definition, for our purposes an appropriate meaning is that a party to the contract cannot deprive the other party of the benefit of the bargain.

Courts have hesitated in imposing a generalized good-faith standard upon at-will employment relationships. The courts fear that a nebulous legal standard will make the delicate relationship too rigid or legalistic. Nevertheless, some courts have made good-faith inroads on at-will employment. Although the courts rarely articulate it in these terms, they tend to make these inroads when investment asymmetries make the employee particularly vulnerable to opportunistic firings....

B. *Regulating Opportunism Over the Life Cycle*

... Unfortunately, an ad hoc "opportunism" test is unsatisfying for several reasons. Courts may have difficulty identifying opportunism when they see it. Even if courts can identify opportunism after the fact, an ad hoc test gives limited prospective guidance to employers and employees. Finally, the amorphous nature of an ad hoc opportunism test may mean it becomes so broadly applied that it is indistinguishable from a just-cause requirement for all terminations. This would weaken the deterrence of employee shirking—the prime rationale for employment at will.

If we recall the life cycle of the career employee, we can identify a more systematic pattern of legal intervention. Over the life cycle of a career employee, a sequence of possibilities for opportunism exists. A career employee is particularly vulnerable to opportunism at the beginning and end of his career. By contrast, employers are especially vulnerable to opportunism at the employee's mid-career. The cases suggest that courts are sensitive to this life cycle. Courts are most likely to scrutinize firings at the beginning and end of the life cycle. Courts do not get involved during mid-career unless they see an obvious case of particular opportunism, such as a firing before a pension vests or a sales commission is due.

1. *Beginning–Career Opportunism*

Employees face a risk of opportunistic termination at the beginning of the life cycle. The risk arises because employees commit irretrievable investments to the relationship before the employer does. Usually the beginning-career cases involve employees who have moved to take a job or quit another job in reliance on a job offer....

Other courts have used a theory of additional consideration to give employees who moved to a new job a reasonable time to recoup their investment before being arbitrarily dismissed. While many courts hold that merely working is insufficient consideration to make a just-cause promise enforceable, some additional detriment to the employee or benefit to the employer may lead to an enforceable promise.... Some courts have held that relocating or leaving secure jobs is evidence that the parties must have agreed on a fixed-term contract rather than at-will employment....

We see, then, that courts sometimes allow claims by beginning-career employees who are arbitrarily fired after moving or quitting a prior job. Some courts use a promissory estoppel or reliance theory, some find an implied contract for a reasonable time to allow the employee to recoup his expenses, and some simply use the decision to move or to quit as evidence of an actual definite-term agreement. Regardless of the theory for recovery, one can explain these cases as attempts to regulate opportunistic firings early in the life cycle. Employers have not yet invested in the relationship and thus are not hurt if they arbitrarily dismiss the new employee. This means that the relationship is not self-enforcing, as it is when both parties have incurred sunk costs.

Nevertheless, protection for beginning-career employees is far from universal. Many or even most courts refuse to find that reliance on an at-will job offer is reasonable....

The ambivalence of courts in this area is understandable. For at least three reasons, the opportunistic termination rationale for protecting employees is weaker in these beginning-career cases than it is later in the life cycle. First, very often the employer also makes substantial investments early in the relationship. Recruiting and training new employees can be a major cost to many firms....

Second, even if recruiting costs are insignificant—as they will be in many cases—so that arbitrarily firing the employee does not penalize the employer, the employer gains nothing from firing a person early in his career. Thus, while employers often suffer no penalty from an arbitrary beginning-career firing, they gain no benefit from them either. This fact distinguishes beginning-career from late-career firings, in which the employer can gain from firing employees whom it pays more than their current output.

A final problem with job protection for new employees is that employers often need a probationary period to sort out hiring mistakes, wherein they can fire employees without explanation or extensive documentation of their reasons....

In sum, in many situations employer opportunism against beginning employees is either a trivial threat or outweighed by legitimate needs to maintain employer flexibility. In these situations, courts do not scrutinize the sudden termination. Still, the potential for opportunistic employer offers is real. An employer engages in opportunistic behavior when it hires a better person before training anyone but after the first job applicant has relied on the offer. Courts protect beginning employees from such opportunism.

2. *Late–Career Opportunism*

Late-career employees face the greatest danger of opportunistic firings. At the end of their life cycle, they often earn more than their current productivity. If they do, the employer has a financial incentive to terminate them, even if it violates an implicit promise to allow the employee to reap the rewards of hard work earlier in his career.

The Age Discrimination in Employment Act provides one check against late-career opportunism. By prohibiting employers from firing workers above the age of forty because of their age, the ADEA protects older workers from discharges based upon stereotypes that lead employers to underestimate their productivity. "We need new blood" and "Doe is slowing down a notch" are classic statements that create age discrimination lawsuits.

However, the ADEA may offer only limited protection against the central concern of the life-cycle model—opportunistic firings when salary and forthcoming benefits outweigh current productivity.... Under the life-cycle model, the employee becomes vulnerable to opportunism with years of service, not with age. The ADEA is therefore of little help....

Greater protection may come from common law courts, which in recent years have begun policing opportunistic firings of late-career employees. The leading case is *Pugh v. See's Candies, Inc.*, in which a thirty-two-year employee was abruptly fired after working his way up from dishwasher to corporate vice president. The employee never had a clear agreement about job security, although managers had given him encouraging evaluations over the years. The court held that this career pattern, including the length of service and the policies and practices of the company, could establish an implied-in-fact promise against arbitrary dismissal. *Pugh* epitomizes the efficiency-wage story and its end-game dangers. Pugh committed himself to a single firm, worked hard to gain promotions to the promised easy life, but then was terminated. *Pugh* also demonstrates the effect of the arrival of new management on job security. In *Pugh*, new management arrived a year before Pugh's firing. Such major corporate changes may diminish the reputational check on firings of late-career employees....

In sum, one can explain these cases as attempts to monitor and enforce the implicit life-cycle employment contract. Late in an employee's career, the usual checks against opportunistic firings unravel. Courts enter to monitor the bargain. The bargain does not give late-career employees complete job security. They can be dismissed for cause, because otherwise the shirking problems would be immense, but the employer does not prove cause simply by proving that salary exceeds current productivity. That is the typical life-cycle pattern that both sides to career employment anticipate and, ex ante, it is in the interests of both sides.

3. *Mid–Career Shirking*

Once the employer has begun to make substantial, asset-specific investments in an employee, the risk of arbitrary firing diminishes. The greater danger of opportunistic behavior—at least, behavior that an appropriate dismissal standard could limit—comes from the employee's side. Because the employer does not want to repeat recruiting and training costs with another employee, the incumbent employee has an opportunity to shirk without fear of dismissal. Shirking at mid-career can occur even if the employer has the right to dismiss at will, but the shirking problem can be exacerbated if the employer must also surmount the hurdle of proving just cause.

This is not to say that the employer cannot exploit the mid-career employee. Indeed, as I emphasized above, being trapped by investments in firm-specific capital and in community roots can make a mid-career employee ripe for exploitation. But the exploitation will not take the form of firing because the employer is making money from the relationship. Rather than fire a mid-career employee, an employer may pay him less than would be called for under a fair division of the gains from the long-term relationship or make his workload or working conditions more onerous. Just cause cannot protect the mid-career employee from these abuses. Better, then, for the law to focus on something it can handle, which is deterrence of shirking by mid-career employees.

The courts seem to have intuited this fact by refusing, in general, to create contract protections against arbitrary terminations for mid-career workers. Mid-career employees have made the fewest contributions to the doctrinal erosion of at-will employment. . . .

In summary, my argument is that the general pattern of good-faith and implied-contract cases reflects an intuitive understanding by the courts that employees are subject to opportunistic discharge at the end, and less consistently at the beginning, of the life cycle. Courts are reluctant, however, to give general protection against arbitrary dismissal to mid-career employees. The economic self-interest of employers should keep such dismissals in check. The greater concern is with employee shirking. . . .

Notes and Questions

1. *Norms and Law.* Schwab shows how employer and employee can jointly benefit from implicit understandings of career employment. It is less clear, however, that the understandings should be legally enforceable. Rock and Wachter emphasize a sharp dichotomy between norms and law in employment terminations. Edward B. Rock and Michael L. Wachter, "The Enforce-

ability of Norms and the Employment Relationship," 144 *University of Pennsylvania Law Review* 1913 (1996). Most employers create a norm of not firing workers without just cause. They hesitate before firing workers for mediocre performance, and many establish elaborate internal procedures that make terminations difficult. At the same time, employers jealously guard their legal right to terminate workers at will, wanting to prevent courts from policing their termination decisions. Rock and Wachter defend this dichotomy, asserting that "when a system of norms is self-sustaining and does not impose costs on third parties, the courts should not enforce those norms." Id. at 1938.

2. *Graduated Severance Pay and the Life Cycle.* Samuel Issacharoff is sympathetic to the life-cycle model, but also worries about turning implicit understandings into legal rights. He says:

> But what is it that the law can or should protect? The difficulty comes in transforming the life-cycle employment model from an analytic device for understanding the operation of labor markets into a legal definition of rights for determining liability. The late-career relational contract model places a great deal of stress on the transformative moment when an employee is subject to special legal solicitude for having entered into the category of employees at risk for opportunistic discharges. This in turn raises a constant concern in imprecise contractual arrangements: how to verify the impropriety of the actions of the allegedly breaching party. Moreover, as Verkerke argues, these problems are compounded in the employment setting in which any measure of low employee productivity could indicate that the employee has reached the furthest reaches of the life-cycle curve, but could also "characterize a late-career employee who has breached his or her side of the implicit contract by 'shirking' under the cover of a life-cycle just cause standard for discharge."

Samuel Issacharoff, "Contracting for Employment : The Limited Return of the Common Law," 74 *Texas Law Review* 1783, 1804–05 (1996).

Unlike Verkerke or Rock and Wachter, however, Issacharoff does not advocate the at-will presumption as a remedy for the vagaries of the life-cycle approach. Rather, he suggests a mandatory severance pay scheme modeled along the lines of most European countries. He would allow employers to specify an at-will contract for the first two years of hiring. After that time, employers must pay terminated workers one month's wages per year of tenure, unless the employer can show in an administrative proceeding that it fired the worker for incompetence or shirking. "The key advantage of this approach," says Issacharoff, "is that it attempts to reflect the asymmetric recovery of value between employee and employer over a life-cycle arrangement.... In addition, the increasing amount of severance pay that would be owed to an employee imprints upon employers the consequences of growing employee dependence on career employment that might otherwise develop invisibly." Id. at 1807.

"An Empirical Perspective on Indefinite Term Employment Contracts: Resolving the Just Cause Debate"*

J. HOULT VERKERKE

. . .

III.　*Empirical Evidence of Employment Contract Practices*

. . . Participants in the just cause debate have relied thus far almost exclusively on speculative assertions about the nature of existing practices. The new data presented in this Part make it possible to impose some empirical discipline on this theoretical debate. . . .

In order to begin to fill what can only be described as a data gap in the literature on employment contracts, I have conducted an exploratory survey asking companies a variety of questions about their employment practices. During the summer of 1994 and the winter of 1994–95, I contacted employers in Virginia, California, Texas, Michigan, and New York. The average response rate was approximately 25%. The total sample size was 221 employers. The mean employer size was 261 employees, with a minimum size of ten and a maximum size of 10,000 employees.

The objective of the survey was to discover what, if any, contractual terms governed discharge at each employer. . . .

Slightly more than one-half of all employers (52%) contract explicitly for an at will relationship. About one-third (33%) use no documents that specify the terms governing discharge. And more than one in seven (15%) contract expressly for just cause protection.

The predominant method of contracting is the employee handbook (61% of all employers). Just over one in ten companies (12%) specify discharge terms on their employment applications. Very few employers communicate such terms in offer letters (5%), and even fewer use form contracts (4%).

Crosstabulations by state suggest that there is little apparent difference in the underlying rate of preference for just cause protection in liberal and conservative jurisdictions. In California, 13.1% of respondents contract for just cause, almost identical to the rate for Virginia (14.9%). This difference is not statistically significant at ordinary confidence levels. Similarly, Michigan and Texas employers provide just cause at nearly identical rates of 15.8% and 16.7%, respectively. Aggregating the liberal jurisdictions of California and Michigan and comparing them to the totals for Virginia, Texas, and New York again reveals virtually indistinguishable rates of 13.8% and 15.6%, respectively.

---

* 4 *Wisconsin Law Review* 838 (1995).

Analogous figures for the percentage of employers contracting explicitly for employment at will show a statistically significant difference between liberal jurisdictions (61.3%) and conservative ones (46.8%). Examining at will contracts by state, however, reveals that the percentage in liberal jurisdictions is higher, principally because Michigan employers are extremely likely to contract for employment at will (73.7%). There have been an unusual number of Michigan cases clearly inviting employers to include disclaimers in their written documents in order to avoid legal enforceability of policy statements. Perhaps these judicial suggestions have influenced Michigan employers' contractual practices.

Crosstabulations by size suggest that employment contracting behavior varies systematically with the number of employees at a company. Small employers are somewhat more likely than midsize or large employers to contract for just cause (17.7%, compared to 12.9% and 12.5%, respectively). Furthermore, small employers are about twice as likely to have no documents providing terms governing discharge (45.8%, compared to 21.2% and 27.5%, respectively). Midsize and large employers have the highest propensity to contract expressly for employment at will (65.9% and 60.0%, respectively, compared to 36.5% for small employers)....

Finally, contract choices do not seem to be influenced by whether the employer has any unionized employees. Employers with at least some union employees contract in roughly the same pattern (44.4% at will, 44.4% none, 11.1% just cause) as those without unions present in the workplace (52.7% at will, 32% none, 15.3% just cause). Moreover, because the sample includes only eighteen employers with union employees, these differences are not statistically significant.

IV. *Choosing a Default Rule*

... The survey data on employment contract practices permit me to determine the majoritarian default rule for indefinite term employment contracts. Assuming first that those who do not contract prefer the prevailing default rule, the revealed preference of market participants is overwhelmingly for the at will contract. A mere fifteen percent of employers contract expressly for just cause. Thus, by more than a five to-one margin, employers either contract expressly for employment at will or choose to adopt the prevailing at will default. If we adopt the alternative assumption that noncontracting employers are expressing no preference about the existing default rule, then employment at will remains the preferred contract arrangement by roughly a three-to-one margin. The available empirical evidence thus appears to provide strong support for the prevailing default rule of employment at will....

My survey data reveal a pattern of contract choices that is inconsistent with the argument that there is a latent demand for life-cycle just cause. First, if a significant proportion of employers wished to offer life-cycle protection, we should expect some fraction of them to choose a just cause contract. Offering express just cause protection increases the reliability of the employer's commitment to a long-term employment relationship. For some employers then, express just cause will be closer to their desired discharge term than the prevailing at will default or the alternative of an express at will contract. Second, recall Schwab's claim that life-cycle just cause is underprovided because of its complexity. Recall also that California law comes closer than any other jurisdiction to offering life-cycle just cause as a default rule. California courts are sensitive to the problems of recent movers; they have expressly relied on longevity of service to support implied just cause protection and seem willing to protect all employees with an economic good faith standard. In contrast, Virginia courts recognize none of these theories and adhere strictly to the traditional at will default.

Employers in California should, therefore, be inclined to contract out of the state's comparatively attractive default rule at a lower rate than will Virginia employers. Virginia firms that fail to contract receive that state's stringent, and thus comparatively unattractive, at will default. In contrast, California employers get a more relaxed version of the at will presumption that more closely approximates the life-cycle just cause default. The multinomial logit results, however, show no statistically significant relationship between state and contractual choice, other than the extraordinary propensity of Michigan employers to contract expressly for at will. Moreover, simple crosstabulations show that, although California employers are slightly less likely (by a statistically insignificant margin) to contract expressly for just cause (13.1% to 14.9% for Virginia), they are also substantially more likely to contract expressly for an at will relationship (57.4% to 49.1% for Virginia). This latter result directly contradicts the empirical implications of the argument for a life-cycle default. . . .

The theoretical case for life-cycle protection also depends on characteristics of employment—the need for firm-specific human capital and the difficulty of monitoring employee performance—that differ systematically across occupations and industries. Thus, the revealed preference for just cause should also vary by occupation and industry. The data reveal a remarkable uniformity across occupations within individual employers and across industries, with no statistically significant pattern emerging. Thus, no support exists for this empirical implication of the life-cycle theory. . . .

D.   *Information-Forcing Default Rules*

. . .

2.   *The Law of Employee Handbooks*

. . . The survey data reveal that handbooks are by far the most important method by which employers communicate the details of their discharge policies to employees. Courts, therefore, will often have to determine whether disciplinary procedures and standards of conduct contained in handbooks should be given legal effect.

An information-forcing rule for employee handbooks involves two complementary elements. First, because employers drafting handbooks are in a better position than employees to avoid misunderstandings, courts initially should construe handbook provisions liberally in favor of employees. Statements that a reasonable employee might read to impose limits on an employer's discretion to discharge without cause should be enforced as contractual commitments. Furthermore, courts should essentially ignore the formal requirements of offer and acceptance, concentrating instead on whether the employer has distributed the handbook to a group of employees of which the plaintiff is a member. These pro-plaintiff rules impose the burden of clarifying the legal effect of an employee handbook on employers—the party best able both to investigate the law and to control the content of the relevant documents.

The second element of the optimal rule follows from the first. If employers must bear the burden of clarifying their contractual intent, then courts must be prepared to honor that intent when employers signal it with sufficient clarity. In the context of employee handbooks, these signals ordinarily take one of two forms. Such documents often include a disclaimer of contractual effect—a clause providing that the terms of the handbook do not form a contract. Many other handbooks include an express confirmation of at will status. Both types of clauses should be enforced. Courts should, however, require that such clauses are sufficiently clear and prominent to inform a reasonable employee that he or she has no contractual protection against discharge.

Existing case law in many jurisdictions reflects precisely this approach to employee handbooks. Thus, the information-forcing theory is useful both as a positive explanation and a normative argument for current practice. . . .

Notes and Questions

1. *Public Policy Violations.* Regardless of their position on whether courts should make contract-based inroads on employment at will, scholars are generally more accepting of tort inroads (except for the direct and indirect costs of such litigation, mentioned above). Examples of the tort of wrongful discharge in violation of public policy would include a worker fired for refusing to perjure himself on behalf of the company or a worker fired for reporting illegal pollution by the company. Recall that Richard Epstein, in his article excerpted in this chapter, does not quarrel with these "infrequent exceptions" to private-contracting autonomy. (See footnote 11 on page 225 and accompanying text.) For an evaluation of these tort cases, arguing that they should be allowed if and only if the termination significantly affects

third parties, see Stewart J. Schwab, "Wrongful Discharge Law and the Search for Third–Party Effects," 74 *Texas Law Review* 1943 (1996).

2. *Penalty Default Rules*. Normally, courts adopt default rules that most parties would write into a contract were they to focus on the issue. Such a "majoritarian" default rule saves on transaction costs, because most parties can by hypothesis rely on the default rule rather than explicitly bargain on the issue. Verkerke argues, based on his empirical survey showing that most employment contracts call for employment at will, that the majoritarian principle should be employment at will. Schwab, by contrast, argues that courts should consider the differential costs of contracting away from at will to a life-cycle contract, which he claims is difficult, compared to the costs of contracting away from a life-cycle default to at will, which he claims is relatively easy. This argues for a life-cycle default rule—not on majoritarian principles but on the principle of minimizing overall transaction costs.

In some situations, the appropriate default rule does not minimize bargaining costs in either of the senses discussed above. Instead, some default rules are designed precisely to be so onerous that one party will want to write around them, in the process revealing information that allows for greater joint gains from the bargain. Ayres and Gertner have labeled these "penalty default" rules. See Ian Ayres and Robert Gertner, "Filling Gaps in Incomplete Contracts: An Economic Theory of Default Rules," 99 *Yale Law Journal* 91 (1989). Others call them "information-forcing" default rules. See Jason S. Johnston, "Strategic Bargaining and the Economic Theory of Contract Default Rules," 100 *Yale Law Journal* 615, 621 (1990). See also Lucian A. Bebchuk and Steven Shavell, "Information and the Scope of Liability for Breach of Contract: The Rule of *Hadley v. Baxendale*," 7 *Journal of Law, Economics & Organization* 284 (1991). Verkerke, in the reading above, applied the information-forcing concept to employment manuals, arguing for a strict construction against the employer as the more informed party. For a rearticulation of their original penalty-default model, with applications to the at-will employment rule, see Ian Ayres and Robert Gertner, "Majoritarian vs. Minoritarian Defaults," 51 Stanford Law Review 1591 (1999).

3. *Adverse Selection and Mandatory Just Cause*. Regardless of how they stand on the value of at-will employment as a general matter, the authors of the previous articles have all agreed that individual employers and employees should be allowed to contract for at-will employment if they so choose. The debate was over the appropriate default rule when the parties fail to contract explicitly about the rule governing termination. This preference for default rules rather than mandatory terms is typical of scholars working within a law-and-economics framework.

Under this vision of default rules, some firms might insist on at-will contracts, while others might promise not to fire workers without just cause. One problem with voluntarily offering just-cause protection, however, is that these firms will attract applicants with a greater tendency to shirk. If these applicants cannot be fully screened out, average productivity in the just-cause firms will tend to fall. This will require the firms to reduce the wage, which will attract even fewer hardworking workers. A downward spiral results, and the just-cause firms may be driven out of business, even if workers overall were willing to pay for the greater costs associated with just cause.

A mandatory just-cause requirement might eliminate this "lemons" problem, as it has been called. Shirkers would no longer disproportionately apply to certain firms, because all would offer just-cause protection. If every firm shares the shirking problem, it becomes more manageable and may be outweighed by the reduced number of opportunistic firings under a good-cause regime. The following reading outlines this lemons story.

"Labor and Lemons: Efficient Norms in the Internal Labor Market and the Possible Failures of Individual Contracting"*

WALTER KAMIAT

[T]his story applies the "lemons problem" described in George Akerlof's *The Market for "Lemons": Quality Uncertainty and the Market Mechanism* to the employment contracting context. Borrowing a phrase from the used car market, Akerlof's "lemons problem" is the inefficiency that characterizes a market in which buyers cannot easily verify the quality of goods offered by sellers, and sellers have superior (but hard to warrant) information regarding the quality of the goods they offer. In such a market, Akerlof shows, the ability of dishonest sellers to misrepresent the quality of the goods they offer (that is, to offer "lemons"), paired with the inability of buyers to distinguish between honest and dishonest sellers (that is, to determine which offers are "lemons"), will mean that prices will fall. As honest sellers disproportionately withdraw from a market that is undervaluing their offers (leaving a market with even more "lemons"), the price will fall further. In the end, a significant number of otherwise willing buyers and willing sellers will find it impossible to contract.

An employee and employer contracting for employment fits Akerlof's model: each possesses unique access to information—information regarding the quality of their offers—that the other party would find highly relevant, but which neither party can easily discover from the other. The employee, for example, has superior information regarding his likely work quality (including his skills and his propensity to shirk). The employer can only discover this information to a limited extent, and, fearing employee strategic behavior, the employer may have little reason to believe any representations of high work quality made by the employee. Similarly, an employer has superior information regarding the employer's likely conformity to worker protective norms, but the employee

---

* 144 *University of Pennsylvania Law Review* 1953, 1957–62 (1996).

has little reason to believe representations of "trustworthiness" made by the employer.

In this context, an employee who seeks an enforceable just-cause provision in the employment contract confronts a serious signalling problem regarding the quality of the employee's likely work. At least two kinds of employees will disproportionately value just-cause protection. A relatively risk averse individual who desires long-term employment may seek just-cause protection as a form of insurance against future employer opportunism ... may be willing to pay a reasonable price for this insurance (in terms of a wage adjustment reflecting the added costs), and may nevertheless be at least equally likely to perform work of outstanding quality. Alternatively, an individual may value this protection precisely because she expects (or wishes to reserve an option) to perform deficiently at the job in question and therefore hopes to take advantage of the costs that a just-cause clause would impose on employer efforts to police against shirking. In Akerlof's terms, the latter employee can be called a "lemon."

The problem is that the employer cannot tell, in any given case, whether the employee who seeks the term is of the former or latter type, and the employee cannot effectively warrant as to which alternative she represents. Given these realities, employees will tend not to seek such a term through individual contracting, fearing that any efforts to obtain the term will signal that they may be "lemons"—that is, shirkers or boundary-testers—whose costs to the employer will be more than the wage adjustment associated with the term. Any disclosure that they place a high value on the term will call into question their fitness for the job.

From the employer's perspective, the employee's signalling problem becomes a problem of adverse selection. Should the employer offer the just-cause term, the employer may become disproportionately attractive to those likely to shirk. Although the "trustworthy" employer might otherwise be quite willing to offer such a term in return for a wage differential (which would reflect that workers no longer require compensation for the risks of employer opportunism), the uncertainties associated with this adverse selection problem discourage the employer from making the offer without an additional wage adjustment to account for the associated uncertainty. Because an employee's acceptance of the term at the lower wage (higher price) would signal that the employee places an even higher value on the term, this might cause the employer to have an even greater concern for the quality of the employee. And this, of course, would make the employer less likely still to offer the term at that wage. Under such conditions, there might simply be no stable price for the term in question.

Given these realities, employers will tend not to offer such a term. The employer who desires a means of warranting his promise not to discharge without just-cause may still be unwilling to offer a binding term to any employee who discloses that she particularly values the term. In essence, the employer may be willing to offer such a term in the abstract, but not to any employee willing to pay for it. This is precisely the pattern documented by Akerlof in a host of situations, where—under circumstances of asymmetric information and unverifiable quality— private markets often generate a situation where "no . . . sales may take place at any price."

[The fact that a just-cause term] is generally never produced through non-union employment contracting may simply reflect this "lemons problem." If so, the absence of the term is absolutely no evidence that employees would not highly value the term if they could get it. In other words, the absence of the just-cause term does not disprove the provision's efficiency. Employees may sufficiently fear employer opportunism that they would be more than willing to pay their share of the term's cost. And this fear of opportunism may prevent optimal match investments in internal labor market human capital. Nevertheless, there may remain an insignificant number of just-cause provisions in individual employment contracts.

This "lemons problem" account is fully consistent with two other factors noted by [commentators]. First, it is consistent with the contracting pattern in unionized employment, where just-cause provisions are as uniformly present as they are absent in non-union settings. When unions negotiate for employees, they can voice employee preferences without attributing these preferences to individual employees. Thus, while each individual employee may fear raising the issue of a just-cause term as an individual—lest she mark herself as one who is more likely to shirk and, thereby, competitively disadvantage herself in the eyes of the employer— the union can advocate the just-cause provision without disadvantaging any individual employee. In this way, the bargaining demands of a union may be far more accurate reflections of "true" employee preferences than the bargaining demands of individual employees.

Similarly, the employer may be less likely to fear an adverse selection problem when the term is sought by a union for the workforce as a whole, precisely because the term is unassociated with the particular preferences of individual employee applicants and, accordingly, says less about the likelihood of particular employees shirking.[12]

12. I say "less likely" because an adverse selection problem may still be present for an employer in this situation. Having a just-cause term may mean that applicants with a predisposition to shirk will be disproportionately attracted to the firm. Although unionized employers overwhelmingly accept contractual just-cause provisions in collective bargaining agreements, such an employer concern may nevertheless explain some part of employer opposition to unionization. In any event, the fact that contracting difficulties persist in unionized employment gives no support to the proposition that non-union employment contracting is efficient.

Second, this "lemons problem" account is consistent with the use of disclaimers ... in those jurisdictions where judicial decisions have implied an enforceable just-cause term from the existence of a just-cause norm. Put simply, reversing the default rule will not solve the "lemons problem." The problems of unverifiable quality and asymmetrical information remain, as do the resulting problems of signalling and adverse selection. To recognize this state of affairs, one need only hypothesize an employer presenting to applicants a boilerplate disclaimer which states that no legally enforceable just-cause term is intended by the statement of the just-cause norm. Should the employee propose deleting the disclaimer, asserting a strong preference for enforceable just-cause protection, the same signalling and adverse selection problems would arise: The employer, viewing any such employee as more likely than average to be a shirker or boundary tester, will be less likely to hire the employee at all. The employer is thus less likely to offer the option of individual just-cause protection and the employee is less likely to express the preference for any such protection.

Given these possible inefficiencies of individual contracting, state intervention may, in this context, enhance efficiency by solving the "lemons problem." Thus, if a just-cause term were efficient—such that its benefits in limiting employer opportunism outweigh its costs—state imposition of the term might be justified, given that the private market will tend not to produce it. As David Levine explains:

> If all firms had policies, then the efficiency gains of just cause might outweigh the burden of [any increased problem of] shirkers. If only a subset of firms have just-cause policies, these firms will be faced with an applicant pool of workers with a concentration of workers who do not work hard but cannot be fired.
>
> As is usual when externalities are present, government policies can increase national income. In this case, laws ... that move toward just-cause employment policies can increase efficiency. If all companies were required to use just cause, the poor workers would be evenly distributed, and the efficiency gains could dominate the loss of productivity from shirkers.

Accordingly, the failure of nonunion individual employment contracting to expressly provide for enforceable just-cause protection hardly demonstrates that legal intervention to provide such protection would be inefficient.

Notes and Questions

1. *Signaling and Symmetry.* Kamiat's signaling story focuses on the problems of workers who want just cause for benign reasons but cannot signal their interest without danger of being lumped with "bad" workers. This might explain, the story concludes, the persistence of at-will agreements

even if each worker is willing to pay for the added costs just cause imposes for that worker (which is small for "good" workers).

One problem with this story is that it is formally symmetrical. Employers wanting at-will arrangements for benign reasons should have an analogous problem of being lumped with "bad" employers who plan on exploiting workers with unfair dismissals. If so, parties might be unable to contract around a legal regime presuming just cause even if employers were willing to pay for the added risks at will imposes on workers (which is small for "good" employers). See J. Hoult Verkerke, "Employment Contract Law," in Peter Newman, ed., *The New Palgrave Dictionary of Economics and the Law* (London: Macmillan, 1998). In an omitted footnote, Kamiat responds that an "assertion that there are multiple contracting problems is hardly a demonstration that current arrangements reflect efficient contracting." Kamiat, "Labor and Lemons," 1953 n.15.

2. *Adverse Selection and Just–Cause Employers.* The signaling story also suggests that employers cannot offer just-cause contracts because they will disproportionately attract unproductive workers. As Verkerke reports in the principal reading above, however, 15 percent of all nonunion employers in his survey contracted for just cause. While Verkerke called this a "mere" 15 percent, it does suggest that a substantial number of presumably viable firms can offer just-cause protection without the adverse selection problem that is the heart of the signaling story.

8

Topics in Employment Regulation: Minimum Wages and Pensions

This chapter examines two important topics in employment regulation, laws mandating a minimum wage and laws regulating pensions.

A. Minimum Wage Regulation

The Fair Labor Standards Act (FLSA) mandates a minimum wage for all covered workers. Originally set in 1938 at 25 cents per hour, by 1997 the federal minimum wage was $5.15. The FLSA allows states to mandate higher minimum wages than the federal standard. This interstate variation allows economists to test the degree to which a minimum wage reduces employment, a subject of controversy in recent years. Two leading economists have recently argued that the employment effects of the minimum wage are far less than earlier thought. David E. Card and Alan B. Krueger, *Myth and Measurement: The New Economics of the Minimum Wage* (Princeton: Princeton University Press, 1995). Our lead article by Daniel Shaviro reviews this issue as well as the major justifications for minimum wage laws.

"The Minimum Wage, the Earned Income Tax Credit, and Optimal Subsidy Policy"*
DANIEL SHAVIRO

. . .

I. *The Minimum Wage as a Subsidy Plus a Tax*

. . .

While regulatory in form, the minimum wage economically resembles a spending program in the form of a subsidy for low-wage employees, financed by a tax on their employers. Suppose that the minimum wage is set at $5 per hour, and that a given employee would otherwise have been paid $4 per hour. Under these circumstances, the regulatory mandate will have one of two effects. Either the wage increases by a dollar, from $4 to $5, compared to what it would otherwise have been, or else the employer decides not to use the employee's services (at least for the same

* 64 *University of Chicago Law Review* 405 (1997).

number of hours). Confining our analysis for the moment to the former case, where the number of hours worked stays constant, an amount equivalent to one dollar multiplied by the number of hours worked changes hands from the employer to the employee relative to what would otherwise have happened. Suppose that the number of affected hours is 2,000 (40 hours a week for a year containing 50 working weeks). Administrative details aside, the outcome is identical, at a first approximation, to that which would have resulted had the government levied a special $2,000 tax on the employer, and paid a $2,000 wage subsidy to the employee.

The analogy to a combined tax and subsidy program becomes no less apt if the employee's hours of work decline due to the minimum wage. Reduced employment would be a standard example of "excess burden" from levying a tax. Similarly, the income tax, by taxing people's wages but not their enjoyment of leisure, may cause them to work fewer hours and earn less pre-tax income, thus in some instances generating excess burden rather than accomplishing the transfer of resources to the government. . . .

Nonetheless, low-wage employees as a group can benefit from being denied the right to accept jobs that pay less than a specified hourly rate. The ban, by applying to them collectively, in effect organizes them as a cartel. It solves the internal organizational and enforcement problems that likely would prevent their establishing, by their own unaided efforts, a cartel (such as a universal labor union) demanding a given minimum wage.

It is well known that cartels can increase their members' aggregate income, albeit by reducing output and imposing a deadweight loss on society. In the case of the minimum wage, this claim of overall group benefit appears to be empirically plausible. The pre-Card and Krueger empirical consensus among economists held that a 10 percent minimum wage increase would likely reduce low-wage hours worked by 1 to 3 percent. This implies the strong possibility of an increase in the total income of low-wage workers (along with increased leisure that could perhaps be used productively, as in housework), although there are countervailing considerations, such as the possible loss of "stepping-stone jobs" leading to better ones down the line.

Still, even if the minimum wage does boost low-wage workers' real income as a group, the internal distributional effect is likely to be quite uneven. . . .

To the extent that job loss is non-random, it will likely fall on those members of the cartel who have the least marketable skills—perhaps the very individuals whom altruistic supporters of the minimum wage law may have wanted to help the most. One might also be concerned about involuntariness: the losers, unless they sought a minimum wage increase through political activity, did not elect to join a cartel and take their chances. . . .

II. *Assessing the Minimum Wage as a Low–Wage Subsidy*

A. *Description of the Tax and Subsidy*

[C]onstruing the minimum wage as a wage subsidy to low-wage employees, financed by a tax on their employers, helps to identify the program's benefits and costs. The subsidy has the following main features:

> (1) It is limited to low-wage employees, determined on the basis of hourly wages. Historically, since its federal enactment in 1939, the minimum wage has fluctuated between 37 and 56 percent of the average nonsupervisory wage in the non-farm private sector.

> (2) The wage subsidy is not means-tested or needs-tested, on either an individual or a household basis. Teenagers from affluent families qualify no less than struggling single heads of households. It takes no account of how many hours the employee has worked during the year, or of the employee's assets, past earnings, or future earnings prospects.

> (3) While benefits are impervious to overall personal circumstances, they increase as the hourly wage that one would otherwise have received declines. . . .

> (4) The employee receives the subsidy directly from the employer, rather than from a government agency. Thus, it does not require separate filing of any kind, and is paid with the employee's regular paycheck. . . .

B. *Possible Reasons for a Low–Wage Subsidy*

In order for the minimum wage to be a defensible program, the subsidy's benefits must exceed the tax's costs. In addition, the subsidy and tax should be reasonably well-designed compared to plausible replacement programs. This section begins the analysis by examining possible rationales for a wage subsidy for low-wage workers.

1. *Progressive wealth redistribution.*

The most commonly advanced reason for a low-wage subsidy is progressive wealth redistribution. If low-wage workers are on average less well-off than others, then increasing their income seems likely to have progressive effects. To be sure, the subsidy only helps those who have jobs, a group that may not include the neediest. It also may help individuals who are well-off despite earning low wages, such as employees with income from capital or other household members' wages. Advocates variously argue, however, that low-wage subsidies restrict benefits to the "deserving" poor (ostensibly, only those who work), minimize adverse work incentives, or are politically more feasible than alternative programs for progressive wealth redistribution.

2. *Reducing the tax and transfer systems' deterrence of market work by individuals in poor households.*

A second argument for a low-wage subsidy, grounded in efficiency rather than distribution, is that it will reduce the tax and transfer systems' discouragement of work effort by individuals in poor households (to the extent they are the ones receiving the subsidy)....

As a general matter, therefore, and even ignoring programs that are regulatory in form, work effort is deterred, reflecting the classic trade-off between efficiency and distributional concerns, along with, perhaps, unnecessary design flaws. Inefficiency results even if overall work effort does not decline. The reason it may not decline is that the substitution effect, which occurs when people shift from market work to leisure because the former's return has been reduced, may be offset by the income effect, which occurs when people decide, by reason of having less money, that they need to work more. Substitution effects are regrettable, however, wholly without regard to the separate occurrence of income effects. Thus, suppose that I forgo an hour of labor that would have paid me $10, because after tax I would have kept only $6 and I valued an hour of leisure at $7. The lost $3 of societal surplus (the excess of what someone was willing to pay for my time over my value for it) is not offset by the fact that some other individual, because taxes have shrunk his bank account, decides to work an hour more (a change in preference generally viewed as efficiency-neutral, since efficiency is measured relative to people's preferences)....

3. *Increasing workforce participation among the poor.*

A third plausible reason for a low-wage subsidy—turning on a claim of positive externalities rather than wealth distribution or minimizing excess burden—is that it may make market work more attractive to marginal workers among the poor, who, at least initially, can command only a modest wage. Suppose that, if low-wage work paid better or were more widely available, individuals who at present do not expect to find appealing stable employment would conclude instead that they could support themselves regularly through market work....

4. *Offering just wages to low-wage workers.*

A final argument for the minimum wage, implicit in the rhetoric of "making work pay," is that it enables low-wage workers to receive the wages to which they are justly entitled by reason of their work. Here the claim—wholly distinct from progressive wealth redistribution or creating appropriate work incentives as such—is that a low-wage worker's labor has a real value, in some sense, that exceeds what the worker can actually command in the marketplace. Thus, justice in the division of national income dictates providing a wage subsidy to narrow the gap between the "real" value the worker has contributed and the market value the worker has received.

[This argument] would seem to lead, however, not to a uniform minimum wage as such, but to subsidizing or taxing at high rates the income earned in different occupations, based on judgments about how their social value differs from their market value. . . .

C. *Effect of the Minimum Wage on the Goals of a Low–Wage Subsidy*

Since the minimum wage is equivalent to a subsidy plus a tax (leaving aside administrative and political considerations), its merits depend on each of these two elements. Most debate concerning the minimum wage has focused on the tax, which economists before Card and Krueger mainly agreed would cause nontrivial disemployment if set high enough to affect wages significantly. However, it is useful to begin by considering the effectiveness of the minimum wage's particular subsidy, ignoring the tax.

1. *Effects of the subsidy.*

The subsidy targets people with low hourly wages, rather than those who are poor. Yet the poor seemingly should be the main beneficiaries under all three of the plausible arguments for the low-wage subsidy—not just progressive redistribution, but also reducing unduly high effective tax rates that result from [the working poor's loss of eligibility for welfare benefits] and increasing workplace affiliation among marginal workers. Thus, the question of fit between those with low hourly wages and those living in poor households is paramount. . . .

[E]mpirical evidence suggests that at one time the fit was fairly good—at least in terms of who got the subsidy, ignoring the question of how many poor households did not get it. Again, in 1939 the percentage of low-wage workers (those earning less than half of the average private sector hourly wage) who lived in households below the poverty line was 85 percent, rising to 93 percent if one included households near the poverty line. By 1989, these figures had declined to 22 percent poor, or 39 percent including the near-poor. This change reflected the weakened link between hourly wages and household income in an era of multiple-earner households, along with the general mitigation of poverty through social welfare programs.

The targeting of the minimum wage's low-wage subsidy seems particularly weak when it is compared to the targeting under the [Earned Income Tax Credit (EITC)], which relies on a measure of annual household income rather than hourly wage rates. [E]ven if one assumes zero disemployment from the minimum wage, the difference in incidence is extreme. Middle-and upper-income families are projected to capture nearly three-quarters of the benefit from the 1996 minimum wage increase, as compared to barely over one-quarter of the benefit from 1993 legislation expanding the EITC....

Despite these problems, the minimum wage's subsidy is generally agreed to be progressive, though only modestly so. It may also, on balance, modestly advance the other plausible goals of a low-wage subsidy, by increasing the appeal of low-wage labor and offering a significant portion of its benefits to low-income households that otherwise face exceptionally high tax rates. Thus, the fact that it is so poorly targeted, while suggesting that alternative low-wage subsidies might be preferable, does not yet make the case for repeal if replacement with a better program is not in fact likely to happen. We next, however, must consider the effects of the minimum wage's imposing a tax on low-wage employment.

2. *Effects of the tax.*

a) *The pre-Card and Krueger consensus.* Despite the poor design of the minimum wage's subsidy, its most controversial element is its tax. One would think that taxing employers when they hire workers who would otherwise receive less than the minimum wage inevitably deters low-wage employment, and thus compromises the various goals of a low-wage subsidy....

On balance, economists widely agreed that the minimum wage simply did not make sense given its disemployment effects and general price distortion. This consensus has now been prominently challenged, however. David Card and Alan Krueger's *Myth and Measurement: The New Economics of the Minimum Wage*, published in 1995, boldly asserts that the economic consensus of the last fifty years, holding that the minimum wage results in disemployment, has simply been wrong. Based mainly on four empirical studies that Card, Krueger, and Lawrence Katz conducted in various combinations in the early 1990s, along with extensive critiques of prior empirical work, they assert the following: (1) modest minimum wage hikes do not reduce, and may even increase, low-wage employment; (2) improved econometric research techniques, representing a substantial advance in the art, permit them to assert this with confidence; and (3) the standard prediction of disemployment from minimum wage increases is based on a faulty theoretical understanding of the labor market. Their book title itself helps to introduce these points, suggesting that they have gone beyond "myth" to achieve "measurement" and are introducing a "new economics" to their readership....

b) *Card and Krueger's proposed "new view."* ... *Myth and Measurement* relies on four asserted natural experiments to support its sweeping conclusion that the "conventional wisdom" and the vast majority of prior studies are wrong, and that in fact modest increases to the minimum wage do not reduce, and may even increase, low-wage employment. [These natural experiments include the 1988 increase in the California minimum wage from the nationally mandated $3.35 to $4.25 per hour; the 1990 increase in the federal minimum wage, which because of differences in states' prior wage levels made it a larger relative increase in some states than in others; and the effects within Texas of the 1990 federal minimum wage increase as demonstrated through before-and-after phone surveys of fast-food restaurants.]

Effects Between New Jersey and Pennsylvania of the 1992 Increase in the New Jersey Minimum Wage: The flagship study underlying *Myth and Measurement*—by far the most ambitious, elaborately designed, and widely discussed—is by Card and Krueger, and concerns New Jersey's 80–cent increase of its minimum wage, from $4.25 to $5.05 per hour, on April 1, 1992. Like the Texas study, this one relied on before-and-after phone surveys of fast-food restaurants. The initial and follow-up phone surveys were seven to eight months apart, and were directed at all Burger King, KFC, Wendy's, and Roy Rogers restaurants in New Jersey and neighboring eastern Pennsylvania (which arguably were subject to similar economic conditions, the New Jersey minimum wage aside).

To improve the study's reliability, it had more than four times the sample size of the Texas study, and a much higher response rate due to aggressive follow-up. It also tried to examine whether mandated wage increases were offset by reductions in fringe benefits, took account of store closings rather than counting only results from surviving establishments, and used national data from McDonald's to examine whether the enactment detectably reduced the rate of new store openings in New Jersey.

Card and Krueger found that low-wage employment actually increased in New Jersey relative to eastern Pennsylvania after the new minimum wage took effect in New Jersey. Noting that this once again seems to contradict the standard view based on competitive markets and the law of demand, they briefly surveyed alternative models of the labor market under which modest minimum wage hikes might plausibly increase equilibrium employment levels. . . .

Despite . . . discordant price data, this study initially seemed to make a stronger case than the first three for Card and Krueger's general theoretical claim that the minimum wage does not reduce and may even increase employment—albeit that one cannot rule out the possibility that unobserved relative changes between the two areas offset the disemployment effects of the New Jersey minimum wage. Critics soon detected grave methodological weaknesses, however. The phone researchers' survey used vague and underspecified questions that may have been interpreted differently, even as between Time One (before the minimum wage increase) and Time Two (afterwards) at the same restaurant. (Presumably out of practical necessity, no effort was made to have the same person answer the questions both times.) For example, the key question, "How many full-time and part-time workers are employed in your restaurant, excluding managers and assistant managers?" was asked without defining any of these terms or otherwise attempting to ensure their consistent interpretation.

Perhaps because of this sloppy execution, the data purported to reveal what Finis Welch called "astonishing changes within stores." Fifteen percent of those reporting full-time employees at Time One reported none at Time Two. Seventy percent of those reporting no full-time employees at Time One ostensibly had them at Time Two. At both Time One and Time Two, the average restaurant had just over twenty-one employees, but the standard deviation of the change in employees was nine. In only eight months, smaller restaurants had an average 71 percent increase, and larger ones an average 42 percent decline, in the stated number of their employees. In various Wendy's restaurants, the price of an "average" hamburger ostensibly increased or decreased by as much as 80 percent in only eight months.

Welch concludes that "there is so much random noise in the data that they should be dismissed altogether." Card and Krueger respond that "reporting errors need not necessarily lead to bias in estimates of employment effects." That is, as sloppy and erratic as the data collection may have been, there was no reason to predict it would hide, rather than exaggerate, any disemployment effects of the increased minimum wage. . . .

Card and Krueger recognize that in Paul Samuelson's words, "it takes a theory to kill a theory; facts can only dent a theorist's hide." The theory behind the standard view is obvious enough: raise low-wage labor's price and demand for it will drop; or, bar certain agreements between employers and prospective workers and they will agree less frequently or for fewer hours. How could one explain the opposite result: that, when the price increases, demand does too, or that the imposition of a cartel by legal fiat increases output?

Card and Krueger make three main suggestions, each of which relies on rejecting the premise of competitive markets that underlies the law of demand.

Monopsony Theory: Under an argument first elaborated, though disbelievingly, in George Stigler's classic 1946 article laying out the standard economic case against the minimum wage, the mandate might increase low-wage employment under two conditions: (1) low-wage employers exercise monopsony power, permitting them to set wages noncompetitively and below the labor's productive value; and (2) employers cannot wage-discriminate by paying different salaries to workers who perform the same job. [George J. Stigler, "The Economics of Minimum Wage Legislation," 36 *American Economic Review* 358 (1946).] If both of these assumptions hold, it may make perfect sense to decline to hire an additional employee even though the value of her labor exceeds the wage that she is asking. . . .

While logically coherent, the monopsony theory is widely regarded as utterly implausible as to low-wage workers. It requires lack of competition between employers, either because there is only one or because they all collude. . . . However, as to low-wage, unskilled workers, the standard monopsony claim makes no sense. In the fast-food industry alone, numerous powerful companies compete nationwide. Their franchises can be found side-by-side nearly everywhere, competing for workers no less than for customers. A range of other employers—such as non-fast-food restaurants and retail trade—compete for low-wage workers as well. Even private households, seeking housecleaning and child care services, may in some cases compete for the same low-wage workers.

Card and Krueger concede this point, but claim that monopsony arises after all because employees, once they have a job, are reluctant to leave. Habituation, search costs, and the like give the employer a kind of monopsony power over current employees who cannot with sufficient ease find and accept competing offers. This explanation does not fit well, however, with conditions in the fast-food industry, where, as Card and Krueger note, fewer than one-half of the nonsupervisory personnel in a typical restaurant have been on the job as long as six months, and more than 80 percent of the restaurants have vacancies at any given time. . . .

Efficiency or Incentive Wages: Card and Krueger next rely on recent insights from labor economics that reflect human workers' being more complicated, less controllable, harder to monitor, and thus more variable in their output, than inanimate productive inputs such as commodities and machines. Hiring and firing workers is expensive, given search and training costs, but workers are free to quit and often cannot bond effectively against doing so. Moreover, they can shirk, or provide less than their best efforts, but whether they are doing so is hard to observe (and thus comparably hard for them to bond against). Getting them to contribute their best efforts may depend in part on providing incentives that make them more reluctant to risk losing their jobs through poor performance.

These considerations often lead employers to pay what economists call efficiency or incentive wages. These are wages set high enough to make job loss more of a sanction than it would be at the reservation wage where the employee was close to indifferent about continuing at the same job (relative both to quitting and to risking being fired for shirking). Wages are bid up by competing employers, with accompanying reduction in employment levels, until there is sufficient queuing for jobs to create the optimal level of sanction.

The implications are twofold. First, employers may receive some compensation in the form of greater output when they are required to pay employees higher wages. Thus, the true tax imposed on employers by the minimum wage is not the entire wage increase, but that increase minus the value of any increase in output. Second, employers often choose between low-wage-high-turnover and high-wage-low-turnover strategies. When the minimum wage bars the former strategy and employers switch to the latter, the result, at least in the short run, may be a stable higher-employment equilibrium.

Unfortunately, Card and Krueger, while rightly ... noting the second implication, ignore the first. Where an employer would have chosen the low-wage-high-turnover strategy but for the minimum wage, there is a strong inference that it was superior overall from the employer's standpoint. Thus, the minimum wage remains a net tax on low-wage employment despite the creation of some offsetting benefit. Over the long run, one would expect this tax to reduce low-wage employment by shifting resources out of low-wage industries, or by encouraging other substitution, as of capital for low-wage labor—even ignoring the problem of setting it at the right level. Thus, the positive employment effect, if any, may be purely short-term....

Shock Theory: Finally, Card and Krueger suggest that the cost of paying minimum wage increases may "shock" firms into adopting better management practices that they otherwise would have overlooked, thus making back the cost of higher wages without any need to reduce employment.... Others have noted that it appears more applicable to one-time upheavals (such as the initial unionization of a plant) than to periodic modest changes in a decades-old policy such as the minimum wage.

c) *Conclusions regarding the minimum wage's choice of tax.* In sum, Card and Krueger's empirical work is unpersuasive, and their theoretical arguments are weak. Thus, one should not accept their claim that minimum wage hikes do not reduce, and may even increase, low-wage employment. The standard view remains more convincing theoretically, and the standard disemployment estimates, although themselves not conclusive, are at least generally consistent both with each other and with what would seem plausible ex ante. In a world where we must make decisions under empirical uncertainty, they provide the best currently available basis for decision.

Again, the standard estimate predicts 1 to 3 percent disemployment for a 10 percent increase, and 3 to 5.5 percent for a 25 percent increase. Based on roughly applying this to the 1996 minimum wage hike of about 20 percent (from $4.25 to $5.15 per hour), which is directly applied to about 4.2 million workers, a total job loss of about 100,000 to 200,000 is widely regarded as plausible. Assuming the general accuracy of these estimates, the minimum wage clearly is inferior to alternative low-wage subsidies....

[In the final sections of the article, Shaviro argues that "the earned income tax credit (EITC) is considerably better than the minimum wage as a device for both progressive redistribution and encouraging work-force participation among the poor," and that a negative income tax might be still better in that it reduces the phase-out problems of the EITC.]

Notes and Questions

1. *Debate Among Labor Economists.* David Card and Alan Krueger, both prominent economists, were at Princeton University when they wrote their book. It sparked enormous debate among labor economists. For a sampling, see the Review Symposium in 48 *Industrial and Labor Relations Review* 827–49 (1995).

The debate can be overstated, however. Richard Freeman declares it to be basically an empirical question. As Freeman explains:

> Economists ... are divided into two basic groups. On one side are those who believe that responses to price incentives are usually large—Big Responders (BRs). On the other side are those who believe that respons-es to price incentives are generally small—Small Responders (SRs). [T]here is little in economic analysis to help us decide whether quantity responses to price incentives are likely to be large or small.... Logic tells us that massive changes in prices ... will have large effects on quantities.... But *whether the BR or SR perspective applies to mini-mum wages in the range observed in the United States is a purely empirical question.* It does not have to do with acceptance or rejection of neoclassical economic theory.

Richard B. Freeman, "What Will a 10% ... 50% ... 100% Increase in the Minimum Wage Do?," 48 *Industrial & Labor Relations Review* 830, 831–32 (1995) (emphasis in original).

Finis Welch, in the same Review Symposium, sharply criticized the empirical methodology of Card and Krueger, and felt the flaws prevented the study from casting doubt on the earlier consensus that minimum wage laws decreased employment. As he put it: "There is confusion between an inconclusive result in a statistical experiment and 'proof' that the answer is indeed inconclusive. When we return empty-handed from a long search, it is tempting to announce that there is no treasure in 'them thar hills,' but the only proof that we have to offer is that we did not find it." Finis Welch, "Comment," 48 *Industrial & Labor Relations Review* 842, 848 (1995).

Charles Brown reflected an intermediate position. He remained con-vinced that minimum wage laws reduced employment, but believed that the magnitude in the short run was smaller than earlier thought. Brown emphasized that Card and Krueger have little to say about long-run effects, which might be considerably larger. Charles Brown, "Comment," 48 *Indus-trial & Labor Relations Review* 828 (1995).

2. *Poorly Targeted Subsidy?* Shaviro carefully reviews whether the mini-mum wage law has the unintended effect of reducing jobs, the issue that has occupied the economists. Shaviro reminds policymakers, however, that the more important issue is how well the minimum wage law achieves its

primary aims. It is a weak antipoverty tool, in his mind, because the link between low hourly wages and low annual family income is tenuous. Many minimum-wage workers are teenagers from nonpoor families. Many poor families have no earners or earners who have hourly wages above the minimum but who cannot find enough work over the year. See Charles Brown, "Minimum Wage Laws: Are They Overrated?," 2 *Journal of Economic Perspectives* 133, 143 (1998); Richard V. Burkhauser, Kenneth A. Couch, and David C. Wittenburg, " 'Who Gets What' from Minimum Wage Hikes," 49 *Industrial & Labor Relations Review* 547 (1996) (arguing that "even if the negative employment effects of the minimum wage are small, it is still a very ineffective method of assisting the working poor").

3. *Trade–Offs Among Low–Wage Workers*. Shaviro emphasizes that even if the minimum wage law increases earnings of low-wage workers as a group, it creates winners and losers among the group. An increase in the minimum wage benefits those low-wage workers able to find or keep a job, but harms those who lose their job as a result. This winners and losers story, however, ignores the fact that turnover among minimum-wage workers is amazingly high, about 12.5 percent per month. With such high turnover, the group of persons "lucky enough to work at a higher wage" and the group "unable to find work" may comprise the same people at different times. See Charles Brown, "Minimum Wage Laws: Are They Overrated?," 2 *Journal of Economic Perspectives* 133, 135 (1998).

B. Pension Regulation

In the Employee Retirement Income Security Act of 1974 (ERISA), Congress preempted most state regulation of pension and other employee benefits in favor of a comprehensive federal statute. This section provides a framework for examining some of the issues in this fast-changing field. We begin with an article by Michael Graetz, outlining the tripartite system of saving for retirement. We then turn to an article by Deborah Weiss, who argues that the economic rationales for pension regulation crumble under close scrutiny, and that paternalism based on psychological short-comings of workers best explains pension regulation.

"The Troubled Marriage of Retirement Security and Tax Policies"*
MICHAEL J. GRAETZ

Commentators typically describe a tripartite system that enables and encourages the provision of income security for individuals in the years following their retirement from the workforce: Social Security, employer-provided pensions, and individual savings. . . .

An effort to analyze these three aspects of retirement security policy as a unified system is inherently complex. It is difficult to conceive of a

* 135 *University of Pennsylvania Law Review* 851, 852–59 (1987).

wider spectrum of public policy mechanisms intended to implement a single goal. At one extreme is Social Security, a mandatory national public program financed by the federal government's power to tax, fulfilled by the government's power to spend, and explicitly redistributional in both purpose and effect—redistributional both across generations and within the same generation. At the opposite extreme is reliance on individual savings as a source of retirement security, a predominantly private program, with the individual (or the family) composing the relevant unit.... Bridging these two public/private extremes are employer-provided pensions, voluntary private programs encouraged through income tax reductions, regulated by government, both directly and as to the many requirements that must be met to qualify for tax benefits, and backed, at least in a limited way, by an insurance system of national scope. Taken together, then, these three retirement security sources reflect a full spectrum of policy initiatives: a federal social program for all Americans, an individualistic program dependent principally upon familial self-reliance, and a pluralistic communitarian program involving both employers and employees....

At the outset one should describe the goals of retirement security policy in order to measure the success or failure of the current mix of public and private programs and to determine whether these programs comprise a coherent whole in addressing the retirement security problem. The shortfall in income upon retirement is lost income from labor. Thus, while there are no doubt disagreements at the margin, replacement of some significant portion of preretirement wages must be the fundamental goal of retirement security policy. Retirement security also implies that the replacement of preretirement labor income will ensure for the retiree the maintenance of an adequate retirement income that will both protect the elderly from widespread poverty and generally ensure against an abrupt decline in a retiree's lifestyle....

Delineating the retirement security goal as a wage-replacement goal helps to clarify the suitable functions of the various elements of our tripartite retirement security system. Social Security—a completely public program—might serve fully to meet the basic income adequacy goal for poorer workers, contribute substantially toward ensuring an adequate threshold retirement income for moderate income workers, and assist somewhat in post-retirement lifestyle maintenance for all workers. This vision of a public Social Security function would require at least all individuals who have enough earnings to satisfy current basic needs to substitute future for current consumption, for example by taxing current wages in exchange for subsequent wage-replacement retirement benefits. In addition, such a view regards as appropriate the redistributional aspects of Social Security and dismisses the contention that a public social security program should resemble an actuarially sound retirement insurance plan for all workers, even those at the highest income levels. The dominant public role of retirement income security policy should be to ensure post-retirement income adequacy for low-and moderate-income workers.

At the other end of the income scale, private individual savings are most likely to ensure retirement income security for those workers who have earned sufficiently high lifetime wages (or who otherwise have sufficient investment assets) to enable them to use current savings to protect themselves from a substantial decline in living standard upon retirement. The public role in this context should obviously permit, and perhaps facilitate, private savings for retirement, but the individual savings component of retirement security for higher-income workers should be a primarily private matter....

The appropriate role of the Social Security and individual savings elements of the tripartite retirement security program thus fits easily within this article's articulation of retirement security goals. Private pensions present more of a problem. While it is clear that these employer-provided pensions often contribute to basic income adequacy, especially for low-and moderate-income workers, it is not nearly so clear to what extent employer-provided plans should serve to facilitate post-retirement lifestyle maintenance for all workers. Specification of the appropriate role for employer-sponsored pension plans depends both on the overall ambitions of the national retirement security program and on the adequacy of Social Security. The voluntariness of such plans links them to individual savings, while their collective nature with respect to benefits and risks as well as with respect to employer and regulatory limitations on employee choices, suggests a public nature. Dominant reliance on income tax incentives as the public stimulus for employer plans necessarily confounds retirement security and income tax policies....

Notes and Questions

1. *The Tripartite Retirement System.* Graetz outlines the three-part American system for providing retirement income: government-provided Social Security, employer-provided pension plans, and individual private savings. These interrelated parts are supposed to fulfill the twin goals of preventing poverty for elderly persons and avoiding abrupt declines in lifestyle. Recall the discussion by Lawrence Summers in Chapter 6 of the trade-off between government provision and employer mandate of benefits. American retirement policy incorporates both approaches.

2. *Focusing on Poorer Workers.* Both Social Security and employer pension plans are "bottom weighted," in the sense that they replace a higher percentage of income for low-paid workers than for high-paid workers. For example, in 1989 a typical worker making $15,000 who retired at age sixty-five would have 44.8 percent of his income replaced by Social Security benefits and another 34.4 percent replaced by an employer pension, for a total replacement rate of 79.2 percent. A worker making $45,000, by contrast, would have only 23.8 percent replaced by Social Security and 29

percent replaced by pension, for a total of 52.8 percent. See Steven L. Willborn et al., *Employment Law*, 2nd ed. (Charlottesville, Va.: Lexis Law Publishing, 1998), 840–41. By contrast, private savings—the third part of the retirement system—provide relatively more retirement income for high-income workers.

"Paternalistic Pension Policy: Psychological Evidence and Economic Theory"*
DEBORAH WEISS

. . .

I. *America's Paternalistic Savings Policy*

. . . The United States attempts to provide retirement income security through two programs: Social Security and the system of tax subsidies for retirement savings. Both of these mechanisms display Congress's desire to protect people from the consequences of their own actions by restricting individual choice.

The design of Social Security most clearly shows Congress's preference for policies that raise savings through restrictions on individual choice. Social Security comprises about fifty-four percent of the average household's post-retirement income. With 1991 Social Security payments estimated to be $235 billion, it is by far the most expensive domestic program. Participation in Social Security is compulsory. Thus, for the individual contributor, the Social Security system is just like forced savings: individuals are required to give up consumption now in return for more consumption later.

Though Social Security is the most obviously paternalistic program, it is by no means the only one. The system of tax incentives also has a paternalistic character, though of a more subtle kind. . . .

The system of tax incentives breaks down into two basic programs: subsidization of employer-sponsored plans and subsidization of Individual Retirement Accounts. This tax-incentive system is more limited than Social Security, with private pensions accounting for fifteen percent of average post-retirement income. Still, it is far from negligible: the tax exemption for employer-sponsored pensions is the largest single tax preference in the Internal Revenue Code, costing an estimated $46.9 billion in lost revenues in 1991. Like Social Security, this costly system disfavors individual choice. It gives the most generous deductions to non-elective employer-sponsored pension plans, in which the employee is not permitted to choose between wages and pension contributions. Such non-elective plans must cover all members of a predetermined group—individual employees of participating employers are forced to contribute

* 58 *University of Chicago Law Review* 1275 (1991).

to their own retirement savings. Non-elective plans receive very favorable tax treatment. Both the employer contributions and the subsequent interest on these contributions are deductible, and these deductions can be taken on contributions of up to $30,000 per year or until a pension annuity of $90,000 per year is reached. . . .

Finally, Congress's decision to disfavor individual choice shows in its treatment of Individual Retirement Accounts (IRAs). The lowest ceilings of all apply to contributions to IRAs, a type of plan wholly unrelated to employment. Eligible persons may deduct contributions to IRAs, but only up to $2000 per year. Additionally, IRAs are generally not available to individuals covered by employer pensions. Congress is thus most generous to those forms of retirement savings that leave the least room for individual choice. . . .

II. *Neoclassical Economics: Policy Without Paternalism*

A. *Economic Savings Theory*

. . . Why do some people not save enough for their old age? From a common sense perspective, individuals who fail to save enough fall into several different groups. Some people, whom I will call myopes, simply do not think very much about the future. They spend money as they receive it. When they retire they are forced to lower their consumption level, and they regret not having saved more. Other people, whom I will call impulsives, worry about providing for their old age, and continually resolve to save more, but find that money burns a hole in their pocket. Such people spend their paycheck the moment they receive it. On Monday they regret the impetuousness of Friday, and promise themselves not to repeat it, yet they find next Friday that temptation is again too great. Still another group, whom I will call impatients, always believe that present consumption needs are especially pressing. Although they see the need to save for future consumption, they believe that it will be easier to save from next year's wages than from this year's. But when next year comes, current consumption seems more pressing than it did in previous years, and the amount that they ultimately save for retirement is far less than what they anticipated while young. The vagaries of cash flow influence the decisions of impatients much less than they do those of impulsives. Impatients have no cycle of Friday binges and Monday morning regret, but rather plan consciously to spend more this year than next. Finally, some people, whom I will call deliberates, plan when young to consume less as they grow old, and follow this consumption plan without any later regret.

The economic theory of savings behavior rejects these distinctions. Economists instead regard all four savings patterns described above as instances of a single type of rational behavior. All four cases are assimilated to that of deliberates, or rational agents who simply prefer present consumption to saving. . . .

Economists apply consumer theory to savings decisions by treating present consumption and future consumption as two distinct goods. An individual's decision to save is a decision to defer present consumption in favor of future consumption. Thus the individual's decision to allocate consumption between temporal periods is analytically identical to the decision to allocate income between two goods in one period.

B. *Efficiency–Based Reform Proposals*

[E]fficiency-oriented economists are not hostile to all pension reform proposals. Although neoclassical economics implies that savings levels are individually rational, it also suggests that they may be below the socially optimal level. This is a result of a simple externality, referred to as the overlapping generations problem: savings affects the welfare of future generations, but those generations play no role in determining today's savings. Thus, the national savings level may be too low to protect the interest of future generations.

Economists who accept this argument offer a number of policy prescriptions. They argue that policies such as capital taxes exacerbate the problem of low savings and are therefore undesirable. They endorse various pension tax subsidies as a subsidiary component of their general advocacy of capital tax cuts....

What about mandatory plans? Here again sophisticated neoclassical economists are willing to support some degree of intervention. The same overlapping generations concern that leads some economists to accept the principle of subsidies also leads them to accept the principle of forced savings. Other concerns are at work as well. Neoclassical economists recognize that individuals may deliberately not save in order to take advantage of welfare-type Social Security. With such concerns in mind, efficiency-oriented commentators insist on the importance of a funded Social Security program, or a mandatory universal pension system (MUPS).

Neoclassical economists also have their own way of looking at restrictions on and protections of pension assets. They believe that restrictions on pension withdrawals serve no good purpose and that the welfare of a consumer can never be improved by reducing the choices available to him. A deliberate consumer who withdraws from his pension fund in the absence of restrictions does so for a good reason. Similarly, the special protection from creditors accorded to pensions cannot be justified....

Neoclassical economics thus provides grounds for rejecting some of the restrictions in the present system, but neoclassicists are still willing to accept a fair range of restrictions on individual choice. Notably, though, the restrictions economists accept are restrictions directed at externalities, not those driven by paternalism. Paternalism thus remains outside the range of the concerns of neoclassical economists. . . .

. . .

IV. *Modified Neoclassical Paternalism: Myopia*

. . . Even those who in general accept the neoclassical argument for consumer sovereignty have misgivings about applying neoclassical welfare analysis to savings. In particular, many economists and philosophers question whether it is rational to value future well-being less than present well-being.

Those who take this approach exclude from the class of deliberates individuals who are "myopes," or who overly discount the future. . . . In common sense terms, myopia is an irrational preference for present consumption over future consumption. In economic terms, myopia is a discount rate that is irrationally larger than zero, or irrationally higher than the interest rate. Thus even consistent preferences may be irrational. . . .

The theory of myopic behavior provides a justification for intervention in individual savings decisions as well as guidance about the optimal savings point and the appropriate corrective tools. Myopes in many respects resemble their deliberate cousins: they make decisions on the margin, and their behavior can be manipulated with neoclassical tools. . . . A tax subsidy in the amount of the difference between the myope's discount rate and the rational discount rate will cause the myope to save at the rational level. The use of tax ceilings will undercut the effectiveness of any subsidy, since myopes are still marginalist creatures. . . .

A satisfactory theory of myopia would thus justify and provide guidance for interventionist pension policy. . . . But if, as the myopia hypothesis requires, some consistent decisions are to be classified as irrational, some substitute criterion for rationality is needed. Without a differentiating criterion, it is hard to explain why a consumer's discount rate can be ignored while the other parameters of his utility function must be respected. And even if discount rates differ from other parameters, why select low discount rates as rational? Why should consumption be smooth or gradually increasing? Why not fluctuating, or decreasing, or rapidly increasing? . . .

V. *The Psychology of Impatience and Impulsiveness*

The theory of myopia has not convinced neoclassical economists to relinquish their model of human behavior, for it provides no precise theoretical reason for distinguishing myopes from deliberates. In this section, I will suggest that impatients and impulsives cannot be forced into the neoclassical model. A look at psychology reveals that their behavior exhibits inconsistency, the one fact that neoclassical economics cannot explain.

A. Time–Inconsistent Preferences

Suppose that on December 25, 1990, an individual is given a choice between $100 on December 25, 1994, and $110 on January 1, 1995; he chooses the $110. However, if he were given the same choice on December 24, 1994, he would prefer the $100 the next day rather than wait eight days for $110. When, as in this example, the individual would make a different decision at a later period, the decision is said to be time-inconsistent or dynamically inconsistent. Intertemporal inconsistencies are a special case of the more general phenomenon of inconsistent choice, which can also occur within a single period.

A growing body of laboratory evidence suggests that many human subjects make dynamically inconsistent choices. The most commonly accepted explanation for this phenomenon is that individual preferences are not stable. . . .

Perhaps the most compelling type of evidence linking time inconsistency to preference change is the phenomenon of precommitment—individuals sometimes deliberately reduce the choices that will be available to them in the future. It is difficult to interpret this as anything but strategic behavior to impose self-control. A perfectly rational subject has no motive to restrict his choices in this way. . . .

[P]references may change as a function of factors other than time. Such factors may produce inconsistencies in intertemporal choice that appear to be time-dependent but are not. Between time t and time $t+1$ an individual's preferences between cs and $cs+1$ may reverse not because of the passage of time but because of changes in situational factors. Both types of inconsistency are dynamic, but I will call inconsistencies caused by the passage of time alone "time-dependent," and those resulting from other factors "situational." Situational preference change produces behavior that corresponds to what most of us would call impulsiveness. . . .

In some important ways, though, an impatient has more in common with a deliberate than either does with an impulsive. Most importantly, the behavior of impatients conforms to the fundamental neoclassical principle of marginalism, while the behavior of impulsives does not. This feature of situational preference change may explain some puzzling facts about savings behavior. Suppose that two individuals, A and B, each have the same tastes and each has a net worth of $100. The principle of marginalism states that both should choose consumption levels that equate marginal utility in the present period with marginal utility in future periods.

Since both have the same level of wealth and the same tastes, both should generally choose the same consumption levels. A qualification to the principle of marginalism occurs if some wealth is held in illiquid form. For example, suppose that both individuals wish to consume $70 today. However, suppose that A's wealth is all in liquid assets such as cash, while B's is allocated half to cash and half to illiquid assets. A will be able to consume $70 today, since his wealth is liquid. B, however, will not. The principle of marginalism acknowledges that marginal utility between periods may not be equated if some impediment (like illiquidity) interferes. But that illiquidity can only interfere if it is on the margin, that is, if it directly prevents consumption of the optimal marginal level. Suppose that both A and B wish to consume $40 today. Under the previous assumption that A's wealth is all liquid, while B's is half liquid, both have liquid assets adequate to finance their desired level of consumption, so both should consume $40. Non-marginal illiquidity—that is, illiquidity that does not directly obstruct the marginal decision— should not affect consumption choices.

Yet in practice it seems to do so: the marginal propensity to consume (MPC) seems strongly positively correlated to non-marginal liquidity as well as to wealth. Under the previous assumption that A has more liquidity than B, A will usually spend more than B in the current period. To some extent this correlation may result from taste differences. Consumers with low MPCs may be more willing than consumers with high MPCs to lock assets away in illiquid form. Likewise, taste differences may contribute to the marginal propensity to consume housing wealth, since housing is endogenous, or chosen by the individual. But non-marginal illiquid assets, such as Social Security and to a lesser extent private pensions, whose levels are exogenously set, also exert the same mysterious effect on spending. These observations are hard to reconcile with deliberate or even impatient behavior, but make perfect sense if people are impulsive. The availability of non-marginal wealth is a situational factor, like the proximity of chocolate, that affects behavior. Impulsive behavior may explain some of the poor performance of the neoclassical savings model in econometric studies. As we will see in the next section, the breakdown of marginalism is of great interest to pension policy-makers....

VI. *Paternalistic Pension Policies for Impulsives and Impatients*

A. *Incentive Plans*

1. *Situational preference change.*

Incentive-based schemes to increase savings run the gamut from a pure, unrestricted capital subsidy such as a capital gains cut, to more narrowly tailored subsidies like IRAs, to heavily regulated employer pensions. Congress has been skeptical about proposals to shift from the present system favoring the more regulated pension assets to a system with increased individual choice and pure tax subsidies. The evidence of situational preference change suggests that this skepticism may be justified, and that pure tax subsidies would be ineffective. The abstract future benefits of a higher return on savings may seem slight at a time when immediate temptation is great. . . .

Capital subsidies, the standard neoclassical means of increasing savings, are thus ineffective in dealing with an impulsive. But the behavior of an impulsive individual can be manipulated with two policy tools that will not affect a person with stable preferences: precommitments and "distraction techniques." Both precommitments and distraction techniques in principle should work without a subsidy, but a mixed policy that combined either with a subsidy might be especially effective.

The simpler of the two is a distraction device. The key lesson of Mischel's work is that factors that focus attention on the possibility of gratification, whether present or delayed, tend to reduce self-control. [See Walter Mischel, Ebbe B. Ebbesen, and Antonette R. Zeiss, "Cognitive and Attentional Mechanisms in Delay of Gratification," 21 *Journal of Personality and Social Psychology* 204 (1972).] For example, thinking about eating reduces the ability to forgo a less desirable food now in return for a more desirable one later. An example of a distraction technique to encourage saving is a payroll withholding plan that would allow employees to elect to have their employers deduct a certain amount from their paycheck every week and deposit it in a savings account. Such plans might even leave the individual perfectly free to terminate his participation or withdraw from the account at any time. Yet the automatic nature of the withholding would tend to discourage current consumption. An individual who must actually force himself each week to divide his paycheck between his checking account and his savings account resembles a child who must look at the candy bar he wants. An automatic withholding plan works in the same way as hiding the candy.

In principle, savings should rise when distraction mechanisms are readily available, even in the absence of any subsidy or other incentive to save. A mere payroll withholding option would probably induce at least some individuals to save more. In practice, many employers and banks offer such schemes through direct deposit arrangements. But such withholding arrangements are not available to all consumers—and even when they are available, implementing them at present involves initiative and planning. Instead, Congress could institutionalize a withholding arrangement by incorporating it into the tax withholding system. Individuals could choose direct savings withholding by simply filling in one more number on a W–4 form. The employer could direct funds where the individual specified or into a Treasury Direct account. This would to some extent mimic the common practice of deliberately overwithholding in order to receive a refund, a habit to which I reluctantly confess.

Withholding policies might be even more effective if combined with a subsidy. But none of the present pension subsidies makes systematic use of people's willingness to engage in distraction techniques. IRAs permit homemade self-control devices: individuals are permitted to make deposits to IRA accounts over the course of the year, and many employers and banks permit direct payroll deposits, which employees can allocate between accounts. But the IRA direct-deposit arrangement takes initiative and organization, and is not a precondition of the IRA tax subsidy. In practice, many [cash or deferred arrangements (CODAs), whereby employees voluntarily contribute part of their salary to pensions] employ withholding arrangements, although the Code does not require or encourage employers to offer withholding. Indeed, the prevalence of withholding arrangements may contribute to Congress's preference for CODAs over IRAs. But CODAs have one substantial disadvantage: employers are not required to provide them, and some people are self-employed, so not all workers can take advantage of them. Congress could better obtain the advantages of withholding by equalizing the subsidy to various pension assets and facilitating withholding arrangements for IRAs through payroll or tax withholding mechanisms. Indeed, even the distributive problem with IRAs—that they serve primarily the affluent—might diminish if withholding mechanisms made IRA participation easier. An impressive body of evidence suggests that the impulsiveness that withholding methods cure is more prevalent among the less affluent.

Besides distraction techniques, a second potential set of remedies for impulsiveness includes measures designed to encourage precommitment against withdrawal. Specifically, legislators might encourage individuals not only to withhold from their pay, but to lock up their wealth in assets from which withdrawal was prohibited, penalized, or merely difficult. Precommitment mechanisms, like distraction techniques, should work in principle without a subsidy, but precommitment, even more than distraction, makes better sense as part of a subsidy plan. A belief in the value of precommitments may in part explain Congress's preference for noncontributory employer plans over CODAs, and for either over IRAs. But there is in principle no connection between the illiquidity of a retirement asset and whether it is employer sponsored. At present, IRAs are subject only to a withdrawal penalty, but a number of other obstacles could be placed in the way of IRA withdrawals. Congress could virtually prohibit withdrawals, as it does for noncontributory employer plans. As with CODAs, withdrawals might be subject to a hardship requirement, whereby individuals would have to make a formal application to the financial institution's plan administrator. Even if generally granted, this added obstacle should discourage impulsive withdrawals of funds. Finally, Congress might require advance notification of an intention to withdraw.

The effectiveness of devices to discourage liquidity illustrates the generally diminished relevance of marginalism to individuals with situational preference change. A corollary is that the usual economic arguments against tax ceilings do not apply to impulsive individuals. Impulsives may replace amounts shifted into IRAs by other liquid assets to a greater extent than deliberates.

A combined scheme of subsidies, precommitments, and distraction devices could take many forms, but it is difficult to discern the ideal structure of tax incentives from the existing experimental evidence. The conventional implementation of a subsidy conditioned on a precommitment would require an irrevocable decision to withhold at the beginning of the tax year, followed by a tax deduction on that year's return. Alternatively, an individual who agreed to the automatic withholding of $50 a week from his paychecks for the next year might receive an immediate tax credit of equal present value, instead of a later deduction. One potential drawback of the conventional approach is that the reward is too far delayed to affect behavior. On the other hand, Mischel's results suggest that focusing on the reward for waiting may be as detrimental to self-control as focusing on immediate gratification. The matter is complicated further by the fact that cool, non-arousing reminders of reward increase self-control, while arousing reminders decrease it. Without further evidence it is difficult to speculate on the timing arrangement that would maximize self-control.

2. *Time–dependent preference change.*

An impatient individual with time-dependent preference change is more like a neoclassical consumer than an impulsive individual, and legislators must use different tools to alter the savings of impatients than to alter the savings of impulsives. Since the impatient's preferences are stable, and are thus immune to situational factors, impatients respond in predictable ways to incentive changes. Tax subsidies that are ineffective with impulsives can be used to increase the impatient's savings. Second, impatients, like rationals, ignore non-marginal illiquidity. The impatient allocates resources so that the marginal costs and marginal benefits are equated within the period. Policies that exploit the effect of non-marginal liquidity on impulsive behavior will not work on impatients. A subsidy with a ceiling below the marginal level will not increase savings, and distraction techniques will not deceive the impatient into ignoring non-marginal wealth.

But legislators can manipulate the behavior of both impatients and impulsives with precommitment mechanisms, which will not affect the behavior of rationals. To be effective, though, precommitment mechanisms probably require a longer time horizon for impatients than for impulsives. The impulsive wants to protect himself from a relatively short, recurring cycle of binging and regret, like spending every Friday's paycheck and regretting that splurge every Monday. In contrast, the time-dependent preference change of the impatient occurs over the course of his lifetime, and evolves at a gradual rate. The effectiveness of precommitment devices increases as the time at which the commitment must be met is pushed further into the future. An impatient finds deferring consumption from tomorrow to the next day easier than deferring consumption from today to tomorrow, but finds it easier still to defer consumption from a day in five years to five years and a day....

Perhaps, though, the desirability of long-term precommitments provides a partial justification for the home mortgage deduction, the most maligned personal tax preference. A mortgage is a kind of precommitment device in which the mortgagee promises to make a series of payments over a long term. In addition, investment in housing seems to exploit situational factors as well, since the present enjoyment of a home may make housing a relatively painless form of savings for most impulsives. Of course, the current housing deduction is not ideally designed: an equity deduction would encourage savings more effectively than the present interest deduction.

3. *Protection from creditors.*

If individuals behave as rational economic agents, the special protection from creditors accorded to retirement assets is difficult to justify. Such protection creates moral hazard problems, especially with respect to pension assets which the debtor controls. However, changing preferences seem to provide a general justification for restrictions on the alienability of pension wealth. Although preference change does not necessarily eliminate moral hazard concerns, it suggests that legislators should address moral hazard issues with narrowly tailored tools, in order to accommodate paternalistic concerns. In this light, the distinction between pension assets which individuals control and those which they do not control seems overly broad, since bankruptcy law contains numerous more finely-tuned protections against fraudulent conveyances.

B. *Mandatory Savings Plans*

Though it is too early to know which of the two is more important, there is evidence for the existence of both time-dependent and situational preference change. Yet our understanding of each phenomenon is nowhere near the point where the exact effects of any given subsidy level or precommitment policy can be even roughly estimated. Perhaps more importantly, the actual workplace is likely to contain a mixture of impatients, impulsives, and deliberates. An incentive-based plan will have different effects on each of these groups. Unlike incentive programs, a mandatory savings plan will increase savings in a predictable way, regardless of why or how much preferences change, and deserves serious consideration. A surprisingly high number of observers take seriously the possibility of a mandatory plan as a substitute either for Social Security or for voluntary employer sponsored pensions. The key point of contention with respect to such a plan is whether it should be implemented through employers, through government, or through private financial intermediaries. Each of these alternatives has problems. Reliance on employer plans is problematic because not all employers are well situated to make long-term contracts and complex financial decisions. Even those skeptical of the power of the market may be dismayed by a government-run plan with a budget of over a trillion dollars, the magnitude of the present private pension system. But the proposed plans that would make use of private financial intermediaries seem based on strong assumptions about the reliability of individual choice, and view increasing choice as an unalloyed good. The problems associated with financial intermediaries seem to be the most tractable. There is no reason why financial intermediaries cannot assume a paternalistic role as well as employers. To the extent that concerns about individual choice center on investment decisions, the same fiduciary requirements, funding rules, and insurance programs that ERISA imposes on employers could be imposed on financial institutions. To the extent that employers supervise such matters as hardship withdrawals, a financial intermediary could provide the benefits of supervised illiquidity just as easily....

Notes and Questions

1. *Paternalism Throughout the Tripartite System.* Professor Weiss argues that a central goal of retirement policy is paternalistic—getting more income for retirees than they would choose to provide for themselves. Weiss shows how paternalism influences policies in all three parts of the system—Social Security, employer pension plans, and individual savings. She gives a number of practical reforms to induce further savings, such as allowing or encouraging greater use of payroll withholding into savings plans. Should paternalistic policies be applied across the board, as Weiss suggests? Or should the government "remain generally neutral about individual decisions by high-income workers regarding the trade-off between their own current and future consumption," as Graetz declares?

2. *Pensions as Discouraging and Encouraging Quits.* Even without the huge tax benefits of pensions, employers might want to offer pensions in addition to current salary. Employers can reduce costly job turnover by promising workers pension benefits that vest only after significant service with the firm. Under current law, accrued benefits must vest, or become nonforfeitable, within five to seven years of service. 29 U.S.C. § 1053.

Employers also use pensions to induce workers to retire. Indeed, now that the Age Discrimination in Employment Act has forbidden age-based mandatory retirement, pension benefits are an important way to encourage retirement. Many plans are designed so that after, say, thirty years of service, the present value of the pension declines if the worker continues to work. This occurs because the extra credits gained by continuing to work are offset by the fewer years in retirement to receive benefits. For an explanation of the retirement effects of pensions, see Edward P. Lazear, "Pensions as Severance Pay," in Zvi Bodie and John B. Shoven, eds., *Financial Aspects of the United States Pension System* (Chicago: University of Chicago Press,

1983), 57. See generally Alan L. Gustman, Olivia S. Mitchell, and Thomas S. Steinmeier, "The Role of Pensions in the Labor Market: A Survey of the Literature," 47 *Industrial & Labor Relations Review* 417 (1994).

3. *Internal Discount Rates and Productivity.* Weiss emphasizes that people differ in how they value future income, and that pension laws should protect people who discount the value of future income too highly. One reason that employers offer pensions is that it enables them to attract workers with low discount rates. Ippolito argues that workers with low discount rates are more productive.

> [I]ndividuals with low discount rates strongly consider the long-term implications of their current work performance. For example, low discounters are less likely to take time off or to quit on a whim, since they appreciate the long-term implications of their reputation for reliability, which reduces the firm's expenditures on duplication and hiring. They are less likely to mistreat machines and equipment, because they recognize the long-term benefit of being labeled a "low cost" employee. They are less likely to value the short-term gains from shirking over the long-term consequences of getting caught. And they are more likely to be motivated to work hard to gain the benefits of promotions.

Richard A. Ippolito, *Pension Plans and Employee Performance* (Chicago: University of Chicago Press, 1997), 108.

4. *ERISA as Protection or Rent–Seeking Rip–Off?* Weiss's arguments assume that Congress is enacting paternalistic legislation with the overall public interest in mind, even if the legislation is perhaps flawed in practice. Others look more suspiciously at the claim that Congress enacted ERISA legislation in the public interest. They point to the rent-seeking potential of forcing people to participate in forced savings or forced insurance plans. For example, Richard Ippolito has argued that a major impact of ERISA was to transfer billions of dollars from well-funded pension plans to those which are underfunded. See Richard A. Ippolito, *Pensions, Economics, and Public Policy* (Homewood, Ill.: Dow Jones–Irwin, 1986).

5. *Opportunism and Termination of Pension Funds.* ERISA requires that accrued benefits "vest," or become nonforfeitable, after an employee has participated in the plan for five to seven years. Thus, employees who leave a firm with a pension plan before normal retirement age have rights to a pension. When a plan terminates, all accrued benefits immediately vest. See Jay Conison, *Employee Benefit Plans in a Nutshell*, 2nd ed. (St. Paul, Minn.: West, 1998), 76–87.

Some scholars have argued that, despite ERISA's vesting requirements, employees are harmed when a plan terminates. For example, consider a defined benefit plan that promises retirement benefits of 1 percent of final salary times years of service. A participant who retires after thirty years with a $50,000 salary will get a pension of $15,000. If the plan terminates after fifteen years, when the worker's salary is, say, $30,000, the pension will be only $4,500. Even if the worker joins an equally generous plan, and after 15 years reaches a final salary of $50,000 (with a resulting second pension of

$7,500), his total pension is less than if he could have participated in a single plan for thirty years.

During the 1980s, a rising stock market caused many pension funds to have excess funds. A number of firms terminated their pension plans, paying out the vested benefits to workers and keeping the surplus. These terminations often occurred in the context of a corporate takeover. Andrei Shleifer and Lawrence H. Summers have argued that these terminations breached an implicit contract between workers and the firm. "Breach of Trust in Hostile Takeovers," in Alan J. Auerbach, ed., *Corporate Takeovers: Causes and Consequences* (Chicago: University of Chicago Press, 1988), 33. For a critique of this theory, see Roberta Romano, "A Guide to Takeovers: Theory, Evidence and Regulation," 9 *Yale Journal on Regulation* 119, 140–42 (1992). In the late 1980s, Congress killed most surplus terminations by imposing a reversion tax of up to 50 percent. See Jeffrey N. Gordon, "Employees, Pensions, and the New Economic Order," 97 *Columbia Law Review* 1519 (1997).

6. *Defined-Benefit and Defined–Contribution Plans*. In a defined-benefit plan, the employer promises a specific retirement pension (a typical promise might be 1 percent of final salary times years of service). The employer, scrutinized by ERISA funding regulations, is responsible for putting sufficient funds into the plan to finance the benefits. The risk of whether the invested funds will cover the promises is on the employer. In a defined-contribution plan, the employer promises to contribute a specified amount (say 10 percent of salary) to an employee's retirement account with no promise of how large a pension this will provide. One form of defined-contribution plans is 401k plans. Employers can make unconditional contributions, but can also allow employees to make additional pretax contributions, which employers can match. In 1979, 83 percent of all workers covered by an employer pension plan had a defined-benefit plan. By 1996 half of covered workers had a defined-contribution plan. This places greater risk on workers, though in recent years it has benefited workers because the stock market has been booming, creating upside risk.

Several factors explain the shift toward defined-contribution plans. First, there has been a shift in jobs from large, unionized firms in manufacturing—which traditionally use defined-benefit plans—to smaller, nonunion service firms. Second, defined-benefit plans became increasingly more costly than defined-contribution plans to administer, especially for small plans. Indeed, defined-benefit plans are still the dominant choice for large firms (95 percent of workers in firms with 5,000 or more employees have defined-benefit plans). Third, employers seem increasingly to like the flexibility of 401k plans and the ability to attract low-discount, high-productivity workers. For example, Ippolito has shown that workers who voluntarily contribute to 401k plans are more likely to receive pay increases, promotions, and high evaluations, and are less likely to quit. Richard A. Ippolito, *Pension Plans and Employee Performance* (Chicago: University of Chicago Press, 1997), 131–37.

7. *Passive Ownership.* Professor Gregory Alexander has criticized American pension law's creation of passivity in ownership among those who have stakes in pension funds. Gregory S. Alexander, "Pensions and Passivity," 56 *Law & Contemporary Problems* 111 (1993). He argues for a relaxation of fiduciary laws to allow a greater voice to pension participants. For example, he proposes that "an obvious step is to abandon the rule barring trustees from following participants' preferences in investment decisions." "Pensions and Passivity," 139. Alexander disagrees with those who argue that the American pension system, and the enormous amounts of funds held by it, is leading to a form of socialism in the United States. See, e.g., Peter F. Drucker, *The Unseen Revolution: How Pension Fund Socialism Came to America* (New York: Harper & Row, 1976). Alexander finds, instead, that the passive nature of the pension system lacks the democratic participation in decision-making required by socialism. "Pensions and Passivity," 113.

*

Part IV
The Future of Labor and Employment Law

In this part of the book, we consider possible alternative futures for U.S. labor and employment law. We begin in Chapter 9 with a look at the different institutional arrangements in Canada, Japan, and Germany, and at the European Community's regulations as sources of possible models for the United States. In Chapter 10, the focus is on proposals to strengthen or alter our system for collective representation of employee interests. The final chapter examines possible reforms from the perspective of an individualistic future in which collective representation is not an available or desired option for most employees.

9

Looking Abroad

The American labor and employment law system differs from that in most other industrialized countries, both in the decentralized, adversarial emphasis of collective bargaining law and in the relatively modest regulation of the content of employment contracts. Do the systems of other countries provide useful models for reconfiguring American institutional arrangements?

A. Perfecting Redistributive Unionism: The Canadian Model

We begin with Canada. Canada shares a common language, culture and increasingly common market with the United States, and its approach to labor relations was initially based on the Wagner Act. During the past few decades, however, Canadian federal and provincial governments have adopted legislation that attempts to bolster the viability of independent union organizations committed to traditional job control and redistributive goals. Whether these rules have succeeded in preserving unionization levels in private industry is discussed in chapter 3, p. 96, note 3; regulation of employer responses to strikes is taken up in Chapter 4, p. 159, note 2. In the principal readings below, Professor Kumar describes some of the differences in institutional arrangements, and Professors Card and Freeman explore differences in unemployment rates and wage inequality between the two countries.

From Uniformity to Divergence: Industrial Relations in Canada and the United States*
PRADEEP KUMAR

In sharp contrast to ... developments in the United States, public policy in Canada ... has been increasingly supportive of collective bargaining and has played an important role in facilitating union representation of workers and the protection of their collective bargaining rights. Although Canadian legislation has some unique features such as compulsory conciliation of disputes before a work stoppage, no strike or lockout during the term of the collective agreement and compulsory arbitration of grievance disputes, designed to secure industrial peace, public policy support of rights to organize and bargain collectively has grown stronger over the years through a series of legislative amendments. Recent legislative changes strengthening the role of unions and the practice of collective bargaining include automatic dues check-off at the request of the union (in the federal jurisdiction and five provinces); first contract arbitration (in the federal sector, British Columbia, Manitoba, Ontario and British Columbia); prohibiting the use of replacement workers during a strike; and legal prohibitions on professional strikebreakers in (Ontario, Manitoba and British Columbia).

Canadian labour relations legislation today differs markedly from U.S. legislation in many respects ...:

- While in the United States collective bargaining in the private economy is governed in most part by a single legislation, there are eleven labour relations jurisdictions in Canada with separate legislation.

---

* (Kingston, Ontario: IRC Press, 1993) 125–127.

- The coverage of labour relations legislation is uniform in the U.S. but varies markedly by jurisdiction in Canada.

- A distinguishing feature of virtually all Canadian collective bargaining legislation is that it provides a relatively simple procedure by which trade unions can acquire collective bargaining rights. In most Canadian jurisdictions a trade union can be certified without a vote upon evidence that 51–60 percent of the employees in the bargaining unit wish to be represented by the union. In the United States, on the other hand, all applications for certification are contested, requiring a vote to establish that a union represents a majority of employees.

- No Canadian jurisdiction has 'right to work laws,' but 21 of the 50 states in the United States have such legislation. Canadian labour legislation permits all forms of union security–closed shop as well as union shop. Dues check-off is a common provision. While some jurisdictions make it mandatory for an employer to collect union dues when requested by a union, others permit it upon authorization by an employee.

- Most Canadian jurisdictions have successor rights provisions, providing that where a business is sold (includes lease, transfer or other disposition) by an employer, the successor employer acquires all the rights, privileges and obligations of the predecessor. The successor is bound by any collective agreement in force. In the United States, the effect of change in ownership upon representative status of a union and the collective agreement is uncertain, depending upon the nature of change and evidence on substantial continuity in the employing enterprise....

- A number of Canadian jurisdictions provide for advance notice and consultation on technological change, a provision not found in U.S. legislation.

- First contract arbitration is available in the federal jurisdiction, British Columbia, Manitoba, Ontario and Quebec. There is no such provision in the NLRA.

- The use of replacement workers during a strike is prohibited in Quebec, Ontario and British Columbia. In the United States there is no prohibition against the use of replacement workers, and workers on economic strikes in some cases may not be reinstated at the conclusion of the strike....

Perhaps the most striking difference between Canada and the United States is the administration of the legislation. Unlike the United States, where employee representation choice is a cumbersome, difficult, and protracted process, the application for certification or decertification is disposed of promptly in all Canadian jurisdictions. Where a vote is required (in Alberta and Nova Scotia), legislation provides for short time limits. . . .

Small Differences That Matter: Canada vs. The United States*

DAVID CARD and RICHARD B. FREEMAN

How similar are labor market outcomes in Canada and the United States? What were the major changes in both economies over the past decade? Table [9.1] gives a capsule summary of patterns in employment, income, and demography in the United States and Canada. . . .

Which country did better in terms of employment generation? The labor market data in the first three rows of the table show that Canada and the United States had similar employment and unemployment patterns at the start of the 1980s. Of particular interest are the relatively high employment-to-population rates for women in both countries. . . . From 1979 to 1989, the proportion of the working age population that was employed grew less rapidly in Canada than in the United States and unemployment in Canada rose compared with unemployment in the United States.

Comparisons of changes in country outcomes in two years, however, can be misleading. The countries may be at different points in their business cycle, or one of the years may be abnormal due to some economic peculiarity. For this reason, we [also look at] the pattern of unemployment rates ... and employment-population rates ... for a longer time period, 1966 to 1990. Consistent with the 1980 to 1989 data in Table [9-1], [the unemployment rates show] that a significant "unemployment gap" emerged between Canada and the United States in the early 1980s. On the employment side, however, there is less evidence of a newly emergent gap. Between 1980 and 1989 Canadian employment grew by 1 percent less than American employment (relative to the population at working age). But 1980 was not a normal year in which to compare American and Canadian employment rates. From the mid–1960s to the early 1970s Canada had a smaller employment-population ratio than the United States. Canada attained a higher or similar ratio in the mid 1970s and in 1980–81, after which the U.S. employment-population rate rose above the Canadian rate. Comparisons of the trend in U.S. and Canadian employment rates using base years other than 1980 show little change in the gap between the countries, or even an increase in employment in Canada relative to the United States. Indeed, ... the gap in employment-population rates in 1989 was actually smaller than that in the late 1960s and early 1970s. The implication is that Canada had a higher rate of unemployment than the United States not

* In Richard B. Freeman, ed., in Working Under Different Rules (New York, N.Y.:Russell Sage Foundation, 1994) 192–196, 203–206.

because the Canadian economy failed to generate additional jobs but because the proportion of the population seeking work rose more in Canada than in the United States (for reasons we will explore later).

Table 9–1. Comparative Statistics on the United States and Canada

	United States		Canada		Relative Percentage Change
	1980	1989	1980	1989	Canada–U.S.
Labor Market					
1. Employment–Population Rate (All Civilians)	59.2	63.0	59.3	62.0	−1.1
2. Employment–Population Rate (Civilian Women)	47.7	54.3	46.2	53.3	0.5
3. Unemployment Rate (All Civilians)	7.1	5.3	7.5	7.5	1.8
Income					
4. Per Capita GNP (in 1989 U.S. Dollars)	$17,670	$19,100	$16,540	$18,140	1.6
5. Median Family Income (in 1989 U.S. Dollars)	$31,637	$34,213	$35,568	$37,603	−2.41
6. Gini Coefficient of Family Income (x100) [1]	39.8	41.1	37.3	37.1	−1.5
Demography					
7. Percent of Female–Headed Families [2]	15.0	17.0	9.3	10.6	−0.7
8. Percent of Births to Unmarried Mothers	18.0	27.0	13.0	23.0	1.0
9. Immigrants Per Year Over Decade (as a Percent of Total Population) [3]	0.2	0.3	0.7	0.4	−0.5

1. Gini coefficients of family income are for 1979 and 1987.
2. 1980 for Canada is 1981; 1989 for Canada is 1987.
3. 1980 for U.S. is 1971–80 change; 1989 for U.S. is 1981–90 change; 1980 for Canada is 1971–80 change; 1989 for Canada is 1981–86 change.

Sources: U.S. Bureau of the Census, *Statistical Abstract of United States* (Washington, DC: U.S. GPO, 1992), Tables 1, 5, 56, 1359; Statistics Canada, *Canada Year Book* (Ottawa: Statistics Canada, 1990) Tables 22, 23, 224; Statistics Canada, *Perspectives on Labour and Income* (Ottawa: Statistics Canada, Spring 1993)....

Rows 4 and 5 of Table [9–1] contain measures of income—per capita GNP and median family income in 1989 U.S. dollars. There are two ways in which to transform Canadian dollars into U.S. dollars: by using exchange rates to convert Canadian currency into U.S. currency or by using purchasing-power parity rates that measure the equivalent cost of a basket of goods between countries. In this table we give the figures in terms of 1989 U.S. dollars using the 1989 exchange rate, but the results would be similar with purchasing power parity figures. Using per capita GNP as a standard, income is slightly higher in the United States. Using (pretax) median family income as a standard, income is slightly higher in Canada. The reversal is attributable to higher taxes in Canada and the smaller frequency of single-person families in Canada. Family income growth was faster in Canada than the United States during the 1970s but slower in Canada during the 1980s. We emphasize the high degree of similarity in average living standards in the two countries.

Average or median incomes give only a partial description of economic well-being. Another important dimension is the dispersion of incomes across families or individuals. An increase in income dispersion, for example, implies that there are more families below any fixed low-income standard, leading to a higher poverty rate. One widely used measure of dispersion of incomes, the Gini coefficient, is shown in row 6 of Table [9–1]. The Gini coefficient represents the fraction of total income that would have to be redistributed to give all families the same income, and varies from 1.00 (the highest possible inequality) to 0.00 (the lowest possible inequality). In 1979 the Gini coefficient was 2.5 percentage points lower in Canada, indicating that Canada had a more even distribution of family incomes than the United States. During the 1980s, family income inequality grew in the United States but fell in Canada, leading to an even greater cross-country difference in inequality....

Labor Participation and Unemployment

The emergence of an unemployment gap between Canada and the United States in the 1980s was initially attributed to the more sluggish Canadian recovery from the 1982–83 recession. However, Canadian unemployment rates were 2 to 3 percentage points higher than U.S. rates at the end of the 1980s—six years into a sustained recovery that saw vacancy rates and GNP growth rates converge in the two countries. Six years of comparable aggregate economic expansion rules out a cyclical explanation for higher unemployment rates.

What else might cause unemployment to be higher in Canada? It turns out that much of the rise in Canadian unemployment took the form of an increase in the fraction of persons without work reporting themselves seeking work. Labor force statistics classify people in three main categories: the employed, or jobholders; jobless persons who are looking for work and thus counted as unemployed; and jobless persons not looking for work and thus out of the labor force. In Canada the proportion of the working age population that was jobless changed little in the 1980s, but the fraction of the jobless counted as unemployed rose. In the United States, in contrast, there was little change in the proportion of jobless persons counted as unemployed. It is this difference that underlies most of the relative rise in Canadian unemployment....

The finding that unemployment rose in Canada relative to the United States largely because jobless Canadians were increasingly likely to seek work compared with jobless Americans is not, of course, a full explanation. Why did jobless women and men increasingly look for work in Canada but not in the United States?

One reason is that unemployment insurance (UI) systems give different incentives for people to seek work in the two countries. In many parts of Canada individuals are eligible for unemployment benefits after working a minimum of ten or twelve weeks per year. In the United States individuals are typically eligible for UI only after they have worked a minimum of twenty weeks per year. Thus Canadians have a special incentive to work for ten to twelve weeks. Not only do they earn money, but they also gain eligibility for unemployment benefits. For comparable Americans the situation is different: if they are welfare recipients, for example, they typically lose welfare benefits, including health insurance, if they work for a short time. The fraction of workers with ten to twelve weeks of work in fact rose in Canada. One-quarter of the rise in Canadian unemployment relative to U.S. unemployment is attributable to the growth in the number of workers in this group and to their reporting that they were unemployed after their two-to-three-month work experience. Still, more generous unemployment benefits are not the only cause of the relative increase in Canadian unemployment. Among men, much of the relative increase in unemployment occurred among those with no weeks of work in the previous year—a group with declining UI recipiency rates in Canada. And reductions in the maximum duration of UI eligibility in the late 1980s failed to reduce the high levels of unemployment. Measured differences in unemployment benefits thus explain only part of the divergence in economic outcomes.

Notes and Questions

1. *Economic Performance.*

   a. *Unemployment.* Canadian unemployment rates since 1980 have consistently hovered at 2 to 3 percentage points above U.S. rates. (We include as Appendix D data on unemployment figures for 1983–1993 for ten major industrial nations.) This unemployment gap, according to Card and Freeman, is not due to differences in the rate of job creation and is only partially attributable to more generous Canadian unemployment benefits. They do not, however, attempt to explain what the other causes of persistently high unemployment might be.

   b. *Competitiveness.* Canada has also experienced sluggish productivity and output growth since the mid–1970s, and rising hourly compensation costs in the 1980s. (We include in Appendix E data on hourly compensation costs for production workers in manufacturing for selected countries, and in Appendices F and G data on labor productivity growth for selected countries). Professors Chaykowski and Verma observe:

   > Several . . . trends suggest that Canada is entering a potentially difficult period in global markets. During the 1980s, productivity in manufacturing was finally surpassed by West Germany, Italy, and France; by 1988, most of the manufacturing industries in Canada had greater unit labor costs relative to those of their U.S. counterparts; and most measures of Canadian competitiveness in technology and science placed Canada at or

near the lowest rank among Japan, the United States, West Germany, the United Kingdom, France, the Netherlands, and Sweden.

Richard P. Chaykowski and Anil Verma, "Adjustment and Restructuring in Canadian Industrial Relations: Challenges to the Traditional System," in Richard P. Chaykowski and Anil Verma, eds., *Industrial Relations in Canadian Industry* (Toronto: Dryden, 1992), ch. 1, 16.

Since trade plays a large role in the Canadian economy (e.g., exports and imports were 43.9 percent of Canadian GDP in 1987), concerns over competitiveness of Canadian firms pose formidable challenges to the country's industrial relations system. These concerns were exacerbated by the Canada–U.S. Free Trade Agreement of 1989 and the later North American Free Trade Agreement (which includes Mexico). For an early assessment, see Morley Gunderson and W. Craig Riddell, "Jobs, Labour Standards and Promoting Competitive Advantage: Canada's Policy Challenge," Labour, IIRS Issue (1995); Brian A. Langille, "Canadian *Labour* Law Reform and Free Trade," 23 *Ottawa Law Review* 581 (1991).

2. *Card–Check Certification of Unions.* Consider the description of Canadian laws on representation issues in Samuel Estreicher, "Labor Law Reform in a World of Competitive Product Markets," 69 *Chicago–Kent Law Review* at 30–31 (1993):

> The laws in Canada on "automatic" certifications without elections are designed to ease the union's organizing task, and exclude the employer from any role in the representational process. In Ontario, if more than 55 percent of the employees in a unit are members of, or have applied for membership (by making a token payment) in, a union, the labor board may (and typically will) certify the union outright. The agency will not consider evidence of membership or disavowal of membership after the date of the union's application for certification. Evidence filed prior to the application date will be considered only if in writing and signed by each employee, but the board will not examine whether the employee made an informed choice. However, such informality does not attend the process of decertification. Petitions will not be entertained during the first year after certification, and if a collective agreement is in place, they will be considered only during the last two months of the third year of the term (or of each succeeding year). They must be signed by 45 percent of the unit, and the signatures must not be tainted by management influence or solicitation going beyond the "acceptable bounds of salesmanship." If the petition satisfies the formalities, the board holds a decertification vote.

Because Canadian labor law (except for federal sector industries such as transportation and communication firms) is a matter for provincial legislation, and political parties are sharply divided along ideological lines, labor laws are often revised when provincial governments change hands. In 1995, for example, the conservative government in Ontario abolished card-check certification, except where employer violations indicate that a representation vote "does not or would not likely affect the true wishes of the employees...." Labour Relations Act of 1995, § 11(1), 1st Sess., 36th Legis., Ont., 44 Eliz. II, 1995.

3. *Fissures in U.S.–Canadian Unions.* Many prominent unions in the United States, including the Machinists, Teamsters, and Electrical Workers, call themselves "international" unions, largely because they have affiliates in Canada. The Canadian–American union relationship is sometimes rocky. It has been observed that "the Canadian labor movement, with its social unionism philosophy, is much more militant than the AFL–CIO, with its business unionism philosophy." John W. Budd, "The Effect of Multinational Institutions on Strike Activity in Canada," 47 *Industrial and Labor Relations Review* 401, 413 (1994). Tensions between Canadian and American bargaining strategies have caused the dissolution of several internationals, the most prominent being the 1985 breakup of the United Auto Workers, when all but one Canadian local split from the American union and formed what is now the Canadian Auto Workers. In a careful empirical study (cited above), Budd could find no significant difference in strike activity between Canadian national unions and international unions, but did find that the propensity to strike by Canadian unions affiliated with a Canadian federation rather than the AFL–CIO was 14–26 percentage points higher.

4. *First–Contract Interest Arbitration.* The Canadian federal sector and several Canadian provinces authorize interest arbitration as a default mechanism to resolve deadlocks in first-time bargaining situations. Unlike grievance arbitration, where the arbitration is limited to interpreting the contract, interest arbitration empowers the arbitrator to dictate contract terms when the parties are unable to reach agreement on their own. By contrast, interest arbitration plays virtually no role in private-sector bargaining in the United States, although American public employers such as police and fire departments often use interest arbitration.

Professor Weiler, while chair of the British Columbia Labour Relations Board, helped shepherd the first of these Canadian laws, limiting interest arbitration as a remedy for bad-faith bargaining rather than the standard impasse-resolution mechanism. See Paul C. Weiler, Reconcilable Differences: New Directions in Canadian Labour Law, (Toronto: Carswell, 1980), 53. In several provinces, according to Roy L. Heenan, a Canadian management labor lawyer, these laws have now become "a standard response to the break-down of bargaining," and typically are resorted to by unions after launching an unsuccessful strike. See Roy L. Heenan, "Issues for the Dunlop Commission: The Canadian Experience," in Bruno Stein, ed., *Proceedings of New York University's 47th National Conference on Labor* (Boston, Mass.: Little, Brown, 1995), ch. 10, 366. Studies indicate that parties infrequently invoke interest arbitration (though its availability may shape the content of first contracts). It is unclear, however, whether arbitrated first contracts result in enduring relationships. See Weiler, *Reconcilable Differences*, at 54; Sabrina Sills, "First Contract Interest Arbitration in Ontario: Success or Failure? 1986–1990" (Master's thesis, Queen's Univ., Kingston, Ont., Aug. 1991), 29–30; Errol Black and Craig Hosea, "First Contract Legislation in Manitoba: A Model for the United States?," 45 *Labor Law Journal* 33, 36–38 (1994); but see Joseph B. Rose and Gary N. Chaison, "Canadian Labor

Policy as a Model for Legislative Reform in the United States," 46 Labor
Law Journal 259, 265–266 (1995).

5. *Decline of Compulsory Mandatory Interest Arbitration in Australia and
New Zealand.* For nearly a century, both Australia and New Zealand
employed a system of compulsory conciliation and arbitration of collective
bargaining disputes. Persisting high levels of unemployment and disappoint-
ing productivity growth in the face of global market pressures have prompt-
ed a change in this system. In the Employment Contracts Act of 1991, New
Zealand abolished mandatory interest arbitration in an effort to promote
decentralized bargaining structures and greater flexibility in outcomes, while
mandating a range of minimum standards for employment contracts. See
Penelope J. Brook Cowen, "Labor Relations Reform in New Zealand: The
Employment Contracts Act and Contractual Freedom," 14 *Journal of Labor
Research* 69 (Winter 1993); Kevin Hince and Martin Vranken, "A Controver-
sial Reform of New Zealand Labour Law: The Employment Contracts Act
1991," 130 *International Labor Review* 475 (1991); Ellen J. Dannin, *Working
Free: The Origins and Impact of New Zealand's Employment Contracts Act*
(Auckland, NZ: Auckland University Press 1997).

A 1992 amendment to Australia's Industrial Relations Act provides for
certification of single-enterprise agreements, and reduces the Industrial
Relations Commission's authority to refuse certification of agreements that
distort the wage structure or exacerbate unemployment or cause inflationary
pressures. In some areas, agreements between unrepresented employees and
their employers can displace previous interest arbitration awards, subject to
meeting certain minimum standards. See Keith Hancock and Don Rawson,
"The Metamorphosis of Australian Industrial Relations," 31 *British Journal
of Industrial Relations* 489 (1993).

Note on Comparative Productivity Data

Productivity is an important measure of a country's competitive position and
the standard of living of its residents. However, comparisons in productivity
growth rates among countries (such as Appendices F and G) are difficult to
evaluate because of a tendency for average labor productivity levels and per
capita incomes among industrialized countries to converge:

> Those countries that were at or near the technology frontier at the start
> of this period [as of 1913] (e.g., the United States and the United
> Kingdom) were limited by the rate of technological advance in determin-
> ing how rapidly on balance productivity could grow. Countries that were
> initially less developed (e.g., Japan and Finland) were able to imitate
> technologies already in use as well as to take advantage of recent
> innovations. The capacity of such countries to grow faster than those on
> the technology frontier makes possible convergence of output per work-
> er, and ultimately standards of living, among these countries. Conver-
> gence implies a negative relationship between countries' initial relative
> position in terms of output per worker and their respective rates of
> growth over the period. . . .

OECD *Jobs Study: Investment, Productivity and Employment* (Paris, France: OECD, 1995) 39. The leading work on the convergence thesis is William J. Baumol, Richard R. Nelson, and Edward N. Wolff, eds., *Convergence of Productivity: Cross–National Studies and Historical Evidence* (New York: Oxford University Press, 1994).

The convergence thesis also places in perspective the fact that although U.S. productivity growth rates have fallen since 1973, the growth rates of its leading rivals also have fallen during this period. The United States continues to hold the lead among OECD countries in overall labor productivity, and its relative position on some measures has improved since the mid–1980s. For a forceful statement of this view, see William J. Baumol & Edward N. Wolff, "Comparative U.S. Productivity Performance and the State of Manufacturing: The Latest Data," 10 *CVS+ Starr Newsletter* (Center for Applied Economics, New York University, 1992) 1ff.

B. Enterprise Unionism: The Japanese Model

Because of American influence during the postwar occupation period, Japan's labor relations system was initially modeled after the Wagner Act. See William B. Gould IV, *Japan's Reshaping of American Labor Law* (Cambridge, Mass.: MIT Press, 1984). Despite this provenance, however, the Japanese system differs in some important respects.

First, the system is based on plural unionism; unions can demand bargaining regardless of the percentage of employees in an enterprise they can count as members or the existence of prior relationships between the employer and other unions. Japan thus offers a decentralized bargaining structure utilizing plural union representation. Little rival unionism occurs in practice; most firms have established relationships with a single union.

Second, even though the Trade Union Law protects the right of employees to establish federations, most Japanese unions confine themselves to the representation of the employees of a single company—hence the term "enterprise unions." These unions are affiliated with national federations and coordinate wage demands in an annual spring offensive:

> Although federations do play a certain role to coordinate bargaining and industrial action of affiliated unions in connection with the spring offensive (*Shunto*), bargaining per se has never been carried out by industrial federations independently....
>
> *Shunto* is a practice that was established ... during the 1950s in order to overcome the weakness of enterprise unionism and enterprise bargaining. Under this practice, a certain number of selected influential unions start bargaining early each spring in a certain number of industries selected on the initiative of the [labor federation]. The chosen strong unions in prosperous industries are more likely to get better settlements in wage negotiations. Once the market price for the wage increase has been established through

these preliminary negotiations, other weaker unions can take advantage of the established market price.

Tadashi Hanami, *Managing Japanese Workers: Personnel Management—Law and Practice in Japan* (Tokyo: Japan Institute of Labour, 1991) 47, 54–55.

Third, Japanese law does not closely regulate the process of bargaining aside from establishing the employer's basic obligation to bargain in good faith with unions of its employees. Distinctions are not drawn between permissive and mandatory subjects of bargaining. Alongside the formal collective bargaining process, many Japanese firms have developed a process of "consultation" with their enterprise unions to deal with issues like dismissals, introduction of new technology, and the closing of facilities. As we shall see below, bonuses form an important part of employee compensation, and it is unclear to what extent bonuses are determined in collective bargaining.

To understand the Japanese system, it may be as important to focus on actual practices as on the formal legal structure. Professors Ulman and Nakata review the literature on the actual workings of the system in the reading that follows.

Enterprise Bargaining and Social Contract in Japan*

LLOYD ULMAN and YOSHIFUMI NAKATA

Large–Scale Employers: Monopsonistic Tendencies and Cooperative Practices

In many cases Japan's major firms have been characterized as oligopolistic competitors in their product markets; and they have exhibited some monopsonistic tendencies within their respective labor markets and vis-à-vis traditional suppliers as well. Having been confronted with labor turbulence in the 1940s and early 1950s (which was accompanied by demands for job security) and with shortages of labor (which were associated with extremely rapid rates of economic growth) in the 1960s and early 1970s, various managerial policies and programs were adopted to help the firm cope with shortages and yet minimize both across-the-board wage increases and turnover, while maintaining high levels and rates of growth of productivity relative to real wages. Four examples might be briefly cited: (1) A postwar revival of the practice of locating plants in rural areas resulted in the establishment of "factory castle towns" and territorial enclaves where local suppliers of labor tended to be reserved to specific firms in the vicinity. (2) Extensive programs of orientation to the firm and its culture, of training in organizational

* In Paula Voos, ed., Proceedings of the 46th Annual Meeting of IRRA (Madison, Wis.: IRRA), 339–347 (1994).

skills, and of employee involvement in management decision making were designed to build up loyalty among employees, detract from their interest in acquiring information about alternative opportunities, and even make them regard quitting as disloyal. (3) The proffer by large firms of assurances of so-called "lifetime" employment has remained popular in a work force with a characteristically high degree of risk aversion (a high marginal rate of substitution of employment for income) even during the period of rapid growth and labor shortage in the 1960s and early 1970s. (4) Age, seniority, and family need are included among the determinants of pay as well as long promotion ladders which are associated with continual training and employee evaluations based on performance and aptitude. In combination these features constitute a stretched-out incentive system with deferred compensation that the worker would have to forfeit in the event of early departure from the firm.

Policies designed to internalize supplies of labor to the firm have also included policies intended to restrict access to them by other employers, that is, by the big firm's smaller suppliers in the same area and by its big competitors in the same product markets. In the former case, any monopsonistic advantage held by the larger firm in traditional commercial relationships with smaller contractors can be utilized so as to enhance its ability to maintain a high relative wage level which would help to insulate its work force and also ensure it preferred access to supplies of new labor. Thus a large firm's monopsonistic position in a product market could reinforce its monopsonistic position in a labor market.

As for labor market competition among oligopolistic competitors, it has not infrequently been restrained by mutual agreement and informal cooperation. "Gentlemen's agreements" against poaching regular employees have been credited with (or blamed for) inhibiting the practice of hiring "mid-career" employees. Thus they tend to maintain the integrity of the large firms' "internal market" systems and also their ability to adjust to shortages of younger workers by raising their relative wages within the establishment rather than bidding up the wages of experienced workers.

Informal agreement has also been described as the "mechanism by which big businesses check their respective labor costs with each other ... to ensure that they are reflected in the negotiations over revision of product prices." Moreover, since wage rates are ultimately established at [the] company level in bargaining with autonomous enterprise-based unions, the latter have been placed in a weaker bargaining position than they might have enjoyed under formal industrywide bargaining (which the employers had successfully opposed).

On the other hand, it has been observed that Japanese managers have always been sensitively attuned to the mood and morale of their employees and that they have feared any outbreak of employee unrest or work stoppages. Accordingly, restraint in the exercise of monopsonistic power to set wages might well reflect an efficiency wage mentality and is not necessarily inconsistent with the long-run profitability of the enterprise. At the same time, employer policies like some of those alluded to above, which can offer nonpecuniary compensation to employees or feature deferred compensation ("investment wages") under implicit contracts of long-term employment, are clearly consistent with the ability of productivity to outpace even rapidly rising real wages. They are also consistent with the input of high levels of effort (including long hours of work) which have characterized the economy at large and have been conducive to its economic growth and international competitiveness.

Enterprise–Based Unions: Weak or Willing?

Can wage behavior that conforms to employer preferences and policies be reconciled with the prevalence of unionism and collective bargaining in the sectors dominated by large-scale enterprise? The answer can be yes if those enterprise-based unions are characterized by bargaining weakness. The answer can also be yes if, whether weak or not, these unions deliberately choose to follow policies which conform to the requirements of economic efficiency and are responsive to (or do not contravene) the wishes of their members.

In fact, according to a recent regression analysis by Tachibanaki and Noda, enterprise unionism has not passed the U.S. economists' standard test for union bargaining power (i.e., the ability to secure higher wage rates than are found in nonunion but otherwise comparable establishments)....

However, the same study finds evidence of union impact on such non-wage conditions as working hours (negative) and length of vacation (positive). Earlier studies of union behavior reveal union attempts to reduce hours, including overtime, and also to raise premium rates for overtime. At the same time, enterprise unions have sought to prevent violations by management of their commitment to "lifetime employment." They have also tried to raise the age of mandatory retirement and have favored seniority-based wages over performance-based wages. Finally, enterprise unions have been consulted or informed extensively by management on a wide range of issues—from transfers, promotions, and working conditions to the firm's investments and development plans and financial condition.

Whether the bargaining power of enterprise unions in the nonpecuniary field is generally more significant than in the area of wages, however, is doubtful. Their influence appears to have been strongest (historically as well as on a current basis) in the area of employment security, but not in the area of employee effort in its several dimensions. Hours of work, as noted above, have remained long by international standards. Workers still elect not to take their paid vacation time, and they compete intensely among themselves for favorable performance evaluations from supervisors. Codetermination and cooperation afford a "voice" to the enterprise unions, but not one as powerful as the negotiated rules of seniority by which American managers are contractually bound....

Yet the enterprise unions have also been awarded a generous share of credit for Japan's outstanding performance in the areas of employment (via the responsiveness of wages to declines in demand) and growth (via wage restraint relative to productivity). In the former case, Shimada claimed that it was the "economic rationality" of Japanese unions which "tends to make [them] accept flexible wages in return for stable employment," adding that "such an inclination may be reinforced by well-developed internal labor markets which they organize."

If it is rational for enterprise unions to accept downward wage flexibility in order to keep their "insider" members employed during downswings in demand, should it not be rational for them to raise wages sufficiently to preclude (or minimize) the employment of additional workers (from the "outside") during expansions? Koike, however, claims that the employment of more workers in the firm (at the entry level only) would ultimately increase, rather than reduce, the incomes of members of the experienced work force by increasing their opportunities to acquire more skills and promotions....

A more plausible motivation has been assigned to enterprise unionists by Koshiro: "Originally as a result of major strike losses under left-wing militant leadership in the late 1940s," they became convinced that "the best way to improve their wages and working conditions is to increase productivity and grow with the respective enterprises which usually promise them permanent employment until the retirement years. In other words, unions do not wish to kill a golden egg-bearing goose to improve the immediate conditions of employment." In this model, risk aversion has dominated insider rationality....

Shunto: From Labor Offensive to Social Contract

... Whereas other systems have been designed from the outset to restrain wages in the belief that union bargaining power was too great, Shunto ... originated in the conviction of its founders that union bargaining power had to be augmented in order (a) to reduce inequitable interfirm wage differentials and (b) to boost wages rapidly to "European levels." Moreover, Shunto began life as a "labor offensive" without strong central or industrywide bargaining institutions to rely on. In their place it has featured the annual construction of a national consensus based (a) on the continuing power and influence of major firms in sectors concurrently chosen to set the wage pattern in early consultations and negotiations: (b) on the preparation and widespread circulation of information prepared by the central, industrywide, and local bodies of industry and labor as well as government agencies; and finally (c) on the knowledge imparted to company managers and their counterparts in the corresponding enterprise unions that their firms' competitors have already followed or are about to follow the same pattern which they are prepared to accept.

Pattern setters have been drawn from the private sectors on the basis of their current economic importance (a function of size, growth, and profitability)—at first private railways and steel, later shipbuilding, autos, and electrical manufacturing. In the 1960s, however, public-sector unions, which were economically sheltered and highly militant, were also included as pace setters, especially in recession years. (For the public sector to lead rather than follow the private sector has frequently been regarded as a symptom of failure in conventional policies of wage restraint.)

Nevertheless, the employers ... were able to adjust readily enough to the new system. The bargaining power of the big firms was not impaired; this was dramatized when the major steel firms defeated a strong national union in a series of strikes in the late 1950s and then imposed a regime of "take-it-or-leave-it" bargaining. Militantly led enterprise unions were in many instances replaced by "second unions" under more moderate leaders who entered into company-level agreements calling for cooperation to increase productivity. Government agencies responded vigorously to challenges by unions in the public sector. And pattern following (or convergence on the *Shunto* norm) did discourage leapfrogging....

Exuberant economic growth and tight labor markets in the 1960s gave way to a regime of slower growth and higher levels of unemployment, which was ushered in by the first oil price shock. In 1974 a "People's *Shunto*" roared in like a March lion, producing an unparalleled wage increase of 32.9 percent, which exceeded increases in both the cost of living and wholesale prices. The 1974 Shunto was also attended by demands for indexation to protect against further price inflation which the 32.9 percent wage hike would generate. And it was accompanied by threats of another special Shunto the next fall and of a general strike to support strikes by public-sector unions for the right to strike. The prime minister pleaded for wage moderation in the national interest, and the ministry of finance called for an incomes policy. Finally, big business caved in out of deference to forthcoming national elections and their Liberal Democratic allies.

But the 1980 Shunto (following the second oil price shock) went like a lamb, with negotiated wages rising by only 6.7 percent, translating into a reduction in both real and product wages—signs that this time wages had accommodated rather than resisted price rises in energy inputs. Meanwhile, public-sector unions and their intransigent left-wing leadership lost influence to unions in the growing export sectors and gave way to moderate, more risk-averse leadership in Shunto pattern-setting roles and within the labor movement. And the calls heard for wage restraint . . . were heeded. . . .

The long-term employment relationship which has been [the] distinguishing feature [of the Japanese "social contract"] has been characterized as an implicit employment contract wherein (in theory) the more risk-averse worker accepts a lower wage in return for the employer's assurance of steady employment. However, the theoretical feasibility of such an arrangement has been questioned on the grounds that wages might have to be driven to such a low level that the firm would be confronted by a shortage of labor. But in the real (if idyllic) Japanese world of the 1960s, monopsonistic employers could cope with equilibrium shortages, and above all, high rates of economic growth could minimize employer risks to the point where "lifetime" guarantees could be accompanied by rising real wages.

However, after growth rates declined, government had to participate in the task of risk containment. In an implicit global contract with workers and employers, government undertook to pursue macroeconomic policies which would maintain employment at high levels and achieve price stability if the unions held their Shunto increases within limits set by economy-wide rates of growth in productivity. In order to achieve price stability, however, the authorities pursued stringent fiscal policies, which precluded the attainment of high levels of employment via expansion of domestic demand. What they counted on instead was export-led recovery and growth. . . . Now, however, it is doubtful whether employment security under collective bargaining can continue to be underwritten by export growth to the extent that it has been thus far.

Notes and Questions

1. *Economic Performance.*

    a. *Unemployment.* Japan has consistently registered the lowest unemployment rate among major industrialized countries. Appendix D indicates that while the rate increases significantly with the addition of discouraged workers (U–7 indicator), Japan's relative standing remains unchanged. See Sara Elder and Constance Sorrentino, "Japan's Low Unemployment: A BLS Update and Revision," *Monthly Labor Review* 56 (October 1993); Richard B. Freeman, "Bonuses and Employment in Japan," in Richard B. Freeman, ed., *Labor Markets in Action: Essays in Empirical Economics* (Cambridge, Mass: Harvard University Press, 1989), 250, 258 n.15 ("Japan's unemployment rate remains outstanding even after adjustment.").

    b. *Competitiveness.* Until recently, Japan's economic system has been a great success story, registering high rates of productivity growth even during the turbulent 1980s (see Appendixes F and G). In the 1990s, however, Japan faced considerable difficulties as a result of a sustained recession, failures in the banking industry, the appreciation of the yen, excess staffing in the services, a slower rate of productivity growth, and hourly manufacturing compensation costs at 125 percent of U.S. costs in 1994 (see Appendix E). The need for less costly labor also spurred an increased use of part-time and temporary employees: part-time employment accounted for 16 percent of paid employment in 1992 (up from 11 percent a decade earlier) and temporary workers accounted for 11 percent of paid employment in 1992. See Susan Houseman and Machiko Osawa, "Part–Time and Temporary Employment in Japan," *Monthly Labor Review* 10, 12 (Table 1) (Oct. 1995).

2. *Judicial Activism and Lifetime Employment.* It is unclear whether "lifetime employment" norms, where they do exist, reflect voluntary business practices or are caused by legal restrictions. For the latter view, see Daniel H. Foote, "Judicial Creation of Norms in Japanese Labor Law: Activism in the Service of—Stability?," 43 U.C.L.A. Law Review 635, 637–638, 680 (1996):

> As early as 1959, one prominent scholar remarked, "there is no other country in the world where dismissal is as strictly regulated as in Japan." The limitations on dismissal in Japan have become even more strict over the intervening years. This state of affairs has come about entirely through judicial lawmaking. Despite statutory provisions that seem in unambiguous terms to permit at-will dismissal (subject only to a notice requirement), courts have developed the doctrine of abusive dismissal (or, literally, "abuse of the right of dismissal") in a long series of opinions dating back to 1950. In doing so, they have built a complex and sophisticated body of law providing workers strong rights against dismissal....
>
> Despite statutory language that seems to permit discharge without cause upon payment of thirty days' wages, faithful workers are entitled to great job security despite their shortcomings. The goal of maximizing profits is not a sufficient cause for discharging a worker. The employer ordinarily must be able to establish a serious ground for the dismissal decision, and the worker may still counter by showing that the discharge, in fact, was based on an improper motive. Moreover, even for an enterprise facing major economic difficulties, discharges should be treated as a last resort, when other alternatives have failed....
>
> All of the above protections are in addition to a statutory prohibition on retaliatory discharge for union activities, and in addition to a broad range of protections either expressly provided by, or implied by the courts from, rules of employment and other sets of internal standards established by the employer. Finally, the remedy for violations of these protections is not just a backpay or frontpay order, it is an award of both backpay and reinstatement.

Foote's emphasis on judicial activism is criticized by David Kettler and Charles Tackney in "Light from a Dead Sun: The Japanese Lifetime Employment System and Weimar Labor Law," 19 *Comparative Labor Law and Policy Journal* 1, 3–4 (1997).

> We do not agree with Foote's central conception that judicial activism is best explained by a pervasive judicial philosophy that aims, wherever there is no explicit state policy or powerful economic interest against it, at the "maintenance of stability and existing relationships by providing the weaker party with protection against unilateral termination of a relationship." ... Not judicial traditionalism but a novel combination of labor activism and imported legal approaches led Japanese courts to assimilate the employment relationship to the older pattern Foote emphasizes.

3. *Lifetime Employment in Practice*. Whatever the source of the job-security norms, only a relatively narrow segment of the workforce experiences lifetime employment with the same employer. See Mashiko Aoki, Information, Incentives, and Bargaining in the Japanese Economy (New York: Cambridge University Press, 1988), 67:

> [E]ven among those who started their careers right after they graduated from school with the expectation of lifetime employment, only a minority may fulfill that expectation.... In the manufacturing industry, the ratio [of male high school graduates who have never changed employers to the total number of employees of similar age and educational level] is as low as 65.6 percent in the 25–29 age category and indicates more frequent job search activity in the early career stage of this group.... [H]igh-school graduates tend to settle down with their original employers if they find good matches. About half of those in the 50–54 age category have remained with their original employers. Also, the turnover of employees, particularly among high-school graduates, is significantly higher in the retail, wholesale, and service industries, where the skills required may be more general and standardized than those required in manufacturing.

Although large Japanese companies continue to be considerably more reluctant than their U.S. counterparts to terminate or lay off "regular" employees during economic downturns, they have responded to the recessionary economic climate and the problem of excess staff (especially in service industries) with measures that jar with traditional norms—canceling new recruits, expanding voluntary-retirement programs, and modifying seniority-based wages. See, e.g., *Management Flexibility in an Era of Changes: The Methods of Accommodating Working Conditions, and Work Organizations*, JIL Report No. 3 (Tokyo: Japan Institute of Labour,1994); Kazutoshi Koshiro, "The Employment System and Human Resources Management," in Kenichi Imai and Ryuturo Komiya, eds., *Business Enterprise in Japan: Views of Leading Japanese Economists* (Cambridge, MA: MIT Press, 1994), ch. 12; Shintaro Hori, "Fixing Japan's White–Collar Economy: A Personal View," *Harvard Business Review* 157 (Nov.–Dec. 1993), 157.

4. *Share Economy*. The Japanese compensation system combines (1) a seniority-based monthly salary keyed to the individual's educational attain-

ment and length of service but without relation to performance; and (2) semiannual bonuses not expressly tied to profits that reflect 20–25 percent of annual compensation. Professor Weitzman and others have argued that because flexible compensation permits the Japanese firm to adjust to downturns by reducing compensation rather than initiating layoffs, Japan is "the only industrial economy in the world with anything resembling a share system." Martin Weitzman, *The Share Economy: Conquering Stagflation* (Cambridge, MA: Harvard University Press, 1984) 76.

Aoki criticizes this view on two grounds. First, he argues that Japanese employers try hard to reduce the size of their workforce (by some combination of slowing down new hires, attrition, and increasing work hours) rather than altering the earnings level of incumbent employees, as Weitzman's model would predict. Aoki, *Information, Incentives, and Bargaining*, 170–171, 178–181. Second, Aoki argues that Weitzman's approach fails to recognize that bonuses may reflect a form of labor-management coalition. *Id.* at 153:

> In [Weitzman's] system, decisions on strategic management variables crucial to the well-being of employees, such as employment, are not shared by the employer and the union, either explicitly or implicitly, but are exclusively in the realm of managerial prerogatives. In contrast, I submit that the Japanese enterprise-based union has acquired implicit bargaining power over such strategic managerial issues as employment and relocation, which are of vital concern to its members, in exchange for its own commitment to a certain level of effort expenditure (and wage restraint, if necessary).

Aoki predicts that the effects of such a coalition include (1) pursuit of "a higher growth rate than the level that short-run share price maximization would warrant to deliver extra benefits to the quasi-permanent employee in the form of enhanced promotability and better prospects for a separation payment"; and (2) restraint on "the size of employment relative to the growth of value-added by adopting capital-intensive technology in order to secure the vested interests of incumbent employees." *Information, Incentives, and Bargaining*, 165, 168.

5. *Are "Enterprise Unions" Independent Unions?* As a formal matter, Japanese labor law, like American labor law, prohibits a company from dominating or assisting a union. In the United States, the National Labor Relations Board, implementing Section 8(a)(2) of the NLRA, polices employer domination and will order the dissolution of company unions. By contrast, the Japanese Labor Relations Commission apparently will never dissolve a dominated union, reasoning that the integrity of a union cannot be effectively addressed by outsiders. See William B. Gould, *Japan's Reshaping of American Labor Law* (Cambridge, Mass: MIT Press, 1984) 84.

As a practical matter, many observers note that Japanese unions have been unable to promote solidarity among workers within a firm. See Knuth Dhose, Ulrich Jurgens, and Thomas Malsch, "From 'Fordism' to 'Taylor-ism'? The Social Organization of the Labor Process in the Japanese Automobile Industry," 14 *Politics and Society* 115, 136–137, 138–139 (1985):

> In Japanese automobile firms, percentage raises in pay are negotiated annually in the "spring" offensive of the labor unions, which, however, only relate to total compensation of the whole work force. Pay increases for individual workers cannot be deduced from this overall percentage. The total wage increase is first allocated between the two main components of pay: the basic wage and work-area-related incentive pay. Incentive pay, which averages about 50 percent of normal monthly pay (excluding such additional wage components as night shift and overtime pay) is calculated according to the efficiency of individual work areas and hence increases the pressure of the supervisors . . . and of the work group on the work effort of the individual. . . .

> The unions have been unable to regulate the internal labor market—in its double sense of promotions to higher status groups and a separate wage-career system. . . . The entire career of the individual worker depends on the good will of management in deciding on his or her advancement. In contrast to the usual emphasis on the formation of Japanese culture by collective norms, this system of individuated treatment leads to pronounced competition among workers. They must continuously demonstrate as individuals their usefulness to the firm through diligence, docility, and flexibility. The result [is a] destruction of solidarity among workers. . . .

> The lack of solidarity among Japanese workers as a result of their being so strongly dependent on management personnel decisions is additionally linked to the lack of union regulation of shop-level labor deployment and work norms. . . .

> One reason this structure has not yet been disrupted is that voting for labor representatives is not secret. . . . The elections take place in the offices of the supervisors. Any opposition, therefore, runs the risk of open discrimination in promotions and personnel evaluation.

> These gaps in independent labor-union interest articulation have been filled by management-controlled communication structures. They extend in many cases beyond the normal work day, reaching into employees' lives outside the plant, although still connected with the firm's system of sanctions and rewards.

On the origin of Japan's enterprise-based welfare and labor relations practices in management responses to the militant unionism of the postwar period, see Young–Hoon Cho, "The Growth of Enterprise Welfare in Japan," 17 *Economic and Industrial Democracy* 281 (1996); Andrew Gordon, "Japanese Labor Relations During the Twentieth Century," 11 *Journal of Labor Research* 239, 249–251 (1990); and Gordon's recent book, *The Wages of Affluence: Labor and Management in Postwar Japan* (Cambridge, Mass: Harvard University Press, 1998).

C.   Codetermination: The German Model

Germany: Codetermining the Future?*

Otto Jacobi, Berndt Keller, and Walther Müller–Jentsch

Workplace Institutions and Relations

Works Councils

Works councils are by law formally independent of the unions and represent the entire workforce of an establishment, not only union members. There are no official statistics on the coverage of works councils, but the [German Federation of Trade Unions (DGB)] collects data for all establishments where ... DGB–affiliated unions are represented, and these are regarded by Ministry of Labour officials as a fairly accurate picture of the overall situation. The DGB figures for 1990 cover more than 33,000 establishments with works councils, in which some 180,000 councillors were elected.

There are no statistics on the number of establishments—with five or more employees—where workers have a legal right to elect a works council. Most estimates put the figure somewhere above 40,000; in other words, works councils exist in 70–80 percent of eligible workplaces. Since it is mainly in the smaller firms that works councils do not operate, a higher proportion of German employees is represented by councils.

Works councillors are elected for a four-year term of office (increased from three years in 1989). The size of works councils varies according to the number of employees. In larger establishments—with more than 300 employees—one or more works councillors can act as full-time employee representatives. The works council cannot be mandated by the work force, but is required to call a quarterly works meeting of all employees, when it reports on its activities. All costs arising out of the activities of the works council have to be paid by the employer. According to an employers' survey, the average annual cost of the system is DM 440 per employee. The bulk of this sum—which is almost certainly an exaggeration—is for the day-to-day activities of the works councils; in larger establishments they have their own offices and secretaries.

The participation rights of the works council are linked to the legal obligation to work with management "in a spirit of mutual trust for the good of the employees and of the establishment." The works council is required to negotiate "with a serious desire to reach agreement"; "acts of industrial warfare" as well as "activities that interfere with operations or imperil the peace of the establishment" are prohibited. There is also a secrecy obligation: information defined by the employer as business secrets may not be shared with the work force.

* In Anthony Ferner and Richard Hyman, eds., Industrial Relations in the New Europe (Clifford, U.K.: Blackwell, 1992), 218–696.

The statutory rights of the works council are prescribed in detail. Codetermination rights exist on "social" matters, such as principles of remuneration and the introduction of new payment methods, bonus rates and performance-related pay, daily and weekly work schedules, regulation of overtime and short-time working, holiday arrangements and the use of technical devices to monitor employees' performance. Codetermination also applies to personnel matters, such as policies for recruitment, transfer, regrading and dismissal. In specific circumstances there is a right of veto over individual cases of hiring, grading, transfer and dismissal. Information and consultation rights apply to personnel planning and changes in work processes, the working environment, and job content. The information and consultation rights concerning the introduction of new technology were extended in 1989. Finally, there is a right to information on financial matters. A standing committee of the works council, the economic committee, must be informed by the employer "in full and good time of the financial affairs of the establishment"; the same applies in case of planned changes "which may significantly disadvantage employees."

In general, works councils' participation rights are strong in relation to social policy; weaker in the case of personnel issues; and weaker still in financial and economic matters. In other words, the potential for works council intervention in managerial decision-making decreases the more closely it impinges on business policy.

Most works councillors are loyal unionists with close ties to their union. Unions and works councils are mutually dependent: the union supplies the council with information and expertise through educational courses or direct advice by full-time officials; while works councillors usually sustain union organization by recruiting new members and in general functioning—despite the legal distinction between the two institutions—as the arm of the union in the workplace. This dependence of the unions on the works councils gives the latter significant autonomy in relation to union officialdom; their power is, however, constrained by the fact that election and re-election usually depend on being nominated on an official union list.

In the 1960s and 1970s it was common in large establishments for works councils to negotiate informally with management for additional wage increases after the settlement of the industry-wide wage agreement. Technically this practice was usually illegal, since matters which form part of the agenda of collective bargaining can be regulated by works agreements only if the collective agreement authorizes this step by a so-called opening clause. In the 1970s some important collective agreements on working conditions and new technology introduced such a clause and prescribed supplementary works agreements to permit the flexible implementation of general rules. This move towards negotiation at the establishment level, as a complement to union collective bargaining at the industry level, has been strengthened in the 1980s with agreements on flexible working time. Thus more than 10,000 works agreements were negotiated in the engineering industry after the 1984 strike for the shorter working week. . . . Today, some works councils complain about the burden of negotiating now imposed on them.

The stable coalition between works councils and the union apparatus that has developed requires that a sufficient number of loyal unionists are elected as works councillors. For this reason the results of works council elections are of primary importance for unions. Challenges are possible, first from competing unions and unorganized groups mobilizing protest votes, and second from oppositional groups within the union itself demanding a more militant policy of interest representation.

DGB-affiliated unions have been fairly successful in warding off the first type of competition; according to union sources more than three-quarters, and according to employers more than two-thirds, of all elected works councillors belong to DGB unions. Hence union dominance in the councils is far in excess of union density among the work force. The exception to this pattern are the management staff committees set up under the 1988 legislation: 80 percent of those elected in the first elections, held in 1990, were non-unionists.

The second type of challenge comes from active union delegates (Vertrauensleute) or militant dissenters in large companies. They usually seek either to break with social partnership or to achieve more democratic grass-roots procedures for nominating works councillors. Since the early 1970s, challenges of this kind have emerged in the motor, steel, ship-building and chemical industries. In several cases, oppositional unionists have submitted their own list, sometimes with spectacular success. In a few establishments, foreign workers also challenged the official union lists following complaints about under-representation. Overall, however, such oppositional initiatives in works council elections have been very exceptional.

Union Delegates

Most—though not all—German unions have their own representatives alongside the works council, the Vertrauensleute. These are union stewards, each of whom usually represents between thirty and fifty workers and is elected by union members in a department or group. Their functions are limited, but include recruitment of members, distribution of union material and serving as a channel of information. . . . In many cases, Vertrauensleute are both messengers of the works council and the mouthpiece of their work groups. In the event of open conflict, such as token or unofficial strikes, they function as informal organizers of industrial action. . . .

Managers quite frequently take advantage of the works councils' authority over the work force to make them share responsibility not only for awkward personnel matters but also for more strategic goals. In general, works councils positively support management policies for modernization and rationalization of the production system, if they are convinced that the establishment's economic position will benefit, and providing two preconditions are met: no dismissals and no drop in wages for employees transferred to other jobs. There is also a broad understanding that work reorganization serves a dual goal: increased productivity and product quality on the one hand and humanization of work on the other. . . .

Collective Bargaining and Industrial Disputes

Types and Mechanisms of Agreement

According to the Collective Agreement Act (TVG) the parties to a collective agreement must be unions on the workers' side and single employers or employers' associations on the other. In practice, bargaining takes place at regional (metalworking, chemicals) or national (public sector) levels between the union and the corresponding employers' association. Company collective agreements are mainly found in smaller firms (Volkswagen is the obvious exception) and cover only a small minority of employees. Industry-wide or sectoral agreements contribute to a high degree of standardization of wages and other working conditions, as does state regulation. Though in many cases sectoral collective bargaining is formally undertaken at the regional level, it is centrally directed by the sectoral peak organizations on both sides. So-called pilot agreements reached in key areas of the engineering industry (usually Baden–Württemberg) are the model for the rest of this sector and exert influence on all other industries as well. This creates a specific German form of "pattern bargaining" with IG Metall [the Metal Workers Union] as pace-setter. In general, other industries settle wage increases within 1 percent of the [IG Metall] agreement.

Such a centralized system needs mechanisms for adapting the general conditions of collective agreements to the circumstances of individual establishments. Works agreements, negotiated between works councils and management, are not allowed to violate or contradict the provisions of the industry-wide collective agreement but are important supplements to it. Large establishments have hundreds of works agreements which are sometimes extensive documents regulating details of wage systems, working conditions, etc. In general the subjects of workplace agreements are restricted to "social" and "personnel" questions on which codetermination rights exist. A 1982 study showed that written works agreements existed in four-fifths of firms with over 200 employees. They are less common in small firms with weaker works councils.

Three different kinds of collective agreements are commonly distinguished: wage agreements (*Lohn-und Gehaltstarifoerträge*) fix the level of wages and periodic alterations; framework agreements (*Rahmentarifoerträge*) specify wage-payment systems; and "umbrella" agreements

(*Manteltarifoerträge*) regulate all other conditions of employment (working time, overtime, holidays, dismissals)....

Despite occasional major conflicts (recently on a four-or five-year cycle) Germany is notable for its low level of industrial disputes. Cooperative conflict management has been encouraged by favourable economic conditions with high rates of growth and low levels of unemployment, and governments relatively sympathetic to labour and to the principle of macro-economic management. Within the collective bargaining system, both parties have been able to change priorities from "quantitative" to "qualitative" issues, and to adapt their collectively created institutions and regulatory methods. Unions in particular have had to adapt to new circumstances. Since the 1970s, with severely reduced scope for real wage increases, pay has had a lower priority and non-wage issues have received enhanced attention. In the late 1970s, bargaining in many industries focused on protection against rationalization. Later, collective agreements on working time were reached in different industries, in response to union demands for the 35–hour week, and management pursuit of increased flexibility.... Working-time arrangements have dominated "qualitative" union demands since the mid–1980s, in part as a strategy for job-creation....

In 1992, conflict over wages has returned to the agenda. The costs of German unification have led the government, and the *Bundesbank*, to press for rigid pay restraint. Union efforts to protect real earnings have led to a bank employees' dispute and the first national public sector strike for eighteen years; and as we write, a major stoppage in engineering seems imminent.

Collective Bargaining Outcomes

Agreements involving the two largest unions—IGM and ÖTV [the Public Services and Transport Union]—cover the largest number of workers, though HBV [the Trade, Banking and Insurance Union], with a smaller membership, covers almost as many as ÖTV. This indicates an important feature of German industrial relations: the scope of collective regulation is not closely related to union membership. Roughly 90 percent of all employees are covered by a collective agreement—almost three times the number of union members.

In 1990 average earnings per employee rose by 5.0 percent to around DM 42,000; the increase was significantly more than that in overall productivity (1.9 percent), continuing the trend of the late 1980s to rising unit labour costs. In much of the private sector, actual wages are higher than the contractually agreed pay-scales. Multi-employer agreements are based on the economic situation of the average enterprise; in more profitable companies, the works council may succeed in securing higher wages through a works agreement. This gap between the contractually agreed wage and actual rates differs greatly from sector to sector

and from region to region as a result of varying conditions in product
and labour markets. . . .

Codetermination: The Fourth Decade*
WOLFGANG STREECK

. . . Co–Determination in the 1950s and 1960s

The concept of "co-determination" refers to two different institutional
channels of employee representation in German industrial organizations:
co-determination at the workplace (*betriebliche Mitbestimmung*) which is
exercised through works councils, and co-determination in the enterprise
(*Mitbestimmung auf Unternehmensebene*) which is exercised through
workforce representatives on the supervisory board and, to an extent,
the management board.[1] The first form of co-determination, which
relates to manpower and employment matters, is provided for all establishments with more than five employees. The second, relating to the
enterprise's general economic decisions, is limited to companies beyond a
certain size and of specific legal forms. Co-determination was first
introduced, shortly after the founding of the Federal Republic, through
two major pieces of legislation: workplace co-determination through the
Works Constitution Act of 1952, and enterprise-level co-determination
through either the Works Constitution Act or the Co–Determination Act
of 1951, depending on the industry.

The main features of the German "Works Constitution" have remained unchanged since 1952. . . . Workers in establishments with a
minimum of six employees have a legal right to elect a works council
(*Betriebsrat*) as a representative of their interests in relation to the
employer, and duly elected works councils are entitled to information,
consultation, and co-decision on a range of specified subjects. At the
same time, works councils have a general obligation to co-operate with
the employer for the benefit of the enterprise and not to engage "in acts
of industrial warfare." The law permits all employees to vote and stand
for election regardless of whether or not they are union members.

Concerning co-determination at the enterprise level, the Works
Constitution Act of 1952 stipulated that in joint stock companies, companies with limited partners holding shares, and limited liability companies
with at least 500 employees, one-third of the seats on the supervisory
board had to be allocated to representatives of the workforce. These were

* In Bernhard Wilpert and Arndt Sorge, eds., *International Perspectives on Organizational Democracy* (Chichester: John Wiley, 1984).

1. German companies have by law two boards: a management board consisting of
professional managers who run the company's day-to-day business, and a supervisory
board consisting of elected representatives of stockholders and workers whose major tasks
are the appointment and dismissal of the management board and the supervision of its
activities. The by-laws of the company may in addition provide that certain decisions of the
management board require the prior assent of the supervisory board.

to be elected by secret ballot by all employees, again regardless of whether voters or candidates belonged to a trade union. If the number of seats for workforce representatives exceeded two—which depended on the size of the board which, in turn, was determined by the shareholders—the additional seats could be filled by representatives who were not employed with the company. In practice, "external" representatives, to the extent that there were any at all, were normally full-time union officials.

The Co–Determination Act of 1951 differed from the Works Constitution Act in that it was exclusively concerned with supervisory board co-determination and was limited in scope to companies in the coal and steel industry with more than 1000 employees. It is important to note that as far as workplace co-determination is concerned, the coal and steel industry is fully under the jurisdiction of the Works Constitution Act. The Co–Determination Act provided for "parity" on the supervisory board, i.e. for an equal number of workforce and stockholder representatives. To prevent deadlock, the board had to co-opt one "additional member." Workforce representatives were elected by an assembly of all works council members from the company's establishments. In the normal case in which the number of workforce representatives was five, two of these—who had to be employees of the company—were nominated by the works councillors. The other three were nominated to the electoral body (i.e. the assembly of works councillors) by the central organizations (of the trade unions represented in the various establishments of the undertaking) after prior consultation with the unions represented in the undertaking and with the works councils. The nomination rights of the central organizations shall be proportional to the strength of their representation in the establishments (Section 6.3). One of the three had to be neither an employee of the company nor a full-time trade union official.

Another difference between the Co–Determination Act and the Works Constitution Act was that, in the former, enterprise-level co-determination extended not only to the supervisory board but also to the management board. The Act made it obligatory for coal and steel companies to add a "labour director" (*Arbeitsdirektor*) to their board of management. The labour director could not be appointed against the majority of the labour representatives on the supervisory board. The Act said nothing on the tasks of the labour director; it merely stated that he had to have the same rights as the other management board members, and that board members had to work together "in closest collaboration." Normally, the labour director was given responsibility for personnel matters and was placed at the head of a newly created manpower department.

"Parity" co-determination has been one of the central issues of German politics throughout the 1950s and 1960s—so much so that to many it became synonymous with *Mitbestimmung* as such. In part, it may have been due to continuous, although fruitless, pressures by the unions for the extension of parity to industry as a whole that many observers have tended to underrate the significance of workplace co-determination, and to overlook the fact that whatever differences there were between parity and the "one-third formula," were qualified by the universal presence of works council co-determination. . . .

The Reforms of the 1970s

In 1969 the government changed again, this time to a coalition of Social Democrats and Free Democrats. Among the central projects on the new government's agenda was new legislation on industrial relations. . . .

In 1972 the Works Constitution Act of 1952 was repealed and replaced with a new Act. It is indicative of the interdependence of the two channels of co-determination that most of the changes introduced by the Works Constitution Act of 1972 in effect amounted to a generalization of important elements of the co-determination pattern in coal and steel: (1) the Act strengthened the organizational base of the works councils; (2) it reinforced the influence of works councils over management, particularly in the area of manpower policy and manpower planning; and (3) it institutionalized formally some of the links between works councils and trade unions.

(1) The Works Constitution Act of 1972 increased the number of seats on works councils, especially in large establishments. It also increased the number of works councillors who are by law released from normal work duties, and it made it easier for unions to initiate the election of a works council in a plant where, normally because of employer resistance, none exists. Perhaps most importantly, the Act prescribed the formation of "central works councils" in companies with more than one plant. Central works councils are composed of delegates of plant works councils, and they negotiate with management on matters concerning the company as a whole. In making central works councils obligatory, the 1972 Act responded to increasing economic concentration and centralization of management functions.

(2) As far as the substantive rights of works councils in relation to the employer are concerned, the Act entitled works councils to co-determination on all matters relating to *working time* unless regulated by law or industrial agreement. Moreover, it extended co-determination to the setting of *piece rates* and the *design of workplaces* and the *work environment*, and it made it obligatory for an employer to ask the works council in advance for its assent on "any *engagement, grading, regrading and transfer*" of employees. Works councils were given a veto on a number of grounds laid down in the Act. Furthermore, the Act granted works councils an unqualified right to be consulted on an employer's "*manpower planning*." It

obliged the employer to inform the works council on his "plans in full and in good time," and it gave the works council a legal right to demand that *vacancies* are *notified for internal competition* within the establishment before they are filled. . . .

(3) Concerning the relation between unions and works councils, the Act removed all legal obstacles for works councillors taking on union office and performing union functions. It also gave works councillors a right to attend trade union courses at the expense of the employer and with their full pay continued. The rights of full-time union officials to take part in works council meetings were considerably extended, and so were their rights to enter establishments with or without prior notification of the employer.

Immediately after it had won a new term in the autumn of 1972 the government began to prepare legislation for parity co-determination at the enterprise level in large companies outside coal and steel. It was agreed at the outset that the 1951 Co–Determination Act was to remain in force, and that the new legislation was not to deal with the coal and steel industry. Moreover, it was to apply only to very large firms so that the one-third model of the old Works Constitution Act would remain in effect for middle-sized firms. In the end, the minimum size for a company to fall under the new legislation was set at 2,000 employees.

The Co–Determination Act of 1976 was the result of protracted struggling within the coalition. During the legislative process it increasingly became a source of sometimes bitter conflict between the government and the unions. While the Social Democratic Party was in principle committed to a general extension of the coal and steel model, its coalition partner was not—and, under pressure from business, grew increasingly hostile to it. The final Act was a compromise that lay somewhere between the coal and steel model and the one-third formula of the Works Constitution Act. In particular, the Act:

(1) Increased the representation of employees to parity but required that one of the labour representatives had to come from the ranks of middle management. (Middle management was thus for the first time officially recognized as a separate group among the workforce, having special interests in need of collective representation.) In addition, the Act gave the shareholders' representatives the right to determine the chairman the supervisory board, and it gave the chairman a casting vote in the case of a tie.

(2) Refused unions the right to appoint the labour representatives on the supervisory board directly, but did not make direct election by the workforce obligatory, as had been demanded by the Free Democrats. As a compromise, the Act provided for direct election in companies with up to 8000 employees, and for indirect election by an electoral college (whose members had to be specifically elected for the occasion) in firms with more than 8000 employees. It also made

it possible for the electorate to change the voting procedure from direct to indirect and from indirect to direct, respectively, in a separate ballot in advance of the election.

(3) Set aside, in response to union demands, some of the labour seats on supervisory boards for representatives of trade unions. These seats could, but did not have to be, filled with persons not employed with the company. Seats for union representatives were fewer in number than the seats for "internal" representatives, and occupants could not be appointed by the unions but had to be elected by the same procedure as their "internal" colleagues.

(4) Provided for a "labour director" on the management board who is, however, appointed in the same way as the other management board members. As a concession to unions, the Act requires that all management board members are appointed by a two-thirds majority of the supervisory board. However, if no such majority can be found, appointments can be made by a simple majority, and the chairman may use this casting vote. . . .

Co–Determination After 1976: A New Company Constitution . . .

Turning to the more specific characteristics of the emerging new "company constitution," the following points are of particular interest in the present context:

(1) More than ever, industrial unions outside coal and steel use the works council system as the institutional framework and the major source of support for their activities at the workplace and in the enterprise. Especially in large establishments, works councils have, just as in coal and steel, become de facto union bodies . . . and the proportion of works council seats won by industrial unions, in spite of various external or factional challenges, approaches that in the coal and steel industry. Like the distinction between workplace and enterprise co-determination, that between voluntary representation through trade unions and legally regulated representation through co-determination has become increasingly blurred since the early 1950s. . . .

(2) Central works councils are even more union-dominated than plant works councils. This is because of their indirect election which makes it possible to exclude competing minority groups from them. The importance of central works councils is increasing as a result of the growing centralization of manpower policy and manpower planning at the company level. With more and more works council functions being moved upwards to the central works council—which is in spite of the fact that the legislators wanted to prevent central works councils becoming "super works councils"—the chairman of the latter, who is always a member of the industrial union and

normally holds important union offices, is increasingly becoming the central figure in a company's system of representation.

(3) The facilities available to works councils in large companies frequently exceed the legal minimum (which is already fairly high, especially since 1972). For example, the number of works councillors who are full-time is often higher than prescribed by the law; works councillors frequently have access to chauffeured business cars and company planes; and some works councils employ, at the expense of the company, their own expert staff of professional lawyers and economists. Also, co-determination rights of works councils in practice extend further than legally prescribed. Works councils, and in particular central works councils, are being consulted earlier and on a broader range of subjects than required under the law, and employers seek the consensus of the works council even if legally they do not have to. In part, this is because the Works Constitution Act of 1972 has given works councils considerable additional powers which they can use to obstruct decisions if the management does not co-operate on subjects that are formally not under co-determination. (According to a manager of a large German enterprise: "Without the works council, nothing goes; with the works council, everything goes.")

(4) Almost all of the "internal" workforce representatives on supervisory boards are works councillors, and the chairman of the central works council fails only in the very exceptional cases to sit on the supervisory board....

Works councillors sitting on supervisory boards have greatly improved access to information, and this holds regardless of whether there is parity on the supervisory board or not. In law, members of supervisory boards are entitled to any information that management may have. Any two supervisory board members can, upon request, inspect any document in the possession of management. The prevailing legal doctrine is summarized in the formula, "Whatever the management knows, the supervisory board may also know." Although much of the information given to supervisory board members can be declared confidential, a works councillor bargaining with management in his capacity as works councillor can hardly be expected to forget what he has learned as supervisory board member....

Notes and Questions

1. *Economic Performance*

a. *Unemployment.* Until the 1980s, Germany enjoyed a low unemployment rate (e.g., one-seventh of the U.S. level in 1973). As Appendix D (indicator U–5) indicates, by the mid–1990s the German rate matched or exceeded the U.S. rate; the numbers increased substantially with the absorption of the states of the former East Germany. German joblessness is also of exceptionally long duration (see indicator U–1 of Appendix D). In 1986, 52.2 percent of total unemployed in Germany were out of work six months or more, and 32.2 percent were out of work for twelve months or more; the comparable U.S. figures were 14.4 percent and 8.7 percent, respectively. See Ronald E. Kutscher and Constance E. Sorrentino, "Employment and Unemployment Patterns in U.S. and Europe, 1973–1987," 10 Journal of Labor Research 5, 15 (Table 5) (1989). There is also a pronounced shift toward contingent employment: "In 1986 . . ., about 25 percent of West Germany's workers were under nonpermanent, nonfulltime contracts, and 1 out of 12 unemployed workers could find work only on a fixed-term basis." "The European Labor Market: Some Background," in Richard S. Belous, Rebecca S. Hartley, and Kelly L. McClenahan, eds., European and American Labor Markets: Different Models and Different Results 119 (Washington:, D.C.: National Planning Association, 1992). The Employment Protection Act of 1985, as amended in 1989, accelerated this trend by permitting initial hires on fixed-term contracts for up to eighteen months. Presumably, employers may terminate such contracts free of the strictures of German wrongful-dismissal law.

b. *Competitiveness.* Germany in 1994 had the highest manufacturing hourly labor cost among developed nations, reaching a peak of 160 percent of the U.S. cost level of $17.10 (see Appendix E). Productivity growth also slowed down substantially in the 1980s (see Appendices F and G). Increasingly, German companies are establishing facilities in other countries, such as the BMW plant in South Carolina and the Mercedes–Benz plant in Alabama; according to one account, in 1985 German capital invested DM 37 billion more in direct investment abroad than foreigners invested in the country. See "Germany: Is the Model Broken?," Economist, May 4, 1996, pp. 17, 18.

2. *Impact of Works Councils on Firm Performance.* German works councils are extolled by American observers as instruments of employee voice that improve, or at least do not detract from, firm performance because they are relieved of the redistributive, "social wage" concerns of extrafirm bargaining agents like trade unions. See, e.g., the essays by Rogers and Streeck in Joel Rogers and Wolfgang Streeck, eds., *Works Councils: Consultation, Representation, and Cooperation in Industrial Relations* (Chicago: University of Chicago Press, 1995); Lowell Turner, *Democracy at Work: Changing World Markets and the Future of Labor Unions* (Ithaca, NY: Cornell University Press, 1991). The extant empirical literature on the German experience, however, points to negative or inconclusive results. See John T. Addison, Kornelius Kraft, and Joachim Wagner, "German Works Councils and Firm Performance," in Bruce E. Kaufman and Morris M. Kleiner, eds., *Employee Representation: Alternatives and Future Directions* (Madison, Wis.: Industrial Relations Research Association, 1993) (reviewing literature and reporting results of survey of manufacturing firms in states of Niedersachsen and Baden–Württemberg). This issue is revisited in Chapter 10 with respect to proposals for U.S. works councils.

3. *Disempowered Shareholders?* What is the impact of codetermination on capital markets? Consider Mark J. Roe, *Strong Managers, Weak Owners: The*

Political Roots of American Corporate Finance 214 (Princeton, N.J.: Prince-ton University Press, 1994) 214:

> Codetermination has three important effects on corporate gover-nance. First codetermination makes powerful intermediaries [i.e., banks as highly influential institutional investors] more politically palatable in Germany than they have been in the United States, because the employ-ees are in the boardroom as a counterweight.
>
> Second, codetermination affects the mechanisms of corporate gover-nance by, for example, impeding takeovers.... [T]akeovers that would disrupt employment are difficult because the shareholders can never capture the entire supervisory board. Codetermination may also affect voting structure by encouraging countervailing big shareholder blocks; in fact, few large German firms lack a big blockholder.
>
> Third, codetermination affects corporate governance in the supervi-sory board, impeding intermediaries from pushing for rapid organiza-tional change that would disrupt employment. Bankers also know that a powerful supervisory board enhances the authority of the employees. [B]ankers have sought to weaken the supervisory board, the arena where the employees are, while hoping the managerial board will act as the bankers wish, perhaps after consulting them outside of the board-room.

4. *Multiemployer, Multi-industry Bargaining.* Collective bargaining in Ger-many takes place on a regional level between large multi-industry unions and employer associations, with agreements covering all employees in the represented industries regardless of occupation. Although union members comprise about 35 percent of German workers, collective agreements cover 90 percent of the workforce, with the overwhelming majority of those agreements negotiated on a multiemployer basis. See Wolfgang Meyer, "Pay Bargaining in Germany," paper prepared for ASAP Conference on Wage Determination (Dec. 1991), 2–5. The industrywide agreement sets minimum terms of employment—there is no statutory minimum wage. Unions must tailor their demands to the ability to pay of weaker firms in the employer federations in order to prevent defections, creating a "wage gap" between the collectively bargained wage and the effective wage paid by the larger firms. See Meyer, "Pay Bargaining in Germany," at 16–18; Samuel Estreich-er, "Labor Law Reform in a World of Competitive Markets," 69 *Chicago–Kent Law Review* at 16 n.49 (discussion of magnitude of wage gap). Supple-mental terms are either unilaterally promulgated by employers or tacitly negotiated with the firm-based works council. See Peter Swenson, *Fair Shares: Unions, Pay, and Politics in Sweden and West Germany* (Ithaca, NY: Cornell University Press, 1989) 81.

Multiemployer bargaining is a creature of contract. German law, howev-er, provides a mechanism for extending agreements covering 50 percent of the employees in the relevant sector in a region to noncontracting parties. Although the provision is rarely invoked, "the mere existence of the mecha-nism may signal enough threat potential to prevent outsiders from undercut-ting wages and working conditions of existing collective agreements." Karl-

Heinz Paque, "Germany: Living with Tight Corporatism," in Joop Hartog and Jules Theeuwes, eds., *Labour Market Contracts and Institutions* (Amsterdam: North–Holland, 1993) 209, 220.

The system is showing some signs of unraveling. A number of companies, especially foreign-owned subsidiaries, have insisted on negotiating single-employer agreements. In 1995, Daimler–Benz, the country's largest industrial conglomerate, forced the Metal Workers' Union to agree to Saturday morning work and wages below the collective rate in order to avoid the transfer of jobs to its non-German plants. See "Germany: Is the Model Broken?," *Economist*, May 4, 1996, pp. 17, 19; Greg Steinmetz, "German Firms Sour on System That Keeps Peace with Workers," Wall Street Journal, Oct. 17, 1995, p. 1, col. 6.

5. *Decline of Centralized Bargaining in Sweden.* Sweden for a time represented the archetypical case of highly centralized bargaining, featuring the dominant role played by the national agreement between the employers' federation (SAF) and the blue-collar union federation (LO). The dominance of the central agreement has declined since1984, with employers insisting on greater leeway for decentralized wage determination. See Harry C. Katz, "The Decentralization of Collective Bargaining: A Literature Review and Comparative Analysis," 47 *Industrial and Labor Relations Review* 3, 4–5 (1993). The dynamics of the Swedish case are analyzed in Richard B. Freeman and Robert Gibbons, "Getting Together and Breaking Apart: The Decline of Centralized Collective Bargaining" (NBER Working Paper No. 4464, Sept. 1993).

D. "Social Charter": The European Community Model

Labor and the Global Economy: Four Approaches to Transnational Labor Regulation*

KATHERINE VAN WEZEL STONE

Models of Transnational Regulation

... Given the many respects in which globalization represents a threat to domestic labor movements and labor regulatory regimes, most trade unionists and many labor relations professionals have viewed the rapid march of globalization with alarm. The question of whether the organized labor movements in the Western world can protect their gains in a global economy has been discussed, debated, and bemoaned at length over the past ten years. Despite a pervasive sense of gloom, there has been some optimistic speculation that alternative forms of labor regulation might emerge in the post-trading bloc world....

Rather than embark on an imaginary journey into possible forms of labor regulation in a post-trading bloc world, it makes sense to begin

* 16 Michigan Journal of International Law 987 (1995).

with an analysis of the types of transnational labor regulation that are emerging in fact. . . .

1.   Preemptive Legislation

The European Economic Community Treaty (EEC Treaty) sets out specific provisions of supranational law in certain areas, and sets up structures for European Union [EU]-wide regulation in other areas. There are very few specific provisions in the EEC Treaty that bear directly on labor law. The few labor provisions that do exist can be found in Title III, The Free Movement of Persons, Services, and Capital. Under Title III, there are provisions concerning the freedom of movement of employees, and provisions concerning the treatment of and social benefits for migrant workers. There are also provisions concerning professional workers. Elsewhere in the EEC Treaty there are provisions that mandate equal treatment between male and female workers.

In addition to the principles of labor protection contained in the EEC Charter, the EU Council of Ministers has the power to enact specific labor regulations (*règlements*) that are consistent with the Charter. To date, the EU has promulgated very few *règlements* on labor matters. The few that have been published deal with migrant workers, occupational safety and health, and equality between men and women.

In 1989, European lawmakers attempted to enact a Community Charter of Fundamental Social Rights of Workers (known as the "Social Charter"). The Social Charter contained a list of "Fundamental Social Rights of Workers," which included occupational health and safety protections, guarantees for the right to organize and bargain collectively, rights to adequate social welfare benefits, workplace consultation and participation rights, and protection for children, older workers, and the disabled. Eleven of the twelve member states approved the Social Charter–all but the United Kingdom. As a result, the eleven states that ratified the Social Charter have treated it as a mandate for the European Commission to formulate directives for the protection of labor and the promotion of collective bargaining.

2.   Harmonization

As discussed, the EEC Treaty makes it possible to unify some employment rights by means of multilateral *règlements*, but the Council of Ministers has not yet pursued this course of action. Rather, in most instances, the Council has attempted to encourage its member nations to "harmonize" their labor and employment laws. The goal of harmonization is to provide incentives for convergence, or what the EU scholars call "approximation," between collective bargaining systems. Harmonization occurs in two ways: through EU Directive, and through indirect pressures imposed by regulation in other areas that have a collateral impact on labor matters.

(a) Direct Harmonization

An EU directive is a regulation enacted by the EU Council which the member states must then enact into their domestic legislation. There is a time period within which the member states are required to "transpose" the directive into their own domestic law. Usually the directive sets minimum standards in a particular area which the member states must then "transpose" in ways that are consistent with their own distinct labor law system.

There are presently EU Directives in effect in several areas of labor regulation. In 1975, the EU lawmakers adopted a directive on collective redundancies, also known as dismissals for economic reasons. This directive provided that firms who intend to implement a mass layoff must notify workers affected and confer with the worker representatives. In 1977 a directive designed to protect workers faced with takeovers and other changes in the ownership of their firms was adopted. The 1977 directive provides that employees of companies that were involved in a transfer of ownership of the entire company or a part thereof must have their preexisting contractual rights, including collective bargaining rights, honored by the new entity. A 1980 directive on insolvencies provided that firms must guarantee payment of workers' outstanding wage claims and benefits prior to the commencement of insolvency proceedings.

There have also been directives addressing workplace safety and health and equal treatment for women and men. In addition, the EU is considering several directives concerning part-time workers, service workers and temporary workers.

In 1992 at Maastricht, eleven of the twelve EU member states agreed to a Protocol on Social Policy. In the negotiations leading up to the Maastricht Agreement, there were considerable pressures to enlarge the EEC Treaty's social policy provisions. Due to the United Kingdom's continued opposition, however, there was no unanimous agreement. Instead, provisions based on the previous Social Charter were annexed as a Social Agreement accepted by all except the UK, and these eleven member states were authorized by the Protocol on Social Policy to utilize the mechanisms of the EEC for the purposes of implementing that Agreement. This UK "opt-out" means that the Social Policy proposals which the UK government is unwilling to accept may be agreed upon among the other member states and become binding on all except the UK.

The Maastricht Protocol, also known as the Social Agreement, made a number of changes in the manner in which labor directives are implemented. Most significantly, it provided that labor directives can be implemented through collective bargaining agreements as well as through legislation and administrative regulation. In addition, the 1992 Maastricht Protocol on Social Policy expanded the legislative capacity of the EU. It set out a series of issues on which the EU could legislate on the basis of majority voting, rather than unanimity which had previously been required. These areas include health and safety protection, working conditions, workers' information and consultation rights, and equality between men and women.

Article 2(6) of the Social Agreement makes it clear that most collective labor rights are excluded from majority voting. It states that "the provisions of this Article shall not apply to pay, the right of association, the right to strike or the right to impose lock-outs." Thus, unanimous voting was retained for directives in the areas of job security, representation, and collective defense of workers' interests.

To date, the EU has not attempted to legislate or harmonize in the field of collective bargaining law. It has, however, attempted to legislate works councils. In September 1994, the first Directive was issued under the Social Agreement, providing for the establishment of European Works Councils or other consultative procedures by all European multinational enterprises. These are workplace-based organizations established for the purpose of consultation and sharing information, not for purposes of providing worker representation. A number of multinationals have moved to set up such Works Councils, and although it is not legally binding on the UK, some have included their UK workers in the arrangements.

EU directives have force only to the extent that they are implemented by the member states. As a consequence, the actual meaning of the directives can vary greatly between states. However, in *Francovich v. Italy* [1991 E.C.R. I–5357, 67 C.M.L.R. 66 (1993)], a landmark decision in 1991, the European Court of Justice ruled that a member country could be held liable to an individual worker for restitution if it failed to enact a labor protection directive. In that case, two Italian workers sued the Italian government for failing to implement the 1980 Directive concerning worker protection in the event of an employer's insolvency. The Court ruled that it is "inherent in the Treaty system" that the member states are liable to individuals who are damaged by the state's failure to implement directives. This decision will give added enforcement power to the directives, and may lead to a uniform interpretation of the precise rights and protections contained in them. If that happens, the directives will come to resemble the preemptive legislation of the *règlements* discussed above.

(b) Indirect Harmonization

In addition to harmonization by means of EU labor directives, the EU can harmonize labor regulation indirectly by means of regulations and directives in other areas of law. For example, labor policy is implicated by regulations and directives in the area of corporate law. The EU has a long-standing draft directive on the structure of stock corporations and a proposal for a European-wide stock corporation. However, the proposals have not yet been enacted, due largely to disagreement about the proper role of labor in the structure of the corporation. Some member states have extensive codetermination rights for workers built into their current laws on corporate structures, while some states do not. The EU states have not been able to agree whether or not to include codetermination rights in the EU directive on corporate structure, so the directive has not yet been adopted. However, if any directive on corporate structure were adopted, it would have a profound effect on labor's participation rights in all EU nations.

Notes and Questions

1. *Directive on European Works Councils.* In September 1994, the Council of Ministers enacted a directive on European Works Councils for eleven of the member states (other than the U.K.). Council Directive 94/45/EC, 1994 O.J. (L 254) 64, described in "European Works Council Directive," 250 European Industrial Relations Review 27 (Dec. 1994). Under the directive, member states must introduce legislation requiring companies with at least 1,000 employees within the Community, including at least 150 employees in each of two or more Member States, to establish a European Works Council "or a procedure for informing and consulting employees" or their representatives about issues affecting the company as a whole in Europe. Such matters would include plans for major reorganizations, plant closings, mass dismissals, or new investments and mergers. An individual company's management and a "special negotiating body" of its workforce (pursuant to rules developed by national legislation) have an opportunity to work out on their own the most appropriate methods for fulfilling these information and consultation objectives within the concerned multinational. If consultations fail, however, the directive requires the creation of a European Works Council in which European-level management will meet at least once a year with representatives from each of the firm's European subsidiaries to discuss issues affecting the company as whole, and to inform and consult with the employee body "[w]here there are exceptional circumstances affecting the employees' interests to a considerable extent, particularly in the event of relocations, the closure of establishments or undertakings or collective redundancies...."

The directive (Art. 5) contemplates that the "central management" will commence a negotiation procedure with a "special negotiating body" on its own initiative "or at the written request of at least 100 employees or their representatives" in at least two establishments in at least two different Member States. Once such a request has been made, the negotiation procedure is mandatory, because the directive sets a default set of conditions which national legislation must provide where firms refuse to commence negotiations within six months of such a request. Apparently, the "special negotiating body" can decide by two-thirds vote not to commence or to terminate negotiations, subject to the right to make a new request after two years. Where such a decision is made, the "central management" would be under no obligation to create a European Works Council. See generally John T. Addison, "European Union Labor Market Directives and Initiatives," in Samuel Estreicher, ed. Global Competition and the American Employment Landscape—As We Enter the 21st Century: Proceedings of New York University 52d Annual Conference on Labor (Cambridge, Mass.: Kluwer, 2000).

2. *Eurosclerosis.* High rates of unemployment and low rates of job creation are serious problems for many of the member countries of the Organization for Economic Cooperation and Development (OECD). In the OECD Jobs Study of 1995, the organization issued a set of recommendations urging members states to, inter alia, "[i]ncrease flexibility of working-time," "nurture an entrepreneurial climate" by eliminating impediments to creation and expansion of enterprises, "make wage and labour costs more flexible," and "reform employment security provisions that inhibit the expansion of employment in the private sector." OECD Jobs Study: Implementing the Strategy (Paris, France: 1995) 15. On the general phenomenon, see Lawrence H. Summers, Understanding Unemployment (Cambridge, Mass.: MIT Press, 1990), 240:

> To take an extreme case, suppose that all wages are set by bargaining between employed workers—the "insiders"—and firms, with outsiders playing no role in the bargaining process. Insiders are concerned with maintaining their jobs, not insuring the employment of outsiders. This has two implications. First, in the absence of shocks, any level of employment of insiders is self-sustaining; insiders just set the wages so as to remain employed. Second and more important, in the presence of shocks, employment follows a pattern akin to a random walk; after an adverse shock, for example, which reduces employment, some workers lose their insider status and the new smaller group of insiders sets the wage so as to maintain this new lower level of employment. Employment and unemployment show no tendency to return to their preshock value, but are instead determined by the history of shocks. This example is extreme but nevertheless suggestive. It suggests that, if wage bargaining is a prevalent feature of the labor market, the dynamic interactions between employment and the size of the group of insiders may generate substantial employment and unemployment persistence.

3. *A Critical View of the "Social Charter".* For a critical perspective on the "social charter" effort, see John T. Addison and W. Stanley Siebert, "Recent Developments in Social Policy in the New European Union," Industrial and Labor Relations Review 5, 48 (Oct. 1994); the essays collected in the book they edited, Labour Markets in Europe: Issues of Harmonization and Regulation (London, U.K.: Dryden Press, Harcourt Brace & Co., 1997); and their article, "The Social Charter of the European Community: Evolution and Controversies," 44 Industrial and Labor Relations Review 597 (1991).

E.   Globalization and Domestic Labor Standards

In this era of global markets, can one country mandate high domestic labor standards without suffering competitively? This depends critically,

of course, on whether the labor standard corrects a market defect and
thus might promote the competitiveness of domestic firms, on the one
hand, or inefficiently imposes costs on firms that exceed gains to workers, on the other. Our first reading, by Ronald Ehrenberg, explores the
effects of economic integration on domestic labor standards.

A related issue is whether developed countries should impose their
labor standards on other countries, through trade sanctions or other
economic weapons. Sometimes imposing "western" or "developed" standards on developing countries is premised on moral grounds or as
helping the people in the developing countries. Other times, the goal is
to prevent developing countries from undercutting domestic standards.
The reading by Howse and Trebilcock explores these distinctions.

Labor Markets and Integrating National Economies*

RONALD G. EHRENBERG

The international economy is becoming increasingly integrated. For
example, between 1950 and 1988 exports as a share of gross domestic
product rose from 9.4 to 15.2 percent in the world as a whole, from 3.5 to
6.7 percent in the United States and from 13.1 to 22.0 percent in the
European Community (EC) nations. Increased economic integration is
due in part to reductions in transportation and communications costs,
and in part to the growth of multilateral and bilateral arrangements that
have reduced the tariff and nontariff barriers to trade and capital
mobility. These include the General Agreement on Tariffs and Trade
(GATT), the EC, and the United States–Canada Free Trade Agreement.
The latter evolved, after much debate, into the North American Free
Trade Agreement (NAFTA) and now includes Mexico. . . .

Pros and Cons of Increased Economic Integration

Policies to increase economic integration can take two forms. Some
policies promote trade or capital mobility, or both. GATT is an example
of this form, as is the recently passed NAFTA. Other policies also
promote, or encourage, the mobility of labor, such as those developed by
the EC that allow for free mobility of individuals across member nations
and that require member nations to recognize professional credentials
(for example, medical degrees) earned in other member nations.

Are both kinds of economic integration desirable? Trade is thought
to increase economic efficiency by allowing nations to specialize in the
production of those goods for which they have a comparative advantage
and by allowing them to benefit from any economies of scale in production that may result from having a larger market for their goods. The
mobility of capital is thought to allow capital-labor ratios to equalize

* Washington, D.C.: The Brookings Institution (1994) 1–3, 6–12, 22–23, 39–40

across nations and thus to cause the equality of marginal productivities of capital (and labor) across nations, which should maximize total world output. Hence, in an efficiency sense, the case for free trade and capital mobility seems strong.

The discussion above ignores, however, the effect of trade and capital mobility on the income distributions in different countries. The passage of NAFTA, for example, may lead to reduced employment opportunities for Mexican agricultural workers and reduced employment opportunities for some U.S. manufacturing workers. To the extent that there is an identifiable group of "losers" in each country, domestic adjustment policies, such as retraining programs or income support programs, may help to guarantee widespread continued support for the legislation in both countries and to reduce changes in the distribution of income in each country that residents consider undesirable.

Of course, free mobility of labor would in some cases eliminate the need for countries to pursue domestic adjustment policies. For example, if free mobility of labor were part of NAFTA (it currently is not), Mexican agricultural workers who became unemployed as a result of free trade could migrate to the United States to seek employment. But that would lead to another set of issues regarding how such a migration flow would influence both the distribution of earnings and infrastructure needs (such as schools) in the United States.

Both types of economic integration also lead to questions whether standards would be adequate and whether the level of labor market standards should be part of trade negotiations. Would increased free trade with poorer nations, like Mexico, cause the United States to reduce its occupational safety and health standards or its minimum wages in an effort to remain competitive with the poorer nations and their lower standards? Or rather than "tolerate" such a situation, should the United States agree to free trade with another nation only if the other nation raised its standards to a level close to ours? Or should free trade be accompanied by attempts to harmonize labor market standards across nations through a regional supranational body, such as the EC, or through a global organization? ...

Unemployment Insurance: An Example

To introduce some of the issues ..., I consider as an example the provision and financing of unemployment insurance (UI) benefits through an employer-based payroll tax.... Here I initially consider a very simplified program in which the UI tax is specified to be a flat rate of $T per worker. Initially, I also assume that exchange rates are fixed between nations; an assumption relaxed [below]....

Are payroll taxes fully shifted onto workers? Some recent European data suggest that in the long run they may be, although not in the short run. More specifically, the data indicate that a 1 percentage point increase in the payroll tax increases labor costs by about one-half of 1 percentage point in the first year, with nearly half of the labor cost increase still persisting after five years. Furthermore, other studies based on the estimation of wage equations that use data from a number of countries find evidence of only a partial shifting of the tax onto workers even in the long run. Thus the generosity of a nation's UI system, and hence the level of the payroll tax needed to finance it, may well influence trade flows, at least in the short run.

This finding suggests that concern over the generosity of social insurance programs in competitor nations will be part of any movement toward increased economic integration. Indeed, it explains the attempts (not yet successful) by the EC to harmonize labor standards and social insurance programs across member nations. It also explains why some European countries, in the face of increased international competition during the 1980s, tried to reduce the "generosity" of their social programs or the level of their standards in an effort to achieve more "economy flexibility." . . .

The analysis of the effects of the UI payroll tax just presented implicitly assumed that a system of fixed exchange rates was in place. This assumption is probably appropriate for trade between states in the United States and for trade between nations that seek to limit fluctuations in the relative values of their currencies, such as the EC nations. Here I discuss how the introduction of flexible exchange rates alters the analysis.

Consider first the simplified world . . . in which an increase in a single flat-rate payroll tax is applied to all employees. To the extent that the tax is not fully shifted onto workers, at least in the short run, their costs, and hence the costs of the nation's products, will rise on the international market. With higher prices, there will be an excess supply of the country's exports, and the country's currency will therefore depreciate relative to its trading partners' currencies. However, the decline in the value of the country's currency will make its trading partners' goods more expensive, and the country will reduce its imports. Thus an increase in the tax will lead to a reduction in trade and a decrease in the nation's standard of living. Put another way, residents of the nation will partially bear the burden of the tax in the form of higher prices for both domestic and foreign goods. . . .

Finally, suppose that as in the U.S. system, the nation's UI tax is based on payroll, not employment, and that the system has a relatively low maximum taxable wage base. Then an increase in the payroll tax rate that is not fully shifted onto workers will increase the costs of low-skilled workers relative to the costs of high-skilled workers. The nation's comparative advantage (disadvantage) in producing goods that require high-skilled workers will therefore increase (decrease). Although the resulting depreciation of the nation's currency will lead to a reduction in its imports, exports produced using skilled labor will rise relative to those produced using unskilled labor. So employment opportunities for skilled workers will rise relative to employment opportunities for unskilled workers. Put another way, the nation's demand for skilled workers will rise, and its demand for unskilled workers will fall.

Flexible exchange rates, therefore, do *not* alter the basic proposition that increase in payroll taxes which are not fully shifted onto workers will influence trade. In a fixed exchange rate world, the rise in the nation's product price discourages exports. In a flexible exchange rate world, the resulting depreciation of a nation's currency helps to reduce the drop in exports but also leads to a reduction in imports. Hence, under either exchange rate regime, the nation's consumers partially pay for the increase in the payroll tax rate by experiencing higher prices for domestic goods and, under a flexible exchange rate system, by also experiencing higher prices for imports.

Likelihood of the Convergence of Hours of Work and the Statutes Governing Them

Will nations need to harmonize their provisions regarding sick leave, maternity leave, personal leave, and holiday and vacation leave to facilitate economic integration and to avoid "social dumping," or the movement of jobs to countries with low benefit levels? Some people argue yes. However, in most EC nations sick leave, maternity leave, and family leave are financed by payroll taxes on employers and employees, and ... the burden of these taxes appears to fall primarily, though not entirely, on employees. That is, the increased worker protection that these types of leave appear to buy is at least partially paid for by workers in the form of lower wages. On balance, then, mandating more generous programs in nations that currently have less generous programs will lead to some, but not a proportionate, increase in labor costs in those nations.

The evidence on mandated benefits provided directly by employers, such as holiday and vacation pay, is less clear. No econometric study conclusively demonstrates that the costs of more generous holiday and vacation leaves are shifted onto workers in the form of lower wages. [Several studies suggest, however,] that workers pay for at least a good share of their benefits in the form of lower wages.

Insofar as this evidence is correct, to require a country to improve its leave policies as a precondition for increased economic integration is unlikely to greatly affect total labor cost per output in the country. Put another way, unless all elements of the compensation package, including wages, are subject to minimum standards, when such standards are imposed employers can adjust other elements of the compensation package to keep their total costs from rising very much. Attempts to harmonize standards will thus not totally prevent social dumping unless wage levels are included in the standards. Except for minimum wages, no one has seriously argued that wage levels in a nation should be part of the negotiations over increased economic integration. Hence harmonization of leave policies will probably not be a precondition for increased economic integration.

Will increased economic integration require, or cause, increased convergence in hours of work? Here again the answer is probably no. To the extent that individuals' preferences for income and leisure differ across nations, so will their hours of work. Increased competitive pressure will put pressure on employers to choose levels of hours that will maximize their profits. But if benefit structures and wage levels continue to vary across nations, so too, form employers' perspectives, will optimal hours. . . .

Employment Standards

Almost all nations establish employment standards, or minimal conditions under which they believe individuals should be employed. Examples are minimum wage and maximum hours laws, child labor and compulsory schooling laws, occupational safety and health laws, equal employment or antidiscrimination laws, and laws governing the conditions under which workers can be dismissed. . . .

Critics of free trade argue that it is both an immoral act and unfair competition for the United States to make a free trade agreement with a nation that has much lower employment standards than we do or fails to enforce its existing standards. In the debate that preceded the passage of NAFTA in 1993, some opponents argued that the treaty should not be signed unless side agreements were established to guarantee Mexico's adherence to its own standards in the areas of, among others, minimum wages, child labor law, and occupational safety and health. . . .

. . . I want to stress that employment standards usually impose costs on employers that they cannot fully shift onto employees. For example, a minimum wage law that sets the minimum wage at a level above that which would prevail in the absence of the law will raise the cost of low-skilled workers unless employers can compensatingly reduce employee benefit levels. Similarly, child labor laws, by restricting the supply of young low-skilled workers, will increase the wage levels employers must pay to employ low-skilled workers. Finally, if the value employees place on the improved occupational safety and health that result from occupational safety and health legislation is less than employers' costs of complying with the legislation, only part of the costs will be shifted onto employees in the form of lower wages, and employers' costs will again rise.

In each case, the impact of the employment standard on employers' costs will vary among employers. Minimum wage laws will increase costs the most for employers who have production processes that make the most use of low-skilled workers. Child labor laws will increase costs the most for the same group of employers. Occupational safety and health legislation will affect employers' costs the most when health and safety conditions are initially poor and major expenditures are required to comply with the legislation.

As regards minimum wage and child labor legislation, suppose that many developing nations, such as Mexico, have a comparative advantage (relative to the United States) in producing goods that use low-skilled, labor-intensive production processes, U.S. employers of low-skilled labor will be placed at a competitive disadvantage if foreign producers are not subject to similar standards.

Following the logic used [earlier], where the effect of a payroll tax with a relatively low taxable wage base was discussed, the comparative advantage of foreign producers of goods that are made using low-skilled, labor-intensive production methods will be decreased and fewer of these goods imported when foreign low-skilled workers are covered by such standards, as compared with when they are not. Put another way, the demand for U.S. low-skilled workers will be higher when foreign low-skilled workers are subject to such standards.

Not surprisingly, then, employers who make heavy use of low-skilled labor and the unions representing these workers are often among the chief opponents of free trade agreements, such as NAFTA. They are also likely to be among the chief proponents of requiring potential trading partners to adopt similar standards as ours and of requiring foreign nations to ensure compliance with their own standards.

Notes and Questions

1. *Viva las differences.* Richard Freeman, in an afterword to the Ehrenberg book, agrees with its basic theme, "that economic integration will not force all developed countries to harmonize labor practices and standards." As Freeman summarizes the evidence:

> Some differences in labor practices and standards have no effect on labor costs. Some costly differences are shifted back to workers. Other costly differences are shifted to the entire population through currency devaluation. Economic integration will not turn us all into clones of the least common denominator country. *Viva las* differences.

Id. at 110. See also Richard B. Freeman, "Are Your Wages Set in Beijing?," 9 *Journal of Economic Perspectives* 15 (Summer 1995).

2. *Harmonization and Outliers.* As Professor Stone recounts in the reading, the United Kingdom refused to go along with EC agreements to provide uniform social and labor standards throughout the Community. With a powerful partner not bound by sometimes costly standards, other countries fear that U.K. businesses will gain at their expense. With the election of the Labour government headed by Tony Blair, however, the U.K. will be subscribing to the EC's Social Charter.

3. *Devaluation Checks and the Euro.* Ehrenberg explains how flexible currencies reduce but do not eliminate the competitive harms that can arise when a country enacts expensive labor standards. For example, to the extent a French standard makes French firms less competitive than German firms, the franc can devalue relative to the mark, alleviating the competitive imbalance. This compensating mechanism will end as the EU (sans the U.K.) turns to a common currency, the euro.

The Fair Trade–Free Trade Debate: Trade, Labor, and the Environment*
ROBERT HOWSE and MICHAEL J. TREBILCOCK

Most free traders see recent demands that trade be linked to compliance with environmental and labor standards as motivated by the desire to protect jobs at home against increased competition from the Third World and view many fair traders as charlatans (protectionists masquerading as moralists). Where the demands of fair traders cannot so easily be reduced to protectionist pretexts, free traders are inclined to portray the advocates of linkage as irrational moral fanatics, prepared to sacrifice global economic welfare and the pressing needs of the developing countries for trivial, elusive, or purely sentimental goals. . . .

This article [rejects] the idea of a blanket prohibition of trade sanctions to affect other countries' policies and advocates a more subtle legal and institutional approach to the relationship between trade, environment, and labor rights. We propose a normative framework for disaggregating and evaluating "fair trade" claims relating to labor and environmental standards. In particular, we draw a critical distinction between claims that trade measures should be used to attain a specific non-trade goal or vindicate a specific non-trade value, and arguments for a "level" competitive playing field, evening the odds, or establishing "fair" rules of the game that are internal to the trading system.

The non-trade-related rationales for environment and labor sanctions. An initial issue is whether the ultimate goals of such sanctions can be justified. Here it is useful to identify the main reasons why concerns about environmental and labor laws and practices may legitimately extend beyond national borders.

[The authors first identify as goals externalities, the global environmental commons, and shared natural resources, which apply more to environmental than to labor issues.]

Human Rights. Human rights are frequently and increasingly regarded as inalienable rights that belong to individuals regardless of their national affiliation, simply by virtue of being human. Such an understanding of rights is implicit in the Kantian understanding of human

* 16 *International Review of Law and Economics* 61 (1996).

autonomy that has profoundly influenced contemporary liberal theory. Certain labor rights or standards have come to be widely regarded as basic human rights with a universal character. These include: the right to collective bargaining and freedom of association; the right not to be enslaved; the abolition of child labor; and equality of opportunity in employment for men and women. These rights are reflected in the Conventions of the International Labor Organization (ILO). Some of the Conventions have been ratified by a large number of countries; others by far fewer countries....

International Political and Economic Spillovers. Some human rights abuses and some labor practices, particularly violent suppression of workers' rights to organize or associate, may lead to the kind of acute social conflict that gives rise to general political and economic instability. Such instability may spill over national boundaries and affect global security. Increasingly (as the cases of the former Yugoslavia, Rwanda, and Somalia illustrate), "internal" conflicts are capable of raising regional or global security, economic, or social (e.g., immigration and refugee) issues.

Altruistic or Paternalistic Concerns. Even if they are not directly affected in any of the ways described above, ... citizens of one country may believe that workers in another country would be better off if protected by higher labor standards. Such a belief may or may not be warranted. For instance, higher minimum wages or other improvements in standards that raise labor costs, may in some circumstances do more harm than good, if the result is a significant increase in unemployment. Proponents of external intervention make the strong assumption that citizens in one country are better able to make these welfare judgments than governments in another country, which seems unlikely to be systematically true, even where the government in the latter country is not democratically elected or accountable. However, the provision of foreign aid, often with major conditions attached as to recipients' domestic policies, by international agencies such as the World Bank and the International Monetary Fund (IMF) suggests that a welfare presumption against paternalism is not irrebuttable.

The nature of the above concerns differs in important respects. In the case of externalities, the global environmental commons, and shared natural resources, the main normative basis may sound in an argument about economic welfare, primarily the welfare of citizens in the state seeking to invoke trade sanctions but perhaps indirectly also global welfare. In other cases, the most obvious and compelling normative basis for insisting on compliance with minimum standards may have little relation to economic welfare; this is particularly true in the case of universal human rights, including labor rights, where the case for universal recognition of such rights is often premised on a deontological conception of human freedom and equality. Alternatively, in welfare terms, one can conceptualize such rights as involving interdependent utility functions between citizens of different states....

Scenario 1: trade sanctions or the threat of sanctions succeed in inducing higher environmental or labor standards....

Welfare Effects in Targeted Country. With respect to the *domestic welfare of the country or countries that change policies,* if the status quo prior to the alteration of the policies is welfare maximizing (either in the Pareto or Kaldor–Hicks sense), then conforming to higher standards will reduce domestic welfare....

With respect to labor rights abuses, some of the practices that have been singled out as justifying trade sanctions—slave labor camps in China, for instance—would be difficult to characterize as the product of political or regulatory processes likely to maximize welfare based on the revealed preferences of individuals. Since the countries concerned are not genuine democracies, the domestic political process is simply not designed to take into account the preferences of all citizens....

In general, the domestic welfare gains from improved labor standards are most likely to exist where, in the first place, there is a strong case for regulation to correct specific instances of market failure (e.g., information asymmetries in the case of occupational health and safety, or where markets fail more radically due, for instance, to the presence of coercion [slave labor, child labor, the use of violence to intimidate workers, etc].

Global Welfare Effects.... With respect to labor rights or standards, international minimum standards may address in some measure a fundamental distortion in the global labor market, i.e., restrictive immigration policies that prevent people from moving to locations where their labor is more highly valued. Without the threat of exit and often without effective voice in their home countries, they may be vulnerable to oppressive domestic labor policies or practices. There may be possible longer-term impacts of the reduction in oppressive labor practices that would have positive impacts on global welfare—such as accelerated political liberalization as workers becomes less intimidated, better organized, and generally more capable of asserting their rights.

Welfare Effects in Sanction–Imposing Country. Depending on elasticities of supply and demand, where foreign producers are faced with higher costs due to higher environmental or labor standards, they may be able to pass on some of these costs to consumers in the country that imposed the trade sanctions. However, it may be the case that compliance with minimum environmental or labor standards will not result in significantly higher prices to consumers, where some producers in the targeted country are *already* meeting minimum standards.... [M]aking the conventional economic assumption that supply curves are never infinitely elastic, some adverse price effects on consumers in the sanction-imposing country seem likely, although in many cases these seem likely to be small. . . .

An issue closely related to the effectiveness of economic sanctions is the relative desirability of sanctions as opposed to other instruments for influencing the behavior of other countries and their producers. For instance, the GATT Secretariat has advocated the use of financial inducements as an alternative means to sanctions for influencing countries to adopt higher environmental standards. This proposal has the virtue of attaching a price to the invocation of such sanctions and thus providing some assurance that these higher standards are truly valued for their own sake in the country desiring the changes, especially in cases of ostensible *ad hoc* paternalism or altruism, whereas trade sanctions, lacking such an explicit price (beyond price effects on consumers), may be easily subverted by protectionists. [On the other hand,] subsidies, as opposed to sanctions, create a perverse incentive for foreign countries to engage in, or intensify, the offensive behavior (or make credible threats to this effect) in order to maximize the payments being offered. Moreover, . . . a principle that victims (or their supporters) should always pay ("bribe") violators to achieve compliance would seem impossible to defend either ethically or politically. However, in some cases financial assistance to enable poor Third World countries to meet higher environmental or labor standards may be warranted on distributive justice grounds.

Another alternative to trade restrictions is environmental and labor rights labeling, which allows individuals as consumers to express their moral preferences for environmental or labor rights protection. Products that are produced in a manner that meets a given set of labor or environmental standards would be entitled to bear a distinctive logo or statement that informs consumers of this fact. Although labeling may enable individual consumers to avoid the moral "taint" of consuming the product in question themselves, if most consumers have a preference for terminating production altogether (rather than merely reducing consumption and production) by changing a foreign country's domestic policies, then a collective action problem arises as in any approach to influencing behavior that depends upon coordinating action among large numbers of agents. Unless she can be sure that most other consumers will do likewise, the individual consumer may well not consider it rational to avoid buying the product in question.

In sum, neither financial inducements nor labeling programs are self-evidently superior policy instruments to sanctions for influencing other countries' environmental and labor practices. Each has its own drawbacks.

The "Systemic" Threat to a Liberal Trading Order

Even in the presence of indeterminate welfare effects many free traders may still reject environmental or labor rights-based trade measures on the basis that such measures, if widely permitted or entertained, would significantly erode the coherence and sustainability of rule-based liberal trade.... [T]he legal order of international trade is best understood as a set of rules and norms aimed at sustaining a long-term cooperative equilibrium in the face of ongoing pressures to cheat on this equilibrium, given that the short-term political payoffs from cheating may be quite high.... In the absence of a lack of fundamental normative consensus as to what constitutes "cheating" on the one hand, and the punishment of others' cheating on the other, confidence in the rules themselves could be fundamentally undermined, and the system destabilized.

In considering the systemic threat from environmental and labor rights-related trade measures, it is important to distinguish between purely unilateral measures and those that have a multilateral dimension. The former measures are based upon an environmental or labor rights concern or norm that is specific to the sanctioning country or countries. Here, there is a real risk of dissolving a clear distinction between protectionist "cheating" and genuine sanctions to further non-trade values—the sanctioning country may well be able to define or redefine its environmental or labor rights causes so as to serve protectionist interests. Measures with a multilateral dimension, by contrast, will be based upon the targeted country's violation of some multilateral or internationally recognized norm, principle, or agreement—for instance, a provision in ... one of the ILO Labor Conventions. These norms, principles, or agreements are typically not the product of protectionist forces in particular countries, nor are they easily captured by such forces....

Competitiveness-Based Arguments for Environmental or Labor–Rights–Based Trade Measures

Unlike the arguments for trade restrictions on environmental and labor rights grounds that we have been discussing up to this point, which have a normative reference point external to the trading system itself, competitiveness-based "fair-trade" claims focus largely on the effects on domestic producers and workers of other countries' environmental and labor policies, and not per se on the effects of those policies on the environment and on workers elsewhere. Competitiveness claims are, in principle, indifferent to the improvement of environmental or labor practices in other countries. Hence, in the case of competitiveness claims, trade measures that protect the domestic market or "equalize" comparative advantage related to environmental or labor standards are a completely acceptable substitute for other countries raising their standards. Competitiveness claims usually refer to one of two kinds of supposed unfairness (and, it is often argued as well, welfare losses) that stem from trade competition with countries that have lower environmental or labor standards:

1. It is unfair (and/or inefficient) that our own firms and workers would bear the "costs" of higher environmental or labor standards through loss of market share to foreign producers who have lower costs due to laxer environmental or labor standards in their own country.

2. It is unfair that downward pressure should be placed on our environmental or labor standards by virtue of the impact of trade competition with countries with lower standards.

Competitive Fairness Claim 1

The first kind of claim is, in our view, largely incoherent and in fact in tension with the basic theory of comparative advantage in trade. Assuming there is nothing wrongful with another country's environmental or labor policies along the lines discussed in the first part of this paper, then why should a cost advantage attributable to these divergent policies not be treated like any other costs advantage, i.e., as part and parcel of comparative advantage? . . .

Precisely because the implicit benchmark of fairness is so illusory—i.e., a world where governmentally imposed labor and environmental protection costs are completely equalized among producers of like products in all countries—trade measures based upon this kind of fairness claim are likely to be highly manipulable by protectionist interests. Since, of course, protectionists are really interested in obtaining trade protection, not in promoting environmental standards or labor rights, the fact that the competitive fairness claim in question does not generate a viable and principled benchmark for alteration of other countries' policies is a strength not a weakness—for it virtually guarantees that justifications for protection will always be available, even if the targeted country improves its environmental or labor standards.

Welfare Effects of Trade Restrictions Aimed at Equalizing Comparative Advantage

Trade restrictions will lead to reduced exports, with consequent welfare losses to firms and workers in the targeted country. . . . Firms and workers engaged in the manufacture of like products to those imports targeted by trade restrictions will benefit where the restrictions in question make imports relatively more expensive than domestic substitutes, thereby shifting demand from imports to domestic production. Consumers will pay more . . . as domestic producers will price up to the duty imposed by the trade restriction. Here, the welfare effects essentially resemble those from the imposition of a tariff or countervailing duty. Inasmuch as production is shifted from lower to higher cost producers, there is also some loss of global allocative efficiency.

Clearly, overall, these welfare effects entail a shift in wealth to firms and workers in the trade-restricting country from firms and workers in the targeted country as well as from consumers in the trade-restricting country. In our view, it is difficult to construct a theory of distributive justice to support the fairness of these transfers. . . .

What seems completely unsustainable on grounds of distributive justice is the shift of the costs of higher environmental or labor standards in the trade restricting country from workers and firms in that country to workers and firms in other countries. If, as fair traders vociferously argue, it is unfair to make workers and firms in one's own country pay for the competitive consequences of higher environmental and labor standards in that country, how could it possibly be fair to make workers and firms in another country pay this price? Indeed, shifting the competitiveness costs of one's own environmental or labor standards to workers in other countries seems distributively perverse. No matter how high an intrinsic or instrumentalist value we may wish to put on high environmental or labor standards in our own country, there is simply an unsupportable leap of logic in the conclusion that someone else should be paying the price for them. First of all, workers in other countries do not even usually directly benefit from these higher standards, whereas workers in one's own country do. Second, most competitiveness-based fair trade claims are targeted against countries that are poorer than the trade-restricting country, often with lower per capita incomes, higher levels of unemployment, and weaker social welfare nets (in some instances, the revenue from trading products may be essential to obtaining foreign exchange to buy essential goods such as medicines and foods).

Competitive Fairness Claim 2

This fairness claim does appear to be based in some concern for environmental and labor rights *per se*, albeit not at the international level but within one's own country. Whereas competitiveness claim 1 presumes that governments will not respond to the competitive implications of higher labor and environmental standards, and simply let firms and workers lose out, the second competitive fairness claim assumes just the opposite—that governments will respond by lowering domestic standards below the optimal level.

We do not believe that, generally speaking, lowering environmental or labor standards is an appropriate response to competitive pressures. There is, in fact, a wide range of alternatives—such as better regulation which reduces compliance costs without lowering standards, investment in training, etc. to increase the productivity of labor. . . .

A variation of the claim about the effect of competitiveness pressures on domestic environmental and labor standards suggests the possibility of a form of beggar-thy-neighbor behavior that may, admittedly, leave all countries worse off. This is the "race to the bottom," whereby countries competitively lower their environmental or labor standards, in an effort to capture a relatively greater share of a fixed volume of trade or investment. Much like the beggar-thy-neighbor subsidies wars that characterized agricultural trade among Canada, the United States, and the European Union and other countries during the 1980s, it is not difficult, using the model of a Prisoner's Dilemma game, to show that competitive reduction in environmental or labor standards will typically result in a negative sum outcome, as long as one assumes that before entering the race, each country's environmental or labor standards represent an optimal domestic policy outcome for that country.

The "race to the bottom" claim has a different normative basis from the other competitiveness-based claims discussed above. Those claims relate to the proper distribution of the competitiveness costs of maintaining higher environmental and labor standards than one's trading partners. The normative basis for concern over the race to the bottom, by contrast, sounds in the language of Pareto efficiency: the race ends, literally, at the bottom, with each country adopting suboptimal domestic policies, but no country in the end capturing a larger share of the gains from trade.

Frequently, beggar-thy-neighbor regulatory competition is able to flourish much more easily where it is possible to reduce on a selective basis labor or environmental standards to attract a particular investment or support a particular industry or firm. It is more difficult and more costly to engage in these activities where the formal statutory framework of labor or environmental regulation must be altered across the board. Here, some of the provisions in the NAFTA Environmental and Labor Side Agreements may create disincentives to beggar-thy-neighbor competition in as much as these agreements oblige the signatories to enforce effectively those environmental and labor rights laws that are formally on the books. At the same time, it must be acknowledged that effectively monitoring whether a country is fully enforcing its own laws is not an easy task, especially for outsiders.

Finally, it is possible simply to ban by international agreement beggar-thy-neighbor competition. This is, for instance, what Article 1114 of the NAFTA attempts to do, albeit in rather weak legal language, with respect to environmental measures, *inter alia*. Article 1114(2) states, in part, that "The Parties recognize that it is inappropriate to encourage investment by relaxing domestic health, safety, and/or environmental measures. Accordingly, a Party should not waive or otherwise derogate from, or offer to waive or otherwise derogate from, such measures as an encouragement for the establishment, acquisition, expansion, or retention in its territory of an investor."

Accepting, however, that cooperation is the ultimate solution to the "race to the bottom," a further difficult question remains as to the appropriateness of trade restrictions as a sanction to induce a cooperative outcome.

Conclusion

Once carefully disaggregated and scrutinized, "fair trade" claims related to environmental and labor standards are not necessarily groundless, nor self-serving of protectionist interests, nor as threatening to the liberal world trading order as free traders often make out. A concern to protect the rules-based liberal trading order from a loss of coherence and integrity, and a corresponding risk of a new protectionist spiral, has led free-trade oriented economists, policy experts, and lawyers to criticize and often reject wholesale trade measures related to labor and environmental standards, even where there is little persuasive evidence that such measures are welfare reducing or are motivated only by protectionist interests. However, a potentially serious threat to a liberal international trading order is posed by competitiveness-based or level playing field forms of fair trade claims, which we almost entirely dismiss as normatively incoherent and as mostly thinly disguised forms of protectionism. The institutional challenge thus posed is designing trade law regimes (both international and domestic) with the capacity to distinguish credibly between these two classes of claims. We have argued in this paper that this enterprise will entail minimizing to the greatest extent possible the scope for unilateral assertions of fair trade claims and maximizing to the greatest extent possible the role of international treaties, agreements, and norms as the basis of such claims. Free traders, by indiscriminately dismissing all fair trade claims and eliding these two classes of claims, run the risk of being discredited as moral philistines and thus being marginalized in political debates that do indeed carry serious risks for a liberal international trading order.

Notes and Questions

1. *Separating Good from Bad Trade Sanctions.* Howse and Trebilcock approve of some trade sanctions to support labor standards, while generally criticizing most complaints that competition from developing countries with low labor standards unfairly constrains domestic workers. Can the two be distinguished in practice? Should the United States, for example, impose sanctions on countries that allow workers (children?) to work at extremely low wages? Does this depend on whether the reason for those low wages is lack of worker productivity, on the one hand, or the discouragement of collective bargaining, on the other?

2. *The Politics of Multilateral Agreements.* In the principal reading, Howse and Trebilcock assume that labor standards promulgated by multilateral organizations will not suffer from the protectionism or cultural imperialism of unilateral efforts by nation-states. Does this not depend on the nature of the political process that generates multilateral standards? Even multilateral organizations can be dominated by special interest groups, whether of the

economic or ideological variety. If so, there is little reason to believe that a multilateral standard on, say, child labor will have taken account of all relevant interests and approximates the social optimum.

3. *NAFTA Labor Side Agreement.* In the 1993 NAFTA Treaty, Canada, the United States, and Mexico created a free-trade zone with minimal trade restrictions. Many persons opposed the treaty for fear that the lack of environmental protection and low labor standards in Mexico would put U.S. firms at a disadvantage. To allay this concern, the final treaty included two side agreements, one on the environment and one on labor called the North American Agreement on Labor Cooperation (NAALC). Under NAALC, each country agreed to "improve working conditions and living standards in each Party's territory"; and to "promote to the maximum extent possible," basic enumerated labor principles such as the right to organize and strike. NAALC created a submission process to achieve these objectives. Each country has a National Administrative Office (NAO); any person or organization can submit a complaint to one country's NAO, asking it to investigate labor matters in another country. The NAO issues a report, which can include a recommendation that the labor minsiters of the two countries consult each other about the matter. The overall point of the process is to create greater transparency and political pressure for the signatory states to enforce their own labor standards. See Lance Compa, "NAFTA's Labor's Side Accord: A Three Year Accounting," 3 NAFTA Law Review 6 (1997).

Professor Clyde Summers has argued that the NAALC "totally fails to enforce the standards set forth in the Labor Principles." Clyde Summers, "NAFTA's Labor Side Agreements and International Labor Standards," 3 Small and Emerging Business Law 173, 178 (1999). He points out that the Agreement creates no private rights or duties, and only obliges governments to enforce their own domestic laws. Summers recognizes, however, that the Agreement may make intangible contributions toward improved labor conditions, in that "the very articulation of the Labor Principles in a formal Agreement gives these labor standards a definiteness and salience with a moral claim to be observed." Id. at 187.

10

Reforming Unions and Labor Law

Reform of U.S. labor law is not a likely prospect on the immediate political horizon. The Clinton administration's labor and commerce secretaries appointed a special Commission on the Future of Worker–Management Relations in 1993 in an effort to create public support for some changes in U.S. institutional arrangements. The Commission, chaired by John T. Dunlop, formerly Secretary of Labor in the Ford administration, issued its report and recommendations in December 1994—a particularly unpropitious moment, after elections resulting in Republican party majorities in both houses of Congress. The Dunlop Commission's report sparked a good deal of controversy, but few legislative initiatives. A Republican-led effort to relax § 8(a)(2) restrictions on workplace committees was vetoed by President Clinton in July 1996.

For instructive examples of the growing labor reform literature, see the special symposium issues of volume 69, no. 1 of the *Chicago-Kent Law Review*, reprinted in Matthew Finkin, ed., *The Legal Future of Employee Representation* (Ithaca, N.Y.: ILR Press, 1994), and volume 17, no. 1 of the *Journal of Labor Research*; and the papers presented at a joint conference of the AFL–CIO and Cornell's School of Industrial and Labor Relations, published as Sheldon Friedman, Richard W. Hurd, Rudolph A. Oswald and Ronald L. Seeber, eds., *Restoring the Promise of American Labor Law* (Ithaca, N.Y.: ILR Press, 1994).

Whatever its political prospects, U.S. labor law reform occupies a central place in the agenda of research and policy analysis for students of the American system, given the diminished presence of unions in private firms, the growth in employment discrimination and employment law litigation, and the challenge of global product markets. This and the next chapter offer some exploratory essays suggesting possible paths for change.

This chapter focuses on changes in the U.S. system of collective representation of employee interests. Section A begins with Professor Finkin's proposal for requiring firms to bargain with nonmajority unions at least until a majority representative is formed. Section B presents articles exploring the transplantability of German-style works councils to the United States. In Section C, Professor Estreicher presents his ideas on introducing greater choice among representation options available to U.S. workers. This section also revisits the issue of what the optimal labor market adjustment policy is for a world of competitive product markets.

A. Nonmajority Unionism

"The Road Not Taken: Some Thoughts on Nonmajority Employee Representation"*

MATTHEW W. FINKIN

... What follows will examine whether the road not taken in 1935 is worth exploring in the search for an alternative to the current system: Whether it would make sense today, with the hindsight of the Labor Act's experience, to think about extending bargaining rights on a "members only" basis.

The benefits of such an extension were dealt with in a comprehensive (and prescient) study by George Schatzki in 1975 and need only be briefly rehearsed. All the regulation and delay attendant to unit determinations, election campaigns, and elections themselves would be eliminated (as well as the whole body of law surrounding successorship). Inasmuch as the employer would be required to bargain with any organization on behalf of its members, all the organization need supply to establish a bargaining relationship is a membership list. (Such, in fact, was part of the 1934 Automobile Settlement.) ...

The ability of a "members only" representative more sharply to focus shared concerns would be offset by a lessened ability to command a broader front in dealing with the employer. But a similar caution has been made with respect to bargaining unit determinations under the existing Act, and that has not deterred the Board from finding units of relatively narrow congruent interests to be appropriate—for example, just the food service workers in a single outlet of a large retail chain like F.W. Woolworth [144 N.L.R.B. 307 (1963)]. . . .

The more difficult or, at least, perplexing problem is the prospect of a proliferation of organizations each demanding to bargain for its members over the same subjects and to which the employer would owe an equal duty to bargain in good faith. The difficulty will be discussed presently. But the perplexity derives from the Act's misleading vocabulary and from the want of any statutory guidance on the question of bargaining structure.

The Act speaks in terms of exclusive representation of "an appropriate bargaining unit"—the group of jobs the union represents. But, what the Board in reality is determining is an appropriate election unit for the designation of a bargaining agent, which may or may not coincide with the group of jobs actually represented at the bargaining table. From this

---

* 69 *Chicago-Kent Law Review* 195 (1993).

perspective, the function of the "community of interests" test the Board applies to decide unit questions is only partly a concern for management's ease of bargaining and more importantly one of assuring sufficient homogeneity of employee interests for the purpose of selecting an exclusive representative and minimizing the number of conflicting interests the representative might be called upon to reconcile.

In the case of the Woolworth outlet adverted to earlier, the union sought a unit of only the food service workers, and the employer insisted that only a unit of all the store's employees would be appropriate. Accordingly, the Board attended to differences in work, supervision, and working conditions as well as to similarities in wages, benefits, and personnel policies to decide whether or not the unit petitioned for represented a true community of interests. But at no point does either the Board majority or the dissenting Board members advert to how an enormous national retail chain, with over a thousand outlets, is to bargain effectively over wages, medical insurance, pension benefits, and seniority (including transfer and "bumping" rights) with either a representative of the employees of just a single store or of only that single store's food service workers; nor does the Board contemplate the company's situation were it required to bargain with representatives of potentially thousands of such units.

The Board's silence is not surprising for it mirrors the statute's silence on this point. The duty to bargain under the Act requires the employer to send a representative to the bargaining table with power to make an agreement; thus, the selection of a union by the single outlet's food service workers compels the employer to bargain on company-wide policies such as wages, hours, and benefits. But the Act is silent about, is unconcerned with, how the employer is to do that. Consequently, the practical difficulty for "members only" representation flows from the Act's lack of concern with bargaining structure.

Under the current state of the law, a union may attempt to rationalize the structure of bargaining for the various units it represents. If it is selected at food service counters elsewhere in the company, it may propose to bargain for them all as a single unit; but it may not insist upon that demand for such an alteration in "the bargaining unit" is only a permissive bargaining subject. If the company agrees, however, the union may negotiate a single company-wide contract even though it was elected counter by counter, store by store. In that case, the actual "bargaining unit" will transcend the election districts from which the union derived its bargaining rights. Further, a group of unions representing different groups of the employer's employees may form a coalition and bargain jointly with the employer; but they may not insist that the employer bargain on that basis for that too would alter "the bargaining unit" which the Board determined to be appropriate. For the same reason, neither may the employer insist upon joint bargaining. In the Woolworth example, the employer could not insist upon meeting

jointly with the separate representatives of the food service workers and
store clerks to negotiate a common issue such as seniority in consequence of employee interchange. Nor may either party condition agreement in one unit upon the satisfactory conclusion of negotiations for
another unit. Thus the prospect of a variety of organizations—some
affiliated with national labor organizations, some entirely indigenous—
each representing its own members, each desiring to bargain about
employer policies that may affect them in common, each owed a duty to
bargain in good faith by the employer has the potential of exacerbating
the difficulties an employer would face under the current state of the
law, where it might be required to bargain with a variety of unions, each
the exclusive representative of one or more of a number of bargaining
units....

   If one were to fashion a statute that accepted the principle of
majority rule but required that units be configured to relatively narrow
sets of congruent interests, an analogous problem of a potential proliferation of bargaining obligations would be presented. Such a statute was
drafted to deal with a rather more rarefied question in public sector
collective bargaining; but the approach it took would seem to be applicable to the possible proliferation of bargaining obligations under a system
of "members only" representation. Assuming that section 9(a) were
amended so to require, section 8(a)(5) could be amended as follows:

   It shall be an unfair labor practice for an employer—

* * *

   (5) to refuse to bargain collectively with a representative of his
   employees; but it shall not be an unfair labor practice—

> (a) for two or more labor organizations to demand joint bar-
> gaining with an employer with respect to matters which have
> customarily been provided on a uniform basis among the em-
> ployees represented by such organizations; or,

> (b) for an employer (i) to demand joint bargaining by two or
> more organizations with respect to matters which have custom-
> arily been provided on a uniform basis among the employees
> represented by such labor organizations, or (ii) if joint bargain-
> ing is not agreed to by those organizations or no agreement is
> reached acceptable to all parties, to conclude an agreement as to
> such matter with the organization or organizations which repre-
> sent the largest number of employees and to refuse to bargain
> further with any other organizations as to such matters unless
> that other organization agrees to accept the terms so negotiated.

   These provisions give the employee representatives and the employer the power directly to confront and to rationalize the bargaining
structure. Subparagraph (a) makes joint bargaining a mandatory bargaining subject. Inasmuch as the statutory concern is for the employer's

ability to bargain, the employer need not be required to bargain with a coalition; but where the employee representatives fear an effort to play one off against another, it permits the different organizations to require the employer directly to confront the issue. Subparagraph (b) is concerned with the reverse situation, where the employer sees the need to rationalize its bargaining structure and the representatives prove resistant. Accordingly, the proposed provision gives the employer the power to impose a coalition in the face of such recalcitrance. But both are limited to issues that have customarily been settled on a uniform basis, to preserve separate negotiations on matters of particular interest to the organization that raise no issue of common concern. . . .

The proposal has its most obvious application where the several organizations represent members in work groups who conceive of themselves as uniquely situated or as having special concerns—those who might be subsumed in a more heterogeneous bargaining unit determined to be appropriate by the Labor Board. But even if one were to speculate that employees doing otherwise the same work for the same pay and under the same supervision might choose different organizations to represent them, such would seem possible because these organizations successfully appeal to different workplace concerns. It would be possible, arguably, for employees to segregate themselves into organizations emphasizing divergent interests, for example, of health insurance and pensions for the older, of job training and retraining for the younger, of flextime and child care, especially for female employees with young children, and of safety in certain hazardous jobs. Even in such a speculative situation, a coalition-forcing provision would compel these groups to make compromises with one another in order to achieve an overall package on matters of common policy. . . .

Thus far this excursion has assumed for simplicity's sake that whatever pluralism emerges in employee representation at the plant or office would occur more or less simultaneously. But the duty to bargain might arise sequentially. . . . [A]ssume that after negotiations have been concluded with organization A, binding only on its members, organization B is formed and insists upon different terms. Because B could not have been subject to an employer demand for joint bargaining, the Company could not refuse to bargain with it. But the Company could insist upon the terms agreed with organization A. Were it to agree to better terms with B, it would in effect be deciding which is to be the dominant organization. To be sure, A's "no strike" obligation would bind only its members. Consequently, in this sequential bargaining scenario B would be free to strike were the Company to insist on the pattern made with A. But in simultaneous bargaining, a nondominant organization would be equally free to strike in an effort to secure better terms than those agreed upon with the dominant organization or coalition. In other words, the "sequential bargaining" scenario does not differ greatly from the situation an employer faces under the current state of the law when it bargains with a number of organizations who differ among themselves as to which will be the pattern setter.

Notes and Questions

1. *Economic Pressure to Obtain Representation by a Minority Union.* Professor Finkin's proposal would require statutory change. Employers may currently bargain with unions on a members-only basis, even though the union does not constitute a majority of an appropriate bargaining unit. But the employer is not required to do so, and it is doubtful that workers engage in protected concerted activity when they picket or strike to compel such recognition. For the view that individual employees have Section 7 rights under existing law to insist, even to the point of striking, on members-only representation by a minority union, see Clyde W. Summers, "Unions Without Majority—A Black Hole?," 66 *Chicago-Kent Law Review* 531 (1990); Alan Hyde, Frank Sheed, and Mary Deery Uva, "After Smyrna: Rights and Powers of Unions That Represent Less Than a Majority," 45 *Rutgers Law Review* 637 (1993).

2. *The Affirmative Case for Nonmajority Unionism.* Is members-only unionism preferable to exclusive representation because it reduces the agency costs of unionism by promoting greater homogeneity of interests among represented groups? If so, why (as Professor Finkin suggests elsewhere in his essay) should the plural-union structure give way once a union acquires majority support in a unit? Is the proposal better understood as providing a means of reducing organizing costs for unions seeking eventual exclusive status?

3. *Costs of Mandatory Bargaining with Nonmajority Unions.* Several costs can be identified:

    a. *Proliferation of Bargaining Obligations.* Finkin recognizes that one difficulty with his proposal is the costs to the firm of dealing with a proliferation of bargaining obligations in a particular plant. These costs are absent, or substantially reduced, in foreign labor systems where collective bargaining occurs, if at all, at the multienterprise level, and typically sets minimum terms of employment, as opposed to the U.S. system where unions are firm-based institutions typically seeking contracts setting forth comprehensive terms. See Samuel Estreicher, "Labor Law Reform in a World of Competitive Product Markets," 69 *Chicago-Kent Law Review* 33–34.

    b. *Employer Strategic Behavior.* Finkin addresses the proliferation objection by permitting employers to insist on joint bargaining among labor groups "with respect to matters which have customarily been provided on a uniform basis"; absent consent to such joint bargaining, employers could bargain with the organization that represents the largest number of employees and impose the agreement on other organizations. Would this solution raise the specter that, by picking and choosing among worker representatives, employers will be able to undermine the conditions for cohesive collective action by their employees? In Japan, where bargaining also occurs on a decentralized basis, the law does not require exclusive recognition, and indeed employers must bargain with any representative of two or more employees. The charge has been leveled that Japanese employers have been able effectively to tame militant unionism by extending favored treatment to "second unions." See Mashiko Aoki, *Information, Incentives, and Bargaining in the Japanese Economy* (New York: Cambridge University Press, 1988), 189; Andrew Gordon, "Japanese Labor Relations During the Twentieth Century," 11 *Journal of Labor Research* 239, 249–251 (1990).

c. *Employee Strategic Behavior*. Professor Gottesman voices the concern that mandatory bargaining with nonmajority unions will allow employees a one-way option to rescind a contract with their employer. For example, two 40 percent groups with separate contracts could join forces at any time, creating a majority, and apply for NLRB certification. Under the holding in *J.I. Case Co. v. NLRB*, 321 U.S. 332 (1994), once a group achieves majority status, any collective agreement overrides prior contracts. See Michael H. Gottesman, "In Despair, Starting Over: Imagining a Labor Law for Unorganized Workers," 69 *Chicago-Kent Law Review* 59, 88–90 (1993).

d. *Individual Rights*. Does members-only unionism pose a danger that the interests of minority groups in the workforce will not receive adequate representation? Even if these groups form their own organizations, under Finkin's proposal the numerically predominant union will effectively set the terms for all the others. See George Schatzki, "Majority Rule, Exclusive Representation, and the Interests of Individual Workers: Should Exclusivity Be Abolished?," 123 *University of Pennsylvania Law Review* 89 (1975).

e. *Union Myopia*. Under current law, a union represents only a subgroup of the workforce—say, production and maintenance workers—even though its bargaining policies may affect the entire workforce. The bargaining unit structure thus does not require the union to take full account of the interests of the affected workforce and the firm. Under Professor Finkin's proposal, units would be further subdivided, suggesting an even greater divergence than under current law between the interests of represented employees and the interests of the firm.

4. *The French Model*. The French labor relations system is based on plural unionism but with collective bargaining occurring at the supraenterprise, industrywide level among unions representing political coalitions with little interest in plant-level issues. Five union federations are deemed to be "representative" organizations. Despite plural union representation, only one collective agreement applies to any one enterprise. Unless the unions form coalitions to bargain in unison, the employer may be able to enter into an agreement with a relatively weak "representative" union and insist that this agreement is binding on all workers in the enterprise. Dissenting unions may, however, try to oppose implementation of the agreement at the enterprise level. See Michael Despax and Jacques Rojot, "France," in Roger Blanpain, ed., *International Encyclopaedia of Labour Law and Industrial Relations* (Deventer, Netherlands: Kluwer, 1987), vol. 5, 251; Jacques Freussomet, "France: Toward Flexibility" ("[T]he agreement is negotiated by all the representative unions but to be legally valid it only needs to be approved

by one of them."), in Joop Hartog and Jules Theeuwes, eds., *Labour Market Contracts and Institutions* (Amsterdam: North–Holland, 1993), 276.

Despite considerable legal support of the representative unions, total union membership is almost as low as the U.S. level (see Appendix E), and French unions have had difficulty establishing an effective presence at the firm level. See Francois Eyraud and Robert Tchobanian, "The Auroux Reforms and Company Level Industrial Relations in France," 23 *British Journal of Industrial Relations* 241 (1985); Mary Ann Glendon, "French Labor Law Reform 1982–1983: The Struggle for Collective Bargaining," 32 *American Journal of Comparative Law* 449 (1984). On the other hand, French workers may participate at the enterprise level through works councils, which are mandatory for enterprises employing more than fifty people. Only the official "representative" unions lawfully may nominate candidates on the first ballot; hence, representatives of these unions are likely to dominate these firm-based organizations.

5. *Employee Caucuses.* Professor Hyde urges facilitating changes in the law to protect the formation of informal protest groups or "caucuses" in the nonunion workplace. He gives the example of employees at a technology firm that used an internal electronic bulletin board to voice their objections to management's announced revision of its profit-sharing plan. Such groups (1) "arise in nonunion workplaces"; (2) "are not experienced by the participants as 'unions,' not even nonmajority unions"; (3) "raise both demands that unions might raise in unionized workplaces, and demands that unions rarely raise"; and (4) "limit themselves to employees of a particular employer." Alan Hyde, "Employee Caucus: A Key Institution in the Emerging System of Employment Law," 69 *Chicago-Kent Law Review* 149, 157–158 (1993).

B. Mandatory Employee Representation Committees

"An Economic Analysis of Works Councils"*
RICHARD B. FREEMAN and EDWARD P. LAZEAR

. . . Works Councils: Mandated or Voluntary?

Most Western European countries mandate elected works councils in enterprises above some size and give the councils rights to information and consultation about labor and personnel decisions. Germany gives councils co-determination over some decisions as well. In contrast to plant-level unions, councils cannot call strikes nor negotiate wages, though they invariably use their power to improve the position of workers within the firm. Their function, often specified in legislation, is to foster labor and management cooperation with the goal of increasing the size of the enterprise "pie." Most observers and participants believe that councils succeed in doing this. . . .

---

* In Joel Rogers and Wolfgang Streeck, eds., *Works Councils: Consultation, Representation, and Cooperation in Industrial Relations*, (Chicago: University of Chicago Press, 1995), ch. 2.

If works councils increase the joint surplus of the firm-worker relationship, why do countries mandate them instead of relying on firms to institute councils voluntarily?

Our answer is based on the proposition that institutions that give workers power in enterprises affect the distribution as well as amount of joint surplus. The greater the power of works councils, the greater will be workers' share of the economic rent. If councils increase the rent going to workers more than they increase total rent, firms will oppose them. It is better to have a quarter slice of a 12–inch pie than an eighth slice of a 16–inch pie. Formally, we show:

> Proposition 1. Employers will give worker institutions within the firm less power than is socially optimal and will fail to establish productivity-enhancing councils when there are high fixed costs to the councils. Analogously, workers will prefer more power than is socially optimal.

The argument is based on two relations. First, let χ denote the amount of power or discretion given to the works council. The rent of the organization, R, depends on χ. If workers are given no discretion, then $R = R_0$. With some worker discretion, decisions improve and R rises. If too much worker discretion is given, then rent falls because management does not have enough control over decisions. The detailed rationale behind these arguments is explored [elsewhere in] the paper; the result is an $R(\chi)$ function that has an inverted U-shape. This is shown in Figure [10–1].

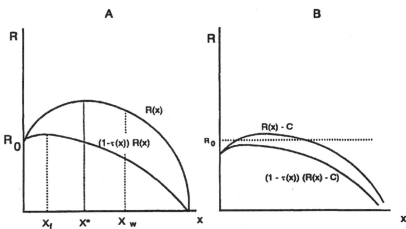

Figure 10–1. A, Firm establishes weak council; B, establishes no council.

Denote the share of total rent that goes to workers as τ. The share τ also depends on χ. It is a standard result of bargaining models (both Nash and Rubenstein) that the share rises with bargaining strength. Thus, $\tau(\chi)$ is monotonically increasing in x. To start, then,

(1a) $R = R(\chi)$,

(1b) $\tau = \tau(\chi)$.

Will the firm voluntarily establish councils with the socially optimal level of worker power? For a profit-seeking firm, analysis of optimizing behavior says "no." The firm will give less than χ^* power to the council, where χ^* is defined as the level of worker power that maximizes joint surplus. Formally, the profit-seeking firm will maximize

(2) $[1 - \tau(\chi)] \, R(\chi)$,

which has the first-order condition

$-\tau'(\chi)R(\chi) + [1 - \tau(\chi)] \, R'(\chi) = 0$,

so that

(3) $R' = \dfrac{\tau'(\chi)R(\chi)}{1 - \tau(\chi)}$

Since τ is increasing in χ, the right-hand side of equation (3) is positive, which implies that $R'' > 0$ at the firm's optimum point. The firm will choose a level of power for the council on the rising part of the rent-producing curve and will voluntarily give workers less power than 3^*. This is shown in Figure [10–1(A)], where χ_f, the optimum point on the firm's profit curve, lies to the left of the social optimum χ^*. Given fixed costs to works councils—time and preparation for elections, meetings, reduction in work activity by elected councillors, and so forth—the firm may lose money at χ_f, so that it will not establish councils at all, even though they raise the social product. This is shown by the curves $R - C$ and $(1 - \tau)(R - C)$ in Figure [10–1], which lie below the surplus in Figure [10–1] by the fixed amount C. In this case the rent to the firm from establishing the council that maximizes its profits, $[1 - \tau(\chi_f)][R(\chi_f) - C]$, is less than R_0, the profit from no works council. Note that a council is socially preferred because $R - C > R_0$ for some values of χ.

What about workers? if they could choose the amount of power for the works council, would they choose the socially optimal level? Workers who seek to maximize their share of the total surplus $(\tau(\chi)R(\chi))$ will, by symmetry with the analysis of the firm, fail to select the socially optimal point. Workers will choose a level of power that exceeds χ^*. They choose 3_w in Figure [10–1(A)], shortchanging the interests of capital.

The preceding analysis has implications for the existence and viability of works councils. It shows that management, on its own, will either fail to institute socially productive councils or give them less power than is socially desirable. If the government knew the R function, it could enact laws giving works councils χ^* power. Absent such knowledge, the fact that the optimum level of power lies between the preferred levels of labor and management suggests that some average of the two sides' desires will move toward the social optimum. Whether the political bargaining mechanism institutes rules that are superior to the outcome of industrial bargaining remains an open question.

Mandating councils does not, however, necessarily mean that they will be developed at particular workplaces. Even in Germany, many (small) companies do not have councils. The condition for a company to introduce a council is that either the workforce or the firm sees a potential benefit. If each believes that instituting a council will cost it more than the benefits accruing to it, neither will go to the effort of introducing the council. Thus, there will be no council when the sum of worker and firm costs exceeds the total surplus created. This shows that a council will only be established when the benefits from the council exceed its total costs.

If it were possible to decouple the factors that affect the division of the surplus from those that affect the surplus, there would be an obvious way to establish the optimum division of power: the state (or some other outside party) could determine a rent-sharing coefficient and then allow firms and workers to choose the power to be given the council. With the division of rents fixed, the division of power that maximizes total profits also maximizes the amount each side receives. Such a decoupling of production and distribution of surplus is, however, unlikely. In most bargaining models, the division of rent depends on threat or reservation points that would be affected by changes in the authority given to works councils. In practice, managers in the Freeman–Rogers interviews took it as fact that councils used their power strategically to gain greater surplus for workers.[5] Still, this "solution" suggests that councils fit better in labor relations systems where pay and other basic components of compensation are determined outside the enterprise (essentially bounding divisions of the rent) than in systems where firms set pay, and may help explain why councils are found largely in economies with relatively centralized collective bargaining.

Figure [10–1] can also be used to show why unions may oppose works councils. Reinterpret "joint surplus" to be the surplus that goes to workers, councillors, and union leaders, and think of as the share of rent that goes to the works council and workers and $1-\tau$ as the share that goes to union leaders. Then, assuming the function that relates this joint surplus to χ is also an inverted U, the result in equation (3) applies. Union leaders would choose a level of power for works councils that falls short of that maximizing overall labor surplus. Giving the council more power would benefit labor but would reduce the well-being of union leaders. This resonates with the fear German unionists had when they first opposed strong works councils, and with American unionists' worry that councils may substitute for unions. . . .

The possibility that councils benefit workers but not unions means that one cannot take unions as speaking for "labor" on this issue. . . .

---

5. In Germany, respondents gave cases in which councils would trade off their legal right to codetermine the timing of vacations or the need for them to gain the right to approve a social plan for redundancies for wages or benefits beyond those in the industry agreement.

"A Future Course for American Labor Law"*
PAUL C. WEILER

The Constitutive Model ...

... My own pessimistic judgment is that if we are ever to provide American workers meaningful involvement and influence in their workplaces, unmediated by the kind of hierarchical union organization that a good many workers would rather not have, it is necessary to take away from the employees (and also the employer) the choice about whether such a participatory mechanism will be present.

That is the thrust of the third strategy of labor law reform, the "constitutive" model.... Public policy would require not collective bargaining, secured with great difficulty, unit by unit, but a guarantee to all employees of easy access to a basic level of internal participation in a specified range of decision in all enterprises....

The specific model I have in mind is the West German *Betriebsrat*, or Works Council—an in-house procedure through which the employees at local work sites address and help resolve a range of employment issues. By all accounts, such mandatory Works Councils have played a valuable role in the evolution of West German human resource policy. So we can draw upon this quite successful experience for at least some of the ingredients of a proposal that must still be tailored to fit the current trends and needs in the American employment relationship.

Assume, then, that one favors a public policy that would require the adoption of what I shall call Employee Participation Committees (EPCs)....

Structure. In every workplace above a certain minimum size—perhaps twenty-five workers—the employees would elect at least one of their fellow employees as a representative to the EPC. As the size of the workplace grew larger, so also would the number of elected representatives (though not necessarily in proportion to the body of workers). Excluded from the employee constituency would be only the senior executive team and those working in the human resource and industrial relations departments. All other employees—ordinary workers in the plant and office, supervisors, professionals, lower-echelon managers—would be eligible to vote and to run for office as a representative....

Responsibilities. The primary responsibility of this committee structure would be to address and react to the broad spectrum of resource policies of the firm. The employer would be required to inform and consult with the EPC about changes in its criteria for wages, benefits, hiring, training and work assignments; about policies and grievances regarding dismissal, discipline, promotion, demotion, and layoff; regard-

---

* In *Governing the Workplace: The Future of Labor and Employment Law* (Cambridge, Mass.: Harvard University Press, 1990), ch. 6.

ing manpower adjustments to plant closings, relocations, technological and organizational innovation, and other such changes in the firm's economic environment. I assume that the range of subject matter appropriate for direct employer-employee discussion in such an in-house procedure would be even broader than that which is now required by the NLRA for employers engaged in full-fledged bargaining with a national union. And the discussions would occur on a regular basis as each new problem arose and had to be dealt with, rather than be confined to triennial rounds of negotiation like a comprehensive union agreement.

The EPC would also take major initial responsibility for the administration of the broad array of legal policies that now shape and control the employment practices of individual firms. Among the programs I have in mind are the following:

(1) *Occupational Health and Safety*. Through their elected representatives, American workers themselves would play the front-line role in implementing and enforcing the Occupational Safety and Health Act (OSHA) regulations, rather than having to rely on the tiny handful of inspectors now available to monitor hundreds of thousands of work sites across the country. The EPC would have the same kind of implementation and enforcement responsibility for pension security regulation under the Employment Retirement Income Security Act (ERISA) and a variety of other protective employment laws.

(2) *Plant Closings*. Now that a statute has been enacted mandating prior notification of plant closings and mass layoffs, the EPC would be an employee organization already in place to receive the notice and to do something constructive with it, whether that be through job banks, work sharing, retraining, early retirement with expedited pensions, or perhaps even an employee buyout of the endangered plant.

(3) *Equal Employment Policy*. The same committee structure would be available to implement the widening array of antidiscrimination laws, affirmative action requirements, programs for securing pay equity or for eliminating sexual harassment, and so on. Needless to say, care would have to be taken to ensure that the EPC itself had appropriate representation from the affected employee constituencies.

(4) *Wrongful Dismissal*. My proposal for a stripped-down guarantee of basic protection against unjustified dismissal, under which only limited compensation would be offered through the rather rough administrative justice of state UI boards, rested on the assumption that there would be no employee base in the typical nonunion workplace. However, if there were a committee structure capable of representing employees in internal grievance and arbitration procedures, one could envisage the viability of broader legal protections

against unjust dismissal, culminating in reinstatement on the job as a standard remedy.

(5) *Employee Stock Ownership Plan*. . . . [O]ver the last fifteen years ESOP legislation has provided American firms with nearly $20 billion in publicly financed tax expenditures to encourage worker ownership of their employers. In practice, though, ESOPs have been designed and utilized primarily as tools of corporate finance and liquidity, and more recently as antitakeover buffers for incumbent management. There has been no guaranteed role for workers in the adoption, let alone the exercise, of any apparent ownership rights over the actual decisions of the firm. The development of an elected employee committee structure might give Congress the vehicle it needs to ensure that the ESOP tax benefits are spent in ways that really enhance the employees' stake in and commitment to the firm. . . .

Resources . . . One such resource would be *information*. The employer should be required to provide the EPC with regular and detailed information not only about its personnel policies, but also about the broader financial, investment, and profit situation of the firm. The employees, through their elected representative, should be just as entitled as are the shareholders and their Board of Directors to the kind of information that is necessary to assess and defend their stake in the enterprise. Such a measure would at the least enhance the operation of labor market incentives and constraints on the firm, as currently happens in the more smoothly operating capital markets.

Along with information goes *access*: once management has supplied the data regarding its plans, it must then sit down and talk with the EPC about the implications of and the alternatives to these plans. That format would provide employees as a group with far more influence than is now exerted by the disconnected and uninformed individual worker, whose only realistic recourse is to exit the firm if he is dissatisfied.

But to maximize the values of its information and access, the EPC will need to draw upon expertise to analyze the issues and the data. Procuring that expertise might involve training EPC members (about OSHA standards, for example) or hiring professional advisors (about more esoteric issues such as ERISA). In either case, the EPC will need adequate *finances* for its activities. Any public policy favoring the EPC model, therefore, must include some provision for financial support by the employer—not simply in relief time from work, but also in money for hiring lawyers, scientists, economists, and so on. In a sense, then, a small but defined part of the firm's revenues would be channeled for the support of an effective EPC component of the human resource function, just as a portion of firm revenues is now regularly expended on its personnel department. I would also require that the employees themselves make some financial contribution, which the employer would have to match according to a specified multiple.

This combination of guaranteed information, access, and financing would markedly increase the importance of the employee voice in the workplace. . . .

At the same time, one would also expect that with respect to a number of matters, especially issues that run counter to major conflicting interests of either shareholder equity or managerial prerogative, such persuasive influence will not be enough. In such cases, under West German law the Works Council is given another lever to put it on a more equal plane via-à-vis management. At least in regard to specifically human resource questions—which include measures to deal with the impact of plant closings or technological change—the German Works Council must give its prior consent to any management action. When mutual consent is not achieved through the parties' discussions, an appeal may be taken by either side to binding outside arbitration.

I do *not* favor the arbitration option for the United States. In West Germany the Works Council has the responsibility for administering and enforcing both the collective agreement negotiated by the union for the industry and a much more extensive body of employment standards law. Thus arbitration, in lieu of a right to strike, evolved as a natural method for resolving what is often a disagreement about the application of these general standards to particular cases. Under American labor policy, at least in the private sector, we have decided for good reasons not to give unions a regime of binding interest arbitration to help them bargain for protective employment standards. It would be incongruous and unwise to reverse that course and provide this too-easy mechanism in a new EPC procedure, which is after all designed primarily for employees who do not have (and may not want) full-fledged collective bargaining.

That judgment would not, however, leave the employees represented by an EPC with no power to move an intransigent employer. Those employees would still enjoy precisely the same right to strike under Section 7 of the NLRA—"to take concerted action . . . for their mutual aid or protection"—as is now used by union members engaged in collective bargaining. The immediate rejoinder, of course, is that a small group of nonunion workers with the limited resources and lack of tradition of an EPC would probably be too timid and inhibited to actually exercise the legal right to strike without the backing and support of a large union. But if it is the case, as I am sure it usually would be, that the purely persuasive efforts of the EPC were not sufficient to move the employer to improve working conditions, then that is a reason for these employees to exercise their further Section 7 legal right—to join a real union.

Relations. That brings me to a final issue: what is the appropriate relationship between the EPC model and union representation itself?

One fundamental objection to the EPC is that American workers will be bewitched by the false allure of in-house representation without real power, and thus will not consider and will not choose the real thing— organization into unions that engage in full-scale bargaining and that will strike if necessary. . . .

Nor should one lightly assume that the supposedly "not as good" EPC procedure is actually the enemy of the "very good" union version. After all, a company union is not a quasi-totalitarian state from which the employees can never extricate themselves in favor of a different governance mechanism. Even in those historical situations in which management was actually the sponsor of an employee representation plan, many such programs eventually did evolve into independent unions. That transformation tends to happen when a group of workers has had the experience of trying to voice their concerns directly to management but eventually feels the need to ally themselves with a broader organization to make real progress in dealing with the employer. . . .

If employees already have a union for bargaining purposes, would there be any need for an EPC as well? In West Germany that is not a problem, because unions there concentrate their efforts on the negotiation of industry-wide agreements and on political action to secure government-imposed employment standards that together set the basic floor of employment terms for all firms. Inside the individual enterprise the Works Council is the body that actually deals directly with management about both the application and the improvement of the standards contained in the basic union agreement and in the law. By contrast, the United States industrial relations system consists of national unions which have a strong base in local entities that negotiate and enforce agreements specifying all the relevant terms of the employment relationship. Given this presence of established local unions and contracts, there is a real risk of confusion and conflict if a new and somewhat mismatched EPC procedure were to be superimposed on them. Would it not make sense, then, simply to exclude present and future unionized establishments from the scope of any EPC policy? . . .

My preferred method of dealing with this problem would be as follows. In those cases in which the union bargaining agent satisfied certain key EPC conditions for direct employee member elections and representatives, the employees in that bargaining unit would be entitled to designate, by a majority vote, their local union as the committee that would represent them in the EPC program. Elected employee officials of the union local would then exercise the variety of rights and duties conferred on EPCs. Another EPC would have to be created for the benefit of the nonunion employees at that work site, but the relations between the two bodies would be coordinated in essentially the same way as they would be handled for EPCs at different plants or office sites of the same nonunion firm. . . .

Notes and Questions

1. *Other Proposals*. For proposals akin to Weiler's, see Joel Rogers, "United States: Lessons from Abroad and Home," in Joel Rogers and Wolfgang Streeck, eds., *Works Councils: Consultation, Representation, and Cooperation in Industrial Relations* ch. 13 (Chicago: University of Chicago Press, 1995); Janice R. Bellace, "Mandating Employee Information and Consultation Rights," in *Proceedings of the 43d Annual Meeting of the Industrial Relations Research Assn.* 137–144 (Madison, Wis.: IRRA, 1990); Clyde W. Summers, "An American Perspective of the German Model of Worker Participation," 8 *Comparative Labor Law Journal* 333 (1987), and his "Codetermination in the United States: A Projection of Problems and Potentials," 4 *Journal of Comparative Corporate Law and Securities Regulation* 155 (1982).

2. *German Works Councils and Firm Performance*. In evaluating Freeman and Lazear's model, consider John T. Addison's review of the empirical literature in "The Dunlop Report: European Links and Other Odd Connections," 17 *Journal of Labor Research* 77, 81–86 (1996):

> Interestingly, the case for German-style participation has often seemed to rest on the fact that works councils are formally independent of unions or that they do not bargain over wages. This divorce of participation from distributive bargaining is actually seen as a plus by Freeman and Lazear, although they make it clear that the works council should have some codetermination power so that workers "have a say over how the firm uses worker provided information." . . .

> This raises the question of the effectiveness of German works councils themselves, widely regarded to be the exemplary participative institution, even if some would see them as still providing only perfunctory participation. . . . It is immediately apparent [from the German empirical literature] that there is no consistent evidence of the assumed beneficial effect of works councils on any outcome measure. . . .

> Some of the evidence actually points to markedly unfavorable effects of works councils. This is true of the most econometrically sophisticated studies. . . . Studies by FitzRoy and Kraft offer a management pressure/competence model that generally sees unions in more favorable light than works councils! The basic idea is that hard driving managers elicit more effort from their work forces and are rewarded with higher salaries and profits. For their part, workers react by joining a union—hence the positive though indirect relation between unions and productivity and profits. The workers are also more likely in these circumstances to elect a works council for reasons of protection and also to obtain a compensating differential for their greater effort. Independently, by limiting managerial discretion, works councils have an adverse effect on productivity (and profits) which better managers are able to avoid by offering better conditions and alternative channels of communication.

FitzRoy and Kraft also argue that the paraphernalia of the works council is inimical to the flexibility essential for innovation and modern technology. In their innovation study, they now interact union density in the plant with works council status on the grounds that a works council will have more influence when density is high and also be more likely to take a hard line in conflict situations. The composite variable has a strongly negative effect on innovative activity....

Overall, these are not the results that one would expect were works councils endowed with the properties traditionally ascribed to them by their advocates. There are of course a variety of statistical problems that attach to the German studies no less than to the U.S. treatments. [One is] the problem of sample size, which quite apart from the issue of representativeness complicates the normal problem of accounting for the likely nonrandom distribution of works councils. Other difficulties include potential differences between types of works council (ignored in all but one of the studies)—the U.S. parallel being the various forms of worker involvement programs and the distinction between substantive versus perfunctory participation—and the lingering ambiguity of the union-works council nexus. The cross-sectional nature of the studies also may mean that the researcher is attributing to participation effects what are instead the result of unobserved firm effects; further progress thus awaits the development of better, principally panel, data sets that will permit the investigator to control for unobservables. Despite these problems, the German exemplar is clearly much more elusive than a number of U.S. observers ... have assured us.

3. *Financing of Employee Participation Committees.* Professor Weiler's proposal envisions that employers will finance most of the operating costs of the EPC. What are the justifications for requiring shareholders to subsidize a mechanism whose objective is in part to enhance the bargaining power of employees to obtain a larger share of the firm surplus? Will employer financing ultimately undermine the independence of the EPC? Weiler does not consider whether employers should continue to pick up the tab when independent unions run the EPC. If the employer-financing mandate applies only in the non-union sector, will this not reduce even further the demand for independent union representation?

4. *Institutional Fit.* Can mandatory works councils coexist with firm-based U.S. unions? Consider Samuel Estreicher, "Labor Law Reform in a World of Competitive Product Markets," 69 *Chicago-Kent Law Review* at 28–30:

If we put aside nagging questions about whether works councils in Germany actually contribute to, rather than detract from, firm productivity and profits, and whether there is a political constituency for such a sweeping change, mandatory works councils of the German variety, in the abstract, offer an attractive framework for ensuring collective employee voice without some of the costs associated with the U.S. system of multienterprise unionism and decentralized collective bargaining. But Professor Weiler's approach differs significantly from the German version. Notably, it preserves a right to strike and the option of converting the EPC into an independent union. By contrast, German works councils are prohibited by law from striking and operate as a body independent of unions with a set of functions and responsibilities separate from the realm of centralized collective bargaining.

It seems doubtful that EPCs of the Weiler strain will function on American soil as integrative organizations. Predictions as to the likely impact of EPCs vary. The French experience suggests that works councils do not function well where unions are weak and multienterprise collective bargaining has been unsuccessful. In the United States, I suspect, they are likely to be seedbeds of traditional unionism, if they take hold at all.

The problem proponents of mandatory works councils have is that our existing system is committed to legal protection of the right to form independent unions that organize and bargain at the level of the firm. Works councils and trade unions are both firm-based organizations. Unless the range of subjects lodged with works councils is severely curtailed, they will either threaten extinction for conventional unions (at least where such unions do not perform a hiring hall function, as in construction), or they will become unions in all but name.

Seeking a way out of this conundrum, Professors Freeman and Rogers advocate withholding "tax breaks" from employers who fail to establish EPCs that would have rights to information and consultation over labor policies and would help enforce government policies in such as areas as occupational safety and health, job training, and job closings, while steering clear of "wage bargaining" and presumably other matters commonly addressed in collective bargaining. They also advocate allowing 40% of the workers in a unit to insist upon EPCs in their shops.

If such proposals envision narrow-purpose works councils set up largely to police conformity with external law, they are, I submit, misguided. If we think it appropriate to mandate, or use tax policy virtually to compel, collaborative representation, such works councils should be allowed to address constructively the entire range of issues— productivity improvements, wages, hours and benefits, as well as occupational safety and plant closings—affecting the welfare of the employees and the competitive position of the firm.

5. *Mandatory Multiemployer Bargaining.* Drawing an analogy to the extension laws of Germany, France and other European countries, some have urged that the law mandate multiemployer or "sectoral" bargaining where unions have organized a specified percentage of firms in a given sector or industry. See Joel Rogers, "Reforming U.S. Labor Relations," 69 *Chicago-Kent Law Review* 97, 115–116 (1993); Howard Wial, "New Bargaining Structures for New Forms of Business Organization," in Sheldon Friedman, Richard W. Hurd, Rudolph A. Oswald, and Ronald L. Seeber, eds., *Restoring the Promise of American Labor Law* ch. 21 (Ithaca, N.Y.: ILR Press, 1994); Howard Wial, "The Emerging Organizational Structure of Unionism in Low–Wage Industries," 45 *Rutgers Law Review* 671 (1993).

C. Creating a Market in Representational Services

Freedom of Contract and Labor Law Reform: Opening Up the Possibilities for Value–Added Unionism*
SAMUEL ESTREICHER

My thesis is that the labor laws overregulate labor markets, and that a greater measure of freedom of contract would open up opportunities for the development of different models of unionism and labor-management relations. The traditional model to which we are accustomed envisions unions as multiemployer organizations pursuing industry-wide standards that all too often raise costs for unionized firms. But this is not the only conceivable form of independent worker organization; nor is it the only conceivable vision of worker objectives. These familiar outcomes of the system may be the product of overly rigid rules. Perhaps, with greater flexibility, we might see emerge a competing model of "value-added" unionism, that is, organizations that give employees greater voice in articulating their concerns and that negotiate and administer collective goods like grievance procedures, but without undermining firm profits or managerial flexibility....

We should not assume that one size fits all. Under a more flexible set of rules, we might see a range of organizations exhibiting varying degrees of independence from the employer. For some settings, what workers need is a consultative organ, financed by the firm, for voicing concerns to management and providing assistance with benefits issues and grievances. Workers elsewhere might form a firm-based organization whose leaders are on paid leave from the firm, chosen by secret ballot and serving for a limited term. This type of organization might provide trained advocates to help resolve disputes and negotiate contracts with management which stress profit-sharing, skill-based pay, and bonuses keyed to performance. Leverage would come from the organization's effectiveness in articulating the employees' perspective rather than the threat of strikes. The organization might have ties to a multiemployer labor organization, but the latter's role would be that of service-provider: offering lawyers, actuaries, and professional development and placement services. In competition with these options, we would find, as we do today, local unions that are simply administrative units of traditional, adversarial organizations pursuing industry wage and job control policies.

. . .

III. A "Freedom of Contract" Agenda

Can we get from here to there? I have a number of proposals to offer as possible candidates for a "freedom of contract" agenda for labor law reform.

* 71 New York University Law Review 827 (1996).

A. *Rethinking Employee Free–Choice: Ex Ante Versus Ex Post Authorization*

One category of proposals involves some rethinking of how the law tries to promote employee free-choice.

1. Prehire Agreements

Current law holds that employers may express their views but should play no direct role in the employee decision either to seek union representation or to be represented by a particular organization. A firm can voluntarily recognize a union but only after the union has presented proof of majority support in an appropriate unit. Conferral of exclusive bargaining status on a minority union is unlawful. A violation occurs even if the union acquires a majority by the time the contract is executed. Nor is it cured where the parties make clear that the agreement will not be enforced and that it is expressly conditioned on the union's subsequent showing of majority support. Similarly, outside of the construction industry, employers may not enter into contracts with unions before a representative complement of the workforce has been hired and has designated a particular representative.

These rules understandably seek an uncontaminated expression of worker preferences for union representation. However, they do so at the cost of locking employers and unions into an unnecessarily adversarial posture before bargaining relationships can begin. . . . Bargaining relationships can be formed in a different manner. This is suggested by the United Auto Workers (UAW) innovative agreement with General Motors' (GM) Saturn division, which was negotiated before any of the employees were hired for the new Spring Hill, Tennessee facility. By stipulating to the union's bargaining authority in advance, the Saturn management encouraged the union to experiment with broadened job classifications and a participative "team structure" that marked a clear departure from the national UAW–GM agreement. A prehire agreement was also reached with the UAW prior to opening up the New United Motor Manufacturing (NUMMI) plant, a GM–Toyota joint venture in Fremont, California.

Saturn's success, which is still an open question, should not obscure the fact that the parties narrowly averted considerable legal difficulties in that case. The agreement, which was accepted by the National Labor Relations Board (NLRB) General Counsel, was saved by the ingenious argument that the parties were really engaged in a form of bargaining over the effects of layoffs for UAW-represented workers laid off in other plants, from whom the Saturn workforce would be drawn.

This approach could not be used by foreign firms establishing plants in this country. Thus, companies like Mercedes and BMW have no opportunity to test the union's receptivity to doing things differently.

Neither do American firms deciding whether to invest in new plants here rather than abroad.

In my view, the law should encourage, rather than hinder, labor-management cooperation experiments in new "greenfield" plants by relaxing the prohibition against prehire agreements. The wishes of the employees ultimately hired can be determined in a more reliable and constructive manner than by barring such agreements altogether. Employers should be able to enter into agreements with nondominated labor organizations without a prior showing of employee support. The key safeguard for protecting employees would be the requirement that a secret-ballot authorization election be held by the end of the first year of operations. If the employees vote to authorize the agreement, the normal contract-bar rules would apply to promote stability. If the employees vote against the agreement, other unions would be free, as they are presently, to attempt to organize the workforce. . . .

2.   Extension Agreements

Consider a similar approach for the question of voluntary extension of labor agreements to unrepresented segments of the workforce. Typically, unions represent only a fraction of an employer's nonsupervisory personnel. Union organizers understandably favor small, cohesive units. However, an unfortunate by-product of such unit determinations is that the union is not expected to take into account the welfare of all of the employees—even if only the nonsupervisory employees—in the enterprise when formulating bargaining goals and administering contracts. Predictably, this limits the union's appeal among the unrepresented portion of the workforce. More importantly, the union is encouraged to pursue an agenda that, while it may benefit the represented group, may also detract from the overall economic position of the firm.

A reform of existing rules similar to the approach suggested above for prehire agreements can help reduce some of the negative effects of fragmented bargaining structures. I propose that an employer and a union representing a threshold percentage of the workforce should be permitted—without an NLRB election and even where different bargaining units are involved under traditional Board criteria—to extend labor agreements throughout the plant and, perhaps, to other plants within the same commuting area. The accreted employees must, however, have an opportunity by the end of the first year to determine by secret ballot (as separate units under traditional NLRB criteria) whether they approve of the extension agreement and of the union's bargaining authority.

3.   Nontraditional Labor Organizations

Under current law, the Labor Board believes it must ensure that organizations petitioning for representation elections are free of any imaginable risk of conflict of interest. These rules hamstring professional organizations that include supervisors, even of third-party employers, in their decisionmaking structure or that perform labor referral services for nonsignatory employers. We essentially require these groups to transform themselves into traditional unions as the price of admission to NLRA processes. Here, too, the law's objectives would be better served by relaxing, ex ante, prophylactic safeguards that inhibit the possible emergence of alternative approaches to worker representation. In their stead, we should facilitate opportunities to poll worker satisfaction after actual experience with the bargaining agency.

B. *Allow Free Collective Bargaining*

1. Broaden the Right to Insist on Permissive Subjects

Under the Supreme Court's decision in *NLRB v. Wooster Division of Borg–Warner Corp.*, 356 U.S. 342 (1958), sharp distinctions are drawn between "permissive" and "mandatory" subjects: the parties have a duty to bargain and a right to press disagreements over mandatory subjects which are defined narrowly to encompass only issues of immediate concern to employees, whereas a party seeking a change with respect to a permissive subject may make a proposal but may not press its position. Such regulation unnecessarily curtails the creative potential of collective bargaining. Bargaining is essentially about registering preferences and placing values on those preferences, and yet important areas— deemed "permissive"—are virtually excluded from this process of contract-making. Employers may "propose" but not "insist" to impasse on subjects like interest arbitration, discretionary merit pay, bond requirements, and submission of employer offers to employee votes. Unions, too, may not press for terms like salary arbitration, guarantees from nonsignatory parent companies, seats on the board, and the like. If collective bargaining is to succeed, the parties should be able to shape a deal that meets their needs without the government deciding which subjects can be deal-breakers. The freedom to forge contractual solutions should not have to await the firm's imminent demise, when concessions sought from unions allow agreements on matters like employee stock ownership, union directors, and joint processes to improve product safety and design. . . .

2. Reopen Some Presently Illegal Subjects

The labor laws presently prohibit certain agreements without good justification. A commitment to expand the range of contractual solutions achievable in collective bargaining would include a reexamination of these restrictions. For example, the 1947 Taft–Hartley amendments to the NLRA permit the states to enact so-called "right to work" laws that effectively allow employees in units that have chosen collective bargaining to refuse to pay their share of the costs of such representation. Legally sanctioned "free riding" undermines the union's effectiveness and is unnecessary to protect the legitimate interests of "conscientious objectors" to unions in view of other statutory safeguards.

Another Taft–Hartley measure that casts too wide a net is section 302's bar of all employer payments to union officials except as expressly set forth in that provision. Congress properly sought to prevent unions from using economic pressure as a vehicle for extorting payments from firms and to prevent firms from co-opting union officials, but the prohibition reaches much further than necessary. Just as a 1978 amendment allows employer contributions to labor-management committees established for certain prescribed purposes, Congress should permit employers to pay the salary of employees who take a leave of absence for a fixed term to serve as an officer of the local union. Such payments might affect the local union's orientation, but they would not, without a good deal more, evidence the bargaining agent's extortion, corruption, or domination.

A third area for expanding the realm of contract is to revisit the legislative judgment in 1959 that employers and unions cannot enter into "hot cargo" agreements. Contracts should not be enforceable where the costs are principally visited on neutral third parties. Congress was particularly concerned that the Teamsters Union was using its leverage over carriers virtually to compel the unionization of employees of firms using those carriers and otherwise disrupt those businesses in the service of disputes over which they had no control. But the "hot cargo" ban in section 8(e) of the NLRA also prohibits agreements when the costs will be either directly borne, or ultimately absorbed, by the contracting parties. For example, unions in the construction industry cannot trade wage concessions for agreements from employers that they will not establish nonunion subsidiaries competing for work in the union's geographical jurisdiction. . . .

C.   *Reducing the Costs and Enhancing the Benefits of Union Representation* . . . .

2.   Arbitration of Employment Discrimination and Other Employment Law Claims

. . . Under *Alexander v. Gardner–Denver Co.* [415 U.S. 36 (1974)], union-represented employees are free to challenge a discharge or other employment decision under the collective agreement, and relitigate the very same controversy in the administrative agencies and courts under federal antidiscrimination and state wrongful discharge laws. From the employer's perspective, this ruling erodes one of the principal advantages of agreeing to a "just cause" limitation in the labor agreement. No longer is it possible to obtain a truly final, binding resolution under a relatively low-cost procedure in which the arbiter is jointly chosen by the parties and attuned to the operational needs of the enterprise. . . .

Admittedly, unions should not be able to trade off individual entitlements in the interest of maximizing benefits for the larger group. However, it is a little difficult to understand why a collective resource—the benefits to both employers and workers of securing a low-cost final and binding resolution of disputes—should be undermined because individuals also have claims under external law arising out of the same grievance.

The labor laws should be amended to empower employers and unions to negotiate arbitration clauses that provide true finality for all grievances submitted to the dispute resolution mechanism. Some quality standards would have to be satisfied. First, the arbitrator must be empowered to resolve both public-law and contractual claims and to issue remedies available under external law. Second, the agreement should clearly provide that resort to arbitration will preclude any independent right of action in the administrative agencies or the courts. Where these safeguards are met, an individual employee properly should be required to make an express and knowing election of remedies. Under such a rule, most employees would opt for the labor arbitration mechanism because it provides a readily available, experienced advocate, an equivalent probability of a successful outcome, and comparable remedies.

Notes and Questions

1. *Saturn Co–Management Model.* The innovative labor-management agreement between General Motors' Saturn subsidiary and the UAW is described more fully in Saul Rubinstein, Michael Bennett, and Thomas Kochan, "The Saturn Partnership: Co–Management and the Reinvention of the Local Union," in Bruce E. Kaufman and Morris M. Kleiner, eds., *Employee Representation: Alternatives and Future Directions*, ch. 10 (Madison, Wis.: Industrial Relations Research Association, 1993). The authors (who include the UAW local president) state (emphasis in original):

> . . . While we have seen other U.S. joint labor-management governance arrangements include off-line labor-management committees and teams, as well as on-line self-directed work groups, we are aware of no other organization which has developed a process for *on-line co-management by the union.*
>
> For example, union leaders have been partnered with nonrepresented Saturn employees through a joint selection process to carry out new roles as operations' middle management replacing the foremen, general foremen, and superintendents found in traditional GM plants. At Saturn, self-directed work teams are organized into modules based on product, process, or geography. Each module has two advisors to provide guidance and resources. While both are jointly selected by the union and Saturn management, one is represented by the UAW, and the other is not. . . . Elected union executive board members are partnered with business unit leaders (plant managers) or have partnership arrangements in staff or line positions. . . . These union partners have had the

opportunity to join directly in the managerial debates and decisions that shape Saturn's strategy. This partnering goes beyond the formal labor-management committee structure. Essentially, what would be considered middle management in most organizations now contains a significant number of one-on-one partnerships between nonrepresented managers and their represented UAW counterparts....

... Saturn's model of worker representation is based on the premise that long-term employment security can not be negotiated independent of the economic performance of the firm nor solely through collective bargaining after all strategic decisions have been made by management. Rather, employment security can only be achieved over the long run by both contributing to the economic performance of the firm and participating directly in business planning and decision-making processes to ensure that worker interests are given appropriate consideration.

2. *Co-optation?* Saturn and other examples of union receptivity to Japanese management techniques have their critics. See, e.g., Clair Brown and Michael Reich, "When Does Union Management Work? A Look at NUMMI and GM–Van Nuys," 31 *California Management Review* 26 (Dec. 1989), arguing that unions cannot at the same time be faithful agents of worker interests and partners in a program of "management by stress". Mike Parker insists that "a kind of worker empowerment takes place" in these settings, "but only insofar as it conforms to an even more carefully regimented shop-floor regime." Parker, "Industrial Relations Myth and Shop–Floor Reality: The 'Team Concept' in the Auto Industry," in Nelson Lichtenstein and Howell John Harris, eds., *Industrial Democracy in America: The Ambiguous Promise,* ch. 10, 249 (New York: Cambridge University Press, 1993). Professor Barenberg offers a similar critique of "team-based production" in Mark Barenberg, "Democracy and Domination in the Law of Workplace Cooperation: From Bureaucracy to Flexible Production," 94 *Columbia Law Review* 758 (1994). The general problem of union involvement in management functions is thoughtfully explored in Michael C. Harper, "Reconciling Collective Bargaining with Employee Supervision of Management," 137 *University of Pennsylvania Law Review* 1 (1988).

3. *Will a Free Market in Representational Services Drive Out Redistributive Unionism?* Current law privileges traditional unionism by limiting representational options. In assessing Estreicher's proposals, a critical question—harkening back to the discussion of Section 8(a)(2) in chapter 4—is whether allowing a broader range of choice will effectively drive out independent unions from the private sector, and with them the redistributive objectives some believe the labor laws are principally about. Would adoption of such proposals require greater receptivity to minimum-terms legislation as a means of filling the "regulatory gap" with respect to standards for competition among workers?

4. *Union as Broker.* Should unions be given authority, within limits, to trade statutory rights for other benefits to their members? Consider Stewart Schwab, "The Union as Broker of Employment–Law Rights" (ms. for University of Pennsylvania conference, Apr. 7, 1995), p. 2:

Unions should reinvent themselves as brokers of employment-law rights. Unions will push for employment rights their workers need. But if certain employment laws do not make sense for a particular workplace, unions should recognize, applaud, and see themselves as able to broker these unnecessary or burdensome laws for other, more valuable items to their workers. Rightly packaged, unions can be seen as enhancing efficiency.

A similar proposal is outlined in Samuel Estreicher, "Freedom of Contract," 71 *New York University Law Review*, at 847–849; and his "Win–Win Labor Law Reform," 10 *Labor Lawyer* 667, 676–678 (1994). Note that permissive rules are not always empowering. Unions may not want the authority to modify statutory entitlements (even within statutorily defined parameters) because this could complicate their bargaining task and create the appearance that they retreating on employee rights.

5. *For-Profit or Oligarchic Bargaining Agents.* For the view that the law should be indifferent to the organizational form of the bargaining, whether oligarchic or democratic, for profit or nonprofit, as long as represented employees have statutory rights to vote on critical economic decisions such as dues level, strike authorization, and contract ratification, see Samuel Estreicher, "Deregulating Union Democracy," 21 Journal of Labor Research 247–263 (Spring 2000).

11

Models for an Individualistic Future

We assume for the purpose of this chapter that the conventional role of unions as collective agents for articulating and advancing employee interests in the workplace either no longer meets the needs of workers, or that the costs to them of obtaining such representation (including the risk of retaliatory discharge or capital flight from the union sector) exceeds the benefits of such representation. What can the law do to facilitate employee voice and participation in an individualistic economic order?

A. Standard Handbooks for Employers

Reconstituting Workers' Rights*

RICHARD EDWARDS

The basic idea of *Choosing Rights* is simple. Every firm over a certain size would be required by law to promulgate and distribute to its workers an employee handbook. The handbook would state the work rights possessed by workers employed by that employer. The handbook would be recognized in law as a binding and enforceable contract. Employers could promulgate handbooks in one of two ways:

1. *The employer chooses and implements a standard handbook.* A specially chartered public-private employee rights commission would be charged with developing a set—ten or more—of standard handbooks. Each standard handbook would define a minimal level for workers' rights but contain a different mix of specific rights. For example, in the area of job security, one standard handbook might permit dismissal only for just cause, another maintain the employment-at-will doctrine but with substantial severance pay rights, and a third provide less job security but enhanced workers' rights to notification and "say" within the company. The employer would have the prerogative simply to elect whichever standard handbook it wished to have prevail in its workplace. It would certify its choice by registering it with the labor board designated to administer *Choosing Rights* (the National Labor Relations Board or a state labor commission).

2. *The employer writes its own handbook, which is promulgated when employees ratify it.* An employer could develop its own handbook,

* In Rights at Work (New York, N.Y.: Twentieth Century Fund, 1993), ch. 9.

tailored to the specific circumstances of its industry, workforce, location, and method of operations, and reflecting its own entrepreneurial preferences and decisions. There would be no restrictions placed upon the content of this handbook.... The handbook would be promulgated when it was ratified by the firm's workers as follows. The specially tailored handbook would be entered in an election alongside one of the standard handbooks, chosen by the employer. The firm's workers would then vote to adopt either the tailored handbook or the standard handbook. The election could be supervised by the NLRB, as is now the case with certification elections.

The employer's handbook would thus become the workers' bill of rights. *Choosing Rights* captures the principal virtues of collective bargaining and statutory mandate without suffering the limitations of either.... On the one hand, like collective bargaining, it would allow for virtually infinite variation in workers' rights, accommodating the vast diversity of the American workplace resulting from factors such as different management philosophies, industry type, markets, regional company customs, and levels of labor availability. It would foster creative local, private-sector solutions to specifically parochial circumstances. It would encourage each employer to develop and implement any set of workers' rights that fits its interests so long as it could convince a majority of its workers that its system, in the firm's specific circumstances, was better than at least one of the standard handbooks....

The standard handbooks would aim, not at comprehensiveness or at mandating ideal work conditions, but rather at providing an acceptable minimum of workplace rights and protections for workers. In this manner the standard handbooks would serve as the mechanism for resolving the market failure based on the inappropriateness of individual bargaining over workers' rights, and so appropriately they are aimed at implementing minimal standards. Nothing in the law should restrain employers from offering, and presumably market competition among employers would encourage them to offer, more expansive rights than contained in the standard handbooks....

An essential element in constructing the standard handbooks would be creating diversity in the mix of rights across different handbooks. Handbooks would need to cover perhaps five major areas of workers' rights, clearly stating within each category what rights, if any, were provided: (a) complaint and grievance rights; (b) rights involving the procedures and nature of discipline; (c) job security, including procedures and permissible reasons for dismissal; (d) rights concerning promotion, career advancement, training, and growth; and (e) rights concerning eligibility for insurance, pensions, leave, and other benefits. Within each of these categories, substantial variation is possible not only in the "amount" of rights but, more relevant here, in the types and content of the rights. The standard handbooks would aim at providing a package of rights such that the "total amount" of rights would be equal across standard handbooks, while the composition or mix of rights within each would vary greatly. It is not necessary nor even desirable that the rights *within* each category be equal between standard handbooks; indeed, they should be unequal to provide greater diversity. However, each total package would offer a comparable level of rights or degree of protection across standard handbooks. It is this diversity in the mix of rights that would permit employers to choose a rights package best suited to the particular circumstances of the firm. . . .

Disputes concerning handbook-derived rights would be settled through currently existing mechanisms supplemented by an arbitration-based system. . . . As proposed, arbitration would not be without cost to the worker, and therefore presumably only the most important disputes, and those for which the worker felt there was a good evidentiary base, would go to arbitration. However, the availability of external arbitration would immediately offer workers a forum to air grievances and obtain redress of serious violations of their rights. Moreover, by its example arbitration would undoubtedly deter other egregious violations of rights by employers.

Notes and Questions

Professor Edwards, unlike some advocates of changes in the "at will" rule for employment contracts, is sensitive to issues of choice and flexibility. The proposal, however, raises a number of questions.

1. *Minimum Terms Legislation in Disguise?* If the proposal simply provides a procedure for compelling employers to place in an accessible form information about workplace policies that they have adopted or would adopt on their own, is a legal mandate necessary? If, on the other hand, the proposal contemplates a restricted choice among a set of "standard handbooks," this would seem a form of minimum-terms legislation. Is it likely that a "special-ly-chartered public-private rights commission," selected to reflect some balance of employee and management advocates, will promulgate a pure "at will" alternative standard handbook? But if new nonmodifiable rules of a constrained labor market are envisioned, those minimum guarantees would have to be justified on their own terms. If, on the other hand, a pure "at will" standard handbook is available, why would any but a handful of employers choose the other alternatives?

2. *Equality Among Packages of Rights?* What does Edwards mean in suggesting that "[t]he standard handbooks would aim at providing a package of rights such that the 'total amount' of rights would be equal across standard handbooks, while the composition or mix of rights within each would vary greatly"? Do we have a common metric by which to convert rights into commensurable qualities? For example, if 30 percent of employees choose Standard Handbook 1 and 30 percent choose Standard Handbook 2, with the other eight handbooks garnering five percent each, do Handbooks 1 and 2 have too many total rights relative to the others? More generally, is the proposed scheme administrable?

3. *Employee Ratification of Nonstandard Handbooks.* Is the employee ratification requirement for nonstandard handbooks a useless formality when employees have no mechanism for independent articulation of their preferences? Presumably, employers currently attempt to coordinate employee preferences (as identified by human resources management and further refined through informational meetings and focus groups with employees), subject to other objectives of the firm such as preserving managerial discretion to make personnel adjustments in light of changing business conditions. If management makes clear that its business requires a "nonstandard" handbook, is it likely that employees in a nonunion environment will vote to impose a standard handbook against management's wishes?

B. Arbitration of Employment Disputes

Professor Edwards also urges allowing employers to adopt internal dispute procedures, with final, binding arbitration to resolve any dispute "concerning rights granted through statute or employee handbooks," as opposed to "wages disputes or normal collective bargaining." This feature may provide an important incentive for employers to support the "standard handbook" scheme because they will be able to obtain some immunity from the risks and costs of civil litigation in exchange for acceding to some restrictions on managerial discretion.

In recent years the use of arbitration in nonunion settings for statutory as well as contractual disputes has emerged as a topic of increasing interest. Employer practices as of July 1995 are surveyed in U.S. General Accounting Office, *Employment Discrimination: Most Private–Sector Employers Use Alternative Dispute Resolution* B–25717 (July 1995). This interest has been spurred in part by the Supreme Court's interpretation of the Federal Arbitration Act of 1925 (FAA), 9 U.S.C. § 1 et seq., as a broad statement of congressional policy in favor of agreements to resolve existing and future statutory and contractual claims. The Court has extended the FAA to employment disputes in the securities industry, where registered representatives of brokerage houses are required by self-regulatory organizations to agree to arbitrate all disputes with their employers. See *Gilmer v. Interstate/Johnson Lane Corp.*, 500 U.S. 20 (1991), and *Perry v. Thomas*, 482 U.S. 483 (1987). The Court has yet to decide whether the FAA applies to arbitration clauses in employment contracts in other industries.

Note on Uniform Law Commissioners' Model Employment Termination Act

In August 1991, the National Conference of Commissioners of Uniform State Laws approved a "Model Employment Termination Act" for adoption by the states. The proposed model act embodies a tradeoff: recognition of a right of action to challenge wrongful termination in exchange for limitations on remedies for common law claims, particularly the exclusion of punitive

damages, compensatory damages, or other recovery for emotional distress
and pain and suffering. The Act would not alter any rights that employees
have under statutes or administrative rules, collective bargaining agreements or more favorable employment contracts. Covered employees are
granted a substantive right to "good cause" protections against discharge,
which cannot be waived except by an individually executed agreement
guaranteeing a minimum schedule of severance payments keyed to length of
service (up to 30 months' pay).

Although the Model Act allows other adjudicative mechanisms, its
preferred approach is to use state-appointed arbitrators who could award
reinstatement, with or without backpay, and severance pay if reinstatement
is infeasible. See Theodore St. Antoine, "A Seed Germinates: Unjust Discharge Reform Heads Toward Full Flower," 67 *Nebraska Law Review* 56, 77
(1988).

Arbitration of Employment Disputes Without Un-ions*

SAMUEL ESTREICHER

... Proponents of wrongful-termination legislation share a common
intuition that such laws will spur a vast surge of litigation that may
overwhelm the civil courts. This is likely to be the case even if statutory
protection is limited to terminations and "constructive dismissal" claims
rather than including all adverse personnel decisions affecting employees. Even so, this anticipated increase in cases argues only for some
adjudicative mechanism outside the civil courts. The Western European
countries that have enacted such laws use labor courts or industrial
tribunals that function as special tribunals within the civil court system.
Because such courts typically involve a tripartite structure of representatives of industry associations, organized labor and the public, this option
is presumably unavailable on an American terrain characterized by
decentralized collective bargaining and low union density. This option
would, moreover, be inappropriate for employees in the nonunion sector.
Administrative agencies, however, provide an obvious alternative that
could be implemented in this country. The argument, then, has to be
that private arbitration enjoys a comparative advantage over administrative agencies.

The usual argument advanced in favor of arbitration over the
alternatives is grounded in a claim of expertise. This claim ... is that
arbitrators have available to them the accumulated wisdom of over a half
century of grievance arbitration under collective bargaining.... Even if
we grant the need for expertise, this part of the claim is particularly
problematic. The principles that have developed in labor arbitration ...
have been applied in disputes typically not involving employees whose

* 66 *Chicago-Kent Law Review* 753 (1992).

jobs involve considerable unsupervised time and the daily exercise of discretion and judgment. Dismissals for poor performance—as opposed to misconduct—in such unstructured settings are rarely encountered, let alone sustained, by labor arbitrators. An insistence on a formal system of progressive discipline as a precondition to a sustainable discharge, for example, may be inappropriate for managerial and supervisory employees who are likely claimants under a wrongful-termination statute. In a unionized environment, moreover, an arbitration award that significantly hampers managerial discretion can be modified in collective bargaining; a similar escape valve would not be available in a statutory "just cause" regime administered by private arbitrators. . . .

There are also reasons to believe that there are comparative disadvantages to private arbitration over administrative agencies. First, private arbitrators sitting as adjudicators under a wrongful-termination statute act as agents of the state. There are difficulties, both of constitutional and policy dimensions, with having arbitrators paid and selected by the parties functioning as public adjudicators.

Second, once this is conceded, private arbitrators (who typically receive a per diem fee of upwards of $400) may provide a considerably less cost-effective means of dispensing industrial justice than an administrative agency.

Third, unlike administrative agencies, private arbitrators do not screen cases for probable merit and are not well-situated to mete out summary dispositions in appropriate cases. Unless the substantive judgment is made that every termination decision requires a hearing on the merits, some mechanism for weeding out plainly nonmeritorious cases and attempting to mediate solutions will be needed to keep costs down to a manageable level and avoid a situation where the sheer queue of cases prevents a prompt decision—thought to be critical to successful implementation of a reinstatement remedy. Since neither of the parties is bearing the cost of the proceeding itself, other than attorney's fees, they are not likely to face the right incentives. A filing-fee requirement is an unpromising means of promoting self-screening, unless set at a more than nominal level that may lead to under-enforcement of statutory norms. A provision shifting attorney's fees to prevailing parties also would deter potentially meritorious claims and is unlikely to secure political acceptance from representatives of claimants' interests. In all likelihood, the appointing agency will be called upon to make the "reasonable cause" screening decision. But this method sacrifices significant efficiencies—and lowers the potential for mediated solutions by separating that screening task from the ultimate decisional responsibility.

Fourth, private arbitrators who sit to dispense public justice will be subject to the due process requirements that govern any form of public adjudication. In the American legal culture, this will, of necessity, result in increasing levels of formality that reduce whatever advantages of speed and informality arbitration traditionally has enjoyed. It is doubtful that a doctrine of stare decisis can be successfully resisted, simply to ensure that statutory norms are being applied—here, as an exercise of direct governmental authority rather than through the filter of a private contract—in a relatively evenhanded and doctrinally coherent manner.

Finally, the tradition of limited judicial review of arbitration awards is not likely to take root in this context. It is difficult to understand how arbitrators functioning *de facto* as an administrative agency under a statute can be immunized from the standards of judicial review applicable to administrative-agency adjudication. A formal exception can be carved out of federal and state administrative procedure acts. However, principles of judicial review inspired, if not required, by constitutional due process and delegation-doctrine concerns will quickly rise to the fore.

In short, arbitration here is not likely to present any real advantage over an administrative agency, and seems a circuitous route to establishing what will ultimately look and operate like an administrative-agency structure.

Notes and Questions

1. *Partial Displacement of Civil Actions.* Note that the Model Termination Act displaces only common law rights and claims, leaving in place the availability of administrative and civil proceedings for an employee's claims under express oral or written contracts and federal and state statutes. Presumably, an adjudication under the Model Act could not include these other claims, and probably issues decided in an adjudication under the Model Act would still be relitigable in other fora. Whatever its political merits, does this "carve out" promote an efficient system for adjudicating employment disputes?

2. *Severance Pay Buy–Out.* Section 4(c) of the Model Act allows the parties to agree to waive the good cause requirement upon the employer's provision of severance pay of one month for each year of service up to 30 months' pay. This provision resembles the scheduled payment feature of the remedy for wrongful termination in some of the European laws surveyed in Samuel Estreicher, "Unjust Dismissal Laws in Other Countries: Some Cautionary Notes," 33 *American Journal of Comparative Law* 310 (1985).

3. *Private Adjudicators for Rights Under Public Law.* If private arbitrators are either enlisted by the state as adjudicators (as the Model Act envisions) or by employers in arbitration agreements required as a condition of employment (as some companies like Philip Morris and Brown & Root have provided in plans adopted after the *Gilmer* decision), does arbitration have to be converted into a public adjudicatory process? Will awards have to be made public? Will they have to contain detailed findings on statutory issues? Will they be reviewable by courts at least on the same basis as orders of administrative agencies? Can lines be drawn to preserve the distinctive

features of arbitration as a relatively inexpensive, informal, low-visibility claims resolution process?

These issues are perhaps most developed in the securities industry where arbitration of employment (and other) disputes has been required as part of the registration process with self-regulatory organizations like the New York Stock Exchange and National Association of Securities Dealers (NASD). To counter concerns that industry panels might not be appropriate to adjudicate discrimination, harassment and other public policy claims, the NASD amended its Code of Arbitration Procedure in 1993 to require "public" panels (i.e., a majority of non-industry members) and publicly available awards in such cases. In August 1997, the NASD voted to eliminate its mandatory arbitration requirement with regard to civil rights claims, although it will continue to administer employer-employee arbitration agreements conforming to the American Bar Association's "Due Process Protocol." See "NASD Proposes Eliminating Mandatory Arbitration of Employment Discrimination Claims for Registered Brokers," NASD press release (Aug. 7, 1997). The SEC has approved this change in the NASD rules. See "Order Granting Approval to Proposed Rule Change Relating to the Arbitration of Employment Discrimination Claims," 63 Fed. Reg. 35,299 (1998). In 1998, the SEC approved a similar rule change by the New York Stock Exchange, under which it would also not administer predispute agreements to arbitrate employment discrimination claims. SEC Release No. 34-40858, 64 Fed. Reg. 1051 (Jan. 7, 199).

4. *Arbitration as a Condition of Employment.* Presumably, once a dispute has arisen, the parties can make a knowing, voluntary agreement to submit the dispute to a jointly chosen private decisionmaker in lieu of resort to administrative agencies or the courts. Should employers, however, be able to require their employees to enter into agreements to resolve future employment law disputes? Should the law take the position that most workers cannot meaningfully enter into binding agreements because of an inherent inequality of bargaining power? Is the right to a judicial forum best viewed as (1) a nonwaivable, nonmodifiable term of the employment bargain similar to the rights to be paid the minimum wage, to petition for a union, or to work free of workplace hazards; or (2) part of the basic substantive terms of the employment relationship, such as compensation, benefits, or job security, that the law allows the parties to craft to meet their joint objectives? Are most workers better off ex ante if the law allows such agreements—provided that any arbitration of employment law respects statutory liability rules and provides for the imposition of statutory remedies for violations—even if some workers ex post lose the leverage afforded by a right to a jury trial on their claims? Compare Patrick O. Gudridge, "Title VII Arbitration," 16 *Berkeley Journal of Employment and Labor Law* 209 (1995), with Samuel Estreicher, "Predispute Agreements to Arbitrate Statutory Employment Claims," 72 *New York University Law Review* 1344 (1997). See generally Steven Shavell, "Alternative Dispute Resolution: An Economic Analysis," 24 *Journal of Legal Studies* 1 (1995) (ex ante ADR agreements raise parties' well-being and should ordinarily be legally enforced, but there is no general call for ex ante ADR to be aided by the state; ex post ADR agreements will not affect

the prior behavior of parties and also provide no general basis for public support).

5. *Financing*. How should an adjudicative mechanism for wrongful dismissal claims be financed? Most employment laws rely on courts or agencies supported by general revenues without levying user fees. On the model of the unemployment insurance laws, should employers in the first instance pay experience-based premiums in order to create incentives for employers to avoid wrongful terminations? Will the costs of the law ultimately be shifted to employees in the form of reduced compensation or employment levels? Should employees also be charged fees to discourage the filing of groundless claims?

6. *A New Role for Unions?* If we move to a world where nonunion employers put in place binding grievance and arbitration processes for resolving disputes with their current and former employees, organizations of employee advocates (both lawyers and others) would form to provide specialized representation services. Is this a new role for unions?

C. Employee Ownership

We move in the final part of this chapter to proposals to expand employee ownership interests in the firm.

In Despair, Starting Over: Imagining a Labor Law for Unorganized Workers*
MICHAEL H. GOTTESMAN

. . .

1. *Is Special Leverage for Employees Justified?*

If legislatures can decree statutory minima where they think them apt, why should they be allowing employees a leg-up in negotiating for benefits above those minima? This is not meant as a rhetorical question; the answer is not self-evident, and champions of legislative empowerment of employees had better be prepared to answer it. Now that Congress has shown itself ready to decree statutory minima (as it was not in 1935), the investiture of enhanced bargaining power cannot be justified as a means to redistribute income. If not that, what?

The strongest justification for legislative leverage is that the legal deck has been stacked unfairly against employees, thus weakening the leverage they might have enjoyed in a world without law and making a compensatory infusion of leverage a kind of righting of the balance. Capital and labor are both needed to make a firm successful. In a world without law it is not predetermined how control of the firm might be divided between the two. But nineteenth-century law defined a corporation as "owned" by those who supplied capital, and remitted those who

* 69 *Chicago–Kent Law Review* 59, 91–96 (1993).

supplied labor to the status of third-party contractors. In consequence, the law imposed a fiduciary duty on corporate officers and boards of directors to administer the affairs of the corporation single-mindedly for the benefit of the shareholders. The law thus compelled corporate agents to treat labor adversarily (i.e., to seek those outcomes that maximized the interests of shareholders at the expense of the employees).

There was nothing "natural" about this choice of legal regime. It was adopted by legal institutions that were more responsive to corporate barons than to working people. Perhaps it reflected the relative degrees of attachment to the enterprise that predominated in that era: investors were likely to be closely affiliated with the corporations they owned, while workers tended to be itinerants with little loyalty or longevity with particular firms.

The nineteenth-century ordering of legal relations between shareholders and employees is ripe for reconsideration. Nowadays, it is the employees who devote a lifetime of investment to the business, while shareholders are often absentees who move their money from one firm to another through stock-market exchanges. Indeed, precisely because shareholders are now an absentee class, many believe that in practice control of many corporations has migrated to corporate managers who run affairs largely for their own benefit. Once the reality diverges from the theoretical model, it is fair to ask why managers, any more than nonmanagerial employees, should be the legally preferred beneficiaries.

Oliver Williamson has argued that the law is right in treating the shareholders as the "owners" of the corporation entitled to determine its fate, as they are the group least able to protect their interests through arms-length contracting with the corporation. Williamson's confidence in employees' ability to contract is predicated upon an optimistic view of the efficacy of collective bargaining. Williamson assumes that the employees are covered by a collective bargaining agreement with a grievance-arbitration clause; he assumes, in other words, that employees are able to bargain effectively and collectively to a contract, and able to include in that contract a mechanism for resolving problems that arise during the life of that contract. Williamson's thesis is inapplicable to the eighty-eight percent of America's employees who are not covered by collective agreements. . . .

2. *Giving Employees Leverage within the Corporate Governing Structure*

If employees cannot contract effectively to protect their interests, and "economic warfare" is antithetical to the national interest, the wiser path to empowerment may be to consider ways to enhance employee influence within the corporate governing structure, rather than from without via third-party contracting with the corporation. To this end,

there are a number of possible approaches.... I simply note the options
here with brief observations about them.

a.   *Employee Voice in Selecting Corporate Directors*

The law could allocate to employees a voice in selecting the corporation's
directors. Under German law, employees are accorded such a voice.
Indeed, nominally employees have equal vote with shareholders in voting
for directors. The reality, however, is that employee voice is limited: in
case of a tie, the shareholders decide. What is more, the "employee" half
of the electorate includes the managers, whose interests often will be
antithetical to those of the workers covered [in the U.S.] by the NLRA.

It seems quite unrealistic to think that American law could be
transformed to provide employees a large voice in selecting corporate
directors—even a voice as ultimately ineffectual as that in Germany—if
they are not also to bear a share of the risks associated with those
directors' decisions (i.e., the risks to the corporation, as distinguished
from the risks to their own job tenure). Thus, voice in governance is
more likely to emerge from the last of the proposals I tender below:
conferring a share of the *ownership* of corporations upon employees.

b.   *Employee Representative Membership on Board of Directors*

A second approach might be to mandate that the board of directors
contain one or more members chosen separately by the employees.
Ultimately, however, this is likely to be of limited value—certainly too
little to justify declaring victory and stopping the search for meaningful
mechanisms for empowering employees. An employee representative on
the board can assure that the other directors are aware of employee
concerns (and the information pertinent to evaluating those concerns)
and would have access to some information that would not otherwise be
available to employees. There is real value in this, and it is worth doing,
but the reality will remain that the directors and managers will reach
decisions that are in the interests of shareholders and managers (perhaps better decisions, because better informed).

c.   *Fiduciary Duties Toward Corporate Employees*

A third approach might be to impose fiduciary obligations upon corporate directors toward corporate employees. A number of states have
enacted "constituency" statutes which *allow*, but do not require, corporate officers and boards to consider the interests of constituencies that
are tied to the corporation (including employees) in reaching corporate
decisions. In other words, these statutes release corporate officials from
the fiduciary obligation to prefer the shareholders over the employees.
These statutes are important symbolically in their recognition that
employees are not strangers to the corporations for whom they work.
But these statutes, which are merely permissive, leave the decision
making in the hands of officers and boards chosen exclusively by the

shareholders. Thus, the choice to forgo an undeviating preference for shareholders is an act of charity, not compulsion.

One could imagine statutes literally mandating that directors owe fiduciary duties to employees equal in power to those owed shareholders. But given the permissiveness of the "business judgment" rule, these statutes would likely be ineffective so long as directors are chosen by, resemble, and are responsive to, the shareholders. Directors' decisions that favored shareholder (or manager) interests could easily be justified under the business judgment rule.

d.   *Mandatory Interest Arbitration*

Another approach would be to retain the existing contractual relationship, but substitute mandatory interest arbitration as the terminal point for negotiations. . . .

The corporate antipathy to surrendering decision-making control is exemplified by experience under the Steel Industry [Extended Negotiating Agreement (ENA)]. During the life of the ENA, negotiations never ended in interest arbitration: the parties settled. At the same time, however, steel industry labor costs rose at a higher rate than auto industry labor costs—and this was so, although auto companies were far more profitable than steel companies. Steel industry negotiators were paying a premium to avoid interest arbitration—a premium higher than auto industry negotiators were prepared to pay to avoid a strike.

If the corporate mentality resists so strongly the surrender of control to a neutral *selected voluntarily by the parties* (recall that the steel industry voluntarily agreed to enter into the ENA, and did so with knowledge of who the interest arbitrators would be—arbitrators that they jointly chose with the union), imagine the vigor with which they would resist legislation to *impose* interest arbitration as the terminal point of negotiation. So long as that corporate mentality can influence legislative decisions, we will not see a conversion to mandatory interest arbitration in the U.S.

e.   *Optional Alternatives*

Another alternative would be to give corporations a choice. Interest arbitration would be the default rule, but corporations could escape it by giving employees sufficient voice in corporate governance. That voice might consist of one of the other versions discussed herein, perhaps made stronger because it is but an alternative.

f.   *Employees Stock Ownership*

The final alternative—and the one that I think has the greatest hope of being both meaningful and politically viable—is to give employees a share of corporate ownership that provides both meaningful voice and meaningful responsibility. Employee stock ownership affords both voting power and an interest in the profitability of the corporation *qua* corporation. A mechanism that assured that employees held significant (not necessarily controlling) ownership of corporate stock would mean that employee interests would be taken into account in corporate decision making, but that employees (both in their wage demands and their stock voting) would have an interest in enlarging the corporate pie rather than simply taking the largest available slice from the existing pie.

Skeptics will note that there is a slight transitional problem with this proposal: who pays to put this stock into the employees' hands? My answer is succinct: "I'm working on it."

In Defense of Employee Ownership*
ALAN HYDE

. . .

III. *A Firm–Specific Model of Successful Employee Ownership*

We are now in a position to describe (or model, if you like) a particular type of firm in which employee ownership might succeed. Employee ownership can be an attractive solution to a firm experiencing:

1. high conflicts of interest between managers and employees.

2. low trust between managers and employees, as a result of ideological, cultural, or firm-specific factors.

3. suboptimum employment contracting as a "solution" to these problems; that is, employment "conventions" that institutionalize:

     a. low incentives for employee productivity, or

     b. high unnecessary supervision costs; or

     c. inefficient allocation of risks. . . .

[T]hree common patterns of "low trust between employees and managers" go a long way toward explaining nearly all observable successful employee ownership. . . .

A. *"Low trust" as the common thread in employee ownership*

First, employees may not trust managers because they are *professional* employees who have been socialized into deep distrust of managerial types. What, after all, is a "professional" but one who, on the basis of specialized learning, can successfully command respect and autonomy from most managerial or nonprofessional authority? When we deal with employee-owned law firms, we deal with an institution close to the experience of many readers of these pages, so I ask you whether you think law firms would be more efficient if organized as corporations, with shareholders, Boards of Directors, career managers. All my experi-

* 67 *Chicago–Kent Law Review* 159 (1991)

ence tells me that they would lose efficiency; that lawyers would never put in the hours, the effort, the initiative for managerial types that they will for a firm owned by themselves or where a future ownership stake is part of the motivational package. Just ask who works harder and smarter, the lawyers who own their own firms or the lawyers working under bureaucratic management.

Second, employee ownership may succeed, at least comparatively, where employees for whatever political or cultural reason simply will never accept or trust managerial authority.

Third, nonprofessional, nonpolitical employees may distrust management for deep if idiosyncratic reasons: they believe that *this* management has through *this* opportunism messed up *this* company, and they will not trust that management any more. For example, the firm may, as a result of conventional capitalist management, be bankrupt or on the verge of bankruptcy.

This third pattern is of the greatest economic interest but is the least intuitively obvious. After all, if cranky professionals or far-out countercultural types won't work for anyone but themselves, then somebody should design situations in which they *will* work, but without any sense that any wider economic questions hang in the balance. What is the connection between internal inefficiency in the typical industrial firm, and work organization or employee ownership?

B. Employee ownership and information costs

Let me answer this question in two steps. First, common to a great deal of observable real world employee relations is a managerial effort to induce employees to share information with management. Second, it is easily demonstrable that, at least in some situations, an ownership stake will induce such information-sharing that other, competing forms of inducing employees will not.

1. What employees know:

To my mind, Karl Marx never wrote anything more beautiful than the famous discussion of the architect and the bee. At the risk of alienating readers who may conclude that an article quoting Marx cannot possibly be for them, let me quote the passage.

> A spider conducts operations which resemble those of the weaver, and a bee would put many a human architect to shame by the construction of its honeycomb cells. But what distinguishes the worst architect from the best of bees is that the architect builds the cell in his mind before he constructs it in wax. At the end of every labour process, a result emerges which had already been conceived by the worker at the beginning, hence already existed ideally.

[1 Karl Marx, *Capital* (Fowkes trans. 1976) 284.]

For over a century, theorists of work and management, whether of the right or left, have often embarked from just this starting point: the idea that employees hold a great deal of knowledge that their employers do not have and would like to get. This was of course true of nineteenth century craft workers, who, through their control of the production process, had more effective control of the pace and quantity of production. This led to the first great managerial campaign to acquire employee knowledge, the "scientific management" program of Frederick Winslow Taylor, in which employees were minutely observed, and their jobs then broken down into comparatively unskilled, repetitive jobs, the holders of no single one of which would be in a position to hold up or restrict production.

Remarkably, however, even after Taylorist "deskilling," ordinary industrial workers today still control information that management lacks. The uneducated machine operator is likely to be the only one in the place who knows exactly how to operate that particular machine, how to keep it maintained and functional, long after management has refused to put any more money into it and the manufacturer has ceased to make replacement parts.

From this perspective, the common thread among quality circles, quality of work life [(QWL)] programs, and team production, all popular management reforms, is that all seek to create environments in which employees will share information with management that they will never share under conventional labor relations . . .

2.   Efficiency advantages of employee ownership:

   . . . However hard to demonstrate, there may in theory be several ways in which structuring an ownership stake for employees in a participatory workplace will induce higher trust and lower information costs than simple resort to quality circles or team production without an ownership stake.

a.   *Workers may disclose even more information for productivity, work smarter, since the result will not necessarily be layoff, and anyway they can determine the result.*

Critics of quality of work life programs have discussed extensively the fact that management normally retains complete discretion over whether or not to implement the suggestions of the participants. This might seem to place an upper limit on the kind of productivity suggestions that astute employees will adduce. With an ownership stake, employees will reveal no less information, and may disclose more. At the same time management loses incentives to misrepresent firm profitability to workers if those workers are also shareowners.

b.   *Workers will reveal preferences on risk-bearing.*

A basic idea of the "efficiency wage" school, also familiar in practice, is that in *some* workplaces, workers would be willing to adopt a more flexible wage system in which at least some wages would be tied directly to individual or group productivity. Such a scheme should in theory be more efficient, since it provides better incentives to employees to work hard and smart, and permits firms to adjust to economic downturns with wage adjustments rather than layoffs. However, in low trust workplaces, workers will not trust management to administer such schemes, and therefore withhold information on their willingness to assume more risk. They continue to withhold such information in QWL groups where they fear management opportunism. They will share such information with themselves. Or in other words, an employee-owned company is a company in which the Board of Directors always has, essentially without cost, information on employee preferences.

c.   *Workers will be willing to bear the risk of tying between performance and wages since they don't have to trust management.*

This has been a feature of every one of the well-publicized, perhaps over-publicized, worker buyouts of failing firms in order to preserve jobs. It always turns out that workers will make concessions to themselves, mostly tying compensation to firm performance, that they would not and did not make to management.

d.   *One of the best-documented, clearest advantages of employee-owned firms is substantial savings in the number of supervisors.*

This is highly significant, as many new computerized work processes have created the technological possibility of eliminating useless supervisors and replacing them with teams of workers, all working on the same data base and monitoring each other. It appears that employee-owned firms will be at a substantial advantage over conventionally-owned firms in realizing these savings.

e.   *Workers with an ownership stake should be likelier to invest in firm-specific education or other investments of their time, energy, or savings that are specific to the firm.*

f.   *There is a possibility that an ownership stake may motivate workers through diffuse psychological mechanisms.*

We are not on firm ground here; the literature does not clearly demonstrate any such relationship in observable employee-owned firms. This fact is puzzling, however, and may simply reflect gaps in techniques of motivation. It would seem that over time, employee-owned firms *should* be able to design cultures of motivation that are more effective than in conventional firms and would also pay off in terms of job satisfaction.

These, then, are the potential efficiency and productivity advantages of the employee-owned firm. Are there any ways in which employee ownership would be negative for productivity? I would say no, for a simple reason: employee-owned firms are always free to be as hierarchical as they like. Workers can of course select any structure of management hierarchy they like, since it is responsive to them. Employee ownership need not resemble food co-ops. If they need managers, they can and do hire them....

In conclusion, then, the efficiency or productivity case for employee ownership seems to me both empirically and conceptually very strong, although likely to be a different case for each firm, and stronger in some firms than others.

C. The Problem of Risk Allocation

There is one very strong argument against an ownership stake for many workers, and that is the problem of allocation of risk. As we have seen, most working people in the primary sector of the contemporary American economy already are tied to their employer by implicit long-term employment contracts that leave them with a great deal of firm-specific and location-specific investment. What investments do working people have? They do not own stocks or bonds and do not have much savings. They may own a home, but in smaller communities the value of that home will not be independent of the economic strength of the leading employers. To an extent unique in the industrialized world, their access to health care and retirement security will also be a function of their employer's health.

These background facts are not inevitable, and may even be internationally deviant, but they are facts about the American economy today, and it cannot be said that there is any strong political likelihood at present of change to a more Western European-style welfare state. Under the circumstances, it is rational for most employees, who already bear quite substantial risks of their firm's poor performance, to take on no risks other than those imposed by the background system.

This fact explains for me both the historic low incidence of worker ownership in most industries, and the tendency of worker owned firms to revert to private ownership....

I believe that risk aversion is the single greatest problem with employee ownership and the single greatest obstacle to its wider spread. This conclusion is fortified by examining the pattern so commonly observed in which businesses become employee owned in recessions, make dramatic recoveries, and sell to private investors. Why do they sell out? Hansmann, as usual discussing few actual examples, answers: "The most likely explanation is that worker ownership is not an efficient mode of organization for the firms involved." This conclusion is preposterous, given that in nearly all such cases studied a firm driven to the brink of bankruptcy by management opportunism and investor ownership has experienced incredible revival under employee ownership to the point where outside buyers are attracted who never were under investor ownership.

The reason they sell out is no secret. It is mentioned publicly in nearly every case of sale to private ownership, including Weirton Steel, the one actual case that Hansmann mentions: risk diversification for employees. This includes at least two components, depending on whether the employees are currently employed, or facing retirement.

First, the company may need more capital, to modernize or expand, and employees simply do not want so much concentrated risk; they seek a partnership with an outside investor in furtherance of their original goals, and for the same reason anyone else would.

A second component is the problem of repurchase liability. By law, ESOPs must stand ready to repurchase the shares of employees, partly so that employee ownership is diluted only by group, not individual, decisions, and partly to permit employees to diversify their own investments. If the company has really turned around under employee ownership, such repurchase liability can be very expensive, in some cases requiring nearly all the company's cash. Yet requiring such repurchases is necessary lest employees be left with an intolerable assumption of risk, in which they would approach the retirement years invested in a solitary investment.

Risk diversification is thus in both theory and practice the most serious problem with employee ownership as now practiced in the United States. It explains why rational employees will normally want only a partial ownership stake in their employer: in order to protect their retirement and health security. Risk diversification also explains why it is so hard to observe majority employee ownership selected by employees without preexisting professional or political disposition towards employee ownership. Essentially, only employees faced with risks of job and benefit loss, that in the particular case outweigh the risk of having retirement and health benefit funds so heavily invested in a single employer, will voluntarily select majority employee ownership. (It further explains once again why theories of employee ownership must be firm-specific). Finally, it explains why we observe both a strong theoretical and empirical case for the efficiency of majority employee ownership, and yet so few firms attempting to achieve those efficiency gains. Once again, economists would describe this as a tradeoff between incentives for performance and allocation of risk.

In my opinion, advocates of employee ownership have given insufficient attention to solving the problem of risk diversification. Partial solutions to this problem exist. There are a number of ways that ESOP investment may be made less risky for employees. Others are not legally permissible, but could become so with regulatory change. As employee ownership spreads, other devices for reducing employee risk would become feasible. Ultimately, however, there is a plain conflict between having the bulk of employee savings and benefits trust funds invested in their own employer, and security for those employees....

Notes and Questions

1. *Leverage vs. Efficiency?* The principal readings approach the issue of employee ownership from two different perspectives. For Professor Gottesman, the question is whether expanding ownership and participation rights will enhance employee bargaining power; Professor Hyde's focus is whether employee ownership will improve the performance of the firm. For related writings, see Hyde's "Ownership, Contract, and Politics in the Protection of Employees Against Risk," 43 *University of Toronto Law Journal* 721 (1993); Katherine Van Wezel Stone, "Labor and the Corporate Structure: Changing Conceptions and Emerging Possibilities," 55 *University of Chicago Law Review* 73 (1988); Maureen A. O'Connor, "The Human Capital Era: Reconceptualizing Corporate Law to Facilitate Labor–Management Cooperation," 78 *Cornell Law Review* 899 (1993); and her "Restructuring the Corporation's Nexus of Contracts: Recognizing a Fiduciary Duty to Protect Displaced Workers," 69 *North Carolina Law Review* 1189 (1991).

2. *Why Capital Hires Labor Rather Than the Other Way Around?* Worker-owners would appear to have strong incentives to monitor themselves and each other to promote an efficient level of effort. Why, then, is the predominant form of industrial organization investor-owned rather than employee-owned? Consider the following arguments that have been prominent in the literature (paraphrased from Greg Dow and Louis Putterman, "Why Capital Hires: A Review and Assessment of Some Proposed Explanations" (ms. for Columbia University Sloan Conference on Employee Ownership (Dec. 1995)):

> (1) The residual claimant (i.e., shareholders) is likely to be the best monitor of worker output under conditions of team production. See Armen A. Alchian and Harold Demsetz, "Production, Information Costs, and Economic Organization," 62 *American Economic Review* 777 (1972).

> (2) Imperfections in credit markets stymie financing for employee-owned firms. See Samuel Bowles and Herbert Gintis, "Contested Exchange: New Microfoundations of The Political Economy of Capitalism," 18 *Politics & Society* 165 (1990).

> (3) Workers are typically more risk averse than investors; employee ownership exacerbates labor's undiversified investment in the firm. In this account, capital in effect insures workers against market risk. See Frank H. Knight, *Risk, Uncertainty, and Profit* (New York: A.M. Kelley, 1964).

> (4) Employee-owned firms suffer from a "horizon" problem: current employees face a disincentive to make optimal investment expenditures because they cannot fully capture the returns on those investments after they retire or leave the firm. See Michael Jensen and William Meckling, "Rights and Production Functions: An Application to Labor–Managed Firms and Codetermination," 52 *Journal of Business* 469 (1979).

> (5) Because worker preferences are more heterogeneous than capital suppliers, worker-owned firms face special problems of collective decisionmaking not faced by capital-owned firms. See Henry Hansmann, "When Does Worker Ownership Work? ESOPs, Law Firms, Codetermi-

nation, and Economic Democracy," 99 *Yale Law Journal* 1749 (1990); and his "Worker Participation and Corporate Governance," 43 *University of Toronto Law Journal* 589 (1993).

3. *Transitional Form?* Professor Jeffrey Gordon's recent article, "Employee Stock Ownership in Economic Transitions: The Case of United Airlines," in Samuel Estreicher, ed., *Employee Representation in the Emerging Workplace: Alternatives/Supplements to Collective Bargaining: Proceedings of New York University's 50th Annual Conference on Labor* (Cambridge, Mass.: Kluwer, 1998) 513, introduces the notion that in some settings employee ownership can help promote the firms' efficient allocation of "transition" costs incurred, for example, when firms face radically altered competitive conditions, as in the airline industry following deregulation. The article also suggests that employee ownership can make a contribution to the ongoing performance of the firm by changing "corporate culture."

4. *Empirical Studies.* For a review of the extant empirical literature on the effects of employee ownership on firm performance, see Douglas Kruse and Joseph Blasi, "Employee Ownership, Employee Attitudes, and Firm Performance," NBER Working Paper 5277 (Sept. 1995). The authors conclude (pp. 24–26):

1) Employee ownership does not magically and automatically improve employee attitudes and behavior whenever it is implemented; and

2) While there are a number of findings that employee attitudes and behavior are either improved or unaffected by employee ownership, it is rare to find worse attitudes or behavior under employee ownership. . . .

3) Where there were differences in attitudes or behavior, they were almost always linked to the status of being an employee-owner, and not to the size of one's ownership stake;

4) Perceived participation in decisions, either by itself or interacting with employee ownership, was often found to have positive effects on employee attitudes;

5) Despite the possible benefits from increased employee participation in decisions, there was no automatic connection between employee ownership and either perceived or desired employee participation;

6) There is no evidence of decreased need or desire for union representation in employee ownership firms. . . .

7) There is no automatic connection between employee ownership and firm productivity or profitability; and

8) While several studies indicate better or unchanged performance under employee ownership, almost no studies find worse performance.

5. *Union Directors.* Union representatives in the corporate boardroom have a difficult time reconciling their roles as worker advocate and board member. See, e.g., Statement of USW Basic Steel Industry Conference's Bargaining Goals, reprinted in (BNA) Daily Labor Report, No. 24 (Feb. 6, 1996), E–1, E–7:

In significant parts of our Union, there is disappointment over the lack
of visibility, communication, and perceived effectiveness of the USWA
nominee to the company board of directors. At several companies, there
needs to be more frequent, meaningful communication between our
members and local leaders on the one hand and the director nominated
by our Union on the other. Companies must not be permitted to
interfere with this relationship. Representing the Union on the board of
directors is a privilege for those we designate. There must be a substantial increase in the responsiveness of the Union-nominated directors.

For a review of U.S. experience, see Tove H. Hammer, Steven C. Currall, and
Robert N. Stern, "Worker Representation on Boards of Directors: A Study of
Competing Roles," 44 *Industrial and Labor Relations Review* 661 (1991).

Appendix A

Union Members in the United States, 1930–1979

Year	Union members (thousands)	Total labor force (thousands)	Union members as a percent of total labor force	Employment in nonagricultural establishments (thousands)	Union members as a percent of nonagricultural employment
1930	3,401	50,080	6.8	29,424	11.6
1931	3,310	50,680	6.5	26,649	12.4
1932	3,050	51,250	6.0	23,628	12.9
1933	2,689	51,840	5.2	23,711	11.3
1934	3,088	52,490	5.9	25,953	11.9
1935	3,584	53,140	6.7	27,053	13.2
1936	3,989	53,740	7.4	29,082	13.7
1937	7,001	54,320	12.9	31,026	22.6
1938	8,034	54,950	14.6	29,209	27.5
1939	8,763	55,600	15.8	30,618	28.6
1940	8,717	56,180	15.5	32,376	26.9
1941	10,201	57,530	17.7	36,554	27.9
1942	10,380	60,380	17.2	40,125	25.9
1943	13,213	64,560	20.5	42,452	31.1
1944	14,146	66,040	21.6	41,883	33.8
1945	14,322	65,300	21.9	40,394	35.5
1946	14,395	60,970	23.6	41,674	34.5
1947	14,787	61,758	23.9	43,881	33.7
1948	14,319	62,080	23.1	44,891	31.9
1949	14,282	62,903	22.7	43,778	32.6
1950	14,267	63,858	22.3	45,222	31.5
1951	15,946	65,117	24.5	47,849	33.3
1952	15,892	65.730	24.2	48,825	32.5
1953	16,948	66,560	25.5	50,232	33.7
1954	17,022	66,993	25.4	49,022	34.7
1955	16,802	68,077	24.7	50,675	33.2
1956	17,490	69,409	25.2	52,408	33.4
1957	17,369	69,729	24.9	52,894	32.8
1958	17,029	70,275	24.2	51,363	33.2
1959	17,117	70,921	24.1	53,313	32.1
1960	17,049	72,142	23.6	54,234	31.4
1961	16,303	73,031	22.3	54,042	30.2
1962	16,586	73,442	22.6	55,596	29.8
1963	16,524	74,571	22.2	56,702	29.1
1964	16,841	75,830	22.2	58,331	28.9
1965	17,299	77,178	22.4	60,815	28.4
1966	17,940	78,893	22.7	63,955	28.1
1967	18,367	80,793	22.7	65,857	27.9
1968	18,916	82,272	23.0	67,951	27.8
1969	19,036	84,240	22.6	70,442	27.0
1970	19,381	85,903	22.6	70,920	27.3
1971	19,211	86,929	22.1	71,222	27.0
1972	19,435	88,991	21.8	73,714	26.4
1973	19,851	91,040	21.8	76,896	25.8

Year	Union members (thousands)	Total labor force (thousands)	Union members as a percent of total labor force	Employment in nonagricultural establishments (thousands)	Union members as a percent of nonagricultural employment
1974	20,199	93,240	21.8	78,413	25.8
1975	19,611	94,793	20.7	76,945	25.5
1976	19,634	96,917	20.3	79,382	24.7
1977	19,695	99,534	19.8	79,382	24.8
1978	20,246	102,537	19.7	85,763	23.6
1979	20,056	107,050	18.7	89,823	22.3

Source: Michael C. Harper and Samuel Estreicher, *Labor Law: Cases, Materials, and Problems*, 4th ed. (Boston: Little Brown 1996), 108–109.

Note: Union Members are the annual average number of dues paying members reported by labor unions. Data exclude members of professional and public employee associations.

Appendix B

Union Membership Density Among U.S. Wage and Salary Workers, 1973–97

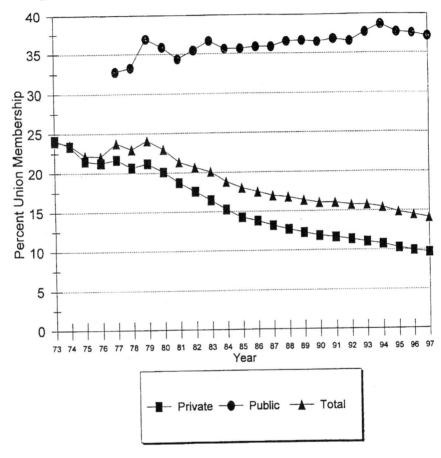

Source: Bureau of National Affairs, *Union Data Book* (1998), 10, Fig. 2.

Appendix C

Union Density Rates, 1900–1989, Eighteen and Twenty–Four Countries

	Employed and unemployed wage and salary earners							
	1900	1910	1920	1930	1940	1950	1960	1970
Sweden	4.8	8.3	27.7	36.1	54.0	66.7	70.1	66.1
Denmark	13.2	17.3	33.4	36.9	40.7	48.9	58.1	57.1
Finland	—	4.5	13.6	7.5	12.7	36.1	34.9	49.1
Norway	3.9	8.2	20.3	19.0	42.9	47.9	57.6	55.6
Belgium	—	5.1	38.6	28.8	33.7	33.2	43.1	44.5
New Zealand	—	—	—	35.8	67.0	60.0	54.0	46.1
Australia	9.0	24.6	42.2	43.5	40.4	50.4	49.1	44.4
Austria	—	5.8	51.0	37.6	—	56.8	59.0	53.0
Ireland	—	—	32.6	27.8	20.6	37.1	43.8	48.6
United Kingdom	12.7	14.6	45.2	25.4	33.1	40.6	40.7	44.6
Italy	6.3	8.3	34.9	—	—	40.3	22.2	33.4
Germany	5.7	18.1	52.5	32.7	—	33.7	35.0	33.0
Canada	—	6.8	15.0	13.5	18.3	32.8	28.3	29.8
Switzerland	—	6.6	26.3	23.6	26.3	39.7	37.0	28.9
Japan	—	—	—	—	6.8	46.2	32.2	34.5
Netherlands	2.9	11.0	31.1	27.7	29.9	42.0	39.4	36.5
United States	5.0	9.1	16.6	9.6	20.3	28.4	28.9	25.9
France	5.8	9.1	10.6	7.8	23.0	31.6	18.6	21.5
Iceland	—	—	—	—	—	—	—	—
Luxembourg	—	—	—	—	—	—	—	46.8
Portugal	—	—	—	—	—	—	—	—
Greece	—	—	—	—	—	—	—	—
Turkey	—	—	—	—	—	—	—	—
Spain	—	—	—	—	—	—	—	—

1980	1989	Employed only			Sectoral rates 1989				
		1970	1980	1989	M	P	1	2	3
78.0	81.3	67.7	80.0	82.5	81	81	99	72	87
75.0	76.0	60.2	76.5	74.9	—	—	99	36	77
69.8	71.6	51.4	69.8	71.3	65	86	80	—	86
55.7	53.8	56.1	56.9	57.0	41	75	87	33	68
55.1	53.4	46.0	56.5	53.0	—	—	95	23	27
53.5	45.9	46.2	55.0	50.2	51	94	58	42	57
47.2	44.7	45.3	50.8	47.9	32	68	48	28	46
52.6	43.6	53.8	53.7	45.2	41	57	53	28	44
52.7	41.7	53.1	57.0	52.4	—	—	—	—	—
48.6	38.9	44.8	50.7	41.5	38	55	41	25	32
44.1	34.0	36.3	49.3	39.6	32	54	47	22	31
35.6	31.5	33.0	37.0	34.2	30	45	48	17	28
33.2	30.4	31.9	36.1	32.9	—	—	38	6	53
31.1	27.6	28.9	31.2	27.7	22	71	34	14	24
30.3	25.9	35.1	31.1	26.7	23	56	32	50	31
32.8	23.6	37.0	35.3	25.4	20	51	25	9	32
21.1	15.4	27.3	23.0	16.4	13	37	22	2	19
17.6	9.7	22.3	19.0	12.0	8	26	5	—	—
68.0	78.3	—	68.1	78.8	—	—	—	—	—
49.0	49.0	46.8	49.6	49.7	43	74	—	—	—
51.9	29.0	—	58.8	30.4	—	—	—	—	—
34.6	25.9	—	35.8	30.1	—	—	—	—	—
—	15.5	—	—	19.2	—	—	48	12	6
17.7	11.4	—	22.0	14.8	—	—	—	—	—

Source: Jelle Visser, "Union Organisation: Why Countries Differ," 9 *International Journal of Comparative Labor Law and Industrial Relations* 206, 208–09 (table 1) (Autumn 1993).

Note: All post-1940 density rates are calculated without retired and self-employed union members.

M = private sector of the economy
P = public and semi-public sector of the economy (except nationalised firms)
1 = manufacturing industries
2 = financial services (banking, insurance, business services, and real estate)
3 = community, social, and personal services

Appendix D

Alternative Unemployment Indicators, Ten Countries, 1983–93

(In percent)

Country and year	U–1	U–2	U–3	U–4	U–5	U–6	U–7
United States							
1983	4.0	5.6	7.5	9.5	9.6	12.6	13.9
1984	2.6	3.9	5.8	7.2	7.5	10.1	11.2
1985	2.2	3.6	5.6	6.8	7.2	9.6	10.6
1986	2.1	3.4	5.4	6.6	7.0	9.4	10.3
1987	1.8	3.0	4.8	5.8	6.2	18.5	9.3
1988	1.5	2.5	4.3	5.2	5.5	7.6	8.4
1989	1.2	2.4	4.0	4.9	5.3	7.2	7.9
1990	1.3	2.7	4.4	5.2	5.5	7.6	8.2
1991	2.0	3.7	5.4	6.5	6.7	9.2	10.0
1992	2.8	4.2	6.1	7.1	7.4	10.0	10.8
1993	2.5	3.7	5.6	6.5	6.8	9.3	10.2
Canada							
1983	6.1	7.0	10.3	11.9	11.8	14.3	15.7
1984	5.4	6.4	9.3	11.2	11.2	13.8	14.8
1985	5.0	5.8	8.8	10.3	10.5	12.9	13.8
1986	4.3	5.3	8.0	9.4	9.5	12.0	12.7
1987	4.0	4.8	7.5	8.7	8.8	11.1	11.7
1988	3.3	4.0	6.7	7.6	7.8	9.8	10.3
1989	3.1	3.9	6.6	7.4	7.5	9.5	9.9
1990	3.3	4.4	7.0	8.0	8.1	10.1	10.6
1991	4.8	6.1	9.0	10.3	10.3	12.9	13.6
1992	5.7	6.7	9.9	11.1	11.3	14.2	14.9
1993	5.9	6.5	9.9	11.0	11.2	14.4	15.2
Australia							
1983	6.2	(1)	7.0	10.1	10.0	12.2	13.6
1984	5.7	(1)	6.3	9.0	9.0	11.0	12.3
1985	5.1	(1)	5.9	8.1	8.3	10.1	11.2
1986	4.7	(1)	5.7	7.9	8.1	10.1	11.1
1987	4.8	2.7	5.9	8.0	8.1	10.3	11.4
1988	4.1	2.3	5.3	6.9	7.2	9.3	10.3
1989	3.2	1.8	4.6	5.8	6.2	8.3	9.2
1990	3.5	2.4	5.1	6.7	6.9	9.4	10.4
1991	5.9	4.1	7.3	9.6	9.6	12.9	14.3
1992	7.4	4.4	8.4	10.9	10.8	14.7	16.2
1993	7.4	3.9	8.7	11.0	10.9	14.8	16.3
Japan							
1984	1.4	.8	2.3	2.2	2.6	3.8	7.6

Country and year	U–1	U–2	U–3	U–4	U–5	U–6	U–7
1985	1.3	.8	2.2	2.2	2.6	3.7	8.0
1986	1.4	.8	2.2	2.2	2.6	3.7	8.1
1987	1.6	.7	2.3	2.3	2.8	3.9	8.6
1988	1.4	.7	2.1	2.0	2.6	3.3	7.7
1989	1.1	.5	1.8	1.8	2.2	3.1	7.1
1990	1.0	.4	1.7	1.6	2.1	2.7	6.4
1991	.9	.4	1.4	1.5	1.9	2.5	6.0
1992	.9	.4	1.5	1.6	1.9	2.7	6.1
1993	1.1	.6	1.8	1.8	2.2	3.2	7.0
Sweden							
1987	.9	1.2	1.6	2.2	2.2	4.9	5.5
1988	.7	.9	1.4	2.0	1.9	4.1	4.5
1989	.6	.7	1.1	1.6	1.6	3.7	4.1
1990	.6	.8	1.3	1.9	1.8	4.1	4.6
1991	1.2	1.7	2.3	3.3	3.1	6.0	6.9
1992	2.7	3.5	4.2	6.2	5.6	9.5	10.8
1993	5.1	6.4	6.7	9.9	9.3	14.3	15.8
France							
1983	6.7	3.4	5.6	8.3	8.0	9.5	(1)
1984	8.0	.9	6.5	10.2	9.6	11.5	(1)
1985	8.9	4.1	7.2	10.9	10.3	12.5	(1)
1986	8.8	4.2	7.7	10.8	10.3	13.3	(1)
1987	9.2	4.7	8.4	11.3	10.8	13.5	(1)
1988	8.6	4.4	8.2	10.7	10.3	12.8	(1)
1989	8.1	4.1	8.1	10.0	9.7	12.3	12.4
1990	7.6	4.5	7.7	9.7	9.5	11.7	11.8
1991	7.5	4.5	7.7	9.7	9.3	11.3	11.5
1992	7.5	5.9	8.7	10.8	10.4	12.7	12.9
1993	8.5	6.9	9.6	12.1	11.5	14.5	14.7
Germany							
West Germany							
1983	(1)	(1)	(1)	(1)	(1)	(1)	(1)
1984	5.4	(1)	5.8	(1)	6.7	(1)	(1)
1985	5.6	2.4	6.2	6.5	6.9	7.2	(1)
1986	5.5	2.3	6.3	6.2	6.7	7.0	(1)
1987	5.6	2.5	6.7	6.5	6.9	7.3	(1)
1988	5.2	2.1	6.2	5.9	6.4	6.7	(1)
1989	4.6	1.7	5.8	5.3	5.8	6.0	(1)
1990	4.0	1.3	5.0	4.6	4.9	5.2	(1)
1991	3.2	1.1	4.2	4.0	4.1	4.5	(1)
Unified Germany							
1992	5.0	3.6	6.4	6.4	6.4	7.1	(1)
1993	6.1	4.4	7.8	7.9	7.7	8.8	(1)
Italy							
1986	6.8	.6	3.3	7.4	7.2	9.7	15.9
1987	7.2	.7	3.7	7.9	7.6	10.3	16.1
1988	7.3	.6	3.9	8.0	7.7	10.1	16.0
1989	7.3	.6	4.3	8.0	7.8	10.0	15.8
1990	6.3	.5	3.8	6.9	6.6	8.5	13.8
1991	6.4	.6	3.9	7.0	6.8	9.0	15.0
1992[2]	8.0	1.4	6.0	9.5	9.5	11.5	6.2
1993	9.3	1.9	6.8	10.4	10.4	12.7	18.0
Netherlands							
1983	10.4	(1)	9.5	11.6	11.9		
1984	(1)	(1)	(1)	(1)	(1)	(1)	(1)
1985	9.2	(1)	8.8	10.2	10.6	12.1	12.4

Country and year	U–1	U–2	U–3	U–4	U–5	U–6	U–7
1986	(1)	(1)	(1)	(1)	(1)	(1)	(1)
1987	7.8	(1)	8.0	7.8	10.0	12.5	13.4
1988	7.5	1.2	8.1	7.5	9.5	12.4	13.3
1989	6.9	1.1	7.6	6.9	8.8	11.8	12.6
1990	5.9	.6	6.9	5.8	7.8	10.5	11.4
1991	5.3	.6	6.4	5.5	7.4	10.2	10.9
United Kingdom							
1983	9.0	(1)	8.5	13.0	11.1	13.1	13.9
1984	8.7	3.2	8.6	12.5	11.0	13.0	13.8
1985	9.1	2.8	9.5	12.5	11.5	13.3	14.1
1986	8.9	2.7	9.5	12.6	11.6	13.4	14.3
1987	8.5	2.6	9.6	12.2	11.1	13.0	13.6
1988	6.8	2.1	7.8	9.7	9.1	10.6	11.1
1989	5.2	1.5	6.6	8.0	7.4	8.7	9.1
1990	4.7	1.4	6.1	7.5	7.0	8.1	8.4
1991	5.8	2.6	7.3	9.6	8.6	10.3	10.6
1992	7.4	4.0	8.4	11.5	9.8	12.2	12.8
1993	8.2	4.2	8.8	12.1	10.3	13.1	13.8

¹ Not available.

² Break in series for Italy. New Jersey methods were introduced in 1992 that raised the adjusted U–5 rate by approximately 1 percentage point.

Alternative unemployment indicators

U–1   Long-duration unemployment rate: Persons unemployed 13 weeks (see footnote 2 in text) or longer, as a percent of the civilian labor force.

U–2   Job loser rate: Job losers, as a percent of the civilian labor force.

U–3   Adult unemployment rate: Unemployed persons aged 25 and older, as a percent of the full-time labor force.

U–4   Full-time unemployment rate: Unemployed seekers of full-time jobs, as a percent of the full-time labor force.

U–5   Conventional unemployment rate: Number of persons not working, but available for and seeking work, as a percent of the civilian labor force. Only persons on layoffs and persons waiting to start a new job are not required to seek work in the past 4 weeks, a necessary condition for all others classified as unemployed.

U–6   Rate encompassing half of the persons working part time for economic reasons: Number of seekers of full-time jobs, plus one-half of all seekers of part-time jobs, plus one-half of all persons working part time for economic reasons, as a percent of the civilian labor force, less one-half of the part-time labor force.

U–7   Rate adding discouraged workers: U–6 plus discouraged workers in the numerator and denominator.

Source: Constance Sorrentino, "International Unemployment Indicators, 1983–93," *Monthly Labor Review* (Aug. 1995): 31, 33–35 (table 1).

*

Appendix E

Indexes of Hourly Manufacturing Compensation Costs, 1975–94

[United States = 100]

Country or area	1975	1980	1985	1989	1990	1991	1992	1993	1994
United States..............	100	100	100	100	100	100	100	100	100
Canada	94	88	84	103	106	110	105	98	92
Mexico...................	23	22	12	10	11	12	14	15	15
Australia.................	88	86	63	87	88	87	81	75	80
Hong Kong...............	12	15	13	19	21	23	24	26	28
Israel	35	38	31	54	57	56	56	53	53
Japan....................	47	56	49	88	86	94	101	114	125
Korea....................	5	10	9	22	25	30	32	33	37
New Zealand	50	54	34	54	56	54	49	48	52
Singapore	13	15	19	22	25	28	31	31	37
Sri Lanka	4	2	2	2	2	3	2	3	—
Taiwan	6	10	12	25	26	28	32	31	32
Austria	71	90	58	99	119	116	126	122	127
Belgium	101	133	69	108	129	127	138	128	134
Denmark	99	110	62	101	120	117	124	114	120
Finland	72	83	63	118	141	136	123	99	110
France	71	91	58	88	102	98	105	97	100
Germany 1	00	125	74	124	147	146	157	154	160
Greece...................	27	38	28	38	45	44	46	41	—
Ireland	48	60	46	67	79	78	83	73	—
Italy	73	83	59	101	119	119	121	96	95
Luxembourg	100	121	59	94	110	107	116	110	—
Netherlands..............	103	122	67	105	123	117	126	119	122
Norway	106	117	80	128	144	139	143	121	122
Portugal	25	21	12	21	25	27	32	27	27
Spain	40	60	36	62	76	78	83	69	67
Sweden	113	127	74	122	140	142	152	106	110
Switzerland	96	112	74	117	140	139	144	135	145
United Kingdom	53	77	48	74	85	88	89	76	80
Trade-weighted measures:									
24 foreign economies 2 ...	60	67	52	77	83	86	88	86	88
less Mexico, Israel	65	72	57	85	91	94	97	94	96
OECD 3	76	85	66	97	105	108	110	107	109
Europe	82	103	62	101	118	118	124	112	115
European Union	80	101	61	98	116	115	122	111	114
Asian NIE's	8	12	13	23	25	28	30	31	34

1 The former West Germany.

2 Twenty-nine countries or areas, less the United States, and four countries for which 1994 data are not available.

3 Organization for Economic Cooperation and Development. Excludes Mexico, which joined the organization in 1994.

Note: Dash indicates data not available.

Source: Janet Kmitch, Pedro Laboy, and Sarah Van Damme, "International Comparisons of Manufacturing Compensation," *Monthly Labor Review* (Oct. 1995): 2, 6 (table 1).

*

Appendix F

Business Sector Productivity Growth
(Average annual percentage change)

	Labour share %	Labor productivity			Change: Columns:	
		Pre–1973 (1)	1974–79 (2)	1980–90 (3)	(2)–(1)	(3)–(2)
Australia	64	2.9	2.2	1.0	−0.7	−1.2
Austria	66	5.6	3.1	1.9	−2.5	−1.2
Belgium	70	5.1	2.7	2.3	−2.4	−0.5
Canada	63	2.8	1.5	1.1	−1.3	−0.4
Denmark	69	3.9	2.3	1.8	−2.6	−0.4
Finland	64	4.9	3.2	3.2	−1.7	0.4
France	65	5.3	2.9	2.4	−2.4	−0.3
Germany	67	4.4	3.0	1.7	−1.4	−1.4
Greece	63	8.5	3.3	0.5	−5.2	−2.8
Iceland	66	—	4.0	1.5	—	−2.6
Ireland	66	4.8	3.4	4.1	−1.4	0.8
Italy	64	6.1	2.8	1.9	−3.3	−0.9
Japan	69	8.0	2.9	2.9	−5.1	0.0
Netherlands	66	4.9	2.6	1.6	−2.3	−1.0
New Zealand	65	1.6	−1.3	1.7	−2.9	3.0
Norway	66	3.6	0.2	1.5	−3.4	1.3
Portugal	58	7.2	0.5	1.6	−6.7	1.1
Spain	65	5.8	3.2	2.8	−2.6	−0.4
Sweden	70	4.0	1.4	1.5	−2.6	0.1
Switzerland	71	3.2	0.8	1.1	−2.4	0.3
United Kingdom	69	3.6	1.5	2.1	−2.1	0.6
United States	68	2.1	0.0	0.6	−2.1	0.5
Unweighted average		4.7	2.1	1.9	−2.6	−0.2
Unweighted standard deviation		1.8	1.4	0.9	−0.4	−0.5

Note: Data begin in 1961 for the United States, Germany, Italy, Austria, Denmark, Portugal, Switzerland, and Australia: 1962 for the United Kingdom, Finland, Greece, and Ireland: 1963 for Japan and New Zealand: 1964 for France and Sweden: 1965 for Spain: 1967 for Canada and Norway: 1971 for Belgium and the Netherlands: 1974 for Iceland.

Source: *The OECD Jobs Study: Investment, Productivity and Employment* (1995), 40 (table 1.3).

*

Appendix G

Indexes of Manufacturing Price Levels, Labor Productivity and Unit Labor Costs, Selected Years, 1970–1993

[U.S.=100]

Country pair and measure	1970	1975	1980	1985	1990	1993 P
France–United States						
Relative producer price level	68.8	102.3	117.8	72.8	129.5	[1]133.9
Value added per hour worked	73.3	78.5	89.8	89.8	91.3	87.8
Labor cost per hour	48.4	86.9	110.5	69.9	117.8	111.3
Unit labor costs	66.0	110.6	123.1	77.8	129.1	126.9
Germany–United States						
Relative producer price level	65.7	96.8	113.2	70.1	132.8	[1]140.0
Value added per hour worked	78.7	87.3	95.2	90.5	85.9	82.5
Labor cost per hour	47.0	83.2	106.8	63.4	121.6	125.9
Unit lobor costs	59.7	95.2	112.3	70.1	141.6	152.6
Japan–United States						
Relative producer price level	66.1	83.2	91.9	75.7	110.3	[1]121.6
Value added per hour worked	44.5	54.1	66.2	69.9	77.9	76.2
Labor cost per hour	21.4	43.0	52.1	45.8	77.5	101.3
Unit labor costs	48.1	79.5	78.6	65.5	99.5	132.9
United Kingdom–United States						
Relative producer price level	70.3	91.6	140.5	86.2	132.9	[1]132.9
Value added per hour worked	51.3	53.0	52.3	58.3	66.0	69.8
Labor cost per hour	[2]38.0	52.9	76.4	51.1	90.4	87.7
Unit labor costs	[2]75.3	99.8	146.1	87.6	137.1	125.7

[1] Data relate to 1992.
[2] Data relate to 1971.

ᴾ = preliminary.

Note: Relative price levels are defined as the average ratio of producer prices between each country and the United States, divided by the currency exchange rate.

Source: Bart Van Ark, "Manufacturing Prices, Productivity, and Labor Costs in Five Economies," *Monthly Labor Review* (July 1995): 56, 57 (table 1).

†